THE CHURCH AS KOINONIA OF SALVATION

ITS STRUCTURES AND MINISTRIES

THE CHURCH AS KOINONIA OF SALVATION

ITS STRUCTURES AND MINISTRIES

LUTHERANS AND CATHOLICS IN DIALOGUE – X

Agreed Statement of the Tenth Round of
the U.S. Lutheran–Roman Catholic Dialogue
with Background Papers

Bishops' Committee for Ecumenical and Interreligious Affairs
United States Conference of Catholic Bishops

Department for Ecumenical Affairs
Evangelical Lutheran Church in America

EDITED BY
RANDALL LEE
JEFFREY GROS, FSC

PREFACE BY
BISHOP CHARLES MAAHS
BISHOP RICHARD SKLBA

United States Conference of Catholic Bishops
Washington, D.C.

The document *The Church as* Koinonia *of Salvation* was developed as a resource by the Committee for Ecumenical and Interreligious Affairs of the United States Conference of Catholic Bishops (USCCB) and the Department for Ecumenical Affairs of the Evangelical Lutheran Church in America (ELCA). It was reviewed by Bishop Stephen E. Blaire, chairman of the USCCB Committee for Ecumenical and Interreligious Affairs, and Presiding Bishop Mark S. Hanson of the ELCA, and it has been authorized for publication by the undersigned.

Msgr. William P. Fay
General Secretary, USCCB

Rev. Lowell Almen
General Secretary, ELCA

First Printing, January 2005

ISBN 1-57455-633-9

CONTENTS

ABBREVIATIONS

AAS	*Acta Apostolica Sedis*
AA	*Apostolicam Actuositatem* (*Decree on the Apostolate of the Laity*)
AB	*Anchor Bible*
AC	*Augsburg Confession*
AELC	Association of Evangelical Lutheran Churches
ACC	*A Common Calling*
AG	*Ad Gentes* (*Decree on the Church's Missionary Activity*)
AJP	*American Journal of Philology*
ALC	American Lutheran Church
AnBib	*Analecta Biblica*
Apol.	*Apology* of the *Augsburg Confession* (1531) (in BC)
ARCIC	Anglican Roman Catholic International Commission
ARCUSA	Anglican Roman Catholic Dialogue in the United States of America
AThR	*Anglical Theological Review*
BC	*The Book of Concord* (Confessions of the Evangelical Lutheran Church)
BCP	Episcopal *Book of Common Prayer*
BDAG	*A Greek-English Lexicon of the New Testament and Other Early Christian Literature*, 3rd ed.
BEM	*Baptism, Eucharist and Ministry*
BibU	*Biblische Untersuchungen*
BS	*Die Bekenntnisschriften der Lutherischen Kirche*
BSac	*Bibliotheca Sacra*
BTB	*Biblical Theology Bulletin*
BU	*Building Unity*
BZ	*Biblische Zeitschrift*
BZNW	*Beihefte zur Zeitschrift für die Neutestamentliche Wissenschaft*
CA	*Confessio Augustana* (*Augsburg Confession*)
CBCR	*Constitution, Bylaws, and Continuing Resolutions of the Evangelical Lutheran Church in America*, 2001 ed.
CBQ	*Catholic Biblical Quarterly*

CCC	*Catechism of the Catholic Church*
CD	*Christus Dominus (Decree on the Pastoral Office of Bishops in the Church)*
CDF	Congregation for the Doctrine of the Faith
CIC	*Code of Canon Law* (1983)
CICO	*Code of Canon Law for the Eastern Churches* (1991)
CN	*Communionis Notio (Some Aspects of the Church Understood as Communion)*
CNT	*Commentaire du Nouveau Testamant*
CSEL	*Corpus Scriptorum Ecclesiasticorum Latinorum*
CT	*Concilium Tridentinum* (Council of Trent)
Directory	*Directory for the Application of Principles and Norms on Ecumenism*
DH	*Dignitatis Humanae (Declaration on Religious Liberty)*
DHn	Denzinger, Heinrich. *Enchiridion Symbolorum Definitionum et Declarationum de Rebus Fidei et Morum,* 37th ed.
DS	Denzinger, H., and A. Schönmetzer. *Enchiridion Symbolorum,* 33rd ed.
DV	*Dei Verbum (Dogmatic Constitution on Divine Revelation)*
EDNT	*Exegetical Dictionary of the New Testament*
ELCA	Evangelical Lutheran Church in America
EN	*Evangelii Nuntiandi (On Evangelization in the Modern World)*
ES	Extraordinary Session of the Synod of Bishops, Final Report
FC Ep	Formula of Concord (1577), Epitome
FC SD	Formula of Concord (1577), Solid Declaration
FR	*Final Report* of ARCIC I (in GA I)
FU	*Facing Unity* (in GA II)
GofA	*The Gift of Authority* (statement by ARCIC II)
GA	*Growth in Agreement* (I & II)
GC	*Growing Consensus* (I & II)
GS	*Gaudium et Spes (Pastoral Constitution on the Church in the Modern World)*

HNTC	*Harper's New Testament Commentaries*
HC	*Heidelberg Catechism*
JAC	*Jahrbuch für Antike und Christentum*
JBL	*Journal of Biblical Literature*
JDDJ	*Joint Declaration on the Doctrine of Justification*
Josephus, Ant.	*Jewish Antiquities*
JSNTSup	*Journal for the Study of the New Testament Supplement Series*
JTS	*Journal of Theological Studies*
JWG	Joint Working Group of the World Council of Churches and the Roman Catholic Church
JWG-LC	*The Church: Local and Universal* (study document commissioned and received by the JWG)
LA	*The Leuenberg Agreement*
LBW	*Lutheran Book of Worship*
LC	Luther's Large Catechism
LCA	The Lutheran Church in America
LCMS	The Lutheran Church–Missouri Synod
LD	*Lectio Divina*
LED	Lutheran–Episcopal Dialogue in the United States (in GC I)
LG	*Lumen Gentium* (*Dogmatic Constitution on the Church*)
LinC	*Life in Christ* (ARCIC II in GA II)
L/RC	Lutheran–Roman Catholic dialogues in the United States (cited with volume numbers 1-9 corresponding to dialogue rounds I-IX)
LV	*Lehrverurteilungen-kirchentrennend?*
LWF/RC	International Lutheran–Roman Catholic dialogues (cited with volume numbers 1-9 corresponding to dialogue rounds I-IX)
LW	*Luther's Works*
LWF	Lutheran World Federation
NA	*Nostra Aetate* (*Declaration on the Church's Relations with Non-Christian Religions*)
NAB	*New American Bible*

NABRNT	NAB *Revised New Testament*
NCCB	National Conference of Catholic Bishops (now United States Conference of Catholic Bishops [USCCB])
NTF	*Neutestamentliche Forschungen*
NJBC	*New Jerome Biblical Commentary*
NPC	*The Nature and Purpose of the Church*
NRSV	*New Revised Standard Version* of the Bible
OE	*Orientalium Ecclesiarum*
PCPCU	Pontifical Council for Promoting Christian Unity (formerly Secretariat)
PA	*Pastor Aeternus* (*Dogmatic Constitution on the Church of Christ*)
PL	*Patrologia Latina*
PO	*Presbyterorum Ordinis* (*Decree on the Life and Ministry of Priests*)
Porvoo	*Together in Mission and Ministry: The Porvoo Common Statement with Essays on Church and Ministry in Northern Europe* (1993)
RBEM	Vatican Response to BEM
RHPR	*Revue d'Histoire et de Philosophie Religieuses*
RSV	*Revised Standard Version* of the Bible
RGG⁴	*Religion in Geschichte und Gegenwart*, 4th ed.
Santiago	*On the Way to Fuller Koinonia*, Official Report of the Fifth World Conference on Faith and Order
SBS	*Stuttgarter Bibelstudien*
SC	*Sacrosanctum Concilium* (*Constitution on the Sacred Liturgy*)
SPCU	Secretariat for Promoting Christian Unity
SupVC	Supplements to *Vigiliae Christianae*
Str.-B	Strack, H. L., and P. Billerbeck. *Kommentar zum Neuen Testament aus Talmud und Midrasch* (six vols., 1922-1961)
TANZ	*Texte und Arbeiten zum Neutestamentlichen Zeitalter*
TBC	*The Belgic Confession*

TDNT	*Theological Dictionary of the New Testament*
TFC	*Toward Full Communion* (Lutheran-Episcopal Dialogue, Series III, in GC I)
TPPP	*Treatise on the Power and Primacy of the Pope*
TRE	*Theologische Realenzyklopädie*
TS	*Theological Studies*
TWNT	*Theologisches Wörterbuch zum Neuen Testament*
UR	*Unitatis Redintegratio* (Decree on Ecumenism)
USCC	United States Catholic Conference (now United States Conference of Catholic Bishops [USCCB])
UUS	*Ut Unum Sint* (That They May Be One)
V II	Second Vatican Council texts
WBC	*Word Biblical Commentary*
WC	*Ways to Community* (Roman Catholic–Lutheran Commission in GA II)
WCC	World Council of Churches
WO	*Die Welt des Orients*
ZNW	*Zeitschrift für die Neutestamentliche Wissenschaft und die Kunde der älteren Kirche*

PREFACE

I t is a joy to celebrate the fifth anniversary of the *Joint Declaration on the Doctrine of Justification* (JDDJ), signed by representatives of the Catholic Church and the churches of the Lutheran World Federation (LWF) in 1999. Pope John Paul II and the leaders of the LWF recognize this agreement as a milestone and model on the road toward visible unity among Christians. Therefore, with great joy we present to the leadership and members of our churches this text, the tenth produced by our United States dialogue, as a further contribution to this careful and gradual process of reconciliation. We hope that it will serve to enhance our communion and deepen our mutual understanding.

Catholics and Lutherans are able to confess "by grace alone, in faith in Christ's saving work and not because of any merit on our part, we are accepted by God and receive the Holy Spirit, who renews our hearts while equipping and calling us to good works" (JDDJ, no. 15). We also recognize together that "our consensus in basic truths of the doctrine of justification must come to influence the life and teachings of our churches. Here it must prove itself. In this respect, there are still questions of varying importance which need further clarification" (JDDJ, no. 43). In this spirit, we offer the following modest clarifications and proposals.

We are united as Christians by our common baptism, common affirmation of Scripture, and common life in Christ; we are united as Lutherans and Catholics by our common commitment to the goal of full communion, our common affirmation of justification, and our common understanding that more agreement is necessary before full, sacramental communion can be restored. In this text we recognize the importance of our agreement, propose new stages of agreement, and celebrate the gifts we can receive from one another in our practice and understandings of ministries and structures within the church as community of salvation.

In this dialogue we also are not proposing to settle all of the church-dividing issues before us. We have not attempted to resolve the important ecclesiological issues of the ordination of women or the authority by which such a decision is made, nor the full meaning of apostolic succession in ordained ministry and how we might be reconciled. We have not addressed the level of communion in ministries and structures that would be necessary for even interim eucharistic communion. Yet we are convinced that the clarifications and research represented by this text make an important contribution in the stages toward reconciling these and other elements along the path toward full communion.

The reader will find this text a bit longer than publications of previous rounds of this dialogue. Biblical and historical material that was prepared and presented in supporting essays over the years of this study is summarized here. Needless to say, not all of the historical, biblical, and theological research on which this text is based is presented here nor is it included in the supporting essays. It will be important for the reader to review some of the earlier research of the U.S. and international dialogues to clarify further the context of these arguments.

This agreed text may be published both by itself and in a volume with some supporting essays. In the volume of essays, only a selection of those which contributed to the dialogue is published. Those that are not summarized in the final document but which further clarify the historical background are included. Some of the biblical, historical research and overview of previous dialogues will be published as articles elsewhere. As we build a common understanding of our biblical and historical heritage, this research becomes an increasingly important resource for our teaching and preaching. It adds to the serious theological literature produced in an ecumenical mode.

The method used to present our conclusions takes account of the "internally differentiated consensus" method employed by the *Joint Declaration*. "Lutheran and the Catholic explications of justification are in their difference open to one another and do not destroy the consensus regarding the basic truths" (JDDJ, no. 40). As our dialogues approach the ecclesiological issues noted above, in the context of the church as community of salvation, we will continue to seek agreement on matters that have been seen as church-dividing. These agreements, of course, will be tested by the faith of our people and the appropriate leadership structures in our churches before they attain the level of reception and authority we now accord the *Joint Declaration*.

Only by reappropriating our common heritage in Scripture and the shared tradition can we follow the call of Christ to that common future for which he so earnestly prayed on the night before he was delivered for us. We can only humbly receive that grace of unity by the power of the Holy Spirit, obediently continuing on the pilgrimage to which God has called us. The labors of our biblical and theological scholarship are one element in the mosaic of our common prayer, service, and life together as we step out into that mysterious and arduous path that lies before the church.

Bishop Charles Maahs, *Lutheran Cochair*
Bishop Richard Sklba, *Catholic Cochair*
Lutheran–Roman Catholic Dialogue in the United States, round X
October 31, 2004

AGREED STATEMENT
THE CHURCH AS KOINONIA OF SALVATION:
ITS STRUCTURES AND MINISTRIES

PART ONE: DEEPENING COMMUNION
IN STRUCTURES AND MINISTRIES

PART TWO: FURTHER BIBLICAL AND HISTORICAL SUPPORT FOR DEEPENING COMMUNION IN STRUCTURES AND MINISTRIES

Part One:
Deepening Communion
in Structures and Ministries

❈

INTRODUCTION

1. From 1965 to 1993, the continuing dialogue between Lutherans and Roman Catholics in the United States addressed doctrines and issues that have united or separated our churches since the sixteenth century. Considerable convergences and even consensus at times have been expressed in nine rounds of discussion on the Nicene Creed (round I); baptism (round II); the eucharist (round III); the ministry of the eucharist (round IV); papal primacy (round V); teaching authority and infallibility (round VI); justification (round VII); the one mediator, the saints, and Mary (round VIII); and Scripture and tradition (round IX).[1] The summaries and joint or common statements in these volumes of findings and supporting studies have been important for relations between our churches and for wider ecumenical discussion.

2. A coordinating committee[2] was appointed by the United States Conference of Catholic Bishops' Committee for Ecumenical and Interreligious Affairs and by the presiding bishop of the Evangelical Lutheran Church in America (ELCA) after the completion of round IX in 1993. It met from 1994 to 1996 to plan for a new round of dialogue and to take part in the development and reception process for a statement on justification by faith and the reassessment of the condemnations connected with justification in the sixteenth century. The Coordinating Committee made a common Lutheran-Catholic response to a draft of the *Joint Declaration on the Doctrine of Justification* (JDDJ) in 1995. It also developed the topic proposal dealt with in this volume, *The Church as Koinonia of Salvation: Its Structures and Ministries*, and in the guidelines[3] accepted by our sponsoring church authorities for a new dialogue team.

3. This tenth round of Lutherans and Catholics in Dialogue, begun in 1998, carried out its study of ecclesiology and ministries with a new basis in the important results from earlier discussions affirmed in a *Joint Declaration on the Doctrine of Justification*. An Official Common Statement confirming the *Joint Declaration*, accompanied by an Annex to the Official Common Statement, was signed by representatives of the LWF and the Roman Catholic Church[4] in Augsburg, Germany, on October 31, 1999.

4. The seventh volume of the U.S. dialogue, *Justification by Faith*, which was completed in 1983, was among the resources[5] that contributed to this worldwide agreement, especially with its own Declaration that set forth the gospel we encounter in Scripture and church life:

> Thus we can make together, in fidelity to the gospel we share, the following declaration:

> We believe that God's creative graciousness is offered to us and to everyone for healing and reconciliation so that through the Word made flesh, Jesus Christ, "who was put to death for our transgressions and raised for our justification" (Rom. 4:25), we are all called to pass from the alienation and oppression of sin to freedom and fellowship with God in the Holy Spirit. It is not through our own initiative that we respond to this call, but only through an undeserved gift which is granted and made known in faith, and which comes to fruition in our love of God and neighbor, as we are led by the Spirit in faith to bear witness to the divine gift in all aspects of our lives. This faith gives us hope for ourselves and for all humanity and gives us confidence that salvation in Christ will always be proclaimed as the gospel, the good news for which the world is searching.[6]

5. The *Joint Declaration* was a harvest from such statements in the U.S. and international dialogues. In Germany between 1981 and 1985, the Joint Ecumenical Commission and Ecumenical Study Group of Protestant and Catholic Theologians dealt with the condemnations by Catholics and Lutherans in the sixteenth century on justification and

related topics.[7] The *Joint Declaration* sets forth a common understanding of justification (§§14-18), in light of the biblical message (§§8-12), with explication in seven problem areas of what Lutherans and Catholics can confess together ecumenically, as well as the distinctive accents of each, now acceptable to the other (§§19-39). In light of the "consensus in basic truths of the doctrine of justification" (§40), the *Joint Declaration* states that "it becomes clear that the mutual condemnations of former times do not apply to the Catholic and Lutheran doctrines of justification as they are presented in the *Joint Declaration*" (Annex, §1; *cf.* JDDJ, §41; Official Common Statement, §1). But it is also recognized that this consensus "must prove itself" in "further clarification" of topics that include "ecclesiology, ecclesial authority, church unity, ministry, the sacraments, and the relation between justification and social ethics" (§43).

6. The *Joint Declaration* has great implications and holds much promise for life in our parishes, in reshaping preaching, teaching, worship, and daily life. It has found expression in agreements and covenants between local congregations, synods, and dioceses, and in national celebrations in the United States, even among Christians neither Catholic nor Lutheran, not to mention reflections in other parts of the world. For our dialogue, it has given fresh impulse and encouragement to our work together.

7. As we have dealt with structures and ministries, we have been mindful of how the dialogue's rounds IV and V (1968-1980) took up the topic of ministry in connection with the eucharist and then papal ministry (also in the sixth volume, *Teaching Authority and Infallibility*). Our review of much of the work done in rounds IV and V made us aware of how helpful and significant these contributions were. Round IV dealt only with local ministry in the local congregation where the eucharist is celebrated and the word is preached. Round V dealt with a universal ministry and the possibility of a renewed papacy. The present round considers the interrelation among local, regional, national, and worldwide ministries and church structures, in the context of an understanding of the church as *koinonia* of salvation.[8] Thus, in continuity with past dialogues and the *Joint Declaration*, our analysis moves from Christ and the gospel of salvation to *koinonia*. We understand this gospel particularly as

the message of justification by grace through faith, and we treat *koinonia* as a lens through which to view ecclesiology and ministries of those ordained, within the whole people of God.

8. This report will proceed from a general consideration of *koinonia* ecclesiology (section I) and the specific concept of the "local church" (section II) to a consideration of the particular structures of *koinonia* in our two churches (section III) and the ordained ministries that serve them (section IV). A brief discussion of the ecumenically significant question of apostolic succession and its relation to ministry follows (section V). All of this analysis and description then forms the background for an argument for a fresh vision of how structures and ministry can be understood, including recommendations (sections VI, VII, and VIII).

9. This new vision confronts us with the wounds to mission and ministry that are the result of our continuing division and calls us to repentance and greater fidelity to the gospel. It invites us to partial mutual recognition of ordained ministry. It opens new paths in the exploration of a universal ministry of unity. The analysis offers a basis for a deeper recognition of each other's churchly reality and of our local, regional, and universal ministries and structures. This recognition will involve stronger acknowledgment of the churchly reality of the parish for Catholics, and of the theological significance of synods for Lutherans.

I. KOINONIA ECCLESIOLOGY

10. There are good reasons why viewing the church as *koinonia* came into prominence ecumenically in the latter decades of the twentieth century (see §§15-20 below). The basic word *koinōnia* in Greek, is ancient, occurring twenty-two times in the Bible,[9] but it was not a term or concept prominent in Catholic or Lutheran documents of the sixteenth century. Thus it has been spared some of the partisan usage that often has made other concepts divisive. *Koinonia* has never been a church-dividing issue for Lutherans and Catholics. It is a useful lens through which this present dialogue reconsiders our differences concerning ministry and church structures. We speak together about this lens in three propositions: the

church shares in salvation; the church shares salvation with others; and the church is a community shaped by salvation. All three are expressed in Scripture through words related to *koinonia*.

A. The Church Shares in Salvation

11. We, the justified, share in salvation from God in Christ in a number of ways. We are called by God into the fellowship of his Son (see 1 Cor. 1:9).[10] We share in the gospel (see Phil. 1:5). We share in Christ's body and blood in the bread we break and the cup we share as presentation for us of Jesus' death on the cross and of its benefits for us (see 1 Cor. 10:16). We participate in the Spirit (see 2 Cor. 13:13; Phil. 2:1) and share in faith in all the good that is ours in Christ (see Phlm. 6). We also share in Christ's and each other's affliction and sufferings (see Phil. 3:10; 4:14), amid which there is consolation (see 2 Cor. 1:7) and the promise of participation in joy and future glory (see 1 Pet. 4:13; 5:1; 2 Pet. 1:4, on future sharing in God's own nature). Witnesses share the kingdom as well as experience persecution and patient endurance (see Rev. 1:9). The sharing in the Spirit that characterizes Christians is also part of the basis for the love and agreement with one another that we, the church, are called to have (see Phil. 2:1). The fellowship that 1 John 1:3-7 depicts is with God the Father and his Son, as well as with one another.[11] In God's plan of salvation, Gentile Christians too came to share, as branches, the riches of the olive tree, Israel (see Rom. 11:17).

B. The Church Shares Salvation

12. *Koinonia* characterizes not only the way we receive salvation but also the way it is offered to others through the church. Through evangelization we share the gospel with others (see Phil. 1:5, 7) as part of its advance (see Phil. 1:12, 25; 4:14-15) in mission (see Mt. 28:19-20). This sharing transforms the church itself as well as the world. The agreement between Paul and other church leaders to evangelize both Jews and Gentiles cuts across boundaries of racial and ethnic divisions of the day; it was a mutual pledge for mission, unity, and support for the poor (see Gal. 2:9-10). We support the proclamation of the gospel through our financial gifts (see Phil. 4:15); we share our resources with the poor and those in need throughout the world. In Paul's time, that meant a

collection from his Gentile churches for "the saints," impoverished Jewish Christians in Jerusalem (see 2 Cor. 8:4; 9:13; Rom. 15:26-27); this economic aid showed concern for the unity of the church (see Gal. 2:9-10).[12] Acts depicts Christians in Jerusalem as sharing not only the gospel message but also their temporal resources (see Acts 2:42, 45; 4:32). In subsequent centuries, such active sharing, *koinonia*, has become the norm for Christian life and has been manifested in sharing food, time, and the results of all sorts of human abilities, as well as money.

C. The Church Is a Community Shaped by Salvation

13. The *koinonia* of salvation has called forth a type of community, the church, appropriate to the grace and calling we have received. We are a *koinonia* called in Christ by and for the gospel (see 1 Cor. 1:9; Phil. 1:5), a community that comes from the Holy Spirit (see 2 Cor. 13:13). The vertical and horizontal fellowship with God and fellow believers (see 1 Jn. 1:2-7) results in a people conformed to Christ's death on the cross (see Phil. 3:10, on the cross and resurrection of Jesus; 1 Pet. 4:13, on suffering and rejoicing). That means for the justified an existence determined by God's love and faithfulness, a life lived with love, in faith and trust, marked by hope. This vertical and horizontal fellowship exists in and with the world and its institutions. It is shaped internally by its relationship with God through Christ and the Spirit and by the participation in Christ and salvation of all members of Christ's body. Externally the church relates to the world not merely as a social institution amid the other public structures (*ta koina*) of the Greco-Roman world, [13] but more important, as a sign of God's will that all share in salvation. Divisions in fellowship blunt the impact of our witness to salvation.

D. Summary

14. In sum, therefore, *koinonia* in the New Testament especially concerns the relationship of justified believers with God and Christ (1 Cor. 1:9; 1 Jn. 1:2-7) and the Spirit (2 Cor. 13:13), thus with the Trinity. (The word "*koinonia*" does not refer in the New Testament to fellowship within the Godhead, as it does in patristic writers who spoke of *koinonia* between the Father and the Son[14]). *Koinonia* also has ecclesiological (Gal. 2:9; 2 Cor. 13:13) and eucharistic connotations (1 Cor. 10:16).

The concept appears as a basis for ethical admonitions (Phil. 2:1) and can also itself be an admonition to share, both in the church and with the poor (Rom. 15:26-27). The New Testament references speak of sharing in sufferings (Phil. 3:10) and of sharing in consolation for people who share in suffering (2 Cor. 1:7). *Koinonia* connects with themes like mission, life together (Acts 2:42), stewardship, and future hope.

E. Recent Developments in Koinonia Ecclesiology

15. From New Testament usage, *koinonia* came to be employed over the centuries as "communion" (*communio*) and in many other renderings, particularly with reference to the church. While the terminology did not play a role of any importance in sixteenth-century Reformation or Catholic theology, it became more prominent in the twentieth century.[15] In Eastern Orthodoxy, *koinonia* ecclesiology has recently centered on eucharistic communion with Christ.[16]

16. Ecclesiology can be called "a chapter of Christology"[17] as long as it also is pneumatological. The terminology also came into the World Council of Churches (WCC), especially through the work of the Faith and Order Commission: "fuller *koinonia*" is the goal of life together in Christ.[18] Bilateral dialogues have found the theme helpful,[19] as have theologians from a variety of traditions.[20]

17. Among Catholics, "communion" was used to speak in a non-juridical way of "a network of sacramentally focused local churches bound together ultimately by the mutual openness of their eucharistic celebrations," with the bishop of Rome "as the focal point of the network of churches linked together in the catholic, or universal, *communio*."[21] Communion as "the permanent form of the unity of the church" was articulated on the eve of the Second Vatican Council.[22] J. M. R. Tillard explored communion ecclesiology as conforming "best to the biblical notion and to the intuitions of the great ecclesiological traditions."[23] The 1985 Synod of Bishops recognized communion ecclesiology as "the central and fundamental idea" of the documents of the Second Vatican Council.[24] The concept of communion came to be applied in a wide range of contexts. The 1992 statement from the Congregation for the

Doctrine of the Faith "Some Aspects of the Church as Communion" explained that "ecclesial communion is at the same time visible and invisible" and this link "makes the church 'sacrament of salvation.'"[25] The 1993 *Directory for Ecumenism* stressed the presence and activity of the universal church in the particular churches.[26] Pope John Paul II said in 1995 that the "elements of sanctification and truth" shared by "the other Christian communities" show that "the one Church of Christ is effectively present in them." This is the reason for the communion that persists between the Catholic Church and "the other Churches and Ecclesial Communities," in spite of their divisions.[27]

18. For Lutherans, the term *koinonia* was used in German discussions on Protestant church fellowship in the 1950s.[28] In the latter part of the twentieth century, the LWF increasingly employed *koinonia/communio* themes.[29] In 1990 the LWF defined itself as "a communion of churches which confess the triune God, agree in the proclamation of the Word of God and are united in pulpit and altar fellowship."[30] Lutherans and Catholics in dialogue have related *koinonia* to the doctrine of the Trinity and ecclesiology.[31]

19. *Koinonia* encompasses all Christians and the salvation of all who share in the gospel. *Koinonia* ecclesiology has many aspects but no uniform definition. The New Testament references to "*koinonia*" do not directly relate the term to "church," let alone to "ministries," but repeatedly deal with all the faithful. In presenting the church as *koinonia*, the Lutheran–Roman Catholic International Commission placed the church within a series of biblical images, beginning with "people of God," and added that, in both our traditions, "we rightly speak of the 'priesthood of all the baptized' or the 'priesthood of all believers.'"[32] All structures and ministries, as instruments of *koinonia*, serve God's people. Whatever is said, then, of "*koinonia* ecclesiology" and "ministry in service of community" is to be embedded in this context: the people of God, all Christian believers.

20. This dialogue now wishes to contribute further to these varied understandings of the church as *koinonia*. The following sections will focus on

koinonia ecclesiology in the context of historical and current Lutheran-Catholic relationships. Our ecclesiologies and our ordained ministries of presbyters and bishops are viewed afresh through the lens of *koinonia*. Our dialogue is intended to foster reconciliation between our churches and is offered to the wider ecumenical community for study and reflection.

II. THE LOCAL CHURCH
WITHIN THE KOINONIA OF SALVATION

21. An important element in much recent *koinonia* ecclesiology of particular significance for this report's analysis is the concept of the "local church," understood in similar but different ways by our two traditions. On the one hand, both Lutherans and Catholics agree that there is a local body which is not merely a part of the church, but is wholly church, even if not the whole church and not in isolation from the rest of the church. Our traditions agree: "The local church is truly church. It has everything it needs to be church in its own situation. . . . The local church is the place where the church of God becomes concretely realized."[33] To say that the local church is "church" in an integral sense is to say that the essential elements of the community—which participates in, shares, and is shaped by salvation—are present in a complete and integral way.

22. On the other hand, Lutherans and Catholics differ over what "local church" designates. For Lutherans, the local church is the congregation; for Catholics, it is most often the diocese.[34] This difference is closely related to a parallel set of differences over the status of the ordained ministers who minister to these two communities: the minister of the congregation or parish (the pastor, priest, or presbyter) and the minister of the regional grouping of these communities (the bishop). This difference is rooted in the complex history of the development of local and regional church bodies (see §§159-195).

23. This complex history begins with the variety of community structures and ministries within first-century Christianity. By the second and third centuries, the pattern was established of local communities gathered for worship around the bishop, who was surrounded by a council of

presbyters and was assisted by deacons.[35] During the profound changes of the late patristic and early medieval periods, the role of the bishop and the nature and size of the communities he headed changed. The primary Christian community for most Christians in the West came to be the parish under the care of a presbyter or priest. The diocese headed by the bishop came to include many such parishes. These shifts contributed to the medieval uncertainties about the relation between priest and bishop and lie at the root of the Lutheran-Catholic difference about what is to be designated "local church" (see §§172-175).

A. The Local Church in Catholic Ecclesiology

24. In continuity with one aspect of the early church, Roman Catholics define the local church (or, more often, the particular church or diocese) as "a portion of the people of God whose pastoral care is entrusted to a bishop in conjunction with his priests. Thus, in conjunction with their pastor and gathered by him into one flock in the Holy Spirit through the gospel and the eucharist, they constitute a particular church."[36] The basic unit of the church is therefore defined both eucharistically and ministerially. The ministry of the bishop is a constitutive element of the most basic ecclesiastical unit, the diocese, which includes all that is necessary to be a church. The link between the parish eucharist and the bishop is not obvious to most Roman Catholics, however, since they only occasionally experience a eucharistic assembly in which their bishop presides, even though they mention the bishop by name in every eucharistic liturgy the parish celebrates.

25. The descriptions of the local or particular church in the documents of the Second Vatican Council emphasize both elements. On the one hand, it is said that "the faithful are gathered together through the preaching of the gospel" and the eucharist.[37] On the other hand, it also is said, "the principal manifestation of the church consists in the full, active participation . . . at one altar, at which the bishop presides."[38] Since the bishop cannot always or everywhere preside over the whole flock, he establishes multiple assemblies of believers. "Parishes, organized locally under a parish priest who acts in the bishop's place, are the

most important of these, because in some way they exhibit the visible church set up throughout the nations of the world."[39]

B. The Local Church in Lutheran Ecclesiology

26. Lutherans, in continuity with a different aspect of the early church, have generally held that the congregation is church in the full sense. As the international Roman Catholic–Lutheran Joint Commission expressed this view in *Church and Justification*:

> Lutherans understand the *una sancta ecclesia* to find outward and visible expression wherever people assemble around the gospel proclaimed in sermon and sacrament. Assembled for worship the local congregation therefore is to be seen, according to the Lutheran view, as the visible church, *communio sanctorum*, in the full sense. Nothing is missing which makes a human assembly church: the preached word and the sacramental gifts through which the faithful participate in Christ through the Holy Spirit, but also the ministers who preach the word and administer the sacraments in obedience to Christ and on his behalf, thus leading the congregation.[40]

This understanding can be seen as a return to the pattern of the early church in which the basic ecclesial unit was a face-to-face assembly. Nevertheless, such a return involves a break with the pattern, both patristic and medieval, in which the bishop heads the local church. The office of ministry is included as an essential element of the local church in the Lutheran understanding, but this office is seen as exercised by the pastor/presbyter.

C. Catholic-Lutheran Similarities on the Local Church

27. This difference between what Lutherans and Catholics designate as the local church masks a deep structural similarity: Lutherans and Catholics each experience the church in a geographically local, face-to-face assembly where the word is preached and sacraments are celebrated: the parish or congregation. In addition, for both of our churches, this

local assembly is not freestanding, but rather exists within a regional community of such assemblies, namely, a diocese or synod. These groupings reach to the national and international level, but the diocese or synod, as the primary regional community, forms the immediate institutional context of the life of the congregation or parish. Lutherans and Catholics differ as to whether the face-to-face assembly or the primary regional community is the local church in the theological sense, but the institutional life of both traditions is shaped by this pairing.

28. This pairing of face-to-face assembly and regional community developed over an extended period without a conscious intent to create this pattern. How is this development to be understood theologically? Is it completely fortuitous, or does it express an institutional truth about how the *koinonia* of salvation is rightly realized, namely, the need both for the immediate experience of *koinonia* in the physical presence of one to another and for the embodiment of the catholicity and diversity of *koinonia* in a community of such face-to-face communities? It may be a theological mistake to insist that one or the other is "local church" in an exclusive sense without also saying that there is something about this pairing of face-to-face assembly and primary regional community that is ecclesiologically normative. If this pairing is normative, we must inquire what significance this structure has for our understanding of the ministries of those who preside over these communities, the pastor and the bishop.

29. Already in the New Testament, the worshiping community did not live in isolation, but rather joined in *koinonia* with other communities. Paul took up a collection (*koinonia*) among his predominantly Gentile churches of Greece and Asia Minor for the church in Jerusalem (see Acts 11:29; Rom. 15:25-27; 1 Cor. 16:3-5). This action extended that initial sharing of common life in Jerusalem by which "distribution was made to each as any had need" (see Acts 4:35).[41] Typically, in the closing of the various letters of the New Testament, churches sent greetings to other churches (see 1 Cor. 16:19; Phil. 4:22; 2 Tim. 4:21; Titus 3:15; Heb. 13:24; 1 Pet. 5:13; 2 Jn. 13; 3 Jn. 15).

30. In the post-biblical period, various ecclesial practices emphasized the communion among local churches. The practice of regional synods and

the development of creedal expressions of the faith and of the common canon of Scripture are exercises of *koinonia*. Individuals presented letters of communion to be admitted to the eucharist of another bishop, indicating that the two sees were in communion with each other. The participation of three bishops in the ordination of a brother bishop signified that he was being admitted into the episcopal college, and bishops frequently visited and corresponded with each other to maintain communion (see §§159-162).[42]

31. Christian communities experience *koinonia* across both space and time. Across space they experience the catholicity of the church in its extension throughout the world as one church consisting of many particular churches in communion with one another. Across time they experience continuity with the apostolic faith of the originating Christian community, the eschatological community founded on the apostles (see Rev. 21:14), and with all communities before and after it that have pursued and will pursue the apostolic mission. The local church is church only within this comprehensive *koinonia*.

III. REALIZATIONS OF ECCLESIAL KOINONIA

32. As the concept of local church indicates, the *koinonia* of salvation is realized in concrete communities with specific structures. The structures and ministries of the church embody and serve the *koinonia* of salvation. It has been a fruitful ecumenical strategy to work from a renewed theology of communion toward a renewed consideration of longstanding, difficult issues in relation to structure and ministries. In this document, we attempt on the basis of a reflection on concrete structures of *koinonia* in our churches to look anew at controversies in relation to structure and ministry that have divided our churches in the past.

33. Lutherans and Catholics affirm together a variety of interdependent realizations of ecclesial *koinonia*: the congregation or parish (i.e., a face-to-face worshiping assembly gathered by word and sacrament), a regional community or grouping of congregations or parishes (the synod in the

ELCA; the diocese in the Catholic Church), a multiplicity of national structures, and a worldwide organization.

34. These realizations and our theological understanding of them, however, are not symmetrical in our two churches. As already noted, Lutheran and Catholic ecclesiologies differ on which realizations may actually be called a "church." In addition, Lutherans, unlike Catholics, have no worldwide body that is itself a church. Roman Catholics do not have national churches in the same sense as Anglicans, Lutherans, or Orthodox do. These differences in ecclesiology involve parallel differences in evaluations of ministry. For example, Catholics consider the bishop to possess the "fullness of the sacrament of order,"[43] while Lutherans follow the teaching of Jerome that there is no difference other than jurisdiction between a presbyter and a bishop.[44] In Catholicism, the ministry of worldwide communion is exercised by the college of bishops, inclusive of the bishop of Rome as member and head, who also can act on the college's behalf. While various ministries occur among Lutherans on a global level, there is no formally recognized minister of worldwide communion.

35. In each of our traditions, the ecclesiological understanding of these various realizations of *koinonia* requires deeper reflection. Larger Lutheran churches around the world are typified by a structure including face-to-face assemblies or congregations, regional groupings of such congregations (called "synods" in the ELCA), and a national or supraregional body with extensive authority to make doctrinal and ecumenical decisions.[45] This structural pattern has rarely, however, been theologically explicated[46] and does not include the universal church. In Catholicism, more recent general councils have primarily focused upon theologies of ministry, which then have shaped the understanding of the structures of ecclesial *koinonia*. For example, the First Vatican Council addressed the theology of the papacy, and the Second Vatican Council developed a theology of the episcopacy from which emerged a theology of the local church. A theology of the presbyterate remained comparatively undeveloped in *Lumen Gentium* (LG), the *Dogmatic Constitution on the Church*, since only one section discusses the priesthood within the chapter on the hierarchy.[47] It is not surprising, then, that the parish has not been the subject of much theological reflection within

Catholicism.[48] An ecumenical reflection on the structures and ministries of *koinonia* thus promises not only new possibilities for the relation between our churches, but also an occasion for consideration of our own ecclesiological blind spots.

A. The Congregation or Parish

36. Lutherans and Roman Catholics affirm together that Christians share in the *koinonia* of salvation most immediately in the worshiping assembly gathered around the baptismal font, the pulpit, and the eucharistic table. Within these communities, the gospel is preached and the faith is professed, the catechumens are evangelized and are formed, the community receives the baptized, and all are nurtured. There the faithful partake of one bread and become one body (see 1 Cor. 10:16). Mission is carried out there, to and for the world.[49] For both Catholics and Lutherans, this face-to-face community is of ecclesiological significance; it is a *koinonia* of salvation, whether or not it is labeled "local church" in the sense discussed above.

1. Lutherans on the Congregation

37. The interdependence of congregation and the wider community finds expression in the definition of a congregation in the ELCA: "a community of baptized persons whose existence depends on the proclamation of the gospel and the administration of the sacraments and whose purpose is to worship God, to nurture its members, and to reach out in witness and service to the world. To this end it assembles regularly for worship and nurture, organizes and carries out ministry to its people and neighborhood, and cooperates and supports the wider church to strive for the fulfillment of God's mission in the world."[50]

38. Each congregation participates with the wider church in God's mission to the world. The sense of relationship, partnership, and commitment to the wider community of faith is reflected in the basic criteria for recognition of ELCA congregations for they must agree to support the life and work of this church (meaning the whole Evangelical Lutheran Church in America).[51] Furthermore, they must pledge to foster and participate in interdependent relationship with other congregations, the synod, and the churchwide organization.[52]

2. Catholics on the Parish

39. For Catholics also, the parish, especially as a place of Sunday eucharistic worship and as the place of Christian initiation, is where the people of God experience the church most immediately. The universal church is actualized in specific places and circumstances, in specific cultures and within particular communities, or not at all. The parish is both gathered together by the preaching of the gospel of Christ[53] and joined together through the flesh and blood of the Lord's body in its celebration of the Lord's Supper.[54]

40. The theology of the parish has been strengthened by the implementation of the Rite of Christian Initiation of Adults, which presumes a local community that helps the candidates and catechumens throughout the whole process of initiation and in their further formation in faith and witness. Within a theology of baptism, the parish is the context and specific *place* of formation in Christian living. The tie to the diocesan church also finds expression within the Rite of Christian Initiation of Adults, in the "rite of election," when candidates are presented to the bishop by name in the cathedral church.[55]

B. The Synod or Diocese

41. Catholics and Lutherans affirm together that congregations and parishes cannot exist in isolation, but rather must be in communion with one another within larger regional communities in order to realize *koinonia* and to carry out mission. In both our churches, essential ecclesial functions are carried out within the regional community of the diocese or synod, such as ordaining pastors and priests, pastoral care of clergy and congregations, and important aspects of ecclesial discipline. In both churches, the diocese/synod is understood to be church in the full sense. Most importantly, this community is the primary location of the congregation's or parish's connection with the wider church.

1. Lutherans on Synodical Realizations

42. The ELCA seeks "to function as people of God through congregations, synods, and the churchwide organization, all of which shall be interdependent. Each part, while fully church, recognizes that it is not

the whole church and therefore lives in a partnership relationship with the others."[56] Furthermore, "congregations find their fulfillment in the universal community of the Church, and the universal Church exists in and through congregations."[57]

43. The interdependence of congregations, synods, and churchwide organization reflects the earliest Lutheran self-understanding. As early as 1523, "Luther does not speak of the local congregation as being . . . self-sufficient. The practical expression of his conviction is seen in the fact that visitations were carried out. In particular, the observance of the 'evangelical doctrine' (*doctrina evangelica*) is not the concern of the individual congregation [alone]; it is the concern of all those who profess this doctrine."[58]

44. In the ELCA, synods are composed of congregations. Congregations in a synod function together both through the synodical assembly and through the ongoing cooperation that is led by the synodical bishop and is guided by the elected Synod Council. The ELCA's churchwide constitution mandates: "Each synod, in partnership with the churchwide organization, shall bear primary responsibility for the oversight of the life and mission of this church in its territory."[59] In the ELCA, synods are the primary locus for the oversight of ordained ministry. All ordinations are regularly performed by synodical bishops. Synods carry out the full range of ecclesial activities and are themselves realizations of the *koinonia* of salvation.[60]

2. Catholics on Diocesan Realizations

45. For Catholics, the particular church, most often a diocese, already embraces a number of parishes—the face-to-face congregations, in which the word is preached, the eucharist is celebrated, and new members are initiated. Every particular church must be in communion with other particular churches and in continuity with its apostolic foundations. Each particular church shows solicitude for the entire church, which includes proclaiming the gospel to the entire world, collaborating with one another, keeping unity with the church in Rome, helping the missions, and extending assistance to other churches.[61]

46. A particular church is not a subdivision of the universal church, although there is an interdependence between the particular and universal church. "In and from these particular churches there exists the one unique catholic church. For this reason individual bishops represent their own church, while all of them together with the pope represent the whole church in the bond of peace, love and unity."[62] Within the episcopal college, bishops represent their particular church in the communion of churches, the collegiality of bishops paralleling the communion of churches.

C. National Realizations of *Koinonia*

47. Lutherans and Catholics affirm together the significance of national elements in the life of the church. Conferences of bishops for the Latin Catholic Church most often serve national groupings. From the time of the Reformation, Lutheran churches have been organized along the lines of national or other political units.[63]

1. Lutherans on National Realizations

48. For historical reasons, such as language and the close relationship between church and state, Lutherans have tended to be organized into national churches for mission, among other purposes.[64] For example, the ELCA is "church" in the theological sense and is not a federation or association of congregations or synods. As church, the ELCA has a pastor, its presiding bishop, who carries out a range of pastoral activities in service of this church.[65] The churchwide organization has extensive authority. Only this churchwide expression can enter into relations of full communion with other churches.[66] Lutherans have rarely sought to provide a theological rationale for the importance that such national churches have played in their life.[67]

2. Catholics on National Realizations

49. In the history of the church, various structures have existed at a level more geographically extensive than the diocese, but less extensive than the church as a whole: e.g., provinces or patriarchates. These structures have varied widely in their powers and responsibilities. The Eastern Catholic Churches have retained synodal structures. Since the Second Vatican Council, national conferences of bishops have come to play an important role in the life of the Latin Catholic Church. They

gather bishops of a given nation or territory and foster a closer *koinonia* among the churches and collegiality among the bishops for the people of that area.[68] The exact theological status of these conferences is not entirely determined.[69] The *motu propio* of Pope John Paul II *Apostolos Suos* describes the extent of the conferences' authority:

> The Conference of Bishops can issue general decrees only in those cases in which the common law prescribes it, or a special mandate of the Apostolic See, given either *motu proprio* or at the request of the Conference, determines it. In other cases the competence of individual diocesan Bishops remains intact; and neither the Conference nor its president may act in the name of all the Bishops unless each and every Bishop has given his consent.[70]

50. The authority of the episcopal conference is limited by the individual responsibility of each bishop as pastor of his particular diocese and by the supreme authority of the church.[71] Episcopal conferences do not have the ecclesial status of the diocese, the patriarchate, or the worldwide church. They are headed by a president who does not have pastoral authority over the churches represented in the conference. The national bishops' conferences do not play the role in the Catholic Church that the autonomous national churches play within Lutheranism.

D. Worldwide Realization

51. Lutherans and Catholics affirm together that the worldwide expression of ecclesial life is a communion of churches, embodying the apostolicity and catholicity of the church. Each understands the universal church to be realized in local or particular churches, and these are not parts of the church, but rather realizations of the one church. They are in communion with one another and with their apostolic origins. The universal church as the comprehensive *koinonia* of salvation forms the context within which all churches are church. Both Lutherans and Catholics have structures of worldwide decision-making and action, no matter how these structures and their authority may differ.

1. Lutherans on Worldwide Realization

52. For most of its history, Lutheranism had no worldwide structural realization. A growing sense of a need for international Lutheran solidarity led first to the gathering of individual Lutherans in the Lutheran World Convention (1923), and later to the organization of Lutheran churches in the LWF (1947). As noted earlier, the LWF does not define itself as a church, but rather as "a communion of churches which confess the triune God, agree in the proclamation of the Word of God and are united in pulpit and altar fellowship."[72] As a communion of churches, the LWF acts on behalf of its member churches in areas of common interest such as ecumenical relations, theology, humanitarian assistance, human rights, communication, and various aspects of mission and development.[73] But it does not perform the full range of ecclesial actions, does not have the authority of a church, and is not structured as a church. The LWF is headed by a president and a general secretary who are not understood as pastors of world Lutheranism. However, the LWF has exercised what amounts to discipline in relation to its German-language churches in Southern Africa during the apartheid era, and it was the organ by which a consensus of its member churches was formed around the *Joint Declaration on the Doctrine of Justification*. The LWF is a realization of the *koinonia* of salvation, even if it is not in itself church.

2. Catholics on Worldwide Realization

53. The Roman Catholic Church understands itself as one church, which finds concrete, historical objectification in a plurality of particular churches: "The Catholic Church herself subsists in each particular church, which can be complete only through effective communion in faith, sacraments and unity with the whole body of Christ."[74] Thus the universal church does not result from an addition or a federation of particular churches. The particular church embodies the universal church in the sense that it is the specific place where the universal church is found, yet it manifests this universality in communion with other particular churches. The bishops in communion with one another and with the bishop of Rome assure the continuity of the particular churches with the apostolic church and represent their churches in communion with other particular churches. LG refers to the mystical body of Christ also as a "body of churches."[75]

IV. MINISTRY IN SERVICE OF COMMUNION

54. Lutheran-Catholic differences in the understanding of the structure of the church at the local, regional or national, and worldwide realizations are paralleled by differences in the understanding of ministry. Distinct ministries serve the *koinonia* of salvation in every ecclesial realization. Lutheran pastors and Catholic priests serve face-to-face assemblies. Bishops serve regional communities of such assemblies. In the Roman Catholic Church, the bishop of Rome has a special role in serving the communion of the universal church. Asymmetry between the two traditions occurs because Catholics locate the basic unit of the church in the particular church or diocese, while for Lutherans the basic unit of the church is the congregation. This asymmetry is paralleled by where they locate the fullness of ministerial office. Catholics locate the fullness of ministry in the bishop, while Lutherans find the office of word and sacrament fully realized in the pastor.

A. A History of the Present Differences between Lutherans and Roman Catholics

55. As shown in the accompanying Explanation (New Testament and history sections), the theological understanding of ordained ministry has varied significantly over the history of the church. The New Testament churches knew offices that were present only at the church's origin (*e.g.*, apostle), but also used terms such as *presbyteros* and *episkopos* which became standard titles of offices in later church history. The exact nature and function of these ministries varied in the New Testament. The threefold ordering of bishop, presbyter, and deacon became widespread in the patristic church, but the function of these ministries changed over time, especially with the rise of the parish presided over by the priest as the most widespread form of face-to-face Christian community. As discussed below (§§168-170), the nature of the distinction between priest or presbyter and bishop was an unsettled matter even in medieval theology. The Lutheran and Catholic understandings of ordained ministry in the sixteenth century were worked out against the background of this medieval uncertainty.

56. Peter Lombard, Thomas Aquinas, and many medieval theologians taught that bishop and priest belonged to the same order (*sacerdotium*). The Lutheran Reformers went further and held that the distinction in dignity and power between bishop and presbyter was not established by divine law (*iure divino*), but instead by human authority (*iure humano*) (see §§176-182 below). Whatever "power" (*potestas*) is needed to "preside over the churches" belongs "by divine right to all who preside over the churches, whether they are called pastor, presbyters, or bishops."[76] Since the congregation is the community gathered by word and sacrament which mediate salvation, the congregation must be church. In a situation of emergency, a church can provide for the needed ministry of word and sacrament by its own pastors' ordaining clergy since in principle a presbyter can do what a bishop can do, regardless of how matters may be ordered in non-emergency situations.[77] On this basis, when the Catholic bishops would not ordain evangelical clergy, Lutheran churches within the Holy Roman Empire proceeded in the 1530s to ordain clergy with pastors acting as the presiding ministers.[78] The Lutheran argument was complex, appealing both to ecclesiological claims about the powers of the church and to claims about the essential equality of presbyter and bishop. This argument reflects the idea that the presbyter could in a situation of necessity exercise all essential functions of the office of ordained ministry.

57. Consistent with this confessional Lutheran understanding, the ELCA is characterized throughout its structures by the interdependence between the assembly and the ordained ministry. The congregation is served by a pastor; the synod is served by a bishop; the ELCA as a whole is served by a presiding bishop. This structure is typical of Lutheran churches, and some Lutheran theologians have seen in this structure a normative expression of the Lutheran understanding of the church.[79]

58. At the Council of Trent, the Catholic Church spoke of "a hierarchy in the church, instituted by divine appointment, consisting of bishops, priests, and ministers," but it stopped short of stating that the office of bishop exists in the church *iure divino* or that the episcopate is an order distinct from the presbyterate.[80] It did affirm, however, that bishops in

particular belong to this hierarchical order (*gradus*), that they have been made by the Holy Spirit rulers of the church of God, that they are higher than priests, and that they are able to confer the sacrament of confirmation and to ordain the ministers of the church.[81] Those who "have neither been duly ordained nor [been] commissioned by ecclesiastical and canonical authority" are not "legitimate" (*legitimos*) ministers of word and sacraments.[82]

59. The Second Vatican Council, in continuity with the implications of the apostolic constitution of Pope Pius XII *Sacramentum Ordinis*,[83] affirmed that episcopal ordination alone confers the fullness of the sacrament of Order.[84] The priest or presbyter participates in the sacrament of Order in a less complete manner.[85] That the bishops as a body are successors to the apostles is by divine institution.[86] However, the Second Vatican Council left open whether the distinction between bishop and presbyter is of divine institution.[87] Only a bishop confers the sacrament of Order. If the local or particular church possesses all that is needed to be truly church, then it must include within itself all ministries essential to the church. If the bishop alone exercises the fullness of the ministerial priesthood, then only that church which includes a bishop can be such a local or particular church.[88]

B. Ordained Ministry Serving the Congregation or Parish

60. Catholics and Lutherans affirm together that the ministry of an ordained pastor or priest is a constitutive element of the *koinonia* of salvation gathered around font, pulpit, and altar. Central to this ministry is preaching the gospel, presiding in the sacramental life of the community, and leading as pastor the community in its life and mission. The activities of this minister are instruments of the life of the congregation as a *koinonia* of salvation.

1. Catholics

61. The pastor, a member of the presbyterate,[89] is the proper shepherd of the parish. He exercises the duties of teaching, sanctifying, and pastoral care in the community entrusted to him under the authority of the diocesan bishop in whose ministry of Christ he has been called to share.[90] In a

certain sense, presbyters make the bishop present in the individual local congregation.[91] Together with the bishop, presbyters constitute one presbyterium,[92] evidence of the collegial character of the order. A presbyter carries out the duties of teaching, sanctifying, and governing with the cooperation of other presbyters or deacons and the assistance of other members of the Christian faithful. In their own locality, priests also make visible the universal church.[93] The pastor of a parish works with the bishop and with the presbyterate of the diocese to ensure that "the faithful be concerned for parochial communion and that they realize that they are members both of the diocese and of the universal church and participate in and support efforts to promote such communion."[94]

2. Lutherans

62. Lutherans have historically emphasized the single office of word and sacrament exercised by all ordained ministers. The vast majority of such ministers are congregational pastors. In preaching the word and celebrating the sacraments, their ministry is essential to the congregation as church and intimately related to the character of the congregation as a *koinonia* of salvation. They "stand both within the congregation and over against it. They stand with the whole people of God because all share in the one ministry of the church. They stand over against the congregation because in God's name they proclaim the saving gospel to God's people, and therefore bear the authority of God's word, but only insofar as their proclamation is faithful to the gospel."[95]

C. Ordained Ministry Serving Regional Communities

63. Lutherans and Catholics affirm together that the realization of *koinonia* in the primary regional community is presided over by an ordained minister, called a bishop. Lutherans and Catholics agree that the bishop exercises a priesthood or ministry of word and sacrament also shared in by the priest or pastor. Episcopal ministry finds its center in word, sacrament, and pastoral leadership. This ministry serves the unity of the church, both within the regional community and in the relation of this regional community with the church of all times and places.[96]

1. Catholics

64. In the Catholic Church, a bishop is a priest who has the "fullness of the sacrament of order."[97] Ordination to the episcopacy confers the offices of sanctifying, teaching, and governing.[98] By virtue of his ordination, the bishop's authority in his diocese is "proper, ordinary, and immediate,"[99] which means that it is not delegated by higher ecclesiastical authority. He is able to exercise this authority, however, only in communion with the college of bishops and the bishop of Rome. Among his duties, "the preaching of the gospel occupies the pre-eminent place."[100] He is the pastor of a particular church, which includes multiple parishes.

65. In the Catholic Church, bishops function within the college of bishops to which they are admitted by virtue of their episcopal ordination and hierarchical communion with the bishop of Rome.[101] A bishop represents his own church within this college, and all the bishops together with the bishop of Rome represent the whole church[102] and share responsibility for preaching the gospel to the whole world.[103] The college of bishops does not constitute a legislative body apart from the bishop of Rome, but instead includes the pope as member and head of the college.

66. The Second Vatican Council did not specify what constitutes the fullness of the sacrament of Order given in ordination as a bishop. This "fullness of the sacrament of order" can refer (among other things) to the regional bishop's representing his particular church in the communion of churches. The very nature of the episcopacy requires that a bishop exercise his office, even within his own particular church, only in communion with the college of bishops into which he is "incorporated" by his sacramental ordination. The college of bishops symbolizes the unity among the particular churches that each bishop represents in his office. The episcopacy is a relational office, connecting eucharistic communities with one another across space and time as well as fostering the ministry of the local church in faith and love. The collegiality of the episcopacy represents the catholicity of the churches. The episcopacy also connects eucharistic communities with the college of the apostles, and thus represents the apostolicity of the churches.[104]

2. Lutherans

67. At the time of the Reformation, Lutherans in the Holy Roman Empire organized ministries of oversight in their territorial churches to replace those of the bishops who, they judged, had abandoned the gospel and who would not ordain evangelical clergy. While these ministers of oversight had various titles, their ministry was understood to be episcopal.[105] Various Lutheran church orders spoke of this office of oversight as necessary to the life of the church[106] because it was oriented to the church's faithfulness in those ministries that served its life as a *koinonia* of salvation. Following 1918 and the end of the state-church system within which the princes played a quasi-episcopal role, the German Lutheran churches reintroduced the title "bishop."[107] The Nordic Lutheran churches, in lands where the entire nation became Lutheran, preserved the pre-Reformation episcopal order, with varying degrees of continuity with their predecessors in office (see §§189-195 below). The predecessor bodies of the ELCA introduced the title "bishop" in the second half of the twentieth century (see §232 below).

68. In the ELCA, a bishop is called to be a "synod's pastor" and as such "shall be an ordained minister of Word and Sacrament."[108] Like all pastors, the bishop shall "preach, teach, and administer the sacraments." In addition, the bishop has "primary responsibility for the ministry of Word and Sacrament in the synod and its congregations, providing pastoral care and leadership."[109] The ministry and oversight of the bishop thus relate directly to that which makes the synod a realization of the *koinonia* of salvation.

69. Lutherans also affirm the role of the episcopacy in linking regional churches to the universal church. The ELCA constitution stipulates that the synodical bishop shall provide "leadership in strengthening the unity of the Church."[110] This responsibility is affirmed by the ELCA–Episcopal Church agreement "Called to Common Mission": "By such a liturgical statement [entrance into the episcopate through the laying on of hands by other bishops] the churches recognize that the bishop serves the diocese or synod through ties of collegiality and consultation that strengthen its links with the universal church."[111] Similarly, in the Northern European *Porvoo Common Statement*, the participating Lutheran and

Anglican churches "acknowledge that the episcopal office is valued and maintained in all our churches as a visible sign expressing and serving the Church's unity and continuity in apostolic life, mission and ministry."[112]

D. Ordained Ministry Serving the Universal Church

70. Catholics and Lutherans affirm together that all ministry, to the degree that it serves the *koinonia* of salvation, also serves the unity of the worldwide church. A specific ministry that serves universal unity is affirmed by Catholics and not excluded by Lutherans. Lutherans and Catholics together need to discuss how such a ministry can be formed and reformed so that it can be received by a greater range of the world's churches and thus better fulfill its own service to unity.

1. Catholics

71. As bishop of the particular church of Rome, the bishop of Rome, successor of Peter, has a unique responsibility as pastor and teacher to the universal church. He is, in his Petrine ministry, the visible "principle of the unity both of faith and of communion."[113] The common statement *Papal Primacy and the Universal Church* spoke of a "Petrine function" to describe "a particular form of Ministry exercised by a person, officeholder, or local church with reference to the church as a whole," a function that "serves to promote or preserve the oneness of the church by symbolizing unity, and by facilitating communication, mutual assistance or correction, and collaboration in the church's mission."[114] Since the pope must ensure and serve the communion of the particular churches, he is the first servant of unity.[115] While the pope does not take the place of the diocesan bishop, his pastoral authority and responsibility extends throughout the church around the world. He must assure that the local churches keep and transmit the apostolic faith with integrity. He promotes and coordinates the activities of the churches in their missionary task. He speaks in the name of all the bishops and all their local churches when necessary and has the authority to declare officially and solemnly the revealed truth in the name of the whole church. The bishop of Rome always fulfills his office in communion with the college of bishops as a member and its head.[116] His office is not separate from the mission entrusted to the whole body of bishops.

72. In *Ut Unum Sint*, Pope John Paul II's concern for the unity of the churches is not limited to the Catholic communion, but extends to all Christian communities. He acknowledges that the exercise of the papacy at times has been an obstacle to Christian unity. Therefore, he seeks "a way of exercising the primacy which, while in no way renouncing what is essential to its mission, is nonetheless open to a new situation."[117] To this end, he has called upon church leaders and theologians to engage with him in a patient and fraternal dialogue on this subject.[118]

2. Lutherans

73. Openness to a rightly exercised primacy is part of the Lutheran theological legacy. The Lutheran Reformers' rejection of the papacy focused on "the concrete historical papacy as it confronted them in their day" rather than on the very idea of a universal ministry of unity.[119] In Luther's *Against the Papacy in Rome, Instituted by the Devil* (1545), perhaps his sharpest writing against the papacy, Luther nevertheless affirms that the pope might have a primacy of "honor and superiority" and "of oversight over teaching and heresy in the church."[120] This "conditional openness" to papal primacy is dependent upon a reformed papacy, subject to the gospel, that would not arbitrarily restrict Christian freedom.[121]

74. The Lutheran argument did not merely contest abuses, however; it also challenged the alleged *iure divino* character of the papacy. Philipp Melanchthon added to his subscription to the Smalcald Articles that, if the pope "would allow the gospel," the papacy's "superiority over the bishops" could be granted *iure humano*.[122] Historical criticism has significantly altered understandings of divine and human law and criteria for distinguishing them.[123] Especially in relation to the papacy, but also in relation to other traditionally controversial questions relating to ministry, the categories of divine and human law need to be re-examined and placed in the context of ministry as service to the *koinonia* of salvation.

V. MINISTRY AND THE CONTINUITY WITH THE APOSTOLIC CHURCH

A. Succession in Apostolic Mission, Ministry, and Message

75. Both Lutherans and Catholics have a strong commitment to maintaining apostolicity in the Christian faith.[124] The *koinonia* of salvation requires continuity in the mission, ministry, and message of the apostles. The discussion of ordained ministry between Lutherans and Catholics, however, often has been dominated by the issue of apostolic succession understood as a succession of episcopal consecrations. As a result, the question of apostolicity has been discussed in a narrowly canonical and mechanistic manner. The renewed ecclesiology of *koinonia* instead has sought first to understand ministry as a bond of *koinonia* within the church and then to recover the rich patristic sense of the bonds of the church to the apostles' mission, ministry, and message across space and time. Lutherans and Catholics agree that the continuity of the apostolic church and the continuity of its mission, ministry, and message are promised to it by its Lord.[125] In the mission given by Jesus to the apostles, the Lord has promised to be present until the end of the age (see Mt. 28:19-20). There is one household of God, founded on the apostles and prophets, with Christ as the cornerstone (see Eph. 2:20). The gates of Hell shall never prevail against this church (see Mt. 16:18).

76. Lutherans and Catholics agree that "apostolic succession" in this comprehensive sense is essential to the church's being. Such succession is continuity with both the past and the future, both with the apostles as witnesses of the resurrection two thousand years ago and with the apostles whose names will be on the twelve foundations of the New Jerusalem (see Rev. 21:14). Such continuity is an element of "the Church's communion which spans time and space, linking the present to past and future generations of Christians."[126]

77. Continuity in apostolic mission, ministry, and message is not a human achievement, but rather a gift of the Spirit. God is faithful to his promise, despite our failings. Our confidence in this continuity is not based upon our fidelity, but upon God's promise. God maintains the

church in the apostolic mission, ministry, and message through concrete means: the apostolic scriptures, faithful teachers, the creeds, and the continuity of ordained ministry. Through these various means, the community as a whole remains apostolic.[127]

B. The Bishop as Sign and Instrument of Apostolic Succession

78. As a regional minister of oversight, the bishop is called to foster the *koinonia* that extends beyond any one local community. The bishop maintains *koinonia* with the church's apostolic foundations through proclamation of the gospel and apostolic faith. A truly evangelical oversight will focus on the church's faithfulness to the gospel and thus seek to safeguard and further its true apostolicity. The episcopal task is thus inherently bound up with a concern for apostolic continuity. As the ELCA–Episcopal Church agreement stated, a ministry of *episcopé*, conferred through the laying on of hands by other bishops and prayer for the gift of the Holy Spirit, is one of the ways "in the context of ordained ministries and of the whole people of God, in which the apostolic succession of the church is visibly expressed and personally symbolized in fidelity to the Gospel through the ages."[128]

79. While a focus on a continuity in ordinations or consecrations can make the concept of succession appear simply human, such a focus should bring to the fore the divine initiative in preserving the church. The laying on of hands is a classical form of intensive prayer. In both of our churches, the laying on of hands for the episcopal office is accompanied by a prayer for the pouring out of the Spirit upon the new bishops to empower their ministry. The church thus celebrates the continuity of apostolic ministry, a continuity that lies ultimately in the hands of God. The church must pray for that ministry to continue, and it prays confidently in the knowledge that God will be faithful to the promise that goes with the command to "go out into all the world" (see Mt. 28:19-20; Mk. 16:14).

80. Prior to the late 1530s, the theme of succession played little role in Reformation debates on the role and authority of the bishop. The

authority and ministry of the bishop, not any particular concept of succession, were the subject of debate. The Lutheran Confessions explicitly regret the loss of the "order of the church"[129] that resulted from the presbyteral ordinations the Lutherans judged to be necessary for the life of their churches, but neither Article 28 of the *Augsburg Confession* on the power of bishops nor the response by the imperial Catholic theologians to it in the *Confutation* refers explicitly to succession.[130] Thus, when the Lutheran churches felt compelled to ordain pastors apart from the Catholic hierarchy, they were not consciously rejecting any concept of episcopal succession, for such a concept was not current in theological discussions of the period. Only with the renewed attention to patristic sources in the subsequent debates was such a concept reasserted.[131] Unfortunately, when the writings of such figures as Irenaeus were taken up in the debate, they were used within a canonical argument over validity which the Lutherans could only reject.[132] More recent ecumenical discussions of succession as a sign of the continuity of the church (*e.g.*, the Anglican-Lutheran *Niagara Report*, 1987) have found much greater (though not universal) acceptance in Lutheran circles.[133] In 2001, the ELCA entered a new relation with The Episcopal Church, committing both to "share an episcopal succession that is both evangelical and historic."[134] Similar Lutheran-Anglican agreements in Canada and Northern Europe in which Lutherans have affirmed episcopal succession put Lutheran-Catholic relations in a new context.

81. The Roman Catholic Church has preserved the succession of episcopal consecrations; this succession was broken in continental Lutheranism, maintained in parts of Nordic Lutheranism, and has been reclaimed by the ELCA. What is the significance of either preserving or breaking this succession? That question must not be isolated and made to bear the entire weight of a judgment on a church's ministry. Whether a particular minister or church serves the church's apostolic mission does not depend only upon the presence of such a succession of episcopal consecrations, as if its absence would negate the apostolicity of the church's teaching and mission.[135] Recent ecumenical discussions of episcopacy and succession do not remove our former disagreements, but they do place them in a richer and more complex context in which

judgments made exclusively on the basis of the presence or absence of a succession of consecrations are less possible.

VI. LOCAL AND REGIONAL STRUCTURES AND MINISTRIES OF COMMUNION

A. The Relationship between Local and Regional Churches

82. The interdependent polarity between "face-to-face eucharistic assembly" and "primary regional community of such assemblies" elaborated above (see §§27-29, 33) forms the background for a reconsideration of the relation between bishop and presbyter. Bishop and pastor are the presiding ministers, respectively, of the synod or diocese and of the congregation or parish gathered around word and sacrament.[136] Church unity rests in *koinonia* or sharing in word and sacrament. Because ordained ministry of word and sacrament is essential to the church's sharing in and sharing of salvation, such ministry is intrinsically related to the church's unity and *koinonia*.

83. The relation between bishop and pastor parallels in important ways the relation between synod or diocese, on the one hand, and parish or congregation, on the other. Within this parallelism, the differing understandings of the structure of church held by Lutherans and Catholics have each grasped an essential dimension of the church: the primacy of the face-to-face community gathered around font, pulpit, and altar, on the one hand, and the essential character of *koinonia* with other such communities for the life of any eucharistic assembly, on the other. In seeking to determine which is "local church" in the theological sense noted above, however, false choices have been forced upon theological reflection. As a result, both Lutherans and Catholics suffer from an imbalance in their theological account of the church.

84. With respect to Roman Catholics, the international Roman Catholic–Lutheran Joint Commission has noted that, despite the definition of the local church as the diocese, "in actual fact it is the parish, even more than the diocese, which is familiar to Christians as the place

where the church is to be experienced."[137] The Second Vatican Council recognized this role of the parish when it stated that "parishes set up locally under a pastor who takes the place of the bishop . . . in a certain way represent the visible Church as it is established throughout the world."[138] For Catholic doctrine, however, the church is identified by the minister who presides over it. The presence of the bishop signals the continuity of the local church in the apostolic faith as well as the communion of that church with other churches, essential components in the definition of a local church in the Roman Catholic tradition. But Catholics do not often perceive their eucharistic community as headed by the bishop. Although the bishop directs and is named in every celebration of the eucharist in the diocese,[139] and there is an understanding that the priest in some sense makes present the bishop,[140] in the experience of most Roman Catholics, the diocese is not the primary eucharistic expression of the church.

85. With respect to Lutherans, the local/presbyteral realization of the church in the congregation has priority. A theological understanding of the need to realize regional *koinonia* with ongoing structures remains underdeveloped. The church is identified as "the assembly of saints in which the gospel is taught purely and the sacraments are administered rightly."[141] But the church is not limited to the congregation, for Luther says, "The church is the number or gathering of the baptized and the believers under one pastor, whether this is in one city or in one province or in the whole world."[142] Herein lies the difficulty. While a community gathered by word and sacrament suggests a local congregation, the Reformers and most of later Lutheranism[143] have stressed the need for regional structures and discipline. In the same text to the Bohemians in which Luther urges them to ordain their own ministers, he also suggests that if a number of communities do this, then "these bishops may wish to come together and elect one or more from their number to be their superiors, who would serve them and hold visitations among them, as Peter visited the churches, according to the account in the Book of Acts. Then Bohemia would return again to its rightful and evangelical archbishopric, which would be rich, not in large income and much authority, but in many ministers and visitations of the churches."[144]

86. Here Luther clearly urges a regional structure. The term "particular church" was applied by later Lutheran theology equally to the congregation and to the regional or national body.[145] What Lutheranism lacks is a clear and convincing theological rationale for its actual practice of embedding the congregation in a regional body, which is also called "church." The temptations of congregationalism and the understanding of regional structures as merely sociological necessity have recurred within Lutheran history.[146] The theological basis for the realization of the essential catholicity of the face-to-face assembly in lived *koinonia* with other such assemblies is theologically underexpressed.

87. Lutherans and Catholics agree that neither the local congregation or parish nor the regional community of these congregations or parishes is sufficient in itself without the other. Due weight must be given both to the assembly of word and sacrament and to the regional community of such assemblies. Catholics are challenged to develop more fully a doctrine of the parish and to address the contemporary implausibility of its depiction of the diocese as "local church" or eucharistic assembly. The Lutheran viewpoint suffers from an incompleteness in its theological account of the significance of the regional church. Each viewpoint tends to treat ministry in the same way that it treats ecclesiology. Lutheran ecclesiology emphasizes the congregation and the pastor, while Catholic ecclesiology emphasizes the bishop and the regional structure.

88. A way forward beyond this contrast between the two traditions is to regard the regional/episcopal and the local/presbyteral difference as a normative complementarity, both in relation to ecclesiology and in relation to the doctrine of ministry. The exclusive prioritizing of either the regional or the geographically local is a false alternative. An initial agreement on this point already has been reached in relation to ministry by the international Roman Catholic–Lutheran Joint Commission: "*If* both churches acknowledge that for faith this historical development of the one apostolic ministry into a more local and a more regional ministry has taken place with the help of the Holy Spirit and to this degree constitutes something essential for the church, then a *high degree of agreement* has been reached."[147] If the difference between a local and a

regional ministry, paralleling a difference between the face-to-face assembly and the regional community of such assemblies, is a development helped by the Holy Spirit, then an ecclesiology that devalues this difference by reducing one side of it to theological insignificance fails to follow where the Spirit has led.

89. If the church as the *koinonia* of salvation is born from and borne by the gospel proclaimed in word and sacrament, and if the eucharist, including the proclamation of the word and the celebration of the Supper, is the event from which and toward which the church lives,[148] then the face-to-face eucharistic assembly must be a basic unit of the church. It is a place where "church" is essentially realized.[149] Indeed, there can be no church without such face-to-face eucharistic assemblies. In that sense, they are fundamental.[150] That which is realized in this face-to-face eucharistic assembly is truly "church," the body of Christ, the assembly of all the saints across time and space. This relation is manifest in the Supper, where the congregation praises God "with the church on earth and the hosts of heaven."

90. Each eucharistic assembly lives out its constitutive relation with the wider church by its concrete relations with other assemblies in a network of *koinonia*. The JWG affirmed the importance of this *koinonia* for the local church. "The local church is not a free-standing, self-sufficient reality. As part of a network of communion, the local church maintains its reality as church by relating to other local churches."[151] This relationship with other local churches is essential to the catholicity that every church must embody. "Communion with other local churches is essential to the integrity of the self-understanding of each local church, precisely because of its catholicity. Life in self-sufficient isolation . . . is the denial of its very being."[152] The same must be said about the relation of the eucharistic assembly to the wider church. For Catholic theology, the communion of the local face-to-face eucharistic assemblies with their bishop is essential for their ecclesiality, and they cannot be considered "churches" apart from that communion. For these communities, catholicity requires not only communion with other local churches, but

also communion with the ministry of the bishop. It was stated forcefully in the context of an LWF study on church unity that "the already
existing spiritual unity of the Church of Jesus Christ demands the realization of concrete, historical, tangible church fellowship."[153] Thus, "all
local *ecclesiae* in the whole world should stand in a concrete, actually
lived, legally effective *koinonia*."[154]

91. The most immediate and concrete way this network of relations
among face-to-face eucharistic assemblies is realized is in some primary
regional community: a Catholic diocese, a Lutheran synod. These primary regional communities embody in an explicit way the essential
interconnection of every eucharistic assembly within the one *koinonia* of
salvation. Such a regional community is itself church, not just a collection of churches, for it is the assembly (even if only representative) of
assemblies, each of which relates to the others internally, not merely
externally,[155] for *koinonia* with other communities is essential to the
catholicity and thus the ecclesiality of each. The assemblies come
together as one church. If the ecclesial reality of any larger grouping is
inseparable from that of face-to-face eucharistic assemblies, the con-
verse is also true: the ecclesial reality and catholicity of face-to-face
eucharistic assemblies requires their existence within regional communities. The complementarity of face-to-face eucharistic assembly and
primary regional community is thus theologically normative.

B. The Relation between
Priest/Presbyter/Pastor and Bishop

92. The preceding analysis leads to the conclusion that the complementarity of local and regional ministry is normative within the ordained
ministry of the church, paralleling the normative complementarity of the
face-to-face eucharistic assembly and the primary regional community. It
would be a mistake to insist that either the parish/congregation or the
diocese/synod is exclusively *the* local church. Likewise, the doctrine of
ministry would be distorted by insisting that either the presbyter or the
bishop is the only theologically necessary ordained minister, thereby dismissing the other, bishop or presbyter, as practically necessary but theologically insignificant. Lutherans often have insisted that the bishop is a
pastor with a larger sphere of ministry, without seeing the distinctiveness

of the role of a pastor to a communion of communities, each led by its own ordained minister. Recent Catholic theology often fails adequately to explain why priests are theologically necessary, in addition to bishops, rather than merely practically necessary to the church.

93. If we think of the ordained ministry as structured by this complementarity, the specific emphases of each tradition might come to be seen in a new light. Because the regional grouping served by the bishop manifests in a fuller way the unity of the church by manifesting the unity of the communities within it more fully than any one of these communities can do alone, one can say that the ministry of the bishop is *in this sense* fuller than that of any single presbyter. As the minister of the actual face-to-face eucharistic assembly, however, the presbyter might be said *in this sense* to have a richer, more fundamental ministry. Each ministry depends upon the other.

94. At the same time that we strive to show what is distinctive and complementary between the office of bishop and that of pastor/priest/ presbyter with respect to their service to different levels of ecclesiality, it is also important that we keep in mind the profound similarities in these two offices. In many ways, they are distinct but inseparable offices. Both bishops and presbyters are ordained to serve word, sacrament, and the pastoral life of the church. For Lutherans, both bishops and pastors exercise the one office of word and sacrament. In Roman Catholic theology, the sacrament of Order is one; both bishops and presbyters are priests; priests are associated with their bishop in one presbyterium. What these ministries share is much greater than that which distinguishes them.

VII. RECOMMENDATIONS FOR AN ECUMENICAL WAY FORWARD

A. Toward a Recognition of the Reality and Woundedness of Our Ministries and Churches

95. What follows for the relations between our churches from the analysis above, supported by the biblical and historical explanations below?

Building upon the earlier Lutheran–Roman Catholic dialogue texts, *Eucharist and Ministry* and *Facing Unity*,[156] we propose steps toward a full, mutual recognition and reconciliation of our ministries and the ultimate goal of full communion. We are aware of common challenges to overcome. Nevertheless, the mutual recognition of ministries need not be an all-or-nothing matter and should not be reduced to a simple judgment about validity or invalidity. In order to assess the degree of our *koinonia* in ordained ministry, a more nuanced discernment is needed to reflect the way that an ordained ministry serves the proclamation of the gospel and the administration of the sacraments, stands in continuity with the apostolic tradition, and serves communion among churches.

96. We recommend that our churches recognize our common understanding of the interdependent structures of church life and ministry, namely, the diocese/synod with its bishop and the parish/congregation with its pastor or priest. This common understanding is reflected in a shared sense of the single sacrament of Order (*sacramentum Ordinis*) or the one office of ministry (Amt). The differences between us in emphasis and terminology need not be church-dividing even though they challenge each church to overcome imbalances in its own tradition.

97. Our affirmations about ordained ministry go together with our affirmations about our communities (see §§85-89), for ministry parallels the ordering of the church. If real but imperfect recognition exists between our ministers and our communities, neither community can lack churchly reality. Movement toward deeper mutual recognition of our ministries is both rooted in and contributes to our growing sense of the ecclesial reality of each of our communities. In particular, the Catholic non-recognition of Lutheran ministries has hindered Catholic affirmation of the Lutheran churches as churches. If our proposal for deeper mutual recognition of ministries is accepted, then new possibilities should open for reconsideration of mutual recognition as churches. Mutual recognition of our churches and ministries need not be an all-or-nothing matter.[157]

98. We recommend that each church recognize that the other realizes, even if perhaps imperfectly, the one church of Jesus Christ and shares in the apostolic tradition.

99. We recommend that each church recognize that the ordained ministry of the other effectively carries on, even if perhaps imperfectly, the apostolic ministry instituted by God in the church.

100. To say that each church understands itself and the other as exercising the apostolic ministry is not to say that either church escapes the damage done to our ministries by the ongoing scandal of our division. To the extent that the ordained ministry of one church is not in communion with the ordained ministry of other churches, it is unable to carry out its witness to the unity of the church as it should. Such a ministry inevitably bears a wound or defect. Ministry carries this wound whenever the *koinonia* among eucharistic communities and different realizations of the church are broken. Because our relationships are broken, our ministry is wounded and in need of healing by God's grace.

101. This need affects both of our churches. The Roman Catholic Church acknowledges that it is wounded by a lack of communion. As the *Decree on Ecumenism* stated, "The divisions among Christians prevent the church from realizing in practice the fullness of catholicity proper to her."[158] The 1992 letter from the Congregation for the Doctrine of the Faith "Some Aspects of the Church as Communion," after noting the wound that lack of communion inflicts on the Orthodox and Reformation churches, concluded that this division

> in turn also wounds (*vulnus iniungitur*) the Catholic Church, called by the Lord to become for all "one flock" with "one shepherd," in that it hinders the complete fulfillment of her universality in history.[159]

The entire Catholic priesthood, including the bishop of Rome, is wounded in an important dimension of its ministry insofar as unity and communion are lacking with other churches and their ministries.

102. The same must be said of the Lutheran churches and their ministries. Lutherans understand their ministries to be realizations of the one ministry of the one church, yet they cannot manifest communion in this one ministry with many other churches. This woundedness provides a helpful basis for a new understanding of the Catholic assertion of *defectus* in the sacrament of Order in Lutheran churches (§§108-109).

103. We recommend a mutual recognition that (1) our ordained ministries are wounded because the absence of full communion between our ecclesial traditions makes it impossible for them to adequately represent and foster the unity and catholicity of the church, and that (2) our communities are wounded by their lack of the full catholicity to which they are called and by their inability to provide a common witness to the gospel.

104. Addressing these wounds in our churches will require repentance and conversion. Each church must examine its theology and practice of ministry and ask whether they truly serve the mission and unity of the church. Division offers occasions for sin, to which our churches have sometimes succumbed.[160] The Second Vatican Council teaches that "there can be no ecumenism worthy of the name without a change of heart."[161] Pope John Paul II concluded on this basis that "the Council calls for personal conversion as well as for communal conversion."[162]

105. We recommend that our churches pray together for the grace of repentance and conversion needed for healing the wounds of our division.

1. Catholic Discernment

106. Repentance and conversion call for steps toward healing the wounds of our division. For Catholics, a necessary step will be a reassessment of Lutheran presbyteral ordinations at the time of the Reformation. This reassessment on the part of proper church authorities now can take into account the nature of the presbyteral ministry and its relation to episcopal ministry, the nature of apostolic succession, the sort of community that decided to carry out such ordinations, the intent behind these ordinations, and the historical situation that led to such a

decision. The argument presented above about the normative complementarity between presbyter and bishop holds significance for the eval-
uation of the ministries in continuity with these Reformation actions.
The historical findings (see §§171-182 below) show that the theology
that supported the Lutheran action was not a conscious rejection of all
earlier tradition, but instead bore significant continuities with New
Testament, patristic, and medieval understandings. The recent commitment of the ELCA to enter into episcopal succession for the sake of
ecclesial *koinonia*[163] is a new and significant factor in this regard.

107. Catholic judgment on the authenticity of Lutheran ministry need
not be of an all-or-nothing nature. The *Decree on Ecumenism* of the
Second Vatican Council distinguished between relationships of full
ecclesiastical communion and those of imperfect communion to reflect
the varying degrees of differences with the Catholic Church.[164] The
communion of these separated communities with the Catholic Church
is real, even though it is imperfect. Furthermore, the decree positively
affirmed the following:

> Our separated brothers and sisters also celebrate many sacred
> actions of the Christian religion. These most certainly can truly
> engender a life of grace in ways that vary according to the con-
> dition of each church or community, and must be held capable
> of giving access to that communion in which is salvation.[165]

Commenting on this point, Cardinal Joseph Ratzinger, prefect of the
Congregation on the Doctrine of the Faith, wrote the following in 1993
to Bavarian Lutheran bishop Johannes Hanselmann:

> I count among the most important results of the ecumenical
> dialogues the insight that the issue of the eucharist cannot be
> narrowed to the problem of 'validity.' Even a theology oriented
> to the concept of succession, such as that which holds in
> the Catholic and in the Orthodox church, need not in any
> way deny the salvation-granting presence of the Lord
> [*Heilschaffende Gegenwart des Herrn*] in a Lutheran [*evangelis-
> che*] Lord's Supper.[166]

If the actions of Lutheran pastors can be described by Catholics as "sacred actions" that "can truly engender a life of grace," if communities served by such ministers give "access to that communion in which is salvation," and if "the salvation-granting presence of the Lord" is to be found at a eucharist at which a Lutheran pastor presides, then Lutheran churches cannot be said simply to lack the ministry given to the church by Christ and the Spirit. In acknowledging the imperfect *koinonia* between our communities and the access to grace through the ministries of these communities, we also acknowledge a real although imperfect *koinonia* between our ministries.

108. Ecumenical understanding would be furthered if, in official Roman Catholic documents, the Second Vatican Council's reference to *defectus* in the sacrament of Order among "ecclesial communities" were translated using such words as "defect" or "deficiency."[167] As Cardinal Walter Kasper has stated, "On material grounds [*aus der Sachlogik*], and not merely on the basis of the word usage of the Council, it becomes clear that *defectus ordinis* does not signify a complete absence, but rather a deficiency [*Mangel*] in the full form of the office."[168] Translations of *defectus* as "lack" misleadingly imply the simple absence of the reality of ordination. Translations of the word as "defect" or "deficiency" would be consistent with the sort of real but imperfect recognition of ministries proposed above. While short of full recognition, such partial recognition would provide the basis for first steps toward a reconciliation of ministries as envisioned, e.g., in the international Roman Catholic–Lutheran statement *Facing Unity*.[169]

109. We recommend that Roman Catholic criteria for assessing authentic ministry include attention to a ministry's faithfulness to the gospel and its service to the communion of the church, and that the term defectus ordinis as applied to Lutheran ministries be translated as "deficiency" rather than "lack."

2. Lutheran Discernment
110. In ecumenical discussions, Lutherans have shown little hesitancy in recognizing the ordained ministries of the Catholic Church. During

the Reformation era, the Lutheran churches did not re-ordain Catholic priests who joined the evangelical movement.[170] At times in the past, Lutherans doubted that the Catholic priesthood was in fact the one evangelical ministry of word and sacrament of the one church, because Lutherans thought the Catholic priesthood was oriented toward an unevangelical understanding of the Mass.[171] These doubts have been removed by convergence and agreement on the gospel[172] and by such affirmations as that of the Second Vatican Council that "among the principal tasks of bishops the preaching of the gospel is pre-eminent."[173]

111. Lutherans also need repentance and conversion to take steps toward healing the wounds of our division. They must constantly reassess some of their own traditions of ordained ministry. Regarding "the order of the church and the various ranks in the church" including bishops, the *Apology of the Augsburg Confession* testifies that the "greatest desire" of the Reformers was to retain this ministerial structure.[174] This desire stated in the Lutheran Confessions still is normative for present-day Lutheranism. The office of bishop as regional pastor is the normal polity of the church, "a gift of the Holy Spirit,"[175] and it implies bishops in communion with other ministers exercising *episcopé*. A church may be compelled to abandon such a shared episcopal office for a time, but it should return to it whenever possible. Recent actions by the ELCA and some other Lutheran churches to reclaim shared episcopal ordering, both among themselves and as an aspect of communion with Anglican churches, are signs of a willingness to engage in such a reassessment.[176]

3. Common Challenges

112. Asymmetry exists between our churches in relation to our mutual recognition of ordained ministry. Lutheran churches are able fully to recognize Catholic ordained ministries on the basis of ecumenical developments, but the Catholic Church has not fully recognized the ordained ministries of a church such as the ELCA.[177] This asymmetry makes life together more difficult. Any reconciliation of ministries needs to find ways of addressing this asymmetry that accord with the self-understanding of each church.

113. The ordination or non-ordination of women is a significant difference between our two traditions. The decision to ordain both women and men to the ministry of word and sacrament involves questions about the church's authority. The ELCA, continuing the practice of its predecessor bodies, holds itself free under the gospel to ordain women.[178] The Catholic Church does not hold itself authorized to make such a decision.[179] The reconciliation or full mutual recognition of ministries will need to address this sensitive difference.

B. Universal Church and Universal Ministry

114. In relation to a universal ministry at the service of the unity of the universal church, this dialogue is far less ready to propose any official actions. The bishop of Rome, the only historically plausible candidate for such a universal ministry, remains a sign of unity and a sign of division among us. Pope John Paul II has called for an ecumenical dialogue on the papacy and its exercise as a pastoral office in service of the unity of Christians.[180] We are hopeful that this invitation for "a patient and fraternal dialogue"[181] on the papacy and its exercise might be taken up with a renewed commitment to overcoming the divisions of the past and present.

1. Catholic Reflections on Universal Ministry

115. Pope John Paul II in *Ut Unum Sint* (1995) emphasized the bishop of Rome's responsibility to serve the unity and communion of the church: "The mission of the Bishop of Rome within the College of all the Pastors [Bishops] consists precisely in 'keeping watch' (*episkopein*). . . . With the power and authority without which such an office would be illusory, the Bishop of Rome must ensure the communion of all the Churches. For this reason, he is the first servant of unity."[182] In this encyclical, Pope John Paul II invited a consideration of reform and change in the papal office in order that this office would not be a stumbling block to Christian unity.

116. Catholics see the papal office as part of the mission entrusted to the whole people of God. A renewed exercise of the papacy will need to witness to its communal dimension by reconciling a number of tensions within the exercise of authority: the bishop of Rome's primacy and the collegiality he shares within the college of bishops; the authority

reserved to clerics and the participation of the laity in governance; the relationship between the proper, ordinary, and immediate authority of a bishop in his diocese and the universal jurisdiction of the pope; the communion within a universal church and a decentralization which respects the particularity of a local church; and finally, a common Catholic identity and increased openness to diversity.[183] The Second Vatican Council's *Decree on Ecumenism* (*Unitatis Redintegratio*) provides a guiding principle for this task:

> While preserving unity in essentials, let all members of the Church, according to the office entrusted to each, preserve a proper freedom in the various forms of spiritual life and discipline, in the variety of liturgical rites, even in the theological elaborations of revealed truth. In all things let charity be exercised. If the faithful are true to this course of action, they will be giving even richer expression to the authentic catholicity of the Church, and, at the same time, to her apostolicity.[184]

117. We recommend that Catholics explore how the universal ministry of the bishop of Rome can be reformed to manifest more visibly its subjection to the gospel in service to the *koinonia* of salvation.

2. Lutheran Reflections on Universal Ministry

118. In light of *Ut Unum Sint* and other Catholic and ecumenical statements on papacy, Lutherans have been involved in considerable discussion of universal ministry. If, as the Nordic and Baltic Lutheran churches affirmed in the *Porvoo Common Statement*, "the personal, collegial, and communal dimensions of oversight find expression at the local, regional, and universal levels of the Church's life,"[185] then the question cannot be avoided of who might exercise such a personal ministry of oversight at the universal level and of how it might be exercised in subservience to the gospel. Again, if the interdependence of assembly and ordained ministry is typical of the structure of the church at the local, regional, and national level, then why should such an interdependence not also be found at the universal level?[186]

119. Lutherans have been concerned with whether the papal office is necessary for salvation. Today, when the pastoral nature of the papacy and its reform have been taken seriously by the Catholic Church itself, the question of the papacy may be perceived in a different way, in terms of the ecclesial necessity of the papal office. To what extent may such an office of universal ministry be needed for the unity of the church in a *koinonia* of salvation?[187] Exploring these questions might clarify what Lutherans mean when they insist that any universal ministry of unity must be "under the gospel." What would be the characteristics of a universal ministry "under the gospel?"

120. We recommend that Lutherans explore whether the worldwide koinonia of the church calls for a worldwide minister of unity and what form such a ministry might take to be truly evangelical.

VIII. TOWARD DEEPER COMMUNION

121. *Ut Unum Sint*, Pope John Paul II's encyclical on ecumenism, echoes the Second Vatican Council's *Decree on Ecumenism* in affirming a certain but imperfect communion between the Roman Catholic Church and other churches and ecclesial communities.[188] Roman Catholics and churches of the LWF agree on the good news of justification.[189] If the ELCA and the Roman Catholic Church are in imperfect communion, it follows that the ministers within these communities are also in imperfect communion with one another, for ministry serves the communion of the church. Too often in our past, the judgment of the "wound" or the "defect" in another's orders based on juridical categories of validity prevented our recognition of the ministry that is truly shared. We share a common ministry of baptism, proclamation of the word, and pastoral care, and we recognize that each other's eucharist gives "access to that communion in which is salvation."[190] This present study of the structures and ministries of the church through the lens of *koinonia* asks our churches to seek ways of implementing the imperfect ministerial communion that we already experience.[191] Truly living out our communion,

albeit imperfect, may provide a foundation for living toward the full communion we seek.

122. We recommend that our churches recognize the real but imperfect communion among our ministers and encourage appropriate forms of pastoral collaboration between our ministries. Specifically, we propose (1) that common activities among Lutheran and Roman Catholic bishops be promoted in order to signify the level of communion that exists between them, such as regular joint retreats, co-authored pastoral letters on topics of mutual concern, and joint efforts on matters of public good; (2) that mutual activities be intensified among ordained ministers, such as regular retreats, homily or sermon preparation study, participation in non-eucharistic prayer services and weddings, and common sponsorship of events or services in the life of the church, including as appropriate other leadership ministries; (3) that the faithful, in light of their common baptism into the people of God, engage together in catechesis, evangelization, peace and justice ventures, social ministry, and attendance at each other's diocesan and synodical assemblies; and (4) that social ministry organizations, educational institutions, chaplaincies, and other church agencies engage together in activities that further the gospel and the common good.

123. On our journey toward full communion, including mutual recognition of ministry and churchly reality, this round of dialogue has sought to help Lutherans and Catholics move toward that goal

- by accepting *koinonia* of salvation as an interpretive lens for this study;
- by proposing an analysis of the varying local, regional, national, and worldwide realizations of the *koinonia* of salvation as a framework within which to consider mutual recognition of ministries;
- by recalling the issues of recognition of ministries as discussed in round IV in *Eucharist and Ministry* and of reconciliation of ministries stressed in *Facing Unity*;

- by relating ministerial communion to ecclesial communion, with recognition of imperfect ecclesial communion leading to recognition of imperfect ministerial communion;
- by clarifying ministerial identity in relation to service to various levels of ecclesial communion;
- by demonstrating the normative complementarity of congregational and regional structures and ministries; and
- by examining in a preliminary way the role of national and worldwide structures and urging a "patient and fraternal dialogue" on the possibility of a worldwide minister of unity.

124. A fuller mutual recognition of ministries cannot be separated from a fuller common life in Christ and the Spirit. Lutherans and Catholics together have found a greater common basis in the gospel as can be seen in the *Joint Declaration on the Doctrine of Justification*. Mutual recognition of doctrine, ministries, and ecclesial realities, rooted in a common existence in the one body of Christ, can bear fruit by the grace of God in life shared together.

125. Ministry and structures of communion are at the service of the *koinonia* of salvation realized in the life of the church. Mutual recognition of ministry and of ecclesial reality are important conditions for our full and uninhibited common participation in the salvation given us in Christ and the Spirit. We offer our work to our respective churches with the prayer that it may foster the *koinonia* in salvation we are convinced is the will of our Risen Lord.

Part Two: Further Biblical and Historical Support for Deepening Communion in Structures and Ministries

I. BIBLICAL FOUNDATIONS FOR THE CHURCH AS KOINONIA OF SALVATION IN JESUS AND THE CHRIST-EVENT

126. "Salvation," "church," and "ministries" will be treated chronologically below in various segments of the New Testament. *Koinonia* as a biblical term has been introduced above (§§11-13). A term with a range of meanings,[192] *koinōnia* and its related verbs and adjectives occur thirty-eight times in the New Testament. The background for this terminology lies entirely in the Greek world, as there is no counterpart term in Hebrew and little significant use of *koinōnia* in the Greek translations of the Hebrew Scriptures.[193] No recorded usage by Jesus of the term exists, and the Gospels contain little about it (see Lk. 5:10; "partners" in the fishing business). *Koinōnia* is preeminently a Pauline term.

127. One possible starting point in the Greek world is the adjective *koinos*,[194] "common" or "communal," as at Acts 2:44, believers "had all things in common (*koina*)," or Titus 1:4, our "common faith" (NRSV: "the faith we share"). Thus, *to koinon* could refer to the state, the public treasury, the commonwealth, or (with *agathon*) the common good. A "public" and financial side may cling to the terminology in Christian usage. The Greek adage "Friends have all things in common," is reflected in Acts 4:32, "No one claimed private ownership of any possessions, but everything they owned was held in common (*koina*)."

128. A second approach is through the verb *koinōnein*, which can mean (1) "have a share" of something (Heb. 2:14; human beings all share in

flesh and blood) or (2) "give a share" of something (the Philippian church shared funds with Paul; Phil. 4:15).[195] Language of participation also can be used, "having a part" in something or being a partner.

129. Pioneering studies, mainly by Protestants, emphasized "participation" or "fellowship."[196] Later commentators, often Catholic, stressed "association," "community," and "(church) fellowship," sometimes with a sacramental emphasis, *cf.* Latin *communio*.[197] Increasingly it was concluded that no single clear-cut meaning is possible; *koinōnia* is a multivalent term.[198] One may speak of church fellowship, grounded in participation in Christ.[199] New Testament studies sometimes have an eye toward ecumenical implications.[200]

130. How much of the structured church as *koinōnia* of salvation can be traced back to Jesus of Nazareth himself? As a general principle, one must take care "not to read in evidence from later sources or theories."[201] "The church" is known from the earliest Pauline writings, which antedate the written Gospels (*e.g.*, 1 Thess. 1:1; 2:14; Gal. 1:2, 22; 1 Cor. 1:2; 4:17; 7:17; 2 Cor. 8:1). *Hē ekklēsia* often denotes in such passages a particular or local church in a certain area, but it eventually comes to mean "the church" in a sense that transcends local or geographical boundaries (see below). Significantly, however, *ekklēsia*, in either a local or a transcendent sense, is not mentioned in the Gospels of Mark, Luke, or John—or in other New Testament writings such as Titus, 2 Timothy, 1-2 Peter, and 1-2 John. *Ekklēsia* (church) is used in Matthew 16:18: "You are Peter (*Petros*), and on this rock (*petra*) I will build my church" (*cf.* 18:17, of the local assembly). This church-founding statement is paralleled in John 21:15-17 in a post-resurrection setting, without the word *ekklēsia*; Peter's role is to feed the "flock" of Christ.[202] There is little more that one can cull from the Gospels about the structure of Jesus' church to be built.[203]

131. Jesus had followers (see Mk. 1:18; 2:15; Mt. 4:20; Lk. 5:11, 28; Jn. 1:37, 40), eventually called "disciples,"[204] *i.e.*, those taught by Jesus (see Mk. 2:16; Mt. 5:1; Lk. 6:13; Jn. 2:2), and even "apostles," *i.e.*, those sent forth by him to carry on his mission (Mk. 6:30; Mt. 10:2; Lk. 6:13). One

can speak of a "Jesus-movement," but such disciples or apostles are not portrayed in the Gospels as aware of themselves as "church" during Jesus' earthly ministry. The charge to "make disciples of all nations" (Mt. 28:19-20; differently formulated in Lk. 24:47) comes from the risen Christ.

132. It is as an effect of the Christ-event that the New Testament speaks of salvation (sōtēria and the verb sōzein), e.g., Matthew 1:21 ("he will save his people from their sins"); John 3:17 ("that the world might be saved through him"); and John 12:47 ("I came not to judge the world, but to save the world"). He is said to "save" individuals as he heals them (Mt. 9:21-22; Mk. 5:34; 10:52), and in Luke, Jesus is announced as sōtēr, "savior" (Lk. 2:11; cf. 19:9-10).

133. Jesus lays hands on individuals during healings or cures (Mk. 6:5; 8:23, 25; Mt. 19:13, 15; Lk. 4:40; 13:13), but never for commissioning or ordaining, as occurs in the Old Testament (e.g., Moses commissioning Joshua, in Num. 27:18-19; Deut. 34:9).[205] Church structures develop as the Jesus-movement evolves after the resurrection.[206]

II. THE SHAPE OF EARLY CHRISTIAN COMMUNITIES

134. In the Acts of the Apostles, "the fellowship" (hē koinōnia) is the first term that occurs for Jesus' followers as they share their faith and life in common (2:42). Another early name for them is "the Way" (hē hodos; 9:2; 19:9, 23; 22:4; 24:14, 22).[207] Ekklēsia becomes in later chapters of Acts the standard and enduring designation of Christians as a group (8:1, 3),[208] in Jerusalem (11:22; 15:4) and elsewhere (11:26; 13:1; 14:23, 27; 15:3, 41). In time, there also appears an awareness of ekklēsia that transcends local boundaries (9:31 ["the church throughout all Judea, Galilee, and Samaria"]; 12:5; 15:22; 20:28 ["the church of God"]).

135. The Twelve and the apostles function in the early chapters of Acts. The Twelve initially guide the early Jerusalem church, with Peter as its spokesman (Acts 1:15; 2:14). Later, the Seven are chosen "to serve tables" (Acts 6:2-5; cf. 21:8): "These men they presented to the apostles,

who prayed and laid their hands on them" (6:6),[209] which is the last time the Twelve are mentioned. The apostle James, the brother of John, is not replaced at his death (12:1-2), as was the case after the death of Judas Iscariot (1:16-17). "Apostles" still are mentioned as having a part in the Jerusalem "Council" (Acts 15:2, 4, 6, 22, 23), where they are always linked with *hoi presbyteroi* in the Jerusalem church. After 16:4, the apostles disappear from the Lucan story. In the subsequent Christian tradition, there is no office called either the "apostolate" or "the Twelve."[210]

136. Pauline use of *ekklēsia* for a local or particular church often involves "house churches" (1 Cor. 16:19; Rom. 16:5; Phlm. 2; Col. 4:15).[211] Such groupings of Christians were usual in the pre-Constantinian period for various functions, but nothing in the Pauline letters links the house church with the eucharistic celebration.[212] In some Pauline letters, the phrase "the church(es) of God" (1 Thess. 2:14; Gal. 1:13; 1 Cor. 11:16; 15:9) seems to refer to the mother-communities of Jerusalem or Judea; but it eventually is extended to the Corinthian community (1 Cor. 1:2; 2 Cor. 1:1), as the idea of the church regional and universal begins to emerge (1 Cor. 6:4; 10:32; 11:22). The latter idea becomes even clearer in the Deutero-Paulines (Col. 1:18, 24; Eph. 1:22; 3:10, 21), even if it is never said to be *mia ekklēsia*, despite the emphasis in Ephesians on the unity of the church.

137. *Ekklēsia* occurs in 3 John 6, 9, 10 for a local congregation, but there is otherwise no awareness in the Johannine Gospel or Epistles of *ekklēsia* in either a local or a universal sense. Commentators speak either of a "Johannine community," "Johannine circle," or "a community of the Beloved Disciple," characterized by their contrast with those they opposed: "the Jews" (*e.g.*, 2:6, 13; 5:1, 16; 6:4; 8:48, 52; 19:40); crypto-Christians (9:22, 30-38); disciples of John the Baptist (4:1).[213]

138. Many Pauline and Johannine verses using *koinōnia* terms have been cited above (§§11-13). No New Testament passage using *koinōnia* is directly related to *ekklēsia*, but "the fellowship of his Son, Jesus Christ our Lord" (1 Cor. 1:9) is the underlying reality expressing the union of Christ and Christians in the "one body" of Christ, which is the church. Passages using *koinōnia* or *koinōnein* tell us little about the structure of such fellowship or the ministries exercised by Christians in it. Paul's

description of Titus as "my partner (koinōnos)" in 2 Corinthians 8:23 says nothing about Titus's specific ministry. Galatians 6:6, in a reference to oral instruction, possibly a baptismal catechesis, says, "Let the one who is taught the word share (koinōneito) all good things with the one who teaches."[214]

139. Salvation, as an effect of the Christ-event, is an important element in Pauline theology. In light of Old Testament imagery of Yahweh delivering his people Israel (Isa. 45:15; Zec. 8:7), Paul sees that deliverance now coming through Christ: Christians "are being saved" by the cross of Christ (1 Cor. 1:18, 21). 1 Corinthians 15:2 speaks of "the gospel . . . by which you are saved" (cf. 2 Cor. 2:15). Paul identifies "the gospel" as "the power of God for the salvation of everyone who believes" (Rom. 1:16). Only in Philippians 3:20 does Paul call Jesus sōtēr, and as such he is still awaited. The end result is still something of the future, having an eschatological aspect (see 1 Thess. 2:16; 5:8-9; 1 Cor. 3:15; 5:5; Rom. 5:9-10; 8:24 ["In hope we have been saved!"]; 10:9-10, 13). He urges the Philippians, "Work out your own salvation in fear and trembling" (2:12), adding immediately, however, "for God is at work in you, both to will and to work for his good pleasure" (2:13), lest anyone think that salvation is achieved without God's grace.[215] In the passages cited, Paul addresses Christians in the plural; a corporate sense of salvation is thereby expressed. Hebrews 2:3 cautions Christians, "how shall we escape if we neglect such great salvation, which was initially announced by the Lord and attested to us by those who heard him?"

140. In the New Testament, explicit indications of the early church's ministries are diverse and lack uniformity.[216] In his earliest letter, Paul counsels Thessalonians to "respect those who labor among you and are over you (proïstamenous) in the Lord and admonish you" (1 Thess. 5:12),[217] but with no details about their specific titles or functions. The three participles (laboring, standing over, admonishing) refer to one group, either a group of leaders or all members of the community together.[218]

141. In Philippians, Paul greets the saints at Philippi, along with episkopoi kai diakonoi, often rendered "overseers and ministers,"[219] possibly meaning two ministries not otherwise defined. Some see "overseers and ministers" as referring to the same reality (a hendiadys), and thus

to one ministry, "overseers who serve."[220] The two titles, however, more likely arose in Philippi out of the Greco-Roman distinct usage of *episkopos* and *diakonos* in government, guilds, and societies.[221] Possibly *episkopoi* designates leaders of Philippian house churches. *Diakonoi* may imply agents of the overseers, perhaps in financial matters.[222]

142. In 1 Corinthians the conception of the church as "the body of Christ" first emerges in 12:27-28 and becomes an important notion in the Deutero-Paulines (Col. 2:17; Eph. 4:12; cf. Col. 1:18; Eph. 1:22-23; 4:15-16). In that body, where all members have some function, Paul lists, among the various gifts (*charismata*) coming from the Spirit and endowing the members, those whom "God has appointed in the church": apostles, prophets, teachers, miracle-workers, healers, helpers, administrators, and speakers in tongues (12:28). Romans 12:6-8 lists them in abstract form: prophecy, ministry, teaching, exhorting, contributing, leading, and acts of mercy. Note also the gifts to the church from the ascended Christ in Ephesians 4:11: apostles, prophets, evangelists, pastors, and teachers. Apropos of such passages, an earlier round of this dialogue commented that "some of these categories belong in the special Ministry of the church (*e.g.*, apostles, prophets, teachers) and that others reflect the ministry of the people of God (acts of mercy, aid, and helping), and that some are hard to categorize (healing, teaching)."[223]

143. In Acts 14, it is said of Paul and Barnabas, "In each church they installed presbyters (*presbyterous kat' ekklēsian*) and with prayer and fasting commended them to the Lord" (v. 23).[224] In Paul's own uncontested letters, "presbyters" are never mentioned. At Acts 20:17, the Apostle addresses the Ephesian *presbyterous tēs ekklēsias*, counseling them to keep watch over themselves and "over the whole flock, of which the Holy Spirit has appointed you overseers (*episkopous*), to shepherd the church of God" (Acts 20:28).[225] Here the "church of God" is clearly under the supervision of "presbyters," who are called "overseers" appointed by the Holy Spirit. So the question arises, What is the difference in the New Testament between *presbyteros* and *episkopos*e. Moreover, it is noteworthy that *episkopoi* in this passage are understood to be "appointed" by "the Holy Spirit," not by apostles; so even if they carry on a ministry

begun by apostles, there is no indication that their authority to do so is transmitted to them by apostles.[226]

144. The Pastoral Epistles stress structured ministry and orthodox teaching, especially Titus and 1 Timothy. But *ekklēsia* appears only three times: in 1 Timothy 5:16 (probably meaning the local congregation in Ephesus); 3:5 (*ekklēsia tou theou*, "God's church," with a more universal connotation); and 3:15 ("the household of God . . . , the church of the living God, the pillar and bulwark of the truth," probably meant in a universal sense). The concept of the body of Christ is absent from the Pastoral Epistles, as is the term *koinōnia*. The church is the collectivity of Christians that must be properly managed and governed in the interest of sound doctrine.

145. In the Pastoral Epistles, ministry is described, first, apropos of Titus and Timothy, and second, of other members of the church. In the first case, Titus and Timothy function as emissaries of the author, but they are called neither *episkopos* nor *presbyteros*.[227] The author seeks to make sure that the apostolic gospel will continue to be preached without contamination or perversion. Timothy is instructed to administer the church of Ephesus, above all to "teach" (1 Tim. 4:11, 16; 6:2; *cf.* 2 Tim. 2:2, 24), and "not be hasty in the laying on of hands" (1 Tim. 5:22).[228] Titus too is to exercise his "authority" (*epitagē*, in Titus 2:15), to amend what is defective in the church of Crete, and appoint presbyters (1:5); he is also to "teach what befits sound doctrine" (2:1). In the second case, among the tasks that others are to carry out in Ephesus and Crete are teaching (1 Tim. 4:13, 16; 5:17; Titus 1:9); "the work of an evangelist" (2 Tim 4:5); preaching the word (2 Tim. 4:2; *cf.* 1 Tim. 5:17); exhorting (1 Tim. 4:13); guarding the deposit (1 Tim. 6:20); caring for the "public reading of Scripture" (1 Tim. 4:13); and common prayer (1 Tim. 2:8). There is, however, no reference to eucharistic ministry in the Pastoral Epistles, nor any indication about who would preside over it.

146. The titles for Paul,[229] "herald," "apostle," and "teacher of the Gentiles" (1 Tim. 2:7), are given to no one else in these letters. Timothy is to be *kalos diakonos*, "a good minister," of Christ Jesus (1 Tim. 4:6),[230] but here *diakonos* is used generically and hardly means that he was a "deacon." Timothy has been commissioned[231] by the laying on of hands

by the presbyteral college (*presbyterion*, 1 Tim. 4:14), and by the laying on of hands by the writer (2 Tim. 1:6); *i.e.*, a grace (*charisma*) has been conferred on Timothy, which was not simply the "authority" (*epitagē*) of an office bestowed. Nothing similar is said of Titus, who is directed "to appoint presbyters in every town" (Titus 1:5).

147. The Pastoral Epistles list qualities to be sought in individuals who are called *episkopos*, "overseer" (in the singular),[232] *presbyteroi*, "presbyters" (in the plural),[233] *diakonoi*, "ministers" or "intermediary agents,"[234] and *chērai*, "widows."

148. The qualifications of the *episkopos* are set forth in 1 Timothy 3:1-7:[235] eight positive, five negative, with the most important being "skillful in teaching" (*didaktikos*, 3:2), but he is also to "provide for (*epimelēsetai*) God's church" (3:5), implying an administrative role.[236]

149. The term *presbyteros* is used in Pastoral Epistles in two senses: (1) as an adjective denoting dignity of age, "older" (1 Tim. 5:1, "older man"; 5:2, "older woman");[237] and (2) as a substantive, a title for a Christian community official, "presbyter" (Titus 1:5; 1 Tim. 5:17, 19). In Titus 1:5-9, the author lists many of the same qualifications, required for the *episkopos* in 1 Timothy 3:1-7, as requirements for the *presbyteroi*, and Titus 1:5-9, which begins with qualifications of "presbyters," suddenly shifts in verse 7 to *episkopos*, "an overseer," where the qualifications are ten positives and seven negatives. The most important difference from 1 Timothy is that the *episkopos* is now called *theou oikonomos*, "God's steward" (1:7), and an exhorter with sound doctrine (1:9). Moreover, in 1 Timothy 5:17, the author speaks of "presbyters who preside well" and "those who labor in preaching and teaching," which may denote two different kinds of presbyters.[238]

150. In the Pastoral Epistles, *diakonos* and *diakonia* are used in a generic sense—"minister" and "ministry" (1 Tim. 4:6; 2 Tim. 4:5)—and also in the specific sense of a group often called "deacons." The qualifications for the latter are given in 1 Timothy 3:8-13, five positive, three negative; some of them echo the qualifications for the presbyters and overseers. This institution in the early church may be a development of the action

taken in Acts 6:1-6, resulting in the appointment of the Seven (Acts 21:8); but they are never called *diakonoi* in Acts, even though their function is said to be *diakonein trapezais*, "to serve tables."[239] Scholars debate whether *gynaikas* (1 Tim. 3:11) refers to women deacons (somewhat like Phoebe of Rom. 16:1) or to the wives of deacons.[240]

151. Finally, mention must be made of the enrolled *chērai*, "widows," of 1 Timothy 5:3-16, where the qualifications are set forth for those who may be considered such. What their function would be in the structured church is not explained.[241]

152. Of the four groups, the most important seems to be *episkopos*, called *theou oikonomos*, "God's steward" (Titus 1:7; 1 Tim. 1:4; *cf.* 1 Tim. 3:15).

153. The problem is how to distinguish *presbyteroi* from *episkopos* in the Pastoral Epistles, to say what is the difference in the function or role that they are thought to play.[242] Interpreters debate whether in the Pastoral Epistles the church-structure involves two or three offices: either deacons and bishop/presbyters; or deacons, presbyters, and bishop, each clearly distinct.[243]

154. In other New Testament writings, presbyters (*presbyteros/-oi*) appear widely for Christians serving as community leaders (Acts 11:30; 20:17; Heb. 11:2; Jas. 5:15; 1 Pet. 5:1, 5; 2 Jn. 1; 3 Jn. 1), with no hint of accompanying *episkopos* or *diakonos*. The author of 1 Peter even speaks of himself as "fellow elder" (*sympresbyteros*) as he exhorts other *presbyteroi*.[244] Whatever its origin, "presbyter" was a frequent designation of office in the New Testament, even if the term tells us little about the nature of this office.

155. Churches in the New Testament period were related to each other in terms of concern and sharing. For instance, in Acts 15, Paul and Barnabas are sent by the Antiochene church to the apostles and presbyters of Jerusalem to consult them about whether Gentiles have to be circumcised and observe the Mosaic law in order to "be saved" (Acts 15:1-2; the so-called Jerusalem Council; *cf.* Gal 2:1-10). Concern for other churches is found in the decision of James and other Jerusalem

leaders to send a letter to the particular churches of Antioch, Syria, and Cilicia about *porneia* ("fornication" [NRSV] or "unlawful marriage" [NABRNT]) and dietary matters (Acts 15:13-29).[245] Here one sees the mother-church of Jerusalem guiding the activity of daughter-churches.

156. Paul manifests concern for *koinōnia* in his appeals to his churches for a contribution for "the saints" in Jerusalem (1 Cor. 16:1; 2 Cor. 8:1-5; Gal. 2:9-10).[246] Often the churches of one area send greetings to other churches (1 Cor. 16:19 [Aquila and Prisca and their house church]; Rom. 16:23; *cf.* Col. 4:13, 15-16). Such a sharing of concern for other ecclesial communities of a certain region is a form of *koinōnia*, even if the term itself is not used.

157. To summarize, the New Testament evidence reveals that after the resurrection of Jesus his followers became aware of themselves as *ekklē-sia*, a community united by faith in him and sharing a destiny of salvation. They spoke of the *koinōnia* in which they shared. Leadership always existed in the earliest Christian churches, some of it Spirit-appointed, some of it established by apostles or others; but no one pattern of leadership emerged. Jesus' words to Simon Peter imply a Petrine function among his followers in his church to be built or flock to be fed, but they supply no specific form of that function. According to Acts, the Twelve impose hands on the Seven, who are to "serve tables," but some of whom act as preachers and teachers. Others appoint presbyters in local churches, and Paul greets *episkopoi kai diakonoi* as distinct from the rest of the Christians of Philippi. Yet the specific function of these ministers is never fully stated. Even when desired qualities of *episkopos, presbyteroi,* or *diakonoi* are spelled out in the Pastoral Letters, the precise function of such ministers of the Christian community remains unclear.

III. HISTORICAL DEVELOPMENT AFTER THE NEW TESTAMENT

158. The ministry and structures which serve the church as a *koinōnia* of salvation have changed in various ways over two thousand years. In

what follows, we attempt to present the phases of that development that are most relevant to this dialogue. There will be a single narrative for developments up to the Reformation (see §§159-170); distinctive Catholic and Lutheran developments starting with the Reformation will receive separate treatments (see §§171-242).

A. Developments in Service to Koinonia

1. Church Structures and Leadership

159. After, or even in some cases contemporary with, the developments exhibited in the New Testament, a certain variety in the structure of the churches[247] began to yield to the pattern that became normal after Constantine. It became customary for each church to have a single principal leader, who was often assisted by counselors and one or more deputies; the terminology used by Ignatius of Antioch has become standard for these roles: bishop, presbytery or group of elders, and deacons.[248] Together these leaders were responsible for the activity and especially the cohesion of the church they served.[249] Cohesion between churches was part of their task, and it was carried out by letter,[250] personal travel,[251] and meetings (synods), even in the second and third centuries.

160. A special role in this maintenance of *koinonia* was played by the consecrated eucharistic bread itself, whether taken to those who were unable to attend the common liturgy,[252] offered as a sign of *koinonia* from one bishop to another,[253] or shared from the bishop's liturgy to the altars of other eucharistic celebrations in the neighborhood of his city, the so-called *fermentum*.[254] The exclusion of a Christian from the eucharistic assembly was intended to bring about conversion, serving as a grave warning to repent, and even in serious cases of apostasy in persecution, this *koinonia* could be restored as death approached.[255] Likewise the refusal to be "in communion" was the most solemn declaration that *koinonia* did not exist.[256]

161. *Koinonia* was exhibited through the participation by other neighboring bishops in the ordination of a new colleague.[257] Letters of communion established the same kind of link with bishops farther away, attesting both to the orthodoxy of a new bishop's belief and the integrity of his

election, thus certifying his place as a successor to the apostles. Among the criteria which made communion with other bishops possible, we should note the use of orthodox scriptures,[258] the common celebration of the principal Christian festivals,[259] and the exclusion of those denounced by other churches as heretics.[260]

162. The oldest and largest churches played a leading role in maintaining these bonds.[261] Sometimes prominence was determined by Roman imperial organization, *e.g.*, the early importance of the see of Caesarea Maritima in Palestine, the Roman provincial capital, whose prerogatives are preserved even at the Council of Nicaea (325); and the sudden rise to prominence of Byzantium, renamed Constantinople, as the eastern capital of the Roman Empire, recognized at the Council of Constantinople (381) and even more emphatically in the twenty-eighth canon of Chalcedon (451), which was not accepted by the church of Rome. Another sort of prominence derived from Christian history: Thus in the fourth century, Jerusalem, which had an insignificant place in the Roman scheme, came to take precedence of honor over Caesarea Maritima in Palestine, the capital city of the province, and was deemed a fifth patriarchate at the Council of Chalcedon (451).

163. Until the third century, there seems not to have been a clear distinction between the titles "bishop" and "presbyter": the former could be seen as a presbyter with the main responsibility for a church and the authority and powers necessary for carrying out that responsibility.[262] At first, churches could be designated by a pair of terms, *ekklesia* and *paroikia*, as in "the church of God which sojourns (*paroikousa*) at . . . "[263] Even if quite small, churches would normally be led by someone who could be called a "bishop"; village and rural churches were headed by country bishops (chorbishops) until the fourth century.[264] The collegial presbyterate was concerned mainly with decision-making and doctrine and cannot be shown to have priestly liturgical duties until the mid-third century.[265] Apart from that, we are poorly informed about the ways in which pastoral leadership and care were exercised in different settings.

2. The Special Nature of Metropolitan Churches

164. In very large city churches such as the one in Rome, there might have been a number of different Christian communities or "schools," existing side by side, serving different populations, sometimes complementing each other, sometimes competing with each other. The several congregations faced the rest of the Christian world with a single voice, which we call that of the "bishop," but the internal arrangements of the church in Rome and in other large centers of Christian population are unclear to us. In Rome a unified structure can be seen by the third century.[266] At the beginning of the 250s, Cornelius lists the membership of his community as, in addition to the bishop, "forty-six presbyters, seven deacons, seven sub-deacons, forty-two acolytes, fifty-two exorcists, readers and door-keepers, above fifteen hundred widows and persons in distress, all of whom are supported by the grace and loving-kindness of the Master."[267] Such large numbers could hardly have met in a single place, but Cornelius does not inform us about the various congregations which must have existed in Rome or how they were related to each other.

165. The church of Rome and its bishop claimed a certain precedence[268] and broad responsibility in the church as a whole, founded upon its connection with the apostles Peter and Paul, who preached in Rome and were martyred there,[269] and this claim was generally accepted by other churches, though they did not hesitate to speak up for their own rights and traditions.[270] Irenaeus of Lyon made a case for the continuous orthodoxy of the church of Rome and its presiding bishops, one after another,[271] and though he insisted that a similar case could be made for the other ancient churches, such as that of Ephesus, the church in Rome's role as a benchmark of orthodoxy only grew with the passage of time.

B. Communion and Ministry in the Patristic and Medieval Church

166. With the legalization of Christianity in the Roman Empire,[272] the number of Christians rose rapidly, and structure and ministry in the church developed to meet the task of assuring continuity of doctrine among those newly added to the church, consistency of discipline in the many new eucharistic communities, and communion in the apostolic faith

in the church as a whole. The boundary between laity and clergy became more distinct, and certain tasks (*e.g.*, catechesis) were absorbed by the clergy, especially the presbyters.[273] Larger churches, instead of subdividing into smaller ones headed by their own bishops, developed in the opposite direction, with the suppression of the institution of chorbishop[274] and the delegation of pastoral responsibility to presbyters under the bishop's authority.[275] Cities in the western church seem not to have been divided into parishes before the ninth century.[276] In rural areas, the rising number of proprietary churches erected by newly converted feudal lords[277] and the many local congregations cared for by monasteries[278] were gradually integrated into this episcopal structure as well. Bishops tried to foster the unity of the congregations under their care by gathering their clergy regularly[279] and by encouraging the urban clergy to live in community.[280]

167. The emperor Constantine and his successors encouraged the bishops to continue the practice of meeting in councils or synods, and canon 5 of the Council of Nicaea, which Constantine convened, legislated that provincial and regional councils should be held regularly. This legislation, which was reiterated by later directives, was observed to a varying degree in different times and regions.[281] Greater councils, including those technically known as "ecumenical" councils,[282] were of great importance for the maintenance of communion, though they were not always successful in achieving church unity.[283] In addition, communion among churches coexisted with and even benefitted from a hierarchical grouping, under the metropolitan (bishop of the metropolis of the civil diocese)[284] and the patriarch, through whom each congregation was in communion with the rest of the church.[285] A high level of leadership, both doctrinal and disciplinary, was offered by the patriarchs: the bishops of Rome, Alexandria, and Antioch, a group to which were later added Constantinople, as the "new Rome" and seat of the emperor, and Jerusalem, as the church of origin of Christianity and a focus of pilgrimage.[286] Although as a practical matter, "the organization of the church in five patriarchates did not last long,"[287] the ideal has continued to be a powerful symbol of the compatibility of distinction between churches and effective communion.[288]

168. While these developments made it difficult to envisage every local parish as embodying everything which is required in order to be "church," the ancient equivalence of presbyter and bishop was not forgotten. Jerome insists upon that equivalence when he is making the argument that it is normal for bishops to be chosen from among the presbyters of the church, rather than from the deacons.[289] He argued, "For also at Alexandria, from Mark the evangelist down to bishops Heraclas and Dionysius, the presbyters always chose one of themselves and, having elevated him in grade, named him bishop—just as if an army might make an emperor by acclamation, or deacons choose one of themselves, whom they know to be hard-working, and call him archdeacon. For what, apart from ordaining, does a bishop do which a presbyter does not?" "Ambrosiaster" (thought to be Pelagius), in his comments on the Pauline epistles, makes the same point regarding New Testament usage.[290]

Both Jerome and Ambrosiaster are reflected in the *De Ecclesiasticis Officiis* of Isidore of Seville (c. 560-636). He tells us that "'Bishop,' as one of the prudent says, is the name of a work, not of an honor. . . . Therefore we can say in Latin that the bishop *superintends*, so that someone who would love to preside but not to assist may understand that he is not a bishop."[291] For Isidore, presbyters correspond to Old Testament priests as bishops do to the high priest. Presbyters and bishops are alike in regard to the Eucharist, teaching the people, and preaching. He adds,

> and only on account of authority is ordination and consecration reserved to the high priest, lest if the discipline of the church were arrogated by many it might dissolve concord and generate scandals.[292]

Isidore, like Jerome and Ambrosiaster, cites 1 Timothy 3:8, Titus 1:5; Philippians 1:1, and Acts 20:28, and his other sources are as follows: the line about bishops as superintendents is from Augustine;[293] the statement about the common duties of bishops and presbyters, with a purely disciplinary restriction of certain powers to the former, comes from an anonymous treatise "On the Seven Orders of the Church";[294] and the comments on Scripture are from Pelagius's commentary on 1 Timothy.

All Isidore's observations about the bishop/presbyter relationship are taken up by later canonical and theological authors, particularly Peter Lombard,[295] and became part of the standard repertory of authorities with which western Christian theologians had to deal.[296]

169. How undefined the distinction between presbyters and bishops was can also be seen occasionally on the practical level, where there were some striking instances of presbyters exercising powers typical of bishops when the occasion called for it. For example, two eighth-century missionaries, Willehad and Liudger,[297] whom Charlemagne had sent to convert the Saxons on his eastern border, ordained clergy for the churches they founded, long before they themselves received consecration as bishops. In the fifteenth century, three different popes delegated the power to ordain to abbots who had not been ordained to the episcopate; in two of those cases, the privilege included ordination to the priesthood.[298] For many medieval theologians, the limiting of ordination to bishops was associated with the episcopal dignity, but not with orders as such. After the introduction of pseudo-Dionysius's *De Ecclesiastica Hierarchia* into Latin theology in the early thirteenth century, Dionysius's pervasive arrangement of everything in patterns of three seems to have deepened the sense of a distinction among the orders of deacon, presbyter, and bishop.[299]

170. While the communion among local congregations was primarily the charge of the bishop, there were various attempts to assure unity in the church on a wider scale during the Middle Ages. In the East, the rise of Islam, the Russian adoption of Christianity, and the growth of autocephalous churches led to the type of structure characteristic of the Orthodox communion. In the West, the church of Rome maintained and developed an ascendancy which was often advanced by the desire of other particular churches to free themselves from domination from lay feudal lords. The bishops of Rome claimed that anyone in the church might appeal to them[300] and that they inherited the power of St. Peter.[301] The Symmachan Forgeries of the sixth century,[302] the "Donation of Constantine" of the eighth century,[303] and the False Decretals brought in from France in the ninth century[304] all tended to support and promote the papal primacy. Bernard of Clairvaux hailed that primacy as universal,[305]

and despite challenges from figures like Marsilius of Padua and scandals like the Great Schism of the West, papal primacy persisted into Reformation times. The struggle against feudal control of the church was not an unmixed success, however: in the process, bishops, abbots, and the popes themselves became feudal lords and consequently, a part of that system;[306] and the pope's success in divesting kings of responsibility for the *ecclesia universalis* laid the groundwork for the rise of the autonomous state and the dichotomy between sacred and secular.

IV. THE LUTHERAN REFORMATION

171. The traditional, though varied and often unsettled, medieval structures of church and ministry provided the background for the Lutheran reformers of the sixteenth century and "the impact of the gospel"[307] that they brought to the fore. They sought removal of unacceptable aspects and renewal of the existing church, not wholesale restructuring, as part of their conservative reformation. But, with some exceptions outside the Holy Roman Empire,[308] the bishops of the day, many of whom had feudal positions to protect, refused to endorse the aims of the Wittenberg reformers and would not ordain candidates committed to the Reformation gospel. In spite of this opposition, the reformers continued the principle of one ordained ministry, employing a variety of approaches to structure, on the basis of biblical and patristic sources and medieval precedents. Self-appointment to the ministry was not even considered, nor was direct appointment by the Spirit. The steps Lutherans took in this emergency situation were not all intended to be permanently normative. New situations in later times stimulated further development and often variety in Lutheran praxis for church and ministry within the framework of the confessional commitments of the sixteenth century.

A. The Nature of the Church as Communion and Its Ministry

1. *Communion and Local Church*
172. "Communion" as a term applied specifically to the church is not found in the writings of the Reformers or their opponents. But Luther

does apply the closely related notions of the communion of saints and eucharistic communion. His sermon on *The Blessed Sacrament of the Holy and True Body of Christ and the Brotherhoods*[309] seeks to provide a basis for Christian life in both church and city. The transforming power of love, the bonds of unity, and participation in the body of Christ (comprehending both Christ and fellow Christians) are all centered in the Lord's Supper:

> The blessing of this sacrament is fellowship and love. . . . This fellowship is twofold: on the one hand we partake of Christ and all saints; on the other hand we permit all Christians to be partakers of us, in whatever way they and we are able. Thus by means of this sacrament, all self-seeking love is rooted out and gives place to that which seeks the common good of all; and through the change wrought by love there is one bread, one drink, one body, one community. This is the true unity of Christian brethren.[310]

The faithful truly participate in Christ and Christ in them.[311] In this relationship, they share the goods or gifts that are the fruits of that communion. These goods include a sharing not only in each other's joys, but also in each other's sufferings.[312] Such mutual participation is communicated through the means of grace, a sacramental reality that presumes ministers of the word.[313] The existence of ministers, in turn, presumes an ecclesiastical ordering or structure, in short, a church as communion.[314]

173. According to the *Augsburg Confession*, "The church is the assembly of saints in which the gospel is taught purely and the sacraments are administered rightly" (CA 7), and "no one should teach publicly in the church or administer the sacraments unless properly called" (CA 14). Because the local congregation has the word proclaimed and the sacramental gifts of God, it is "church," in that place, in the full sense. In lands that embraced the teaching of Luther, the local church continued to be geographically and often physically the same as that which had existed previously, in village, town, or city. Lutheran immigrants in the United States and Canada formed local congregations where they settled.[315] In such assemblies, Lutherans participate in Christ and live out their faith.[316]

174. For Luther and the Lutheran tradition, the local church, to use biblical language (as in Ezek. 34, Jn. 10, 1 Pet. 5:1-4), consists of a shepherd and the flock. The term "shepherd" refers to the pastor with tasks of word and sacraments, "the flock," to the people of God in a particular place. The pastor as minister of word and sacrament also has oversight responsibilities in the congregation. Luther could describe the pastor/bishop as a supervisor or watchman, i.e., one who carefully observes his flock to see to it that among them the word is taught and proclaimed in its purity, that the sacraments are used rightly, and that the community strives to live according to the word and command of God.[317] Such a function is common to all ordained ministers whether they preside over a congregation or a diocese, and it takes the form of personal oversight.[318]

175. It can further be argued, as of critical importance, that all visible means and structures, all the institutional realities of the church, must reflect and embody the gospel in as clear and as unmistakable a manner as possible. Therefore *koinonia* can neither be forced, nor can it exist apart from *faith*. A true faith (*i.e.*, one that is a participation in *Christ*) will foster a communion that is authentic (*i.e.*, one that is a real *participation* in Christ).

2. The One Office of Pastor/Bishop

176. That the office of presbyter and bishop was one and the same was a teaching widespread in the Middle Ages inherited ultimately from Jerome and the New Testament. Luther asserted the position from 1519 on.[319] He wrote in 1520:

> according to the institution of Christ and the apostles, every city should have a priest or bishop, as St. Paul clearly says in Titus 1[:5]. . . . According to St. Paul, and also St. Jerome, a bishop and a priest are one and the same thing. But of bishops as they now are the Scriptures know nothing. Bishops have been appointed by ordinance of the Christian church, so that one of them may have authority over several priests.[320]

Luther's point was "that originally the *episcopus* was the leader of the congregation in one city, *i.e.*, the pastor, and not the leader of a diocese with many such congregations."[321]

177. In the Lutheran Confessions, this position is forcefully expressed in the *Treatise on the Power and Primacy of the Pope*:

> It is universally acknowledged, even by our opponents, that this power is shared by divine right by all who preside in the churches, whether they are called pastors, presbyters, or bishops. For that reason Jerome plainly teaches that in the apostolic letters all who preside over churches are both bishops and presbyters. . . . What, after all, does a bishop do, with the exception of ordaining, that a presbyter does not?"[322]

178. The Reformers, while denying any *iure divino* difference between presbyter (pastor) and bishop, also allowed, however, for the later, historical development of the episcopal office beyond the individual congregation and even for "distinctions of degree" between bishops and pastors. But this is by human authority, not by divine right.[323]

179. This understanding of the relation between bishop and presbyter not only opened possibilities for needed reform of the episcopate, but also justified the establishment of new (though recognizable) forms through which the ministry of oversight could be exercised alternatively, if necessary and as circumstances required. Melanchthon applied this reasoning and developed it to meet the urgent practical problem of providing for the orderly succession of ministers in areas that embraced the movement for reform. He maintained that, inasmuch as in the ancient church presbyters had been permitted to ordain, presbyters may once again assume this function in the absence of responsible bishops, as the current crisis clearly demanded, for the sake of the gospel. When bishops become heretics or refuse ordination, Melanchthon said, then "the churches are by divine right compelled to ordain pastors and ministers for themselves."[324] Luther also had claimed that the church should not be deprived of ministers on account of neglectful, cruel, or renegade bishops. "Therefore, as the ancient examples of the church and the

Fathers teach us, we should and will ordain suitable persons to this office ourselves."[325] Such action should not be regarded as a deliberately provocative or independent attempt to forge a new ecclesiastical structure. One index of their firm hope to avoid schism is that, while one Lutheran ordination may have taken place in Wittenberg in 1525, there were no more until 1535.[326] The Lutherans believed they were proposing the *more* ancient, and thus original, ministerial structure more conducive to authentic *koinonia*.

180. The Reformers, as indicated above, embraced the view that the office of bishop developed historically, after the New Testament period, as that of a presbyter with special oversight in an area larger than a single congregation or town. While established by human authority, this structure "was instituted by the Fathers for a good and useful purpose."[327] As early as 1522, Luther sketched what an Evangelical bishop would be like, oriented to the gospel of justification and the church as a *communio* for salvation. His tract *Against the Falsely Named Spiritual Estate of the Pope and Bishops* was an appeal for support from, and reform by, the then-reigning bishops.[328] It has been argued that, "Had this attempt been successful, the German Lutheran churches—and most of the United ones [Lutheran and Reformed]—would today have a similar appearance to those of Scandinavia."[329] But none of the bishops within the Holy Roman Empire supported the Reformation. Therefore the Lutheran charges against them increasingly became that they were not true bishops, but rather princes, and that they ultimately opposed the gospel.

181. Fundamental was the problem of the *power* of bishops. The *locus classicus* of the Lutheran argument regarding this power is found in *Augsburg Confession* Article 28, "In former times there were serious controversies about the power of bishops, in which some people improperly mixed the power of the church and the power of the sword." The reformers requested that bishops restrict themselves to doing what is according to the gospel: "the power of the keys or the power of the bishops is the power of God's mandate to preach the gospel, to forgive and retain sins, and to administer the sacraments. . . . If bishops possess any power of the sword, they possess it not through the command of the gospel but by human right, granted by kings and emperors." The reformers'

indictment of the bishops was that they were using the power of the sword to impose and enforce religious practices contrary to the gospel.[330]

182. While *Augsburg Confession* Article 28 was immediately concerned with the practical need to distinguish temporal from spiritual power, it also contained a positive proposal to reform and reorient the church's episcopal structure by returning it to its evangelical, spiritual, and pastoral foundations.

> Consequently, according to the gospel, or, as they say, by divine right, this jurisdiction belongs to the bishops as bishops (that is, to those to whom the ministry of the Word and sacraments has been committed): to forgive sins, to reject teaching that opposes the gospel, and to exclude from the communion of the church the ungodly whose ungodliness is known—doing all this not with human power but by the Word. In this regard, churches are bound by divine right to be obedient to the bishops according to the saying [Lk. 10:16], "Whoever listens to you listens to me."[333]

B. Structures for Regional Oversight

1. The German Lands

183. It soon became apparent in Reformation territories that, if the aims of the reformers were to be carried through in the life of the churches, the oversight that they believed was a special task of the bishops continued to be necessary to congregations embracing the Evangelical faith. A number of steps were taken to carry this out in an Evangelical way.

184. (a) The traditional system of episcopal *visitation* of congregations had collapsed, and the reigning bishops would scarcely carry out visits with encouragement and admonishment along the lines of Reformation theology. Therefore Melanchthon provided an "Instruction" for visitation of the churches and schools of Electoral Saxony, to which Luther wrote a preface (1528). This *episkopē* was to be conducted by centrally appointed visitors from outside the individual parish, to measure what was being done by the standards of the word of God.[332] Catholicity and accountability to the gospel criterion were involved.[333]

185. (b) In some exceptional instances, Catholic bishops in German lands joined the Reformation.[334] Luther watched such developments with interest but was disappointed that no similar cases of a bishop's and region's becoming Lutheran occurred within the Empire.[335] Thus, outside of Prussia (and Sweden and Finland), existing bishops did not come into the Lutheran orbit with their regional churches.

186. (c) In three instances, pastors holding to the Reformation were appointed bishops of existing dioceses in Saxony.[336] In one case, an attempt to involve an existing bishop in the consecration came to nothing.[337] Luther and superintendents and pastors from nearby cities conducted the laying on of hands in the ordination/installation service for two of these bishops; neighboring superintendents laid hands on the third. An episcopate without political power and finance proved unworkable within the structure of the Holy Roman Empire.[338] With the Smalcald War and eventually the Peace of Augsburg, such experiments with Evangelical bishops came to an end. The Protestant princes took over as governors of the episcopal sees, an inheritance of the prince-bishop of the Middle Ages. It was not until 1918, after World War I and the collapse of the Empire and creation of a republic in Germany, that the role of the prince as *summus episcopus* finally was abolished.[339]

187. (d) There emerged, nonetheless, an office of oversight for the German Lutheran churches, called *Superintendent*[340] (etymologically a Latin-derivative equivalent of *episkopos*, one who oversees), *Dekan*, or *Propst*. In so doing, the reformers "held fast to the episcopal office itself."[341]

188. The domination of the church by the princes, especially after the Peace of Augsburg, and the appropriation by the princes of the authority of the former bishops meant that the church in Germany tended to be organized along the political lines of the principalities (not nationally, as in Sweden and England, which were more unified politically). The problem that *Augsburg Confession* Article 28 originally addressed, namely, the confusion of temporal and spiritual authority that had existed with the medieval episcopate, continued to require solution.

2. Nordic Countries

189. The political and ecclesiastical situation in the Nordic lands was different from that of the Holy Roman Empire. In both Nordic kingdoms (Sweden-Finland and Denmark-Norway-Iceland), civil wars, which were more political than religious in their motivation, opened the way for the introduction of the Reformation. Since the ruling authorities in both kingdoms came to support the Reformation, the political realities that forced the creation of new church structures in continental Europe did not exist in the North. Thus, the Lutheran intention to preserve the episcopal structure was realized in the Nordic countries.[342]

190. In Sweden and Finland (under Swedish rule until 1809), the medieval episcopal structure was preserved relatively intact. In the Swedish Lutheran *Church Ordinance* of 1571, the importance of episcopacy was stressed as "an irreplaceable order of the church."[343] This document maintains that, while "the distinction which now exists between bishops and simple priests was not known at first in Christendom, but bishop and priest were all one office," the "agreement that one bishop among them [the pastors] should be chosen, who should have superintendence over all the rest . . . was very useful and without doubt proceeded from God the Holy Ghost . . . so it was generally approved and accepted over the whole of Christendom," a ministerial function that has remained in the church "and must remain in the future, so long as the world lasts, although the abuse, which has been very great in this as in all other useful and necessary things, must be set aside."[344] This text has been reaffirmed in modern Swedish church statements.[345]

191. While a succession of episcopal consecrations was threatened during the sometimes tumultuous sixteenth century, it was not broken and has been continued in Sweden to the present.[346] In 1884, all three Finnish bishops died within a short period of time. As a result, no bishop was available to consecrate a new bishop. After some debate, focusing on the question of inviting a Swedish bishop to consecrate a bishop in Russian-ruled Finland, a new archbishop was consecrated by a professor of theology at the University of Helsinki.[347] After independence from Russia in 1917, Swedish bishops were invited to participate in Finnish episcopal consecrations and a succession of consecrations was re-established.

192. In 1536, the Reformation was carried through in Denmark, which at that time ruled Norway and Iceland.[348] The previous bishops were replaced in 1537 by "superintendents"[349] for the Danish and Norwegian dioceses, consecrated by Johannes Bugenhagen, city pastor of Wittenberg. While a succession of consecrations was thus broken, the medieval diocesan and cathedral structures were preserved and bishops continued to exercise a ministry of oversight.[350] A significant episcopal continuity or *sucessio sedis* or *localis* was preserved.

193. The ecclesial structures of the Baltic lands went through complex changes as political power shifted among the Teutonic Knights, Poland, Sweden, and Russia.[351] Episcopal structures remained in place for the most part in Estonia until Russian rule arrived in the early eighteenth century. Lutheran churches in Latvia and Lithuania tended to follow patterns more like those in Germany, with consistories and superintendents. In the early twentieth century, following the independence of all three of the Baltic republics, the Estonian and Latvian churches turned to episcopal structures. Swedish and Finnish bishops were invited to participate in their episcopal consecrations, and thus these churches deliberately entered episcopal succession. World War II and the Soviet annexation led to a severe disruption of church life, including the interruption of succession, but in both countries such succession was reestablished when it again became possible to invite foreign bishops to participate in episcopal consecrations. The Lithuanian church gave the chair of the consistory the title "bishop" in 1976, and the first bishop was consecrated by the Estonian archbishop.

194. In the Porvoo declaration (see §§69, 111, 118, 241), all the Nordic and Baltic Lutheran churches (with the exception of the churches in Denmark and Latvia) have committed themselves theologically to "the episcopal office . . . as a visible sign expressing and serving the Church's unity and continuity in apostolic life, mission and ministry" and procedurally "to invite one another's bishops normally to participate in the laying on of hands at the ordination of bishops as a sign of the unity and continuity of the Church."[352] As a result, all the Nordic and Baltic churches are episcopally structured, and all but Denmark's have taken on succession as a sign of unity and continuity.

195. In other nearby countries, the Swedish episcopal succession was reintroduced into Finland early in the twentieth century;[353] into Latvia after World War I (but later interrupted);[354] and into Estonia in the 1960s.[355] *The Porvoo Common Statement* envisions the process extending to the churches in Norway and Iceland (to the church in Denmark otherwise).[356]

C. Beyond the Local and Regional: the Universal Church

196. Reformation critiques of the papacy were shaped by the contrast developed during the Middle Ages between that which was *iure divino* and that which was *iure humano*. For the Lutheran Reformers, this distinction was exhaustive and exclusive: every practice in the church was either *iure divino* or *iure humano*. No practice could be both; no practice could be neither. For the most part, the Lutherans held that only practices mandated by God within Scripture or practices directly implied by the gospel could be *iure divino*. That which was *iure divino* could not be changed by human design; that which was *iure humano* was open to human alteration. Because the Lutherans could not find an unambiguous institution of the papacy in Scripture, they denied its *iure divino* character.

197. Luther subscribed to the universal ministry of the bishop of Rome, but especially in view of what he saw as a long history of abuses, he could not accept the claim that papal primacy existed by divine right (*iure divino*). The bishop of Rome could claim such primacy (even given the history of abuse), he acknowledged, but only by human right (*iure humano*). As Luther became convinced that the pope was deliberately obstructing the preaching of the gospel, he did not hesitate to draw on the traditional popular apocalyptic imagery and call the pope "Antichrist."[357] Luther saw the pope's intransigence as a sure indication that the last days were at hand. Such a strong reaction need not be read as a simple rejection of his earlier acknowledgment of a possible universal ministry, but rather as an expression of despair regarding the apparently irreformable nature of the papacy. The pope appeared unlikely to do what all ministry was established to do, namely proclaim the word of God, administer the sacraments, and guard the truth of the gospel.[358]

198. This negative assessment of the papacy did not rule out the possibility that Lutherans might accept a universal ministry involving the bishop

of Rome, provided its authority was based clearly in the gospel and spoke for it.[359] As Luther states in his commentary on Galatians (1531-1535),

> All we aim for is that the glory of God be preserved and that the righteousness of faith remain pure and sound. Once this has been established, namely that God alone justifies us solely by his grace through Christ, we are willing not only to bear the pope aloft on our hands but also to kiss his feet.[360]

V. THE SIXTEENTH-CENTURY CATHOLIC REFORMATION

199. Even before the Council of Trent, priestly ministry had begun to develop in new ways in the Catholic Church. The need for renewal, which was already widely recognized, was answered by the creation of specially trained priests not restricted to particular parishes or dioceses in their work. More than a dozen new religious orders of priests were founded in the sixteenth and early seventeenth centuries, e.g., Jesuits and Theatines, to preach the gospel both in Europe and in newly discovered lands, to promote deeper piety among the clergy and the faithful, and to work in education and care for the sick. Reform of the older orders and of the diocesan clergy took place in many countries and was reinforced by the Council's insistence that bishops reside in their dioceses and visit parishes regularly. While the religious priests were ordained for the work of their orders, not as pastors of local churches, they brought a more vigorous and consistent preaching of the gospel and a revival of congregational life to Catholic parishes, and their example stimulated the diocesan clergy to greater zeal.[361]

A. The Council of Trent

200. In the face of the controversy and restructuring of the church involving the Lutherans, the Council of Trent attempted to sort out what it understood to be Catholic teaching regarding ordination. It undertook this task cautiously and conservatively, with a view toward addressing the most pressing of the contemporary challenges enumerated above. During the debates at the Council of Trent, many of the issues with which this

dialogue is concerned made their appearance.[362] Long discussion was devoted to questions about the ministry of bishops, including whether bishops' ministry was *de iure divino*: how could one avoid eroding papal primacy or dismissing the respectable tradition which saw *sacerdotium* as adequately exemplified in the simple priest?[363] Regarding the latter issue "it became clearer and clearer that the gradations of Order, the steps of the *sacramentum ordinis*, lead not to the simple priest but to the bishop,"[364] but the issue of the relation between bishop and pope remained intractable.[365] In the end, lest there be no decree on the sacrament of Order at all, the Council fathers produced simplified canons which left untouched several matters in dispute.[366] While the debate about the sacrament of Order was longer and more complex than any other besides the debate over justification, the decree itself with its canons was brief, owing mainly to the variety of theological and canonical approaches which existed to the understanding of priesthood. Both the Lutheran attempts at reforming the presbyterate and episcopate described earlier and Trent's extended and sometimes contentious debates on the sacrament of Order should be considered in light of this variety.

201. Trent's doctrine on the sacrament of Order was formulated in a decree of session XXIII (July 15, 1563).[367] Priesthood (*sacerdotium*) itself is linked to sacrifice in the Old Testament; the new visible priesthood to which Jesus Christ entrusted "the power to consecrate, offer, and administer his body and blood," along with the power of forgiving sin, is linked to the eucharist, the sacrifice of the New Testament. The New Testament prescribes only how priests and deacons are to be ordained, but other orders of ministers, ascending by degrees to the priesthood, go back to the beginning of the church. Scripture, the apostolic tradition, and patristic tradition all say that grace is conferred by ordination, which must therefore be accounted a sacrament of the church. Because ordination, like baptism and confirmation, "imprints a character that cannot be destroyed or removed," the Council insists that the priesthood that ordination confers is permanent and not to be confused with the spiritual power received by all the baptized. Regarding the difference between priests and bishops, the Council says that bishops, who succeed the apostles and receive from the Spirit the task of "ruling the church of God," are superior to the priests and can confer confirmation, ordain,

and "do many other functions for which the lower order has no power."
As for the laity, whether congregations or civil magistrates, the Council
denies that they have a necessary, much less a sufficient, role in ordination. It is important to note, however, that while the council fathers
maintained that the hierarchy was instituted by divine ordinance, they
took no position on whether the declared superiority of bishops over
priests was instituted *iure divino*.[368]

202. Eight canons condemning views opposed to the Council's doctrine
were attached to the doctrinal decree. It can be said of them that they
"are purely 'defensive.' They simply defend the legitimacy and validity of
Catholic ordinations but say nothing whatever about the ministries of
the Protestant churches."[369] While canon 3 boldly says that ordination is
"a sacrament . . . instituted by Christ the Lord" (*a Christo domino institutum*), canon 6 says that the hierarchy of bishops, presbyters, and other
ministers was "instituted by divine ordinance" (*divina ordinatione institu-
tam*), a slightly less lofty claim which still distinguishes hierarchy from
mere human invention.[370] Canon 7 insists upon the power of bishops, in
particular that power which they do not have in common with presbyters and which makes them higher than the latter,[371] namely the power
to confirm and ordain.

203. The eighteen canons of the reform decrees of session XXIII reinforced the connection between the power of Order and the power of
jurisdiction, located above all in the bishop. Between the first canon, on
the requirement of residency for all who have the care of souls, and the
eighteenth, which prescribed the formation of seminaries, come canons
concerned with fitness for ministry and the proper procedure for
advancing people though the degrees of ordination. The central role of
the bishop was underlined again and again, and privileges granted earlier to other prelates or church bodies were rescinded.[372] This reorienta-
tion of the sacrament of Order in the direction of the bishop could not
be carried through completely at Trent because the Council was unable
to clarify the relation of episcopacy and papal primacy, but it did succeed
in articulating the difference between bishop and priest in sacramental,
and not merely jurisdictional, terms.[373]

204. Modern ecumenical dialogue has included a re-examination of the decrees of the Council of Trent and the debates which led up to them. One of the fullest studies of the eight canons on the sacrament of Order has been produced by the *Ökumenische Arbeitskreis* (Ecumenical Working Group)[374] as part of their study of the Tridentine anathemas on the sacraments. It noted a difference of emphasis between the Reformers, who stressed the primacy of the task of proclamation of the gospel including the administration of the sacraments, and the bishops at Trent, who "still held fast to the concept of *sacerdos*, or priest, and the relationship of this to the sacrifice of the mass."[375] It is not apparent whether the decree describes or refutes the positions of the Lutheran reformers, and with what accuracy; canons 2, 6, and 8 rejected opinions of radical Reformers such as the Anabaptists, opinions which were not shared by Luther. The group's study concluded that canons 1, 3, 4, 5, and 6 are not applicable to Lutherans today; canon 7 is still applicable in part, since in Catholic teaching and practice priests are ordained by bishops only.[376]

B. The *Roman Catechism* (1566)

205. While the Council of Trent itself was quite guarded in many of its statements about the sacrament of Order, the *Roman Catechism* issued at the Council's behest attempts some simple explanations. It distinguishes between the internal priesthood by which "all the faithful are said to be priests" and the external priesthood which pertains "only to certain men who have been ordained and consecrated to God by the lawful imposition of hands and by the solemn ceremonies of holy Church, and who are thereby devoted to a particular sacred ministry."[377] In regard to the external priesthood, whose office "is to offer Sacrifice to God and to administer the Sacraments of the Church," the *Catechism* says,

> Now although (the sacerdotal order) is one alone, yet it has various degrees of dignity and power. The first degree is that of those who are simply called priests. . . . The second is that of Bishops, who are placed over the various dioceses to govern not only the other ministers of the Church, but the faithful also, and to promote their salvation with supreme vigilance and care.[378]

Three higher degrees follow: archbishops, patriarchs, supreme pontiff.[379] The bishop is declared to be the exclusive administrator of the sacrament of Order, although "it is true that permission has been granted to some abbots occasionally to administer those orders that are minor and not sacred."[380] One can observe in these texts the absence of the sharp polemic or analytical intensity that appear in other genres and later Catholic authors.

VI. SUBSEQUENT CATHOLIC DEVELOPMENTS REGARDING STRUCTURES AND MINISTRY

206. The Council of Trent itself, as we have just noted, defended Catholic doctrine about the sacrament of Order without dealing specifically with the Reformers' arguments. After the Council of Trent, Catholic theologians like Robert Bellarmine (1542-1621) responded more directly to the Protestant Reformers' views on church structure and ministry. In his *Disputations on the Controversies of the Christian Faith*,[381] Bellarmine defended the traditional medieval doctrine that bishops and presbyters share one priesthood, but he argued for bishops' superior power of both order and jurisdiction.[382] He dealt at length with the New Testament texts in which bishops and presbyters seem to be one and the same (Phil. 1, 1 Tim. 3-4, Titus 1, Acts 20), and especially with arguments drawn from Jerome's interpretation of those passages in his Letter to Evangelus. In an apparent rebuttal to Reformers like Melanchthon, Bellarmine questions the inference from the letter that every presbyter is a bishop. If at the start all presbyters were true bishops, then the distinction which was already known to Jerome must have arisen when some accepted ordination of a lower degree. This, says Bellarmine, would not help Jerome to prove his argument that presbyters had more claim than deacons to be promoted to bishop; therefore it is more likely that bishops arose as a higher degree of Order than the presbyterate.[383]

207. Bellarmine was influential, but his solution to this question of the origin of the hierarchy was not the only one proposed by Catholic scholars. At the end of the nineteenth century, Pierre Batiffol proposed a more

complicated evolution. First, the successors of the missionary leadership in the primitive church were overseers (*i.e.*, *episcopoi*) in each community, perhaps several of them working in partnership at first but eventually just one. Presbyter, thought Batiffol, was the name applied in each place to the first converts, benefactors, and owners of house-churches.

> Thus one could be a presbyter without priesthood, and that must have been the case with many of the first presbyters. But it was from among these presbyters without priesthood that they chose—if not by necessity, at least in fact—the members of the community who were raised to the function of *episkopé*. . . . This primitive presbyterate was the original envelope of the hierarchy; as a simply preparatory form, it disappeared. Just the word was preserved to designate the priests, that is, the bishops subordinated to the chief bishop.[384]

Thus, unlike Bellarmine, Batiffol theorized that later presbyters *did* come into being as bishops of inferior rank: the role of bishop began as

> a liturgical, social and preaching function, the episcopate—an episcopate of several persons, like the diaconate; the plural episcopate disappears when the apostles disappear, and separates to give rise to the chief episcopacy of the bishop and the subordinated priesthood of the priests.[385]

That meant that later priests were really descendants of the bishops, not of the early presbyters.[386] While this might seem to favor the Reformers' view, Batiffol's theory was diametrically opposed to an ecclesiology which saw bishops as a human invention, necessary only for practical reasons; such a description would apply more properly to presbyters.

208. For two centuries after Trent, Catholic theology took the form of treatises (often polemical) on particular topics; but eventually the demand for comprehensive theological education called forth new-style scholastic textbooks known as "manuals." One of the first of the sets of manuals included a volume on the sacrament of Order by Thomas Holtzclau, SJ (1716-1783).[387] He set himself against many of the

Reformers' ideas. He denounced any claim that civil rulers have a God-given right to authorize ordinations[388] and argued that Jerome's Letter to Evangelus "attributes to bishops a different degree of Order, by apostolic tradition or *jure divino*, a greater dignity in the Church as Aaron excelled the Levites."[389] He was aware of disagreements among Catholics concerning the extraordinary minister of Order, including whether a simple priest could ordain by papal delegation.[390] He rejected the idea that a simple priest could confer the presbyteral order under any circumstances, even with papal delegation, and he could find neither actual instances nor plausible arguments, though he cited alleged instances.[391] Later manuals continued to report the view of some other Catholic theologians that all the powers of bishops are radically contained in the sacrament of Order conferred in the ordination of presbyters, though these powers are incapable of being exercised until enabled by the granting of appropriate jurisdiction.[392] Already in Holtzclau, we can observe a trait of the manuals which contributes to the incomplete way in which more recent Catholic tradition has treated the issues of the present dialogue: the theology of the church appears early in the manuals, as an argument for the authority and credibility of the church's teaching[393]; the theology of the sacrament of Order, on the other hand, resides in the final section of the manuals, usually between anointing of the sick and marriage.[394] In this arrangement of the material, there is no occasion to ask how the relation of bishop and presbyter might be paralleled by the relation between diocese and parish.[395]

A. Vatican I and Subsequent Developments

209. The First Vatican Council (1869-1870) approved two dogmatic constitutions: *Dei Filius*, the *Dogmatic Constitution on the Catholic Faith*, on the relationship between faith and reason, and *Pastor Aeternus*, the *Dogmatic Constitution on the Church of Christ*, on the primacy of the papacy and the infallibility of papal pronouncements *ex cathedra*. Three positions were represented at the Council: a group of ultramontane infallibilists led by Manning and Senestrey, who upheld the infallibility of all papal teaching, including the Syllabus of Errors, and who advocated papal infallibility as the source of the Catholic Church's infallibility; the majority of the bishops who wanted to strengthen papal authority, and who were thus open to defining papal infallibility; and a third group,

comprising about one fifth of the Council, who vehemently opposed defining papal infallibility. Because more than sixty members of this third group deliberately left Rome before the final vote, the *Dogmatic Constitution on the Church* (*Pastor Aeternus*) was passed on July 18, 1870, with only two negative votes. Because of the outbreak of the Franco-Prussian War, the council adjourned prematurely on October 20, 1870.

210. *Pastor Aeternus* teaches that "a primacy of jurisdiction over the whole church of God was immediately and directly promised to the blessed apostle Peter and conferred on him by Christ the Lord."[396] Furthermore, "whoever succeeds to the chair of Peter obtains, by the institution of Christ himself, the primacy of Peter of the whole church."[397] It also teaches that the Roman pontiff is the successor of Peter, vicar of Christ, head of the whole church, and father and teacher of all Christian people. He has been given full power to rule and govern the universal church. Consequently, "the Roman church possesses a pre-eminence of ordinary power over every other church. And that this jurisdictional power of the Roman pontiff is both episcopal and immediate."[398] The Council added that this power of the supreme pontiff does not detract from that ordinary and immediate power of episcopal jurisdiction by which individual bishops govern their particular churches. Nevertheless, because of the premature adjournment of the Council, the theology of the papacy was not inserted into a larger theology of the episcopacy.

211. The Council defined papal infallibility as a divinely revealed dogma, but it specified strictly limited conditions under which infallibility is given by God:

> that when the Roman pontiff speaks *ex cathedra*, that is, when in the exercise of his office as shepherd and teacher of all Christians, in virtue of his supreme apostolic authority, he defines a doctrine concerning faith or morals to be held by the whole church, he possesses, by the divine assistance promised to him in blessed Peter, that infallibility which the divine Redeemer willed his church to enjoy in defining doctrine concerning faith or morals. Therefore, such definitions of the Roman pontiff are of themselves, and not by the consent of the church, irreformable.[399]

The Council's definition of papal infallibility limited its scope far more than what the Ultramontanes had advocated. Infallibility is assistance given by God first and foremost to the church. Like a council, the pope teaches infallibly on the church's behalf under certain conditions. Infallibility protects the pope from error only when he speaks in his official capacity as "the shepherd and teacher of all Christians," not as an individual theologian. The content of the teaching must be directly related to revelation. The pope does not teach infallibly out of his own abilities, but by virtue of "divine assistance." His definitions are not subject to the juridical ratification of the church.

212. The treatment in the 1917 *Code of Canon Law* does not explicitly lay out the relationships between bishop and pastor, diocese and parish. Some slight attention to dioceses and parishes is prefaced to the treatment of clerics, *i.e.*, canons 215-216 of the 1917 Code. Canon 215 names the major territories, including dioceses, of which it is the prerogative of supreme ecclesiastical authority, *i.e.*, the pope, "to erect, reconfigure, divide, merge, suppress." Canon 216 lists lesser territories, which include parishes. Thereafter the nature of those forms of church must be inferred from what the Code says about bishops and pastors, as if they were functions of their ordained ministers, not realities in their own right. What is clear is the sense that smaller realizations of church are formed by subdivision of larger ones, not larger ones by the accumulation of smaller. As a canonist's study of pastors says, parishes arose relatively late: but, in the fourth century,

> there appeared among the chapels and oratories that dotted the Gallic and Spanish countryside a more permanent pastoral institution called the "*ecclesia baptismalis*" or "*ecclesia major*." Here for the first time there was established a stable, juridic relationship between the faithful in a definite locality and one individual church that was presided over by a priest.[400]

Until the ninth century, cities were not divided into parishes, but instead were served from the cathedral church.[401]

213. In the 1947 apostolic constitution *Sacramentum Ordinis*, Pope Pius XII revised the ritual of ordination to the diaconate, presbyterate, and episcopate, spelling out what is essential for the validity of each rite.[402] Pope Pius XII brought the Latin rite back into conformity with Eastern tradition by insisting upon the laying on of hands and prayer, rather than the presentation of the liturgical vessels, as the essential rites of ordination. This also was the practice of the Reformers. For purposes of this dialogue, it is important to note the pope's insistence on the "unity and identity" of the sacrament of Order, "which no Catholic has ever been able to call in question," despite the fact that there are slightly different rites for ordaining deacons, presbyters and bishops,[403] and that the pope refers to the three "orders" in the plural when discussing the rites. The new prayer for the ordination of the bishop asks God to "complete in your priest the fullness of your ministry."[404]

B. The Second Vatican Council

1. The Papacy

214. The Second Vatican Council (1962-1965) confirmed the teaching of the First Vatican Council regarding the institution, the permanence, and the nature and import of the sacred primacy of the Roman pontiff and his infallible teaching office.[405] The Roman pontiff is a visible source and foundation of the unity of the Catholic Church both in faith and in communion.[406] The council situates this teaching, however, within a theology of the episcopacy that balances and complements the teaching on the papacy of the Second Vatican Council with an emphasis on collegiality. Thus the teaching on the episcopacy provides a context for the teaching on the papacy and yet is itself interpreted within a teaching on papal authority.

2. Episcopacy

215. Bishops represent an historical continuation of the apostolic office and therefore are essential to the Roman Catholic understanding of the apostolicity of the church.[407] LG speaks of a succession that goes back to the beginning by which the bishops are the "transmitters of the apostolic line."[408] They thus serve the church's communion in apostolic faith. Among the principal tasks of bishops, preaching of the gospel is preeminent.[409]

216. By virtue of their episcopal consecration and hierarchical communion with the bishop of Rome and other bishops, bishops constitute a college or permanent assembly whose head is the bishop of Rome.[410] A bishop represents his own church within this college, and all the bishops, together with the pope, represent the whole church.[411] The bishop is responsible for the unity and communion of his church with the other churches. The college of bishops does not constitute a legislative body apart from the pope, but rather includes the pope as member and head of the college. The episcopal college exercises its collegiality in a preeminent way in an ecumenical council. Bishops chosen from different parts of the world may also serve in a council called the Synod of Bishops where they act on behalf of the whole episcopate in an advisory role to the bishop of Rome.[412] Episcopal conferences, "a kind of assembly in which the bishops of some nation or region discharge their pastoral office in collaboration,"[413] are another form of collegial activity. Collegiality is also exercised by the solicitude of the bishops for all the churches, by contributing financial resources, training lay and religious ministers for the missions, and contributing the services of diocesan priests to regions lacking clergy.[414]

217. Although the Roman pontiff can always freely exercise full, supreme, and universal power over the church, the order of bishops is also the subject of supreme and full power over the universal church, provided it remains united with the head of the college, the pope.[415]

218. The Second Vatican Council documents teach that the fullness of the sacrament of Order is conferred by episcopal consecration.[416] The priesthood of the bishop is a sharing in the office of Christ, the one mediator.[417] By virtue of his ordination, a bishop's authority is proper, ordinary, and immediate.[418] This means that a bishop possesses authority by virtue of his ordination that is not juridically delegated by the bishop of Rome. The exercise of this authority, however, is ultimately controlled by the supreme authority of the Church.

3. Presbyterate
219. The Second Vatican Council documents define the nature and function of the presbyterate in relation to the episcopacy. The

Constitution on the Liturgy (*Sacrosanctum Concilium*) subordinates both the local parish to the diocese and a priest to the bishops: "since the bishop himself in his church cannot always or everywhere preside over the whole flock, he must of necessity set up assemblies of believers. Parishes, organized locally under a parish priest who acts in the bishop's place, are the most important of these, because in some way they exhibit the visible church set up throughout the nations of the world."[419] Priests depend on bishops for the exercise of their power and are united with them by virtue of the sacrament of Order.[420] In a certain sense, presbyters make the bishop present. The "unity of their consecration and mission requires their hierarchical communion with the order of bishops."[421] As the fellow-workers of bishops, priests "have as their first charge to announce the gospel of God to all."[422]

220. Through the sacrament of Order, priests are "patterned to the priesthood of Christ so that they may be able to act in the person of Christ the head of the body."[423] Priests exercise their sacred function above all in the eucharistic worship. They also exercise the office of Christ, the shepherd and head, according to their share of authority in their pastoral work.[424] In addition to their care of individuals, priests are exhorted to form real Christian community, embracing not only the local but also the universal church.[425] In their own locality, priests make visible the universal church.[426] Priests are to "take pains that their work contributes to the pastoral work of the whole diocese, and indeed of the whole church."[427]

221. Along with their bishop, priests constitute one presbyterium.[428] By virtue of their common ordination and shared mission, all priests are bound together in a close fraternity. This is symbolized by their laying on of hands with the ordaining bishop in the ordination rite. No priest can adequately fulfill his charge by himself or in isolation. Thus "priestly ministry can only be fulfilled in the hierarchical communion of the whole body."[429]

222. The Second Vatican Council balanced a theology of the papacy and the universal church with a renewed emphasis on the episcopacy and the local church, with the help of resources that had been recovered from the

biblical and patristic heritage. The understanding of church as communion shaped its teaching on collegiality. These Catholic developments have been driven by the desire to be faithful to its tradition, and at the same time to be open to renewing its structures of ministry.

223. Throughout Roman Catholic history, the emphasis on the unitary nature of the office of ordained ministry has remained constant. There is but one sacrament of Order conferred in discrete ordinations of bishops, presbyters, and deacons. The unitary nature of the sacrament mitigates differences between Lutherans and Roman Catholics on the distinctions between presbyter/pastor and bishop.

VII. SUBSEQUENT LUTHERAN DEVELOPMENTS

A. The Reformation Heritage Continued

224. The impact of Luther and the Confessions (IV.A. above) continued over the centuries through "one order of ordained Ministers, usually called pastors, which combines features of the episcopate and the presbyterate,"[430] in local congregations and in structures for regional oversight, including episcopacy (IV.B. above). In contrast to the Middle Ages, there was emphasis on preaching of the word and administration of the sacraments in concrete relationship with a congregation; church office was seen "over against" (*gegenüber*) congregation, an office grounded in the priority of the word of God which constitutes the church (*cf.* §62).[431]

225. For all the adherence to "one office of ministry," there were varieties of structural patterns among Lutherans in church organization and different emphases in the periods of Lutheran Orthodoxy and Pietism (in its emphasis on the priesthood of all baptized believers), the Confessional Revival in the nineteenth century, and later, under the influence of the ecumenical movement.[432] As Lutherans emigrated from Europe to other parts of the world and mission work produced new churches, especially in Africa and Asia, the Lutheran confessional tradition adapted to new needs and possibilities.[433]

226. A significant step in Germany was the introduction of the office of bishop as spiritual leader in the decade after World War I, when princes ceased to exercise the role of "bishops *pro tempore*" or *Summepiskopat* in Protestant territorial churches (see §190 above). "[L]egislative features were entrusted to the synod, but the administrative functions more or less to single individuals," standing vis-à-vis or *gegenüber* the synod, just as the office of ministry stands "over against" the local congregation.[434] Luther's ideas were recovered to become part of a picture of what an Evangelical bishop would be, in distinction from the usually congregational *Pfarramt* (pastoral office), a distinction only by human law. During the Nazi period (1933-1945) and *Kirchenkampf* (Church Struggle), "'spiritual leadership' became in an unexpected way concrete;"[435] a dubious *Führerprinzip* (leader principle) was introduced into the church, even while some bishops opposed the Nazi take-over of the Protestant churches. After 1945 the term "bishop" came to be used in additional *Landeskirchen*. The concept of "synodical episcopate" (*synodales Bischofsamt*) developed, with emphasis on the bishop as preacher and "pastor of the church" (speaking for the church, ecumenical contacts) as well as *pastor pastorum* (e.g., in ordination and visitation).[436] The United Evangelical Lutheran Church in Germany (VELKD) developed a conference of bishops (from member churches), with a presiding bishop; the Evangelical Church in Germany (EKD) did not.

B. Specific Developments in North America

227. The ELCA reflects the backgrounds of many immigrant streams from Lutheran lands in central, northern, and eastern Europe. Their coming, settling in, and amalgamation stretch from the seventeenth century (Dutch and Swedish colonies in New Amsterdam [New York] and the Delaware Valley) until the present, when immigrants are more likely to come from Africa or Asia. The ELCA is "the child of *many* mergers, not just the one that occurred in 1987-1988."[437]

228. The pioneer pietist mission pastor Henry Melchior Muhlenberg (1711-1787) illustrates the situation in colonial America and the beginnings of the United States. His experiences are reflected by many later clergy serving Lutheran immigrants. Muhlenberg was sent by Gotthilf

August Francke, of Halle, to serve three "United Congregations" (Philadelphia, New Hannover, and Providence ['Trappe]), "the Lutheran people in the province of Pennsylvania."[438] He traveled there via London in order to meet with the Court Preacher to the Hannoverian king of England. Muhlenberg, in the face of self-appointed itinerants and congregations sometimes beguiled by them, demonstrated his authority in America by exhibiting his letters of call and instruction from "the Rev. Court Preacher," whom he regarded—along with the revered fathers in Halle, Germany, to whom he sent regular reports—as his ecclesiastical superiors.

229. In many ways, Muhlenberg was more a unifier of congregations, to be served by trained and properly called pastors, than a planter of new congregations. His efforts led to the formation of the first Lutheran synod in North America, the Ministerium[439] of Pennsylvania and Adjacent States, in 1748. The history of "the three dozen or so church organizations and church bodies that finally were united in the Evangelical Lutheran Church in America" often parallels aspects of Muhlenberg's ministry and the founding of the Ministerium of Pennsylvania. The sheer number of synods formed over the years[440] suggests how strong the desire of individual congregations was to work with other congregations for larger purposes beyond the local community of word and sacrament. The concern to have pastors ordained by other Lutheran pastors, often across lines of language, ethnicity, and even views on ministry, can be seen in the histories of these groups.[441]

230. Lutherans in North America inherited from Europe, and took part in, debates over the ministry in the nineteenth century, and the outcomes were sometimes reflected in the positions and practices of synods in America. At one extreme was the "transference theory" (*Übertragungslehre*) that authority is transferred from the local priesthood of believers to one of its members to serve as minister.[442] This position found reflection in The Lutheran Church–Missouri Synod,[443] *e.g.,* C. F. W. Walther (1811-1887): "The holy ministry is the authority conferred by God through the congregation, as holder of the priesthood and of all

church power, to administer in public office the common rights of the spiritual priesthood in behalf of all."[444] But a statement for the Missouri Synod in 1981 moves away from the transference theory: "The office of public ministry . . . is not derived" from "the universal priesthood of believers."[445]

231. At the opposite extreme, opposing any transference theory, were views that stressed ministerial office and its authority as divine institution, apart from or at least prior to the local congregation or universal priesthood. In a time of change in society, there was a revival of emphasis on the Lutheran Confessions. F. J. Stahl (1802-1861) saw the contemporary preaching office as identical with the New Testament office of apostle. He favored episcopacy because "it alone can guarantee authority of administration and spiritual care," authority in contrast to majority or mob rule.[446] A. F. C. Vilmar (1800-1868) emphasized that only pastors can ordain, determine doctrine, and decide who is qualified for ordained ministry.[447] J. K. Wilhelm Loehe (1808-1872), pastor in Neuendettelsau, Bavaria, emphasized presbyter-bishops closely connected with the divine order of salvation.[448] His vision of the church remained rooted in the local congregation.[449] The institutions he created in Neuendettelsau had great influence in America through support of pastors for Lutheran immigrants who became part of the Missouri Synod and, more importantly, the Iowa Synod.[450] In between what have been called "low"and "high church" extremes were a variety of views on ministry, though differences on ministry were not the chief obstacle to American Lutheran unity.

232. Because the ministry is a matter on which Lutherans, while having certain confessional and theological commitments, possess degrees of flexibility to meet changing situations and needs in church, society, and culture, there have periodically been studies and action on the topic by Lutheran bodies. In the course of the 1970s, the predecessor bodies of the ELCA all adopted the term "bishop," which was carried over into the ELCA.[451]

233. The ELCA mandated in 1988-1994 "an intensive study of the nature of ministry" with "special attention" to the following: "1) the tradition of the Lutheran Church; 2) the possibility of articulating a

Lutheran understanding and adaptation of the threefold ministerial office of bishop, pastor, and deacon and its ecumenical implication; and 3) the appropriate forms of lay ministries to be officially recognized and certified by this church, including criteria for certification, relations to synods, and discipline." The study presented recommendations in four areas, of which two are of particular relevance to this dialogue.[452]

234. First, the reaffirmation of the universal priesthood and of all baptized Christians in their various callings in the world and in the church was received with probably the greatest enthusiasm of all proposals.[453]

235. Second, the final report found that "threefold ministry" (or other "folds") "is not the way in which most of the people of this church approach the issues either of unity or mission."[454] Recommendations fol-lowed the heritage of, as an LWF study put it (see §237 below), "basically one ministry, centered in the proclamation of the Word of God and the administration of the Holy Sacraments," by pastors "within and for a local congregation" and by bishops "with and for a communion of local churches."[455]

236. Specifically, the ELCA Churchwide Assembly voted as follows:

> To reaffirm this church's understanding that ordination commits the person being ordained to present and represent in public ministry, on behalf of this church, its understanding of the Word of God, proclamation of the Gospel, confessional commitment, and teachings. Ordination requires knowledge of such teachings and commitment to them. Ordained persons are entrusted with special responsibility for the application and spread of the Gospel and this church's teachings.[456]

And with regard to bishops, they decided the following:

> (1) To retain the use of the title "bishop" for those ordained pastoral ministers who exercise the ministry of oversight in the synodical and churchwide expressions of this church; and

(2) To declare that the ministry of bishops be understood as an expression of the pastoral ministry. Each bishop shall give leadership for ordained and other ministries; shall give leadership to the mission of this church; shall give leadership in strengthening the unity of the Church; and shall provide administrative oversight.[457]

C. Aspects of Ministry in the Evangelical Lutheran Church in America in Light of World Lutheranism and Ecumenism

237. American Lutheran churches, in dealing with ministry issues in the second half of the twentieth century, did not do so in isolation, but rather often cooperatively and with international Lutheran and ecumenical resources. The Lutheran Council in the U.S.A. (1966-1987), involving The Lutheran Church–Missouri Synod and the bodies that merged into the ELCA, produced studies on the Ministry and on Episcopacy.[458] Its study on women's ordination is noted in §235 above, note 455. The LWF provided studies on the ministry, episcopacy, the ordination of women, and laity.[459] LWF leadership at times was active in advocating bishops in episcopal succession. There was also Lutheran involvement in producing and responding to the Faith and Order Commission report *Baptism, Eucharist and Ministry*.[460] In such ways, the ELCA received and participated in worldwide treatments and understandings on ministry and structure, while being able to act appropriately for its own particular situation.

238. Ordaining women to the ministry of word and sacrament occurred in German, Scandinavian, and other European Lutheran churches prior to the decision to do so in the United States. The significant debate in Sweden and its decision to ordain women as priests in 1958 was a turning point for many.[461] A Lutheran Council study, carried out in 1968-1969, centered especially on scriptural questions. The Lutheran Church in America and American Lutheran Church voted at conventions in 1970 to ordain women.[462] The practice, found also in the Association of Evangelical Lutheran Churches, was readily carried into the ELCA. Since Lutherans have one office of ministry, no theological obstacle existed to female pastors' becoming bishops.[463]

239. The ELCA, in addition to sharing in the *Joint Declaration on the Doctrine of Justification* with the Roman Catholic Church, has entered into full communion[464] with Reformed, Episcopal, and Moravian churches in the United States.[465] Although Reformed polity and ordering of elders and deacons differ from Lutheran practices, the ministry did not emerge as an issue in *A Formula of Agreement*.[466] The ELCA entered into full communion with two Moravian provinces in North America in 1999; ministry was treated in the section "Mutual Complementarities."[467] Thus the ELCA has entered into full communion with churches holding varying views of ministry.

240. Anglican emphasis on episcopacy made Lutheran-Episcopal dialogue toward full communion a more complicated matter. After narrowly failing to achieve the necessary two-thirds majority at the 1997 Churchwide Assembly of the ELCA, a proposal for full communion between the ELCA and The Episcopal Church, entitled "Called to Common Mission,"[468] was approved by the ELCA Churchwide Assembly in 1999[469] and subsequently affirmed in 2000 by The Episcopal Church. In this agreement, the two churches commit themselves "to share an episcopal succession that is both evangelical and historic" (see §12). Lutherans and Episcopalians promised "to include regularly one or more bishops of the other church to participate in the laying-on-of-hands at the ordinations/installations of their own bishops, as a sign, though not a guarantee, of the unity and apostolic continuity of the whole church"; *episcopé* is valued as "one of the ways, in the context of ordained ministries and of the whole people of God, in which the apostolic succession of the church is visibly expressed and personally symbolized in fidelity to the gospel through the ages" (see §12). Each church "remains free to explore its particular interpretations of the ministry of bishops in episcopal and historic succession," whenever possible in consultation with one another (see §13).

241. "Called to Common Mission" was able to refer to the 1993 full communion agreement between British and Irish Anglican Churches, on the one hand, and Nordic and Baltic Lutheran Churches, on the other, the *Porvoo Common Statement*.[470] The Meissen Agreement between the Church of England and the Evangelical Church in

Germany[471] represents the stage of "interim eucharistic hospitality," not full communion. The Waterloo Declaration[472] between the Evangelical Lutheran Church in Canada and the Anglican Church of Canada, adopted in 2001, provides for full communion. "Called to Common Mission" and these other Lutheran-Anglican agreements represent variations on a common vision of apostolicity and episcopacy in the church.

242. The ELCA and other Lutheran churches, in varied relations of communion with other churches, have reflected their Lutheran commitments, demonstrated ecumenical openness, and honored the heritages of their partners in dialogue. These agreements, with their differences, all reflect a firm belief in the church as *koinonia* of salvation.

NOTES

1 Lutherans and Catholics in Dialogue, nine volumes: (1) *The Status of the Nicene Creed as Dogma of the Church* (1965) (L/RC-1); (2) *One Baptism for the Remission of Sins* (1966) (L/RC-2); (3) *The Eucharist as Sacrifice* (1967) (L/RC-3); (4) *Eucharist and Ministry* (1970) (L/RC-4); (5) *Papal Primacy and the Universal Church* (1974) (L/RC-5); (6) *Teaching Authority and Infallibility in the Church* (1980) (L/RC-6); (7) *Justification by Faith* (1985) (L/RC-7); (8) *The One Mediator, the Saints, and Mary* (1992) (L/RC-8); (9) *Scripture and Tradition* (1995) (L/RC-9). Volumes 1-4 were originally published by the Bishops' Committee for Ecumenical and Interreligious Affairs, Washington, D.C., and the U.S.A. National Committee of the Lutheran World Federation, New York, New York. Volumes 5-9 were published by Augsburg Fortress, Minneapolis. Volumes 1-3 have been reprinted together in one volume by Augsburg Fortress (n. d.), as has volume 4 (1979).

2 Its Catholic members included the Rev. Avery Dulles, SJ, Bronx, New York; the Most Rev. Raphael M. Fliss, Bishop of Superior, Wisconsin; the Rev. Patrick Granfield, OSB, Washington, D.C.; Brother Jeffrey Gros, FSC, Washington, D.C.; the Rev. John F. Hotchkin, Washington, D.C.; Dr. Margaret O'Gara, Toronto; the Most Rev. J. Francis Stafford, Archbishop of Denver (chair); the Rev. Georges Tavard, Milwaukee, Wisconsin; and Dr. Susan K. Wood, SCL, Collegeville, Minnesota. Its Lutheran members included the Rev. H. George Anderson, Decorah, Iowa (elected presiding bishop of the ELCA in 1995); the Rev. Sherman G. Hicks, Chicago; Dr. David Lotz, New York, New York; Dr. Daniel F. Martensen, Chicago; the Rev. Joan A. Mau, Washington Island, Wisconsin; Dr. John H. P. Reumann, Philadelphia; Dr. Michael J. Root, Strasbourg, France; Dr. William G. Rusch, Chicago (until 1995); and Bishop Harold C. Skillrud, Atlanta (chair). A consultation involving U.S. and European Lutherans and Catholics, held February 18-21, 1993, at Lake Worth, Florida, had assessed the dialogues to date and examined future possibilities.

3 The Objectives were described thus: "The ultimate goal is to establish full communion between our churches. This round of dialogue should focus on church-

dividing issues and communion-hindering differences. There may result mutual instruction of our churches, learning from each other, and convergences that contribute to deeper *koinonia* between Lutherans and Catholics." "Structures" and "Ministries as Servants and Bonds of *Koinonia*" were to include the local, regional, national, and international, with "the themes of authority and freedom (collegiality, conciliarity)" running "through the entire document."

4   *Joint Declaration on the Doctrine of Justification: The Lutheran World Federation and the Roman Catholic Church* (Grand Rapids, MI: Eerdmans, 2000). *Gemeinsame Erklärung zur Rechtfertigungslehre* (Frankfurt am Main: Verlag Otto Lembeck/Paderborn, Bonifatius-Verlag, 1999; Lutherischer Weltbund, Päpstlicher Rat zur Förderung der Einheit des Christen).

5   Others, listed in the *Joint Declaration*, 27-28, include *The Condemnations of the Reformation Era: Do They Still Divide?* ed. K. Lehmann and W. Pannenberg (Minneapolis: Fortress, 1990), from the work by the Joint Ecumenical Commission of the Roman Catholic Church and churches of the Reformation (Lutheran, Reformed, United), published as *Lehrverurteilungen—kirchentrennend?* (LV) *I. Rechtfertigung, Sakramente und Amt im Zeitalter der Reformation und heute*, Dialog der Kirchen 4 (Freiburg im Breisgau: Herder/Göttingen: Vandenhoeck & Ruprecht, 1986); *II. Materialien zu den Lehrverurteilungen und zur Theologie der Rechtfertigung*, Dialog der Kirchen 5 (1988); *III. Materialien zur Lehre von den Sakramenten und vom kirchlichen Amt*, Dialog der Kirchen 6 (1990). The study in Germany dealt especially with the condemnations (anathemas) attached by the Council of Trent to its decree on Justification (1547) and statements of condemnation in the Lutheran Confessions.

6   The reading continues: "This gospel frees us in God's sight from slavery to sin and self (Rom. 6:6). We are willing to be judged by it in all our thoughts and actions, our philosophies and projects, our theologies and our religious practices. Since there is no aspect of the Christian community or of its life in the world that is not challenged by this gospel, there is none that cannot be renewed or reformed in its light or by its power.

"We have encountered this gospel in our churches' sacraments and liturgies, in their preaching and teaching, in their doctrines and exhortations. Yet we also recognize that in both our churches the gospel has not always been proclaimed, that it has been blunted by reinterpretation, that it has been transformed by various means into self-satisfying systems of commands and prohibitions.

"We are grateful at this time to be able to confess together what our Catholic and Lutheran ancestors tried to affirm as they responded in different ways to the biblical message of justification. A fundamental consensus on the gospel is necessary to give credence to our previously agreed statements on baptism, on the Eucharist, and on forms of church authority. We believe that we have reached such a consensus." (L/RC-7, §§161-164, 73-74)

7   See LV, n. 5, esp. Vol. III, and *The Condemnations of the Reformation Era*, where 147-159 deal with the ministry.

8   In the international dialogue, attention was given to *Church and Justification: Understanding the Church in the Light of the Doctrine of Justification* Lutheran–Roman Catholic Joint Commission (LWF/RC-9) in *Growth in Agreement II* (GA II), ed. J. Gros, H. Meyer, and W. G. Rusch, Faith and Order Paper No. 187 (Geneva:

WCC/Grand Rapids, MI: Eerdmans, 2000), 485-565. Apostolicity is the theme of the new round of international dialogue, begun in 1994.

9   Nineteen of them in the New Testament, three in the Septuagint Old Testament; see further §§126-129.

10   This calling depends on God's faithfulness and involves election (1 Cor. 1:2, "called [to be] saints"; 1 Thess. 1:4; Rom. 8:33). Paul regularly assumes a response in faith to the message of the gospel (as in 1 Thess. 1:5), followed by baptism (1 Cor. 6:11, "washed, sanctified, justified"), with a resulting *koinonia* (1 Cor. 1:9, with Christ). No passage in Paul, however, connects *koinon*-terms with baptism. But note 1 John 1:6-9, *koinonia* with God, the blood of Jesus cleanses us from sin; "if we confess our sins, God who is faithful and just will forgive us our sins and cleanse us from all unrighteousness"; *cf.* R. Brown, *The Epistles of John*, AB 30 (Garden City, NY: Doubleday, 1982), 242-245.

11   Both aspects are stressed by J. Hainz, *Koinonia: "Kirche" als Gemeinschaft bei Paulus* (*Biblische Untersuchungen* 16; Regensburg: Pustet, 1982). A. Weiser, "Basis und Führung in kirchlicher Communio," *Bibel und Kirche* 45 (1990), 66-71, speaks of "spiritual" dimensions (with God) and "societal."

12   *Cf.* O. Cullmann, *Katholiken und Protestanten. Ein Vorschlag zur Verwirklichung christlicher Solidarität* (Basel, Reinhardt, 1958); trans. J. Burgess, *Message to Catholics and Protestants* (Grand Rapids, MI: Eerdmans, 1958). Cullmann, later a Protestant observer at the Second Vatican Council, suggested, as early as 1957, "a yearly offering by both sides for one another; by Protestants for needy Catholics, and by Catholics for needy Protestants" (9-10) as a step toward Christian solidarity. The collection and *koinonia* in the New Testament are mentioned, 33-39. It could today take the form of parish and diocesan gathering of gifts.

13   Thus, *e.g.*, "diocese" (Latin *dioecesis*) reflects terminology from Roman provincial administration, likewise "synod" and "council." *Cf.* A. Brent, *The Imperial Cult and the Development of Church Order: Concepts and Images of Authority in Paganism and Early Christianity before the Age of Cyprian*, Supplements to Vigiliae Christianae 45 (Leiden: Brill, 1999), who claims (77), "The Order of the Christian community, constituted by an apostolate whose *koinōnia* continued the teaching and healing ministry of Jesus along with the breaking of bread (Acts 2,42), was the true means of producing the *pax dei*, in contrast to Augustus's *pax deorum*," (*cf.* Lk. 2:14; 19:38), thus "a refashioned Christian version of the Augustan *saeculum aureum*."

14   *A Patristic Greek Lexicon*, ed. G. W. H. Lampe (Oxford: Clarendon, 1964), "*koinōnia*" B.3.b., "*community* of essence," of Father and Son, citing Athenagoras (second century), Dionysius Alexandrinus (third century), Basil and Gregory of Nyssa (fourth century), of the Trinity, and Chrysostom (fourth-fifth century).

15   Christoph Schwöbel, "Koinonia," RGG[4] 4 (2001), 1477-1479; Rolf Schäfer, "Communio," RGG[4] 2 (1999), 435-438.

16   Nicolai Afanasev, *L'Eglise du Saint-Esprit* (Paris: Le Cerf, 1975). John D. Zizioulas, *Being as Communion. Studies in Personhood and the Church* (Crestwood, NY: St. Vladimir Seminary Press, 1985) interpreted *koinonia* in light of the anti-Arian trinitarianism of St. Athanasius. It is an ontological reality founded on the identity of

Jesus Christ with the eternal Word of God. Because, by virtue of the Incarnation, substance is seen to possess "almost by definition a relational character," the faithful who are united with Christ by faith and the Spirit are necessarily in the mutual relationships of a Communion that is at the same time spiritual and sacramental. John D. Zizioulas, *Eucharist, Bishop, Church*, trans. Elizabeth Theokritoff (Brookline, MA: Holy Cross Orthodox Press, 2001).

17 G. Florovsky, "Le corps du Christ vivant," in Florovsky et al, *La sainte Eglise universelle. Confrontation oecuménique* (Paris: Delachaux et Niestlé, 1948), 12, quoted in Zizioulas, *Being as Communion* (n. 16 above), 124. Thus a synthesis of Christology and Pneumatology is manifest in the Communion of the Church and the Churches. Since pneumatology implies eschatology and communion, which coincide in the Holy Liturgy, one may say that "*eschatology* and *communion* have determined Orthodox ecclesiology" (131).

18 See Thomas Best, Gunther Gassmann, eds., *On the Way to Fuller Koinonia* (Geneva: WCC, 1993) (Santiago) and the earlier working document and discussion paper "Towards Koinonia in Faith, Life, and Witness," 263-295. "The unity of the Church to which we are called is a koinonia given and expressed in a common confession of the apostolic faith; a common sacramental life entered by the one baptism and celebrated together in one eucharistic fellowship; a common life . . . ; and a common mission" (Canberra 1991, §2.1, 269), thus a gift, as well as a calling.

19 The *Final Report* of ARCIC-I (1982), in *Growth in Agreement*, Ecumenical Documents I, ed. H. Meyer and L. Vischer (New York/Ramsey: Paulist/Geneva: WCC, 1984) (GA I), 62-67; ARCIC-II, *The Church as Communion*, in GA II, 328-343; ARC-USA, "Agreed Report on the Local/Universal Church" (1999) summed the matter up thus, "'Communion' has emerged . . . as the concept that best expresses the reality of the Church as diverse yet one on faith, as both local and universal," *Origins* 30:6 (2000): 85-95; Pentecostal–Roman Catholic, "Perspective on *Koinonia*" (1989), in *Pneuma* 12 (1990): 117-142, in GA II, 735-752; Christian Church/Disciples of Christ–Roman Catholic, "The Church as a Communion in Christ" (1992), GA II, 386-398; Anglican/World Methodist Council, "Sharing in Apostolic Communion" (1996), GA II, 55-76; Catholic/World Methodist Council, "The Church as Koinonia of Salvation" (2001). *Cf.* S. Wood, "Ecclesial Koinonia in Ecumenical Dialogues," *One in Christ* 30 (1994): 124-145.

20 Miroslav Volf, *After Our Likeness: The Church as Image of the Trinity* (Grand Rapids, MI: Eerdmans, 1998) and "Kirche als Gemeinschaft: Ekklesiologische Überlegungen aus freikirchlicher Perspektive," *Evangelische Theologie* 49 (1989): 52-76. Veli-Matti Kärkkäinen, *An Introduction to Ecclesiology: Ecumenical, Historical and Global Perspectives* (Downers Grove, IL: InterVarsity Press, 2002).

21 Ludwig Hertling, *Communio: Church and Papacy in Early Christianity*, trans. with introduction by Jared Wicks (Chicago: Loyola University Press, 1972), 4-5 and 2; German, in *Xenia Piana: Miscellanea historiae pontificiae* 7 (1943): 1-48; *cf.* "Communio und Primat," *Una Sancta* 17 (1962) [J. Reumann, "Toward U.S. Lutheran/Roman Catholic Dialogue on Koinonia," paper for L/RC Coordinating Committee, April 1996]. For a survey of theologians on this, see Dennis M. Doyle, *Communion Ecclesiology: Vision and Versions* (Maryknoll, NY: Orbis, 2000).

22   See Jérôme Hamer, *L'église est une communion* (Paris: Cerf, 1962; English trans. Ronald Matthews, New York: Sheed and Ward, 1965). Jan Jacobs, "Beyond Polarity: On the Relation between Locality and Universality in the Catholic Church," in *Of All Times and Places: Protestants and Catholics on the Church Local and Universal*, ed. Leo J. Koffeman and Henk Witte (Zoetemeer: Meinema, 2001), 49-68, at 55-58.

23   *Church of Churches. The Ecclesiology of Communion* (Collegeville, MN: Liturgical Press, 1992), xii. This very defective translation of *Eglise d'Eglises: L'ecclésiologie de communion* (Paris: les Editions du Cerf, 1987), 9 ("au donné biblique") should not be used without checking the French text. *Cf.* also Walter Kasper, *Theology and Church* (New York: Crossroad, 1989, German 1987), "The Church as a Universal Sacrament of Salvation," 111-128, and "The Church as Communion: Reflections on the Guiding Ecclesiological Idea of the Second Vatican Council," 148-165 (literature in n. 5). Avery Dulles, *Models of the Church* (Garden City, NY: Doubleday, 1974), 56, treated *koinonia* as "a network of friendly interpersonal relationships" and as "a mystical communion of grace" under "The Church as Mystical Communion" (43-57), rev. ed. (1987), 60-61 and 47-62.

24   The Second Extraordinary General Assembly of the Synod of Bishops (1985), *Ecclesia sub Verbo Dei Mysteria Christi Celebrans pro Salute Mundi. Relatio Finalis*, II. C. 1. Available in English in *Origins* 15:27 (December 19, 1985): 448. Pope John Paul II reaffirmed this in his post-synodal apostolic exhortation *Christifideles Laici* (December 30, 1988), §19.

25   *Communionis Notio* (CN), in *Origins* 22:7 (June 25, 1992): 108-112. This text (1) equates "the Church of Christ" with "the worldwide community of the disciples of the Lord" (§7), which is more than "a communion of Churches"; (2) while there is a close connection between the eucharist and the Church, the eucharist is not sufficient by itself to ensure the being of a church; and (3) the communion is also served by institutions, like religious communities, that are not confined to one particular church; unity in diversity is one aspect of the communion. *Cf.* also Jörg Haustein, "Entmythologiseirung einer Zauberformel: Schreiben der Glaubenskongregation über die Kirche als Communio," *MD: Materialdienst der Konfessionskundlichen Instituts Bensheim* 43 (1992): 61-62.

26   *Directory*, §§13-15; Pontifical Council for Promoting Christian Unity, "Directory for the Application of Principles and Norms on Ecumenism" (Directory), in *Origins* (June 29, 1993): 129, 131-160.

27   *Ut Unum Sint* (UUS), §11, in *Origins* 49 (June 8, 1995): 51-72, §§11-14.

28   *Koinonia: Arbeiten des Oekumenischen Ausschusses der Vereinigten Evangelisch-Lutherischen Kirche Deutschlands zur Frage der Kirchen- und Abendmahlgemeinschaft* (Berlin: Lutherisches Verlagshaus, 1957). The essay by Werner Elert, "Abendmahl und Kirchengemeinschaft in der alten Kirche," 57-78, was expanded as a book translated by Norman Nagel as *Eucharist and Church Fellowship in the First Four Centuries* (St. Louis: Concordia, 1966).

29   Harding Meyer, "Zur Entstehung und Bedeutung des Konzepts 'Kirchengemeinschaft.' Eine historische Skizze aus evangelischer Sicht," in *Communio Sanctorum: Einheit der Christen–Einheit der Kirche, Festschrift für Bischof Paul-Werner Scheele*, ed. Josef Schreiner and Klaus Wittstadt (Würzburg: Echter

Verlag, 1988) 204-230; Eugene L. Brand, *Toward a Lutheran Communion: Pulpit and Altar Fellowship*, LWF Report 26 (Geneva: LWF, 1988); *Communio/Koinonia: A New Testament–Early Christian Concept and its Contemporary Appropriation and Significance*, A Study by the Institute for Ecumenical Research, Strasbourg, 1990, repr. in *A Commentary on 'Ecumenism: The Vision of the ELCA,'* ed. W. G. Rusch (Minneapolis: Augsburg, 1990), 119-141; *The Church as Communion: Lutheran Contributions to Ecclesiology*, ed. Heinrich Holtze, LWF Documentation 47 (Geneva: LWF, 1997), including "Toward a Lutheran Understanding of Communion," 13-29 [Reumann, April 1999, "'Koinonia' in Lutheran Use"].

30 LWF Constitution, Art. 3; text in *From Federation to Communion: The History of the Lutheran World Federation*, ed. J. H. Schjørring, P. Kumari, N. A. Hjelm; V. Mortensen, coordinator (Minneapolis: Fortress, 1997), 530; the 1947 Constitution said simply "a free association of Lutheran churches" (527).

31 LWF/RC-9.

32 *Ibid.* (§§51-62).

33 Joint Working Group of the World Council of Churches and the Roman Catholic Church (JWG), *The Notion of "Hierarchy of Truths" and The Church: Local and Universal.*, Faith and Order Paper No. 150 (Geneva: WCC Publications, 1990), §13ff.

34 Within Roman Catholicism, the terms "particular church" and "local church" are often used interchangeably. Most often the Second Vatican Council documents use the term "particular church" to refer to the diocese, but this term can also refer to churches in the same rite, region, or culture. There is no standard practice governing the use of this terminology. In spite of the Second Vatican Council's use of the term "particular church," this term has not enjoyed widespread acceptance. Whether or not it refers to a diocese or a larger region has to be discerned from its context. The present document explores the asymmetry between Lutheran and Roman Catholic understandings of what constitutes the basic unit of ecclesiality implied by the term "local" or "particular" church.

35 A forthright expression of this pattern is found in Ignatius (Smyr. 8.1), but the bishop as head of a local community came to be the common pattern.

36 CD, §11.

37 LG, §26, states that "the faithful are gathered together through the preaching of the Gospel of Christ, and the mystery of the Lord's Supper is celebrated 'so that, by means of the flesh and blood of the Lord the whole brotherhood of the Body may be welded together.'"

38 *Sacrosanctum Concilium* (SC), §41, states, "The principal manifestation of the church consists in the full, active participation of all God's holy people in the same liturgical celebrations, especially in the same eucharist, in one prayer, at one altar, at which the bishop presides, surrounded by the college of priests and by his ministers."

39 SC, §42.

40 LWF/RC-9, 85.

41 Nicholas Sagovsky, *Ecumenism, Christian Origins and the Practice of Communion* (Cambridge: Cambridge University Press, 2000), 128.

42   Council of Nicaea, canon 4.

43   LG, §26. The Latin text speaks of a "sacrament of order" (singular) rather than "of orders" (plural); "Episcopus, plenitudine *sacramenti ordinis* insignitus, est 'oeconomus gratiae supremi sacerdotii'" (emphasis added).

44   *Treatise on the Power and Primacy of the Pope* (TPPP), §63. *The Book of Concord* (BC), ed. Robert Kolb and Timothy J. Wengert (Minneapolis: Fortress Press, 2000), 340.

45   On Lutheran church structures around the world, see E. Theodore Bachmann and Mercia Brenne Bachmann, *Lutheran Churches in the World: A Handbook* (Minneapolis: Augsburg, 1989). The German Lutheran churches are organized regionally within the nation rather than nationally, but they still have this threefold structure. Lutheran churches of course recognize the one, holy, catholic, and apostolic Church.

46   An exception is Wolfgang Huber, *Kirche*, 2nd ed. (Munich: Chr. Kaiser, 1988).

47   LG, §28. *Cf. Presbyterorum Ordinis* (PO), §§4-6.

48   For some exceptions, see James A. Coriden, *The Parish in Catholic Tradition: History, Theology and Canon Law* (Paulist Press, 1997); U.S. Bishops' Committee on the Parish, "The Parish: A People, A Mission, A Structure," in *Origins* 10:41 (March 26, 1982): 641, 633-646; Philip J. Murnion, "Parish: Covenant Community," *Church* 12.1 (Spring 1996): 5-10.

49   AG, 37; Provision 9.11., in the *Constitution, Bylaws, and Continuing Resolutions of the Evangelical Lutheran Church in America* (CBCR), 2001 ed. (Chicago: ELCA), 58.

50   Provision 9.11. in CBCR, 58.

51   See Provision 9.21. in CBCR, 58.

52   Provision 9.41. in CBCR, 60. The same text is found in required provision *C4.03. in the *Model Constitution for Congregations* as contained in the ELCA churchwide constitution, 221-222.

53   LG, §26.

54   LG, §26. Even though the document does not actually say that these groups are parishes, it does refer to them as local congregations. The text affirms that Christ, by whose power the one, holy, catholic, and apostolic church is gathered together, is present in these communities.

55   *Rite of Christian Initiation of Adults*, §9.

56   Provision 8.11. of CBCR, 50.

57   Provision 3.02. of CBCR, 20.

58   Werner Elert, *The Structure of Lutheranism*, trans. Walter A. Hansen (St. Louis: Concordia, 1962), 369.

59   Provision 10.21. in CBCR, 75.

60   Provisions †S6.03. and †S8.12. in the *Constitution for Synods* as printed in CBCR, 187-189 and 193-195.

61   LG, §23.

62   LG, §23.

63   The Church of Sweden and the German Landeskirchen are examples.

64   The ELCA is only a slight exception to this pattern of national organization; it includes a Caribbean Synod in Puerto Rico and the U.S. Virgin Islands.

65   Provision 13.21. in CBCR, 90.

66   Provision 8.71. in CBCR, 54.

67   This lack was noted in an important address by E. Clifford Nelson to the 1963 Assembly of the Lutheran World Federation, "The One Church and the Lutheran Churches," in *Proceedings of the Fourth Assembly of the Lutheran World Federation*, Helsinki, July 30–August 11, 1963 (Berlin: Lutherisches Verlagshaus, 1965).

68   CD, §38. "Pope Paul VI, in his 1966 *motu proprio Ecclesiae Sanctae* called for Episcopal Conferences to be established wherever they did not yet exist; those already existing were to draw up proper statutes; and in cases where it was not possible to establish a Conference, the Bishops in question were to join already existing Episcopal Conferences; Episcopal Conferences comprising several nations or even international Episcopal Conferences could be established. Several years later, in 1973, the Pastoral Directory for Bishops stated once again that 'the Episcopal Conference is established as a contemporary means of contributing in a varied and fruitful way to the practice of collegiality.' These Conferences admirably help to foster a spirit of communion with the Universal Church and among the different local Churches." (Pope John Paul II, *Motu proprio On the Theological and Juridical Nature of Episcopal Conferences [Apostolos Suos]* May 21, 1998, §5; *Ecclesiae Sanctae* and the *Pastoral Directory of Bishops*, in *Origins* 28:9 (July 30, 1998): 153, §5.

69   *Ibid.*

70   *Ibid.*

71   LG, §23 stipulates that "individual bishops, in so far as they are set over particular churches exercise their pastoral office over the portion of the people of God assigned to them, not over other churches nor over the church universal. But as members of the Episcopal college and legitimate successors of the apostles, by Christ's arrangement and decree, each is bound to be solicitous for the entire church; such solicitude, even though it is not exercised by an act of jurisdiction, is very much to the advantage of the universal church."

72   LWF Constitution, Article III: Nature and Function.

73   *Ibid.*

74   Pope John Paul II, Address on September 12, 1987, in *Origins* 17:16 (October 1, 1987): 258. Here Pope John Paul II extends the assertion in LG, §8, that the Church of Christ subsists in the Roman Catholic Church to the relationship between the universal church and particular churches.

75   LG, §23.

76   TPPP, 60f.

77   TPPP, 72.

78   See §§187-188 regarding ordinations in continental Lutheranism by pastors with responsibilities as superintendent; regarding bishops' continuing to ordain in Nordic countries, see §§189-195.

79   See the discussions in Kurt Schmidt-Claussen, "The Development of Offices of Leadership in the German Lutheran Church: 1918-Present, "in *Episcopacy in the Lutheran Church? Studies in the Development and Definition of the Office of Church Leadership*, ed. Ivar Asheim and Victor R. Gold (Philadelphia: Fortress Press, 1970), 72-115; Wilhelm Maurer, *Das synodale evangelische Bischofsamt seit 1918, Fuldaer Hefte* 10 (Berlin: Lutherisches Verlagshaus, 1955).

80   Council of Trent, Session 23, Canons on the sacrament of Order, 6.

81   Council of Trent, Session 23, chap. 4.

82   Council of Trent, Session 23, Canons on the sacrament of Order, 7.

83   DHn 3860. Pope Pius XII, *Sacramentum Ordinis*, in *Acta Apostolicae Sedis* (AAS) 40 (1948): 5-7.

84   LG, §21.

85   LG, §28; PO, §2.

86   LG, §20.

87   Avery Dulles, "*Ius Divinum* as an Ecumenical Problem," *Theological Studies* 38 (1977): 689.

88   The Second Vatican Council defines the diocese as "a portion of the people of God whose pastoral care is entrusted to a bishop in cooperation with his priests" (CD, §11).

89   *Code of Canon Law* (CIC), canon 521 º1.

90   CIC, canon 519.

91   LG, §28.

92   LG, §28. PO, §8.

93   LG, §28.

94   CIC, canon 529 §2.

95   LWF, *The Lutheran Understanding of Ministry* (1983), reprinted in *Ministry: Women, Bishops*, LWF Studies (1993), §21.

96   Presbyterian polities stress the interrelation of the face-to-face assembly and the regional community of such assemblies. Ministry at the regional level, however, is exercised by the presbytery as a college rather than by a single ordained minister such as a bishop. The possibility of such a polity has not been a part of the discussions of this dialogue. While Lutheran churches have generally included a regional ordained minister of oversight, a presbyterian polity has not been seen as unacceptable, and the ELCA is in full communion with the Presbyterian Church (U.S.A.). Catholic theology requires the presence of a bishop.

97   LG, §26.

98   LG, §21.

99   LG, §27.

100 LG, §25.

101 LG, §19.

102 LG, §22.

103 LG, §24.

104 LG, §20.

105 See especially Luther's Preface to the 1528 Saxon Visitation Articles (LW 40, 271) and, more comprehensively, Werner Elert, "Der bischöfliche Charakter der Superintendentur-Verfassung." *Luthertum* 46 (1935): 353-367.

106 See orders cited in Werner Elert, "Der bischöfliche Charakter der Superintendentur-Verfassung." *Luthertum* 46 (1935): 355f.

107 Kurt Schmidt-Clausen, "The Development of Offices of Leadership in the German Lutheran Church: 1918-Present," in *Episcopacy in the Lutheran Church? Studies in the Development and Definition of the Office of Church Leadership,* ed. Ivar Asheim and Victor R. Gold (Philadelphia: Fortress Press, 1970), 72-115.

108 Provision †S8.11. of CBCR, 193.

109 Provision †S8.12. of CBCR, 193.

110 Provision †S8.12.h. of CBCR, 194.

111 "Called to Common Mission: A Lutheran Proposal for a Revision of the Concordat of Agreement" (CCM) (Chicago: ELCA, November 1998), 12.

112 *Porvoo Common Statement,* in *Together in Mission and Ministry: The Porvoo Common Statement* (Porvoo) (London: Church House Publishing, 1993), §58a vi.

113 LG, §18; *cf.* §§22-23.

114 *Papal Primacy and the Universal Church.* Lutherans and Catholics in Dialogue V (L/RC-5), ed. P. C. Empie and T. A. Murphy (Minneapolis: Augsburg, 1974), II, 34, 30. As early as 1972, the "Malta Report" stated "But in the various dialogues, the possibility begins to emerge that the Petrine office of the Bishop of Rome also need not be excluded by Lutherans as a visible sign of the unity of the church as a whole 'insofar as [this office] is subordinated to the primacy of the gospel by theological reinterpretation and practical restructuring'" (66).

115 UUS, §94.

116 *Ibid.,* §95.

117 *Ibid.*

118 *Ibid.,* §96.

119 L/RC-5, §30.

120 WA, 54, 231; LW 41, 294; *cf.* Harding Meyer, "Suprema auctoritas ideo ab omni errore immunis: The Lutheran Approach to Primacy" in *Petrine Ministry and the Unity of the Church,* ed. James Puglisi (Collegeville, MN: The Liturgical Press, 1999), 16-18.

121 On the shape of such reforms, see *Papal Primacy and the Universal Church*, §§23-25.

122 BC, 326.

123 This ambiguity with regard to the precise nature of the *ius divinum/ius humanum* distinction was pointed out in the international Roman Catholic–Lutheran dialogue on "The Gospel and the Church" ("Malta Report," 1972) (LWF/RC-1), §31: "Greater awareness of the historicity of the church in conjunction with a new understanding of its ecclesiological nature, requires that in our day the concepts of the *ius divinum* and *ius humanum* be thought through anew. . . . *Ius divinum* can never be adequately distinguished from *ius humanum*. We have *ius divinum* always only as mediated through particular historical forms." The problem was addressed by George Lindbeck in his article, "Papacy and *Ius Divinum*: A Lutheran View" in L/RC-5.

124 The issue of "apostolic succession" was taken up by L/RC-4, 138-188, in articles by McCue, Burghardt, and Quanbeck. Note the Common Statement, §44. It expands the notion of apostolic succession beyond that of a succession in episcopal office to include transmission of the apostolic gospel and grants that Lutherans have preserved a "form of doctrinal apostolicity," leading to the tentative conclusion of the Catholic participants that they "see no persuasive reason to deny the possibility of the Roman Catholic Church recognizing the validity of this Ministry" (54). See more recently the Lutheran–Roman Catholic Joint Study Commission, *The Ministry in the Church* (1981), (LWF\RC-5), 62: "The apostolic succession in the episcopal office does not consist primarily in an unbroken chain of those ordaining to those ordained, but in a succession in the presiding ministry of a church, which stands in the continuity of apostolic faith and which is overseen by a bishop in order to keep it in communion with the Catholic and Apostolic church" (quoted also in *The Niagara Report. Report of the Anglican-Lutheran Consultation on Episcope*, 1987, §53). See also *Baptism, Eucharist, Ministry*. Report of the Faith and Order Paper No. 111 (BEM) (Geneva: WCC, 1982), 35: "The primary manifestation of apostolic succession is to be found in the apostolic tradition of the church as a whole." *Cf.* CCM, 12.

It should be noted that the dogmatic constitution of the Second Vatican Council on the church stated that "among those various ministries which, as tradition witnesses, were exercised in the Church from the earliest times, the chief place belongs to the office of those who, appointed to the episcopate in a sequence running back to the beginning (*per successionem ab initio decurrentem*), are the ones who pass on the apostolic seed." (LG, 20 [trans. W. M. Abbott (ed.), 39]). Other translations of the cited Latin phrase wrongly use the word "unbroken." Thus A. P. Flannery (ed.), *Documents of Vatican II* (Grand Rapids, MI: Eerdmans, 1975), 371: "in virtue consequently of the unbroken succession, going back to the beginning." Similarly, S. Garofalo (ed.), *Sacro Concilio Ecumenico Vaticano II: Constituzioni, Decreti, Dichiarazioni* (Milan: Editrice Ancora, 1966), 189: "per successione che decorre ininterrotta dall'origine." See also *Ecclesia de Eucharistia*, in *Origins* 32:46 (May 1, 2003): §§28, 29, 753-768.

125 AC VII.1; LG, §20.

126 ARCIC, *The Church as Communion*, §31.

127 Anglican-Lutheran International Continuation Committee, *The Niagara Report*, §§28-30; in GA II, 17f.

128 CCM, 12.

129 Apol. XIV.1.

130 BC, 90-103; Robert Kolb and James A. Nestingen, *Sources and Contexts of the Book of Concord* (Minneapolis: Fortress Press, 2001), 137-139.

131 Georg Kretschmar, "Die Wiederentdeckung des Konzeptes der 'Apostolischen Sukzession' im Umkreis der Reformation," in *Das bischöfliche Amt: Kirchengeschichtliche und ökumenische Studien zur Frage des kirchlichen Amtes*, edited by Dorothea Wendebourg (Göttingen: Vandenhoeck and Ruprecht, 1999), 300-344.

132 For an example of a vehement rejection by the Reformers of the argument that episcopal succession is essential to a valid ministry, see Philipp Melanchthon, "The Church and the Authority of the Word," in *Melanchthon: Selected Writings*, translated by Charles Leander Hill (Minneapolis: Augsburg, 1962), 130-186. Latin original in *Melanchthons Werke im Auswahl*, vol. 1, 323-386.

133 See also BEM, M38.; Warren A. Quanbeck, "A Contemporary View of Apostolic Succession," in L/RC 4, 187; The Lutheran responses to BEM on ministry and succession are analyzed in Michael Seils, *Lutheran Convergence? An Analysis of the Lutheran Responses to the Convergence Document "Baptism, Eucharist and Ministry" of the World Council of Churches Faith and Order Commission*, LWF Report 25 (Geneva: Lutheran World Federation, 1988), 126-131. A more positive reading of Lutheran responses is in Michael Root, "Do Not Grow Weary in Well-Doing: Lutheran Responses to the BEM Ministry Document," *dialog* 27 (1988): 23-30.

134 CCM, 12.

135 Cf. *Niagara Report*, §§54-55.

136 This analysis presumes that bishops and pastors working within congregational, parochial, and diocesan structures are paradigmatic for ecclesiology.

137 Roman Catholic–Lutheran Joint Commission, 1994 (LWF\RC-8), §93.

138 SC, §42.

139 CD, §15.

140 LG, §28.

141 AC, §7.

142 WA 30II: 421 quoted in Althaus 1966, 288, n. 10.

143 The major exception here might be The Lutheran Church–Missouri Synod. For a significant Missouri discussion of these issues, see Pieper 1950-1957, vol. 3, 419-435.

144 "Concerning the Ministry," LW 40.41.

145 See Quenstedt, cited in Heinrich Schmid, *Doctrinal Theology of the Evangelical Lutheran Church* (1899; rpt. Minneapolis: Augsburg, 1961), 591.

146 See Conrad Bergendoff, *The Doctrine of the Church in American Lutheranism*, The Knubel-Miller Lecture, 1956 (Philadelphia: Board of Publication of the United Lutheran Church in America, 1956).

147 LWF/RC-6, 49 (emphasis in original text).

148   See SC, §10.

149   See SC, §41. Karl Rahner makes this point in "Theology of the Parish," in *The Parish: From Theology to Practice,* ed. Hugo Rahner (Westminster, MD: The Newman Press, 1958), 23-35. He identifies the parish as "the representative actuality of the Church; the Church appears and manifests itself in the event of the central life of the parish" (25). Rahner argues that the church is necessarily a local and localized community. It achieves its highest degree of actuality where it acts, that is, where it teaches, prays, offers the Sacrifice of Christ, etc. For Rahner the parish is not a division of a larger segment of the church, but "the concentration of the Church into its own event-fullness" (30). The parish is "the highest degree of actuality of the total church" (30). See also Jerry T. Farmer, *Ministry in Community: Rahner's Vision of Ministry,* Louvain Theological and Pastoral Monographs, §13 (Leuven: Peeters Press; and Grand Rapids, MI: Eerdmans, 1993), 134-136.

150   In the reference just cited, Rahner also makes the point that the parish and the pastor are *iure divino* in the same way that the Church, papacy, and episcopate are, even though a canonist would not easily concede this point. *Ibid.,* 25.

151   JWG, §13.

152   ARCIC, 1991, §39.

153   Peter Brunner, "The Realization of Church Fellowship," in *The Unity of the Church: A Symposium,* papers presented to the Commission on Theology and Liturgy of the Lutheran World Federation (Rock Island, IL: Augustana Press, 1957): 22.

154   *Ibid.,* 18f.

155   CN, §7.

156   L/RC-4, proposed, "As Lutherans, we joyfully witness that in theological dialogue with our Roman Catholic partners we have again seen clearly a fidelity to the proclamation of the gospel and the administration of the sacraments which confirms our historic conviction that the Roman Catholic church is an authentic church of our Lord Jesus Christ. For this reason we recommend to those who have appointed us that through appropriate channels the participating Lutheran churches be urged to declare formally their judgment that the ordained Ministers of the Roman Catholic church are engaged in valid ministry of the gospel, announcing the gospel of Christ and administering the sacraments of faith as their chief responsibilities, and that the body and blood of our Lord Jesus Christ are truly present in their celebrations of the sacrament of the altar" (§35); and "As Roman Catholic theologians, we acknowledge in the spirit of the Second Vatican Council that the Lutheran communities with which we have been in dialogue are truly Christian churches, possessing the elements of holiness and truth that mark them as organs of grace and salvation. Furthermore, in our study we have found serious defects in the arguments customarily used against the validity of the eucharistic Ministry of the Lutheran churches. In fact, we see no persuasive reason to deny the possibility of the Roman Catholic church recognizing the validity of this Ministry. Accordingly we ask the authorities of the Roman Catholic church whether the ecumenical urgency flowing from Christ's will for unity may not dictate that the Roman Catholic church recognize the validity of the Lutheran Ministry, and, correspondingly, the presence of the body and

blood of Christ in the eucharistic celebrations of the Lutheran churches" (§54). The international Lutheran–Roman Catholic Commission text *Facing Unity*, which built on earlier agreements, outlines a proposal for Lutheran-Catholic unity by stages including mutual teaching of the apostolic faith, mutual engagement in apostolic mission, and recognition and reconciliation of apostolic ministries by mutual installation/ordination of bishops. Unlike "Called to Common Mission," it does not propose immediate, full mutual recognition of ministry, but rather a phased recognition and reconciliation.

157 UR, §3. Lutherans long had a complex view of the ecclesial status of the Roman church, stressing both its character as church and its perceived failings that were asserted to undercut its faithfulness in a fundamental way. On Rome as church despite its failings, see LW 26.24; for an apparently contrary assertion, see LW 41.144.

158 UR, §4.

159 CN, §17.

160 *Cf.* LWF\RC-9, 153-156.

161 UR, 7.

162 UUS, §15.

163 "Called to Common Mission" describes the ELCA's relationship of full communion with the Episcopal Church.

164 UR, §3.

165 UR, §3.

166 Briefwechsel von Landesbischof Johannes Hanselmann und Joseph Kardinal Ratzinger über das Communio-Schreiben der Römischen Glaubenskongregration," *Una Sancta* 48 (1993): 348.

167 LWF\RC-8, §§75-77. *Defectus* is translated as "lack" in the English edition of *UR* on the Vatican website (§22c), in UUS, §67, and in the official English translation of the *Catechism of the Catholic Church*, §1400. See also *Ecclesia de Eucharistia*, in *Origins* 32:46 (May 1, 2003): §30, 753-768.

168 Walter Kasper, "Die apostolische Sukzession als ökumenisches Problem," LV, III, 345.

169 *Growth in Agreement II*, 443-484.

170 See Arthur Carl Piepkorn, "A Lutheran View of the Validity of Lutheran Orders." In L/RC-4, 215; Wolfgang Stein, *Das kirchliche Amt bei Luther* (Wiesbaden: Franz Steiner Verlag, 1972), 192f.

171 For example: "It is a definite conclusion that no one confers holy orders and makes priests less than those under the papal dominion. A semblance, indeed, of ordination and of making priests is magnificently present but it behooves the king of semblance to grant nothing but semblance so as to guarantee his abominations" (LW 40.15; WA 12, 176). See further Helmut Lieberg, *Amt und Ordination bei Luther und Melanchthon* (Göttingen: Vandenhoeck & Ruprecht, 1962), 168-171.

172 JDDJ, §40.

173 LG, §25.

174 BC, Apol., 14, 222-223.

175 Church of Sweden Church Ordinance of 1571, in John Wordsworth, *The National Church of Sweden* (London: Mowbray, 1911), 232; on this Ordinance and its importance for later Swedish theology, see Sven-Erik Brodd, "The Swedish Church Ordinance of 1571 and the Office of Bishop in an Ecumenical Context," in *The Office of Bishop: Swedish Lutheran-Roman Catholic Dialogue* LWF Studies (Geneva: LWF, 1993), 147-157.

176 CCM, esp. §§15-21; Porvoo, esp. §§34-57 of the Common Statement; *Called to Full Communion: The Waterloo Declaration* (*http://generalsynod.anglican.ca/ministries/ departments/doc.php?id=71 &dept=primate*) (May 1, 2004), esp. §§A 3, 5.

177 Although there is no general Catholic ruling on Lutheran orders, consistent Catholic practice has been to re-ordain Lutheran ministers entering the Catholic priesthood.

178 John Reumann, "The Ordination of Women: Exegesis, Experience, and Ecumenical Concern," in *Ministries Examined* (Minneapolis: Augsburg Fortress, 1987).

179 *Ordinatio Sacerdotalis*, §4 (*cf. Origins* 24 [June 9, 1994]: 51). Cf. Congregation for the Doctrine of the Faith, *From "Inter Insigniores" to "Ordinatio Sacerdotalis,"* (Washington: United States Catholic Conference, 1996).

180 UUS, §79.1.4.

181 UUS, §96.

182 UUS, §94.

183 Recent discussion on the reform of the papacy in the light of UUS includes Carl Braaten and Robert Jenson, eds., *Church Unity and the Papal Office: An Ecumenical Dialogue on John Paul II's Encyclical Ut Unum Sint* (Grand Rapids, MI: Eerdmans, 2001); Michael J. Buckley, *Papal Primacy and the Episcopate: Towards a Relational Understanding* Ut unum sint: Studies on Papal Primacy (New York: Crossroad, 1998); William Henn, *The Honor of my Brothers: A Short History of the Relation between the Pope and the Bishops* Ut unum sint: Studies on Papal Primacy (New York: Crossroad, 2000); Hermann J. Pottmeyer, *Towards a Papacy in Communion: Perspectives from Vatican Councils I & II Ut Unum Sint:* Studies on Papal Primacy (New York: Crossroad, 1998); John R. Quinn, *The Reform of the Papacy: The Costly Call to Christian Unity* (New York: Crossroad, 1999); ed. James Puglisi, *Petrine Ministry.*

184 UR, §4.

185 Porvoo, §45.

186 "Therefore we ask the Lutheran Churches: 1) if they are prepared to affirm with us that papal primacy renewed in the light of the gospel, need not be a barrier to reconciliation; 2) if they are able to acknowledge not only the legitimacy of the papal Ministry in the service of the Roman Catholic communion but even the possibility and the desirability of the papal Ministry, renewed under the gospel and committed to Christian freed, in a larger communion which would include the Lutheran

churches; 3) if they are willing to open discussion regarding the concrete implications of such a primacy to them." from "Toward the Renewal of Papal Structures" Part C, "Lutheran Perspectives," §32, 22-23.

187 Cf. L/RC-5, its use of the "Petrine principle" and questions to Lutheran churches, including "that papal primacy, renewed in light of the gospel, need not be a barrier to reconciliation" (§32), and including to the Roman Catholic Church, "if it is prepared to envisage the possibility of a reconciliation that would recognize the self-government of Lutheran churches within a communion" (§33); LWF/RC-6, §§67-73 = Growth in Agreement, 269-271; Harding Meyer, "Suprema Auctoritas" in Petrine Ministry and the Unity of the Church, 15-34, esp. 29.

188 UUS, §11. Cf. UR, §3.

189 JDDJ, §15.

190 UR, §3.

191 LWF\RC-8, §§92-93; §§120-122.

192 A Greek-English Lexicon of the New Testament and other Early Christian Literature, 3rd ed. (hereafter BDAG), rev. and ed. F. W. Danker (Chicago: University of Chicago Press, 2000), 552-553, offers four basic definitions (in boldface type, meanings, functional use; English equivalents in italics):

[1] "close association involving mutual interests and sharing, association, communion, fellowship, close relationship," as in marriage or friendship or the bond of life that unites Pythagoreans; Phil. 1:5 a close relation with the gospel, or with the poor (Rom. 15:26);

[2] "attitude of good will that manifests an interest in a close relationship, generosity, fellow-feeling, altruism," 2 Cor. 9:13, generosity in sharing;

[3] abstract term for the concrete "sign of fellowship, proof of brotherly unity; even gift, contribution"; Rom.15:26 might fit here, so might 1 Cor. 10:16ab, "a means for attaining a close relationship with the blood and body of Christ";

[4] participation, sharing in something, Christ's sufferings (Phil. 3:10), the body and blood of Christ (1 Cor. 10:16), the Holy Spirit (2 Cor. 13:13), faith (Phlm. 6).

Cf. further F. Hauck, "koinos, . . . koinōnia, etc.," (German 1938), Theological Dictionary of the New Testament 3 (Grand Rapids, MI: Eerdmans, 1965), 789-809, supplement in Theologisches Wörterbuch zum Neuen Testament 10:2 (Stuttgart: Kohlhammer, 1979) , 1145-1146; J. Hainz, "koinōnia etc.," (German 1981), Exegetical Dictionary of the New Testament 2 (Grand Rapids, MI: Eerdmans, 1991), 303-305.

193 In the Old Testament, the noun, verb, and adjective occur twenty-five times. There are seven more New Testament examples if compounds (synkoinōnos, synkoinōnein) are counted, for a New Testament total of forty-five instances. There are a maximum 119 occurrences in the entire Greek Bible if koinos, "common" or "impure," is included. Examples that do occur are mainly in later (deuterocanonical) books under Hellenistic influence; koinōnia occurs only at Wisdom of Solomon 6:23 and 8:18, for associating with wisdom and her words. Charts on koinon-terms in J. Reumann, "Koinonia in Scripture: Survey of Biblical Texts," in On the Way to Fuller Koinonia,

ed. T. F. Best and G. Gassmann, Faith and Order Paper No. 166 (Geneva: WCC, 1994), 39, where all New Testament passages are treated, and bibliography provided, some of which cannot be included here.

194 BDAG, 551-552.

195 BDAG, 552. The verb *metechō*, "have a share in, partake of something," is sometimes associated with *koinōnein*, as at 1 Cor. 10:17 (*cf.* 16) and 10:21, 30; and Heb. 2:14. *Cf.* N. Baumert, *KOINŌNEIN und METECHEIN—synonym? Eine umfassende semantische Untersuchung*, SBB, 51 (Stuttgart: Katholisches Bibelwerk, 2003) distinguishes them and gives a variety of meanings to *koinonein*, not a single sense that some like Hainz (n. 11 above) sought.

196 J. Y. Campbell, "*KOINŌNIA* and Its Cognates in the New Testament," *Journal of Biblical Literature* 51 (1932): 352-382; H. Seesemann, *Der Begriff KOINŌNIA im Neuen Testament*, BZNW 14 (Giessen: Töpelmann, 1933); Hauck (n. above). A. R. George, *Communion with God in the New Testament* (London: Epworth, 1953), took communion as "have a share, give a share," and sharing, partly in reaction to those who made "the Fellowship" a name for the church, as was argued by C. A. Anderson Scott, *Christianity According to St Paul* (Cambridge: Cambridge Univ. Press, 1927, reprinted 1961), 158-169.

197 K. Kertelge, "Abendmahlsgemeinschaft und Kirchengemeinschaft im Neuen Testament und in der Alten Kirche," in *Interkommunion–Konziliarität. Zwei Studien im Auftrag des Deutschen ökumenischen Studienausschusses*, Beiheft zur Ökumenischen Rundschau 25 (1974), 2-51, reprinted in *Einheit der Kirche: Grundlegung im Neuen Testament*, ed. F. Hahn, K. Kertelge, and R. Schnackenburg, *Quaestiones Disputatae* 84 (Freiburg: Herder, 1979), 94-132, and "Kerygma und Koinonia: Zur theologischen Bestimmung der Kirche des Urchristentums," in *Kontinuität und Einheit*, Festschrift for F. Mussner, ed. P. G. Müller and W. Stenger (Freiburg: Herder, 1981), 317-339. R. Schnackenburg, "Die Einheit der Kirche unter dem Koinonia-Gedanken," in *Einheit der Kirche* (1979), 52-93. J. Hainz, *Koinonia* (1982) (n. 11 above).

198 See J. M. McDermott, "The Biblical Doctrine of KOINŌNIA," *Biblische Zeitschrift* N.F. 19 (1975), 64-77 and 219-233. J. Hainz, *Koinonia* (see n. 11 above), was critical of earlier studies for failing to find an underlying unity or for reading in traditional dogmatic theology (178, 185, 188); history of research and results, 162-204.

199 F. Hahn, "Einheit der Kirche und Kirchengemeinschaft in neutestamentlicher Sicht," in *Einheit der Kirche* (n. 197 above), 9-51. Hahn (13-14) suggested that the Greek *koinōnia* is like the Latin *participatio* and partly like *communio*, while the German *Gemeinschaft* is like Latin *societas*.

200 J. G. Davies, *Members One of Another: Aspects of Koinonia* (London: Mowbray, 1958), originally presented to the WCC's Division of Interchurch Aid and Service to Refugees; G. Panikulam, *Koinōnia in the New Testament: A Dynamic Expression of Christian Life*, Analecta Biblica 85 (Rome: Biblical Institute Press, 1979); J. Hainz, *Ekklesia: Strukturen paulinischer Gemeinde-Theologie und Gemeinde-Ordnung*, Biblische Untersuchungen 9 (Regensburg: Pustet, 1972); Hainz' *Koinonia* (n. 11 above) includes sections on Roman Catholic, Reformation, and Orthodox views on the concept (206-272). Reumann's tradition-history approach (n. 193 above) was presented at the Fifth World Conference on Faith and Order in 1993. Further, S. Brown,

"Koinonia as a Basis of New Testament Ecclesiology?" *One in Christ* 12 (1976), 157-167; J. D. G. Dunn, "'Instruments of Koinonia' in the Early Church," *One in Christ* 25 (1989), 204-216; K. Kertelge, "Koinonia und Einheit der Kirche nach dem Neuen Testament," in *Communio Sanctorum: Einheit der Christen–Einheit der Kirche, Festschrift für Bischof Paul-Werner Scheele*, ed. Josef Schreiner and Klaus Wittstadt (Würzburg: Echter Verlag, 1988), 53-67.

201   J. Reumann, "Church Office in Paul, Especially in Philippians," *Origins and Method: Toward a New Understanding of Judaism and Christianity: Essays in Honour of John C. Hurd* (JSNTSup 86; ed. B. H. McLean; Sheffield: Sheffield Academic Press, 1993), 82-91, esp. 83. See J. P. Meier, "Are There Historical Links between the Historical Jesus and the Christian Ministry?" *Theology Digest* 47/4 (2000): 303-315; E. Schweizer, *Church Order in the New Testament* (SBT 32; London: SCM, 1961), 20-33 (2 a-m).

202   Today it is widely recognized among New Testament interpreters that the added assertions in Matthew 16:16b-19 may be a retrojected account of an episode in the gospel tradition rooted in a post-resurrection appearance of the risen Christ, such as that preserved in John 21:15-17. In other words, Matthew 16:16b-19 may be a Matthean version of the "feed my lambs/sheep" conversation of John 21. See, e.g., R. E. Brown et al. (eds.), *Peter in the New Testament: A Collaborative Assessment by Protestant and Roman Catholic Scholars* (Minneapolis: Augsburg; New York: Paulist, 1973), 83-101. Cf. J. Roloff's estimate: "Vielmehr tritt Petrus an dieser Stelle lediglich als Garant der Jesusüberlieferung in Erscheinung, die die Grundlage von Verkündigung und Leben der Gemeinde darstellt," *Exegetische Verantwortung in der Kirche: Aufsätze* (ed. M. Karrer; Göttingen: Vandenhoeck & Ruprecht, 1990), 339. Cf. P. Perkins, *Peter: Apostle for the Whole Church* (Minneapolis: Fortress, 2000), 86. Such an interpretation of the Caesarea Philippi scene would not deny that Jesus founded a "church," but it would reveal rather an awareness that his early followers had of themselves as the "flock" or "church," which developed during the course of the decades between AD 30 and 90, when the Matthean and Johannine Gospels were eventually composed. In other words, Matthew would have interpreted with hindsight the meaning of Peter's acknowledgment and the implications of Jesus' reaction to it in thus formulating the church-building statement, which appears on Jesus' lips.

203   In Luke 22:31-32, Jesus prays for the repentant Simon that he might "strengthen" his "brethren." This supportive Petrine function, however, is set out in a context making no mention of *ekklēsia*.

204   This title seems to be derived by the evangelists from the Hellenistic world, because *talmîd* is almost wholly absent from the Old Testament (save in 1 Chr. 25:8, used of pupils in the Temple choir!). *Mathētēs* occurs in the Septuagint of Jer. 13:21; 20:11; 46:9, but always with a variant reading that makes the deriving of the New Testament usage from it problematic. See further J. A. Fitzmyer, "The Designations of Christians in Acts and Their Significance," in Commission Biblique Pontificale, *Unité et diversité dans l'Eglise* (Vatican City: Libreria Editrice Vaticana, 1989), 223-236, esp. 227-229.

205   See further E. Lohse, *Die Ordination im Spätjudentum und im Neuen Testament* (Göttingen: Vandenhoeck & Ruprecht, 1951), 19-21. Cf. J. Newman, *Semikhah*

(*Ordination*): *A Study of Its Origin, History and Function in Rabbinic Literature* (Manchester: Manchester University, 1950), 1-3. From Old Testament passages, rabbinic tradition developed its practice of ordination, a practice attested only several centuries later in the Tannaitic Midrashim (*Sifre* Num. 27:18 §140; *Sifre* Deut. 34:9 §357); *cf.* Str-B, 2. 647-648.

206   J. Roloff has summed up the matter: "Jesus, to be sure, neither founded the Church nor installed office-holders, but even so by his *calling of followers*, by *establishing a community of disciples*, and by his *summons to service* he supplied the momentum, without which the post-Easter development of the Church would not be explicable" ("Amt / Ämter / Amtsverständnis IV," TRE 2 [1978], 510). Similarly, H. von Lips, "Amt, IV. Neues Testament," RGG⁴ 1 (1998), 424-426.

207   See further J. A. Fitzmyer, "The Designations of Christians in Acts" (n. 204 above), 227, 229-232.

208   The first occurrence (Acts 5:11) is a comment of the author himself about the effect of Ananias's deception as he uses a term current in his own day to report how "fear fell upon the whole church," *i.e.*, the whole Jerusalem church.

209   J. Fitzmyer, "The Acts of the Apostles," *Anchor Bible* 31 (New York: Doubleday, 1998), 343. Although the Seven are chosen *diakonein trapezais*, "to serve tables," they are not called *diakonoi* by Luke. The later ecclesiastical tradition often considered them to be the first "deacons." See *1 Clement* 42:4. Luke hardly intended his readers "to see the origin of the diaconate in this episode."

210   Bishops in the Catholic tradition are regarded as successors of the apostles (Second Vatican Council, LG, §20); *cf.* F. A. Sullivan, *From Apostles to Bishops: The Development of the Episcopacy in the Early Church* (New York: Newman, 2001). Does that mean successors of the "Twelve Apostles" (Mt. 10:2; Rev. 21:14)? In the New Testament, others beyond the Twelve bear the title *apostolos*: Matthias, Acts 1:26; Barnabas and Paul, Acts 14:4, 14; unnamed "apostles," 2 Corinthians 8:23; and possibly Andronicus and Junia, Romans 16:7. See further J. Hainz, *Kirche im Werden: Studien zum Thema Amt und Gemeinde im Neuen Testament* (ed. J. Hainz; Munich/Paderborn: Schöningh, 1976), 109-122.

211   Although the phrase *hē kat' oikon ekklēsia* does not occur in Acts, the idea may be found in Acts 2:46; 5:42; 12:12 and may be derived from the conversion of individuals and their "households" (Lydia, Acts 16:15; the jailer, 16:34; Crispus, 18:8; possibly also "the house of Jason," 17:5). On the house church, see R. Banks, *Paul's Idea of Community: The Early House Churches in Their Historical Setting* (Grand Rapids, MI: Eerdmans, 1980); F. V. Filson, "The Significance of the Early House Churches," JBL 58 (1939) 105-112; H. J. Klauck, *Hausgemeinde und Hauskirche im frühen Christentum* (SBS 103; Stuttgart: Katholisches Bibelwerk, 1981); A. J. Malherbe, "House Churches and Their Problems," *Social Aspects of Early Christianity* (Baton Rouge, LA: Louisiana State University, 1977), 60-91; W. Rordorf, "Was wissen wir über die christlichen Gottesdiensträume der vorkonstantinischen Zeit?" ZNW 32 (1986): 476-480.

212   In such gatherings the *paterfamilias* or *prostatis*, "patroness" (Rom. 16:2), presumably provided the leadership in the house church, which eventually came to be called *episkopē* (1 Tim. 3:1).

213　See further P. Benoit, "L'Unité de la communion ecclésiale dans l'Esprit selon la quatrième Evangile," *Unité et diversité dans l'Eglise* (see n. 204 above), 265-283; R. E. Brown, *The Community of the Beloved Disciple* (New York: Paulist, 1979); F.-M. Braun, "Le cercle johannique et l'origine du quatrième évangile," RHPR 56 (1976): 203-214; R. Fernández Ramos, "La comunidad joánica," *Ciencia Tomista* 106 (1979): 541-586; H.-J. Klauck, "Gemeinde ohne Amt? Erfahrungen mit der Kirche in den johanneischen Schriften," BZ 29 (1985): 193-220.

214　See further J. Hainz, *Koinonia: "Kirche" als Gemeinschaft*, 62-89 (n. 11 above); idem, "*Koinōnia*," EDNT 2: 303-305, esp. 304. *Cf.* J. Reumann, "Koinonia in Scripture" (n. 193 above), 48-49.

215　See further N. Brox, "*Sōtēria* und Salus: Heilsvorstellungen in der Alten Kirche," EvT 33 (1973), 253-279; K. H. Schelkle, "*Sōtēr*" and "*Sōtēria*," EDNT, 3, 325-329.

216　In 1 Corinthians 3:5-15, Paul hints at the role that all ministers in the church are to play for its upbuilding; they are there as "God's fellow workers," as he comments on his own and Apollos's role.

217　As translated by the RSV, similarly in NABRNT; the NRSV has "those who labor among you, and have charge of you in the Lord and admonish you." So too J. Roloff, "Amt," TRE 2 (1978), 521: "Vorsteher"; F. Neugebauer, *In Christus: En Christō. Eine Untersuchung zum paulinischen Glaubensverständnis* (Göttingen: Vandenhoeck and Ruprecht, 1961) 139-140; C. Masson, *Les deux épîtres de saint Paul aux Thessaloniciens* (CNT 11a; Neuchâtel/Paris: Delachaux et Niestlé, 1957), 71-72.

In Romans 12:8, the same participle appears, *ho proistamenos en spoudē*, which the RSV there renders, "he who gives aid, with zeal," but the NRSV has, "the leader, in diligence"; and the NAB, "if one is over others, with diligence." Compare 1 Tim. 5:17, where the perfect participle of the same verb is used, *proestōtes presbyteroi*, "elders who rule" (RSV, NRSV), "presbyters who preside" (NAB). *Cf.* 1 Tim 3:4, 5, 12; Josephus, *Ant.* 8.12.3 §300 ("govern"); 12.2.13 §108 ("chief officers").

Some commentators, however, would rather translate the three verbs thus: "who labor, give care, and admonish." Thus J. Reumann, "Church Office" (n. 201 above), 89; A. J. Malherbe, *First Thessalonians* (AB 32B; New York: Doubleday, 2000), 310-314; R. F. Collins, "The First Letter to the Thessalonians," NJBC, art. 46, §37; E. J. Richard, *First and Second Thessalonians* (*Sacra Pagina* 11; Collegeville, MN: Liturgical Press, 1995), 267-268.

218　See J. Hainz, *Ekklésia: Strukturen paulinischer Gemeinde-Theologie und Gemeinde-Ordnung* (BU 9; Regensburg: Pustet, 1972), 37-42; also idem, "Die Anfänge des Bischofes- und Diakonenamtes," and "Amt und Amtsvermittlung bei Paulus," in *Kirche im Werden* (n. 210 above) 91-108, 109-122.

219　The NRSV has "bishops and deacons," but with a marginal note, "overseers and helpers." The same twosome occurs later in *1 Clement* 42,4-5 (supposedly based on the LXX of Isa. 60:17); *Didache* 15:1.

220　See G. F. Hawthorne, *Philippians* (WBC, 43; Waco, TX: Word, 1983), 9-10; A. Lemaire, *Les ministères aux origines de l'église: Naissance de la triple hiérarchie: évêques, presbytres, diacres* (LD 68; Paris: Cerf, 1971) 27-31, 96-103, 186; "The Ministries in the New Testament," BTB 3 (1973), 133-166, esp. 144-148.

221 The origin of the office of "overseer" is debated. See H. Lietzmann, "Zur urchristlichen Verfassungsgeschichte," ZWT 55 (1914) 97-153, repr. in *Das kirchliche Amt im Neuen Testament* (Wege der Forschung 189; ed. K. Kertelge; Darmstadt: Wissenschaftliche Buchgesellschaft, 1977) 93-143; J. M. Balcer, "The Athenian Episkopos and the Achaemenid 'King's Eye,'" AJP 98 (1977) 252-263; H. W. Beyer, "*Episkopos*," TDNT, 2. 618-620; L. Porter, "The Word *episkopos* in Pre-Christian Usage," ATR 21 (1939) 103-112; A. Adam, "Die Entstehung des Bischofsamtes," *Wort und Dienst* 5 (1957) 104-13; W. Nauck, "Probleme des frühchristlichen Amtsverständnisses (I Ptr 5, 2f.)," ZNW 48 (1957) 200-220, esp. 202-207; H. Braun, *Qumran und das Neue Testament* (2 vols.; Tübingen: Mohr [Siebeck], 1966), 2. 329-332; W. Eiss, "Das Amt des Gemeindeleiters bei den Essenern und der Christliche Episkopat," WO 2 (1959) 514-19; J. A. Fitzmyer, "Jewish Christianity in Acts in Light of the Qumran Scrolls," *Studies in Luke-Acts: Essays Presented in Honor of Paul Schubert* (ed. L. E. Keck and J. L. Martyn; Nashville: Abingdon, 1966) 233-257, esp. 245-248; J. Hainz, "Die Anfänge des Bischofs- und Diakonenamtes," *Kirche im Werden* (n. 210 above), 91-107; R. E. Brown, "*Episkopē* and *Episkopos*: The New Testament Evidence," TS 41 (1980): 322-338. On house churches and episcopacy, see E. Dassmann, "Zur Entstehung des Monepiskopats," JAC 17 (1974), 74-90; "Haus-gemeinde und Bischofsamt," in *Vivarium: Festschrift Theodor Klausner* (JAC Ergänzungsband 11; Münster in W.: Aschendorff, 1984), 82-97; *Ämter und Dienst in den frühchristlichen Gemeinden* (Hereditas 8; Bonn: Borengässer, 1994); G. Schöllgen, "Hausgemeinden, *Oikos*-Ekklesiologie, und monarchischer Episkopat," JAC 31 (1988), 72-90; "Bischof, I. Neues Testament," RGG[4] 1. 1614-1615; J. Reumann, "Church Office" (n. 201 above), 87-89; "One Lord, One Faith, One God, but Many House Churches," *Common Life in the Early Church: Essays Honoring Graydon F. Snyder*, ed. J. V. Hills et al. (Harrisburg, PA: Trinity Press International, 1998), 106-117. Cf. B. L. Merkle, *The Elder and Overseer: One Office in the Early Church*, Studies in Biblical Literature 57 (New York: Peter Lang, 2003).

222 See J. N. Collins, *Diakonia: Re-interpreting the Ancient Sources* (New York: Oxford University Press, 1990) 235-237; cf. BDAG, 230: "agent, intermediary, courier." J. Roloff suggest that it was "aus der Funktion beim Gemeindemahl entwickelt" ("Amt," TRE 2 [1978], 522).

223 L/RC-4, 10, n. 6.

224 J. Fitzmyer, "Acts" (n. 209 above), 534-535. Roloff considers this as unhistorical ("ganz sicher ungeschichtlich"), "Amt," TRE 2 (1978), 521.

225 J. Fitzmyer, "Acts" (n. 209 above), 673.

226 See F. A. Sullivan, *From Apostles to Bishops*, 65 ("such authority was seen as coming directly from the Holy Spirit or the risen Christ").

227 "The anachronistic comparisons of these figures with 'apostolic delegates' or 'metro-politans' or 'monarchical heads' or 'coadjutors' are seductively charming, but the text of the Pastoral Epistles employs the father-child model for expressing the way in which the apostolic task was shared and transmitted" (J. D. Quinn, *The Letter to Titus* (AB 35; New York: Doubleday, 1990), 71.

228 Our translation. This might refer to the commissioning or ordaining of an *episkopos* or *presbyteroi*, but its meaning is debated. Some commentators have even understood

it as a penitential rite because of the following clause about participation in the sins of another. See N. Adler, "Die Handauflegung im NT bereits ein Bussritus? Zur Auslegung von 1 Tim. 5,22," *Neutestamentliche Aufsätze: Festschrift für Prof. Josef Schmid* (ed. J. Blinzler; Regensburg: Pustet, 1963), 1-6; J. P. Meier, "*Presbyteros* in the Pastoral Epistles," CBQ 35 (1973): 323-345, esp. 325-337.

229 The Pastoral Epistles are widely regarded as Deutero-Pauline, perhaps by a disciple or disciples in the Pauline School. *Cf.* Raymond E. Brown, *An Introduction to the New Testament* (New York: Doubleday, 1997), 662-668: "*about 80 to 90 percent of modern scholars would agree that the Pastorals were written after Paul's lifetime,*" having "some continuity with Paul's own ministry and thought, but not so close as manifested in Col. and Eph. and even 2 Thess." (668). On various hypotheses, see J. D. Quinn, "Timothy and Titus, Epistles to," *Anchor Bible Dictionary* 6 (New York: Doubleday, 1992), 568-569.

230 In 2 Timothy 4:5, the author charges: "Do the work of an evangelist (*ergon euangelistou*), fulfill your ministry (*diakonian*)."

231 Or "ordained," since it is not easy to say precisely what is implied by this "laying on of hands." Acts 8:18 associates it with the gift of the Spirit. Note also *lectio varia* in some MSS of 1 Timothy 4:14: *presbyterou. Cf.* Hebrews 6:2.

232 Often translated later "bishop."

233 This term often is rendered "elders." That translation is acceptable for members of local councils in various towns in pre-Christian Judaism: *e.g.*, among Jews in Jerusalem (Acts 4:5; 6:12), or in the Old Testament (Josh. 20:4; Ruth 4:2). As a designation for those with a special function among Christians, "presbyters" is preferred (as in Acts 11:30; 15:2, 4, 6, 22; 21:18).

234 Later called "deacons."

235 The abstract noun *episkope* means "the act of watching over" or "visitation," as in Luke 19:44 and 1 Peter 2:12; in Acts 1:20 it denotes a "position" or "assignment"; but in 1 Timothy 3:1 it is used in the sense of "engagement in oversight, supervision," of leaders in Christian communities, *i.e.*, the office of overseer (BDAG, 379).

236 The term is used in a generic sense in 1 Peter 2:25 of Christ, who is called *episkopos ton psychon hymon*, "guardian of your souls."

237 Corresponding substantives *presbytes* and *presbytis* occur in Titus 2:2-3.

238 See R. E. Brown, *Priest and Bishop: Biblical Reflections* (New York: Paulist, 1970), 34-40.

239 It is debatable whether one should understand "tables" in a dining sense or in a banking sense (*i.e.*, "to look after financial tables"). See W. Brandt, *Dienst und Dienen im Neuen Testament* (NTF 2/5; Gütersloh: Bertelsmann, 1931; repr. Münster: Antiquariat Th. Stenderhoff, 1983); E. Schweizer, *Church Order* (n. 201 above), 49 (3 o), 70 (5 i).

240 See Ambrosiaster, *Ad Tim. prima* 3.11 (CSEL, 31/3. 268); J. N. D. Kelly, *Commentary on the Pastoral Epistles* (HNTC; New York: Harper & Row, 1963) 83-84; R. M. Lewis, "The 'Women' of 1 Timothy 3:11," *BSac* 136 (1979), 167-175.

241 See B. B. Thurston, *The Widows: A Women's Ministry in the Early Church* (Minneapolis: Fortress, 1989), 36-55.

242 Even though one might argue from Titus 1:5-9 that *episkopos* and *presbyteroi* stand for one administrative office in the Cretan church, one cannot predicate that one office so easily of the Ephesian church, because the qualifications of the *episkopos* are treated in 1 Timothy 3, quite distinctly and independently of what is said about *presbyteroi* in 1 Timothy 5, so that the church in Ephesus might have been structured with these administrators separately considered. This might affect one's consideration of regional churches and the way they received each other in hospitality or eucharistic sharing more so than in structural uniformity. See J. Reumann, "Koinonia in Scripture" (n. 193 above), 63 (§52); R. Schnackenburg, "Ephesus: Entwicklung einer Gemeinde von Paulus zu Johannes," BZ, 35 (1991), 41-64; W. Thiessen, *Christen in Ephesus: Die historische und theologische Situation in vorpaulinischer und paulinischer Zeit und zur Zeit der Apostelgeschichte und der Pastoralbriefe* (TANZ 12; Tübingen/Basel: Francke, 1995).

243 See G. W. Knight, "Two Offices (Elders/Bishops and Deacons) and Two Orders of Elders (Preaching/Teaching and Ruling Elders): A New Testament Study," *Presbyterion* 12 (1986): 105-114; F. M. Young, "On *episkopos* and *presbyteros*," JTS 45 (1994), 142-148 (on the origin of the presbyterate as distinct from that of the episcopate and the diaconate); R. A. Campbell, *The Elders: Seniority within Earliest Christianity* (Edinburgh: Clark, 1994); J. D. Quinn, "Ministry in the New Testament," *Eucharist and Ministry* (see n. 183 above), 69-100, esp. 97.

244 For *presbyteroi* as derived from the "elders" of the Jewish synagogue, see J. T. Burtchaell, *From Synagogue to Church: Public Services and Offices in Earliest Christian Communities* (New York: Cambridge University Press, 1992); and "Amt, III. Antikes Judentum," RGG^4 1 (1998), 424. For backgrounds in the Greco-Roman world, see in contrast R. A. Campbell, *The Elders* (n. above), 67-96, 246, 258-259.

245 Note that Paul is informed about this decision in Acts 21:25, on his return to Jerusalem at the end of his third missionary journey. Nothing is said about it in Galatians 2. See further J. A. Fitzmyer, *The Acts of the Apostles* (AB 31; New York: Doubleday, 1998), 538-567, 691-694; on *porneia* as "illicit marital union," rather than the traditional "unchastity" or "prostitution," 557-558; i.e., BDAG *porneia* 2, rather than 1.

246 In Romans 15:26, *koinonia* is the word for "contribution," which in this case comes from Achaia and Macedonia.

247 In the New Testament, Apostolic Fathers, and apologists we encounter apostles, prophets and teachers, then bishops and deacons, presbyters (*Didache* 11,3-12; 13,1-7; 15,1-2; *1 Clement* 42,4; 44,1-6; Polycarp, *Ep. Phil.* praef.; 5,1-6,3), teachers and leaders (Justin speaks of the "president," *1 Apol.* 61, 65 and 67; he himself was a teacher [*Mart. Iust.* recension C, 3,3]), and various others in service to their communities.

248 For the three titles in conjunction with each other, see Ignatius, *Magn.* 2; 6; 13,1; *Trall.* 2,3; *Philad.* praef. and 7,1; *Polyc.* 6,1. For the presbytery as a group, see *Eph.* 2,2; 4,1; 20,2; *Magn.* 6,1; 7,1; 13,1; *Trall.* 2,2; *Philad.* 7,1. The bishop is to be respected as the grace of God, in the place of God, as Jesus Christ or the Father or the commandment, or followed as Jesus Christ follows the Father. The presbytery is to be

respected as the law of Jesus Christ, God's council or the apostles. The deacon is to be respected as the one who serves Jesus Christ or his mysteries, or as Jesus Christ himself, or as God's commandment.

249 In the bishop Ignatius says he meets the bishop's church (*Ephes.* 1,3 and *Magn.* 6,1; in *Magn.* 2 he meets their church in all three ranks). He asks for messengers to be sent to his own people to give them encouragement, and for his church to be remembered in prayer.

250 See the section "*Communio* through Letters" in Hertling, *Communio* (n. 21 above), 28-36; Werner Elert, *Eucharist and Church Fellowship in the First Four Centuries*, trans. N. E. Nagel (St. Louis: Concordia, 1966), 125-160; and also the papyrus letters of recommendation studied by Hans Reinhard Seeliger, "Das Netzwerk der *communio*: Überlegungen zur historischen Soziologie des antiken Christentums und ihrer Bedeutung für die Ekklesiologie," in Communio—*Ideal oder Zerrbild von Kommunikation?*, edited by Bernd Jochen Hilberath (Freiburg: Herder, 1999), 19-38.

251 *1 Clement, e.g.,* 51,1-4 (Rome even sends official emissaries: 65,1).

252 Justin, *1 Apol.* 65,5 and 67,5. The absent are not only the sick: Otto Nussbaum, *Die Aufbewahrung der Eucharistie* (Bonn: Hanstein, 1979), 177.

253 The practice of sending *eulogia*, portions of consecrated bread from one bishop—especially a metropolitan—to bishops of nearby or dependent churches was condemned by a Synod of Laodicea in the late fourth century (Synod of Laodicea, canon 14 [Mansi 2.566E]), which implies that the practice existed earlier. See Robert F. Taft, "One Bread, One Body: Ritual Symbols of Ecclesial Communion in the Patristic Period," in *Nova Doctrina Vetusque: Essays on Early Christianity in Honor of Fredric W. Schlatter*, ed. Douglas Kries and Catherine Brown Tkacz (New York: Peter Lang, 1999), 30-31.

254 In Rome in the fifth century, the bishop sent a particle of his eucharist to presbyters conducting services at *tituli* within the walls (but not beyond), according to a letter of Innocent I to Decentius of Gubbio, March 19, 416; see Taft, art.cit. 32-34.

255 Tertullian, *Apol.* 39,4; on readmission to communion in the end, Cyprian, *ep.* 18,1; 55,13 (but repentance is required, 55,23).

256 Hertling, *Communio* (n. 21 above), 36-42, *e.g.,* "In some circumstances, a layman or the people could break off communion with their own bishop. . . . In these ruptures of fellowship, the essential issue is sharing in eucharistic communion (37). . . . From our point of view, it is striking that nowhere in antiquity do we find a precise statement as to who had the right to excommunicate someone. Instead, it appears that everyone had this right—which, however, corresponds exactly with the early Christian conception of *communio*" (41).

257 Council of Nicaea I (325), canon 4, says that all the bishops of a province should take part, but in any case at least three.

258 The growth of agreement concerning authoritative texts, what is called the "formation of the canon" of scripture, involved the inclusion of some texts and the exclusion of others. The condemnation of Marcion in the 140s solidified the Christian commitment to their Jewish biblical heritage, and through exchange and copying the churches came to possess and use quite similar collections of their own basic texts.

259 Easter is a good example. See the controversy described in Eusebius, *H.E.* 5,23-25, and the resolution of the date at the Council of Nicaea (325), mentioned in its synodal letter, §3, Socrates, *H.E.* 1,9.

260 Warnings about heretics, *e.g.*, Eusebius, *H.E.* 4,7,6; 5,13,1-4; 5,18,1; 5,19,1-4; 6,43,3; 7,30; Socrates, *H.E.* 1,6 and Theodoret, *H.E.* 1,4 (regarding Arius).

261 On the importance of the principal churches in maintaining and documenting *koinonia* via letters and lists of the orthodox, see Hertling, *Communio*, (n. 21 above), 30-35.

262 New Testament texts cited by the Fathers in this connection include especially Acts 20:17-28; Phil. 1:1; Titus 1:5-10; 1 Tim. 3:1-7 and 4:14. Ignatius of Antioch addresses Polycarp of Smyrna as "bishop" (*ep. ad Polyc.* praef.), but Polycarp's own letter to the Philippians never mentions the term, suggesting that titles were fluid in the mid-second century.

263 Numerous examples include *1 Clement*, Polycarp *To the Philippians*, the Letter of the martyrs at Lyons and Vienne (Eusebius, *H.E.* 5,1-3). When the term "dioecesis" was taken into Christian use later, it bore no resemblance to the imperial (civil) diocese.

264 See the *Dictionnaire de Droit Canonique*, ed. R. Naz, s.v. "Chorévèque" (Jacques Leclef). In the East, the institution survived into the eighth century, although canon 57 of the Synod of Laodicea (Mansi 2.574B) in the fourth century calls for the replacement of such village or country bishops by pastors who travel amongst these small communities (*periodeutas*). The Synods of Ancyra, Neocaesarea, and Nicaea's "regulations consistently emphasize the full dependence of the *chorepiscopus* on the real head of the community, who alone defined the sphere of his functions," says Karl Baus in *The Imperial Church from Constantine to the Middle Ages*, volume two of *History of the Church*, edited by Hubert Jedin and John Dolan (New York: Seabury Press, 1980), 233.

265 Alexandre Faivre, *Ordonner la fraternité: Pouvoir d'innover et retour à l'ordre dans l'Église ancienne* (Paris: Cerf, 1992), 33 and 80-82.

266 Peter Lampe, *Die stadtrömischen Christen in den ersten beiden Jahrhunderten*, 2nd ed. (Tübingen: J. C. B. Mohr [Paul Siebeck], 1989), 334-342, suggests as early as the late second century; Allen Brent, *Hippolytus and the Roman Church in the Third Century* (Leiden: Brill, 1995), 417-432, would put the date of a monarchical bishop in Rome later.

267 Eusebius, *H.E.* 6,43,11.

268 One of the best treatments of the development of Rome's preeminence, up till the sixth century, is Robert B. Eno, *The Rise of the Papacy* (Wilmington: Michael Glazier, 1990). Eno participated in many earlier rounds of the U.S. Lutheran-Catholic Dialogue. See also James F. McCue and Arthur Carl Piepkorn, "The Roman Primacy in the Patristic Era," in L/RC-4, 43-97.

269 Irenaeus, *haer.* 3,1,1 (*cf.* Eusebius, *H.E.* 5,8,2-4) and 3,3,2. Willy Rordorf, "Was heisst: Petrus und Paulus haben die Kirche in Rom 'gegründet'? Zu Irenäus, Adv. haer. III,1,1; 3,2.3," in *Unterwegs zur Einheit*, FS Heinrich Stirnimann, ed. Johannes Brantschen and Pietro Salvatico (Freiburg/Schweiz: Universitätsverlag, 1980), says that they "founded" it by their oral preaching, constituted it by the installation of bishops.

270 See the examples of Victor and Irenaeus in the Easter controversy (Eusebius, H.E. 5,23-25); Stephen, Firmilian, Dionysius of Alexandria and Cyprian in the dispute about rebaptizing heretics (Cyprian, ep. 69-75 and Eusebius, H.E. 7,9,1-5).

271 Irenaeus, haer. 3,3,3. In the huge literature on this passage, which has been rather tendentiously summarized by Domenic Unger in "St. Irenaeus and the Roman Primacy," Theological Studies 13 (1952): 359-418, and "St. Irenaeus on the Roman Primacy," Laurentianum 16 (1975): 431-445, one can discern the desire of scholars to maximize or to minimize the basis of the Roman church's importance. Walter Ullmann, "The Significance of the Epistola Clementis in the Pseudo-Clementines," Journal of Theological Studies n.s. 11 (1960): 310-311, contends that Linus and Cletus may have been Roman bishops, but the first proper successor or "heir" of Peter, succeeding to his powers, was Clement, and that the language in Irenaeus supports this. Enrico Cattaneo, "Ab his qui sunt undique: una nuova proposta su Ireneo, Adv. haer. 3,3,2b," Augustinianum 40 (2000): 399-405, thinks that Irenaeus is referring to the succession of presbyters, and emends undique to presbyteri.

272 Edict of Galerius, 311, Eusebius, H.E. 8,17,3-10; Licinius and Constantine's declaration of toleration ("Edict" of Milan), 313, Eusebius, H.E.10,5,2-14. In 380, Christianity was given almost exclusive legal status in the Roman Empire (Codex Theodosianus XVI 1,2; see Creeds, Councils and Controversies, edited by J. Stevenson [New York: Seabury, 1966], 160-161). We are less well informed about the legal circumstances in other parts of the Christian world.

273 Faivre, Ordonner la Fraternité, 77-84, 93-96. Faivre calls the process "sacerdotalization."

274 In the West, these first appear early in the eighth century in Germany, especially Bavaria and Frankish lands, but have virtually disappeared by the eleventh and twelfth centuries. From the first they are assistants to the bishop, and teach, oversee, confirm, consecrate altars and churches, ordain clergy (even major orders), take part in synods. Dictionnaire de Droit Canonique, (DDC) s.v. "Chorévèque," 691-693. Archpriests were an earlier phenomenon (Merovingian times): as the number of country converts grew, they needed more service than a deacon could give, and the priest in charge of them came to live with them. He did not have authority over several churches, nor could he ordain (A. Amanieu, "Archiprêtre," DDC 1, 1007-1009). See also n. 264 above.

275 The late ninth century saw the replacement of earlier archpriests and chorbishops by rural deans and archdeacons, who supervised all types of parishes. Ewig, in Friedrich Kempf, Hans-Georg Beck, Eugen Ewig and Josef Andreas Jungmann, The Church in the Age of Feudalism, "History of the Church 3," ed. Hubert Jedin and John Dolan (New York: Herder and Herder, 1969), 165-166.

276 Bernard M. Kelly, The Functions Reserved to Pastors, The Catholic University of America Canon Law Studies 250 (Washington: Catholic University of America Press, 1947), 4; he adds (8), "This parochial unity of the city (civitas) was one of the most characteristic marks of the ancient diocese. The cathedral was the only parish church in the city. Around the ninth century, however, other parishes appeared in the city, administered by collegiate chapters."

277 See the article by R. Schieffer, "Eigenkirche," Lexikon des Mittelalters III (München: Artemis-Verlag, 1986): 1705-1708.

278 Pierre Riché, in *Évêques, moines et Empereurs (610-1054)*, ed. Gilbert Dagron *et al.* (Paris: Desclée, 1993), 768-769, writing about the late ninth and early tenth century, says that some bishops sold off churches to lay patrons, and rural churches were fortunate if they belonged to monasteries. On 697, he gives as a rough estimate that during the ninth century, the proportion of monks who were priests and deacons rose from 20 percent to 60 percent.

279 See Riché (n. 278 above), 695: "Every year the bishop gathered the urban and rural clergy at his palace. At that time, the diocesan statutes would be formulated." He is speaking of the ninth century.

280 One focus in the Carolingian reform of the clergy under Louis the Pious (814-840) was to bring urban priests together in a canonical life and to draw rural priests closer together. Kempf, in Kempf *et al.*, 307-311; *cf.* 330-332.

281 Ewig points out, in Baus *et al.*, 532, that while church synods were separate in the sixth century, later "the boundaries begin to become blurred" with royal councils. Y. M.-J. Congar, *L'Ecclésiologie du haut Moyen Age* (Paris: Cerf, 1968), 133, n. 11 speaks of a great number of councils in the sixth through eighth centuries, declining in the ninth and especially the tenth.

282 For example, the first reference to Nicaea I (325) as "ecumenical" came in 338, borrowing a term used by the worldwide associations of professional athletes and Dionysiac artists, according to Henry Chadwick, "The Origin of the Title, 'Oecumenical Council,'" *Journal of Theological Studies*, n.s. 23 (1972): 132-135. Constantinople I (381) was called "ecumenical" soon after the fact, in 382. The ecumenical status of Ephesus II (449) never was achieved, despite the fact that it seems to have complied with the proposed conditions for that designation as well as the acknowledged ecumenical councils; see Wilhelm De Vries, "Das Konzil von Ephesus 449, eine 'Räubersynode'?" *Orientalia Christiana Periodica* 41 (1975): 357-398.

283 The conciliar attempts to hold the churches of the East together in the face of disagreements over the theology of the Incarnation, from Ephesus I (431) through Constantinople III (680-681), ended in church division. For the painful story, see W. H. C. Frend, *The Rise of the Monophysite Movement: Chapters in the History of the Church in the Fifth and Sixth Centuries* (Cambridge: Cambridge University Press, 1972), or *Les Églises d'Orient et Occident*, ed. Luce Pietri (Paris: Desclée, 1998), 387-481: "Justinien et la vaine recherche de l'unité."

284 Wilhelm de Vries, "Die Patriarchate des Ostens: Bestimmende Faktoren bei ihrer Entstehung," in *I Patriarcati orientali nel primo millennio*, "Orientalia Christiana Analecta 181" (Roma: Pontificium Institutum Studiorum Orientalium, 1968): 20-21, says, "The bishops were fundamentally equal, but their cities were not." The leader of the Christian churches of each province was the bishop of its metropolis; he oversaw the election and ordination of bishops, presided at synods and served as a court of appeal from the local bishops.

285 These groupings were reflected in an important liturgical affirmation of communion, where in the eucharistic prayer itself, the presider prayed explicitly for the bishop of the place and for the patriarch or patriarchs through whom the congregation was in communion with the rest of the church. This practice is well attested from at least the sixth century in both the East (the "diptychs") and the West (the prayer

"Memento" in the Roman rite); see Joseph A. Jungmann, *The Mass of the Roman Rite*, trans. Francis A. Brunner (New York: Benziger Brothers, 1955), II, 154-156.

286 Constantinople's importance was recognized at the Council of Constantinople (381); Jerusalem was first under the metropolitan of Caesarea in Palestine and overseen by the church of Antioch, but its unique place in Christian history and piety was recognized when it was named a fifth patriarchate at the Council of Chalcedon (451). Bernard Flusin, in *Les Églises d'Orient et d'Occident*, ed. Luce Pietri (Paris: Desclée, 1998) 510-511, says that "if the system of five patriarchs ever existed, it was not yet fully developed"; at the time of Chalcedon, "patriarch" was not yet a technical term.

287 Vittorio Parlato, *L'ufficio patriarcale nelle chiese orientali dal IV al X secolo: Contributo allo studio della 'communio'*, (Padova: Edizioni Cedam, 1969), 26-27, assigns several causes: "heresies, schisms, political factors, persecutions, occupation of Christian territories by the Muslims, and not least the revival of nationalism in the Greek-speaking parts of the empire." By 543, Antioch had a Monophysite hierarchy, and its Melkite (imperial or Chalcedonian) bishop preferred to live in Constantinople from 609-742, so a third patriarch of Antioch was chosen by the North Syrians; from 566 there were competing Monophysite and Melkite patriarchs in Alexandria.

288 See H. Marot, "Notes sur la Pentarchie," *Irénikon* 32 (1959): 436-442; Ferdinand R. Gahbauer, *Die Pentarchie-Theorie. Ein Modell der Kirchenleitung von den Anfängen bis zur Gegenwart* (Frankfurt: Josef Knecht, 1993).

289 Hieronymus, *ep.* 146 1,6, ed. I. Hilberg, CSEL 66 (Vienna: F. Tempsky, 1918), 310: "nam et Alexandriae a Marco euangelista usque ad Heraclam et Dionysium episcopos presbyteri semper unum de se electum et in excelsiori gradu conlocatum episcopum nominabant, quomodo si exercitus imperatorem faciat aut diaconi eligant de se, quem industrium nouerint, et archdiaconum uocent. quid enim facit excepta ordinatione episcopus, quod presbyter non facit?"

290 Pelagius, Commentarii in Ep. 1 ad Tim. 3, 8, ed. A. Souter (three volumes), Texts and Studies 9: 1-3 (Cambridge: University Press, 1922-1931), reprinted in *Patrologiae Latinae Supplementum* 1.1110-1374; the treatment of 1 Timothy 3.8 is at PLS 1.1351.

291 "Episcopatus autem, ut quidam prudentium ait, nomen est operis non honoris. . . . Ergo episcopum Latine superintendere possumus dicere; ut intelligat non se esse episcopum qui non prodesse sed praeesse dilexerit." Isidorus Hispaliensis, *De ecclesiasticis officiis* II 5,8, ed. Christopher M. Lawson, Corpus Christianorum Series Latina 113 (Turnholti: Brepols, 1989), 59 (PL 83.782).

292 II 7,2 (ed. Lawson [n. 291 above], 65): "Praesunt enim ecclesiae Christi, et in confectione diuini corporis et sanguinis consortes cum episcopis sunt, similiter et in doctrina populorum et in officio praedicandi; ac sola propter auctoritatem summo sacerdoti clericorum ordinatio et consecratio reseruata est, ne a disciplina ecclesiae uindicata concordiam solueret, scandala generaret."

293 Augustine, *Civ. Dei* 19,19.

294 The treatise, *De VII ordinibus Ecclesiae*, appears among the *spuria* of Jerome in PL 30.148-162; the cited text from chapter 6 is in columns 155-156. J. Lécuyer, "Aux origines de la théologie thomiste de l'Épiscopat," *Gregorianum* 35 (1954): 65, n. 24,

says that PL gives a faulty text; see the critical edition by A. Kalff (Würzburg, 1935). Lest we assume that the unknown author of "De VII ordinibus Ecclesiae" thought of bishops as simply presbyters with special duties, we should note that the quoted words come from section six of that little treatise; the seventh section exalts the *ordo episcopalis* remarkably (PL 30.158-159A). In contrast to later lists of the seven orders, this treatise lists diggers (*fossarii*), porters, readers, subdeacons, levites or deacons, priests, bishops.

295   *IV Sent.* dist. 24, c. 11 and 12.

296   Thomas Aquinas, for example, in his lectures on Philippians 1:1, 1 Timothy 3:1, 4:14, and Titus 1:6 accepts the New Testament equivalence; *Super Epistolas S. Pauli lectura*, ed. Raphael Cai, 8. ed. revisa (Torino: Marietti, 1953) II, 91, 231, 245, 305.

297   *Vita s. Willehadi* 5-8, in Monumenta Germaniae Historiae, Scriptorum t. II, 380-383; *Vita s. Liudgeri* 19-20, same volume, 410-411. These presbyters were mentioned already in a paper by the late A. C. Piepkorn, a member of an earlier round of the present dialogue, L/RC-4, 221-222.

298   The popes were Boniface IX (Bull "Sacrae Religionis," February 1, 1400), Martin V (Bull "Gerentes ad Vos," November 16, 1427), Innocent VIII (Bull "Exposcit Tuae Devotionis," April 9, 1489). See Ludwig Ott, *Das Weihesacrament*, Handbuch der Dogmengeschichte IV 5 (Freiburg: Herder, 1969), 106-107, and his *Fundamentals of Catholic Dogma*, 6th ed. (St. Louis: B. Herder, 1964), 459, and other Catholic manuals since the discovery of Martin V's bull in 1943, such as H. Lennerz, *De Sacramento Ordinis* (2 vols.; Rome: Gregorian University, 1953), 145-153 (Appendix I). A. C. Piepkorn cited these instances in *Eucharist and Ministry*, 222-23. For a full discussion, see John de Reeper, "Relation of Priesthood to Episcopate," *Jurist* 16 (1956): 350-358.

299   Dionysius was thought to have been Paul's convert, so his testimony conflicted with the equivalence of bishop and presbyter in the New Testament. Medieval theologians like Thomas Aquinas tried to resolve the conflict by postulating a very rapid development from Paul to Dionysius. Not until the sixteenth century did theologians recognize that Dionysius wrote much later than the first century. In two of the passages of Thomas Aquinas cited above, he notes that Dionysius gives the triple order; Thomas explains the difference by saying it was not that way at the very beginning.

300   Baus, 38-39 and 260, n. 58, describes the origins of this claim, which was strongly resented by the Eastern churches. Hamilton Hess, *The Canons of the Council of Serdica A.D. 343* (Oxford: Clarendon Press, 1958), 52, says, "None of the early references to the canons which were made by the Roman church ascribe them to the Council of Serdica. Their attributed source, when given, is invariably the Council of Nicaea."

301   According to Walter Ullmann, "Leo I and the Theme of Papal Primacy," *Journal of Theological Studies* n.s. 11 (1960), 25-51. Leo's innovation was a legal theory of the pope's inheritance of Peter's fullness of power, which Peter in turn had received from Christ. The notion of heir turned up first in a letter written by Siricius (384-399): "We carry the burdens of all who are heavy laden—or rather, the blessed apostle Peter in us bears them, he who protects us and keeps us safe as his heir in all points of his ministry, as we believe" (30-31). As Ullmann observes, the heir in Roman law

acts in all things with the full rights of the testator, and if he were not of the same moral stature as the testator, he would be unworthy (*indignus*), but heir nonetheless–in this case, of Peter's office and fullness of power. Ullmann insists on several points: that it is Peter's office which is inherited, not his apostolic commission; "that no pope succeeds another pope, but succeeds St. Peter immediately"; that this is not a matter of orders, so a layman can become pope; and that "bishops received their (jurisdictional) *office* (not their sacramental *ordo*) from the pope" (33-35; 43; 50; 44-45). No unbroken line of succession is needed in this theory.

302 Their "aim . . . was to prove by the example of alleged cases from the history of the papacy the principle that the first episcopal see cannot be subjected to any court–*Prima sedes a nemine iudicatur*" (Baus, in Baus *et al.*, 621). The Latin axiom has been retained in the Roman Catholic *Code of Canon Law* (1917 Code: canon 1556; 1983 Code: canon 1404; 1990 *Codex Canonum Ecclesiarum Orientalium*: canon 1058).

303 Itself based on fifth-century forged acts of Pope Silvester (Baus, in Baus *et al.*, 247), the *Constitutio Constantini* or "Donation of Constantine" appeared in Rome under mysterious circumstances "not later than the early fifties of the eighth century," writes Walter Ullmann, *The Growth of Papal Government in the Middle Ages*, 3rd ed. (London: Methuen, 1970), 74-86.

304 Ewig, in Kempf *et al.*, 168. On 169, he adds that the effect of these texts was not fully felt until they were incorporated into canon law collections in the 11th century. For the decretals themselves, see PL 130 or the edition by P. Hinschius, *Decretales Pseudo-Isidorianae et Capitula Angilramni* (Leipzig, 1863).

305 Colin Morris, *The Papal Monarchy: The Western Church from 1050 to 1250* (Oxford: Clarendon Press, 1989), 206, says that *plenitudo potestatis*, fullness of power, "had a long history beginning with the letter of Leo I [*ep.* 14,1], but up to the time of Gratian it had attracted little notice. Its use was confined to Leo's letters and two pseudo-Isidorian texts based on it, and it simply contrasted the authority of the apostolic see with those (such as legates or metropolitans) who had been authorized to perform a subordinate function. It was Bernard's *De consideratione* [*consid.* II 8,16; *Opera* III 424] which introduced a new interpretation. . . . Bernard understood it as referring to the universal power of the Roman pontiff to intervene in all parts of the church."

306 Morris, *Papal Monarchy*, 388, observes, "The prince-bishop was not (or not only) produced by original sin, but by the structure of ecclesiastical property."

307 The phrase "der evangelische Ansatz" is from Werner Elert, *Morphologie des Luthertums*, Bd. 1: *Theologie und Weltanschauung des Luthertums hauptsächlich in 16. und 17. Jahrhundert* (Munich: C. H. Beck, 1931, 3rd ed. 1965); Bd. 2, *Soziallehren und Sozialwirkung des Luthertums* (1932), as trans. by Walter A. Hansen, *The Structure of Lutheranism, Vol. 1, The Theology and Philosophy of Life of Lutheranism in the Sixteenth and Seventeenth Centuries* (St. Louis: Concordia, 1962), xix, for discussion on the rendering; on this impact and "The Office of the Ministry," 1:297-307 = Eng. trans. 339-351.

308 For example, Georg von Polentz, Bishop of Samland, and Erhard of Queiss, Bishop of Pomesania.

309 Preached in 1519; LW 35.49-73.

310 LW 35.67. The "Brotherhoods" (*Brüderschaften*) were societies of laymen who practiced devotional exercises and good works (BC, 54, n. 103). They are here regarded by Luther as a distortion of true *communio*.

311 While Luther and his colleagues emphasized Christ the word, they did not exclude the Trinitarian tradition; see, *e.g.*, Luther's explanation of the Third Article of the Creed in his *Large Catechism*. *Cf. Luther und die trinitarische Tradition: Ökumenische und philosophische Perspektiven*, Veröffentlichen der Luther-Akademie Ratzeburg, 23, ed. Robert W. Jenson (Erlangen: Martin-Luther-Verlag, 1994).

312 From the New Testament understanding of koinonia and this Sermon by Luther on "The Blessed Sacrament," Paul Lehmann has, more recently, understood the church as a place where God's acts become concrete in the world, a place or field of relationships for ethical reflection; see his *Ethics in a Christian Context* (New York: Harper & Row, 1963); Nancy J. Duff, *Humanization and the Politics of God: The Koinonia Ethics of Paul Lehmann* (Grand Rapids, MI: Eerdmans, 1992).

313 CA 5; 28.8-9.

314 See several articles in *The Church as Communion*, ed. Heinrich Holze, LWF Documentation No. 42/1997 (Geneva: LWF, 1997), especially Alejandro Zorzin, "Luther's Understanding of the Church as Communion in his Early Pamphlets," 81-92; Simo Peura, "The Church as Spiritual Communion in Luther," 93-131. David Yeago, "The Church as Polity? The Lutheran Context of Robert W. Jenson's Ecclesiology" in *Trinity, Time, and Church: A Response to the Theology of Robert W. Jenson*, ed. C. Gunton (Grand Rapids, MI; Cambridge, U.K., 2000), 236, states, "[T]he goal of Luther and the early Lutheran movement was not to isolate the eschatological from the outward and bodily church but to ask how the communion of the church could and should 'take up space in the world' in a manner appropriate to its eschatological character as the body of Christ. On this reading, therefore, the Lutheran tradition already contains elements of something like a 'communion-ecclesiology' in its normative sources."

315 E. Clifford Nelson, ed., *The Lutherans in North America*, (Philadelphia: Fortress Press, 1980), 52-56.

316 *Cf.* Gerd Haendler, *Luther on Ministerial Office and Congregational Function* (Philadelphia: Fortress, 1981); Dorothea Wendebourg, "The Ministry and Ministries," *Lutheran Quarterly* 15/2 (Summer 2001) 159-94, esp. "The Local Ministry of the Pastor as the Primary Form of the Ordained Ministry," 163-166.

317 LW 28.283; LW 39.154-155. *Cf.* LW 37.367: "The bishops or priests are not heads [of the church] or lords or bridegrooms, but servants, friends, and—as the word 'bishop' implies—superintendents, guardians, or stewards." Such tasks are so important that subsequently in local congregations the elected leadership of lay people, usually the congregational council, is assigned also a part in the task of oversight, shared with the pastor(s); ELCA *Model Constitution for Congregations*, C12.04., "The Congregational Council shall have general oversight of the life and activities of this congregation, and in particular its worship life, to the end that everything be done in accordance with the Word of God and the faith and practice of the Evangelical Lutheran Church in America." *Cf.* *C9.03. for what ordained ministers are to do,

including (besides preaching) sacraments, conduct of public worship, and pastoral care, "and supervise all schools and organizations of this congregation."

318 See Dorothea Wendebourg, "The Reformation in Germany and the Episcopal Office" in *Visible Unity and the Ministry of Oversight* (London, 1997), 54: "the Wittenberg theologians generally envisage [*episcope*] as taking place in personal rather than synodical form" (this is in the context of visitation in parishes, on which see §184 of this text).

319 Martin Brecht, "Die exegetische Begründung des Bischofsamt," 10-14, and Heinz-Meinolf Stamm, "Luthers Berufung auf die Vorstellungen des Hieronymus vom Bischofsamt," 15-26, esp. 15-17, in *Martin Luther und das Bischofsamt*, ed. M. Brecht (Stuttgart: Calwer, 1990).

320 LW 44.175 "An Open Letter to the Christian Nobility," *The Christian in Society I* (ed. J. J. Pelikan, H. C. Oswald, and H. T. Lehmann) =WA 6:440.21-29.

321 Wendebourg, "The Ministry and Ministries," 184, n. 32, but she goes on, "Luther does recognize a difference between bishops and presbyters at a time as early as that of the Pastoral Epistles, but it is a difference—and this is his point—within a single congregation led by one pastor-bishop: Here the bishop had presbyters and deacons as his assistants." Cf. WA 6:440, 33-35; LW 44.175, the pastor or bishop should "have several priests and deacons by his side. . . , who help him rule the flock and the congregation through preaching and sacraments."

322 BC, 340. On Jerome, see §§163, 168 above.

323 As Melanchthon put it in the TPPP: "Jerome, then, teaches that the distinctions of degree between bishop and presbyter or pastor are established by human authority [*humana auctoritate*]. That is clear from the way it works, for, as I stated above, the power is the same. One thing subsequently created a distinction between bishops and pastors, and that was ordination, for it was arranged that one bishop would ordain the ministers in a number of churches. However, since the distinction in rank between bishop and pastor is not by divine right [*iure divino*], it is clear that an ordination performed by a pastor in his own church is valid by divine right." BC, 340. In this connection, Wendebourg speaks of "the office of diocesan bishop" as "a secondary phenomenon, owing its existence to historical circumstance"; the tasks of pastor and bishop remain the same, though their areas of jurisdiction differ; in principle, even the right to ordain is still embodied in the office of the local pastor. "The Ministry," 165.

324 TPPP, 72. On the historical and political context of the early Lutheran situation concerning the problem of episcopacy, see especially Wendebourg, "The Reformation in Germany," 49-55.

325 *Smalcald Articles*, Part 3, Art. 10.3, Kolb and Wengert, 324; *Cf.* Formula of Concord Solid Declaration 10.19.

326 Archdeacon Georg Rörer was ordained to some office in the *Stadtkirche* at Wittenberg, on May 14, 1525; see Wendebourg, "The Ministry," 191, n. 91; at least this was Rörer's claim, Schwiebert, *Luther and His Times*, 621; *cf.* WA 16:226; 17, xvii, xxxviii, 243; 38, 403. BC, 324, n. 159 (on Smalcald Articles III.10,3) says, "The first ordination by the Wittenberg reformers in Wittenberg took place on 20 October

1535." See the more detailed note in *Die Bekenntnisschriften der lutherischen Kirche* (1930 ed., 458, n. 2); involved is Luther's understanding that call (by a congregation) was the decisive matter (WA 38, 238, 7f.; 41, 240-242 and 457f.).

327 Apol. 14.2, BC, 222.

328 WA 10:2, 105-158; *cf.* Gottfried Krodel, "Luther und das Bischofsamt nach seinem Buch 'Wider den falsch genannten geistlichen Stand des Papstes und der Bischöfe,'" in *Martin Luther und das Bischofsamt*, 27-65.

329 Wendebourg (n. 318 above), "Reformation," 55. The pre-Reformation dioceses would have had bishops "who could look back to a chain of predecessors into the Middle Ages and in some cases even into antiquity" but after acceptance of Reformation teaching "committed to proclaiming the Gospel according to the teaching of the Wittenberg Reformation and to undertaking their specific duties in accordance with it."

330 CA 28.1, 5, 19. BC, 91-93.

331 CA 28.20-22. BC, 95.

332 In the sense of Luke 19:44, oversight visitation; *Besuchdienst*.

333 WA 26:195-240; LW 40.269-320; Wendebourg, "The Ministry" 169-170.

334 *Cf.* J. Höß, "The Lutheran Church of the Reformation. Problems of its formation and organization in the middle and north German territories," in *The Social History of the Reformation. Festschrift H. J. Grimm*, ed. L. P. Buck, J. W. Zophy (Columbus, 1972), 317-339; "Episcopus Evangelicus. Versuche mit dem Bischofsamt im deutschen Luthertum des 16. Jahrhunderts," in *Confessio Augustana und Confutatio*, ed. E. Iserloh (Münster, 1980), 499-516. See also Merlyn E. Satrom, "Bishops and Ordination in the Lutheran Reformation of Sixteenth-Century Germany," *Lutheran Forum* 33:2, Summer 1999, 12-15; Gerhard Tröger, *Das Bischofsamt in der evangelisch-lutherischen Kirche* (1965) and "Das evangelische Bischofsamt," TRE 6. Two of these were in Prussia, which was not part of the Holy Roman Empire, namely, Georg von Polentz, bishop since 1519 of the Samland (his see in Königsberg) and Erhard von Queiß, elected bishop of Pomesania in 1523 but not yet confirmed by the pope or consecrated.

335 Wendebourg, "Reformation," 56-57. In the 1540s, Hermann von Wied, Archbishop and Elector of Cologne, was forced to abdicate when he sought to reform his diocese along Evangelical lines (and died under excommunication in 1552), and Franz von Waldeck, in Osnabrück, had to renounce his turn to Protestantism in order to remain bishop. The one exception was the Bishop of Brandenburg, Matthias von Jagow (bishop 1516-1544), who continued to serve as a Lutheran bishop, for the territory under his secular control was not under the Emperor. Literature in Wendebourg, "Reformation," nn. 63-66.

336 Nikolaus von Amsdorff (1483-1565) in Naumberg (1542), Georg von Anhalt (1507-53) in Merseburg (1544), and Bartholomäus Suave in Pomeranian Kammin (1545).

337 Hermann von Wied of Cologne, Matthias von Jagow, or one of those in Prussia.

338 See Wendebourg, "Reformation," 58-62.

339 A. F. von Campenhausen, "The Episcopal Office of Oversight," 175.

340 A *Superintendent* was usually a prominent pastor from one of the cities who frequently worked with a consistory, to supervise, coordinate and provide for the area's pastoral needs. Pastors of principal congregations in the territorial capitals, as was the case, *e.g.*, in Electoral Saxony, were sometimes called *Generalsuperintendenten*. Whatever the drawbacks might have been, such arrangements preserved a personal (rather than collective) form of oversight, involving the authority (delegated by the prince) to make visitations.

341 A. F. von Campenhausen, "The Episcopal Office of Oversight in the German Churches, its Public Status and its Involvement in Church Decision in History and the Present," in *Visible Unity and the Ministry of Oversight. Second Theological Conference held under the Meissen Agreement between the Church of England and the Evangelical Church in Germany* (London: Church House Publishing, 1977), 171-183, who gives the other terms sometimes used, like *Landessuperintendent*, *Kreisdekan*, or *Prälat*; quotations from 173 and 181, n. 10 (P. Brunner, who thought that "superintendent" matched well the office of bishop in the early church). See further, D. Wendebourg, "The Office of Superintendent as a Distinct Type of Episcopate," in "Reformation," 63-66, noting the "flexibility in the practical exercise of *episkope*" that "characterizes the form which the episcopal office takes in protestant churches to the present day."

342 Dorothea Wendebourg, "The Reformation," 55f.

343 So Sven-Erik Brodd, in an excursus, "The Swedish *Church Ordinance* 1571 and the Office of Bishop in an Ecumenical Context," attached to *The Office of Bishop*. Report of the Official Working Group for Dialogue between the Church of Sweden and the Roman Catholic Diocese of Stockholm (Geneva: LWF, 1993), 148; compare 45-47 and 82 in the dialogue report itself. Brodd notes that in Petri's other writings both the monarchy and the episcopacy are divinely ordained institutions.

344 The translation is that of John Wordsworth, *The National Church of Sweden* (London: A. R. Mowbray, 1911), 232-233.

345 See Bishops' Conference [Church of Sweden], *Bishop, Priest and Deacon in the Church of Sweden: A Letter from the Bishops Concerning the Ministry of the Church* (Uppsala: Bishops' Conference, 1990), 23-24.

346 On the history of episcopacy in Sweden, see Sven-Erik Brodd, "Episcopacy in Our Churches: Sweden," in Porvoo, 59-69.

347 On these events, see "The Church of England and the Church of Finland: A Summary of the Proceedings at the Conferences Held at Lambeth Palace, London, on October 5th and 6th, 1933, and at Brandö, Helsingfors, on July 17th and 18th, 1934," in *Lambeth Occasional Reports 1931–1938* (London: SPCK, 1948), 154-155, and Fredric Cleve, "Episcopacy in Our Churches: Finland," in Porvoo, 77-78.

348 On these events in Denmark, see Lars Österlin, *Churches of Northern Europe in Profile: A Thousand Years of Anglo-Nordic Relations* (Norwich: Canterbury Press, 1995), 83-87 and Svend Borregaard, "The Post-Reformation Developments of the Episcopacy in Denmark, Norway, and Iceland," in *Episcopacy in the Lutheran Church? Studies in the Development and Definition of the Office of Church Leadership*, Episcopacy in Lutheran Church? (Philadelphia: Fortress Press, 1970), 116-124.

349 The use of the term "superintendent" alongside that of bishop is not seen as indicative of a significant break with earlier understandings of the role of the bishop; see
Österlin, *Churches of Northern Europe*, 85 and Gerhard Pedersen, "Episcopacy in
Our Churches: Denmark," in Porvoo, 87. The term "bishop" was made standard
again in 1685.

350 On the episcopate in Denmark, Iceland, and Norway, see the essays in Porvoo, 85-108.

351 Information in this paragraph is all taken from Porvoo, 109-123.

352 Porvoo, §§58a(vi) and 58b(vi); in Porvoo, 30-31.

353 Martii Parvio, "Post Reformation Developments of the Episcopacy in Sweden,
Finland, and the Baltic States," in *Episcopacy in the Lutheran Church? Studies in the
Development and Definition of the Office of Church Leadership*, ed. Ivar Asheim and
Victor Gold (Philadelphia: Fortress Press, 1970), 132-135; Frederic Cleve,
"Episcopacy in Our Churches: Finland," in Porvoo, 77f.

354 Ringolds Muziks, "Latvia," in Porvoo, 117-120.

355 Tiit Pädam, "Estonia," in Porvoo, 109-115.

356 Porvoo (n. 352 above), 31; Gunnar Lislerud, "Norway," and Hjalti Hugason,
"Iceland," in Porvoo, 93-99 and 101-108.

357 *Cf.* Scott Hendrix, *Luther and the Papacy: Stages in a Reformation Conflict*
(Philadelphia, 1981), who, on the basis of Luther's later reflections on his early
career, labels Luther's attitude toward the papacy even prior to 1517 as essentially
"ambivalent" (7). Melanchthon, in TPPP, 38, expressed himself similarly: "Even if
the Bishop of Rome did possess the primacy by divine right, he should not be obeyed
inasmuch as he defends impious forms of worship and doctrines which are in conflict
with the gospel. On the contrary, it is necessary to resist him as Antichrist." Bernard
McGinn, *AntiChrist: Two Thousand Years of the Human Fascination with Evil* (San
Francisco: Harper San Francisco, 1994). Luther's usage is consistent with venerable
predecessors of the period, such as St. Birgitta of Sweden.

358 See *e.g.*, Hendrix, 42-43, 69-70, 84, 156-159. *Cf.* Luther's *Babylonian Captivity of the
Church* (LW 36.113). See also LW 36.115.

359 L/RC-4, 23-32, *cf.* Raymond Brown, et. al., *Peter in the New Testament* (New York:
Paulist Press, 1973).

360 LW 26.99.

361 For a brief overview of the new orders, particularly the Society of Jesus (Jesuits), see
Karl Bihlmeyer and Hermann Tüchle, *Church History* (Westminster, MD: Newman
Press, 1966), III, 83-98.

362 A summary can be found in Josef Freitag, "Church Offices: Roman Catholic
Offices," in *The Oxford Encyclopedia of the Reformation*, ed. Hans J. Hillerbrand (New
York: Oxford University Press, 1996) I, 342-346, and in A. Duval, "The Council of
Trent and Holy Orders," in [Centre de Pastorale Liturgique], *The Sacrament of Holy
Orders* (London: Aquin Press, 1962), 219-258. Fuller particulars are in Josef Freitag,
"Schwierigkeiten und Erfahrungen mit dem 'Sacramentum ordinis' auf dem Konzil
von Trient," *Zeitschrift für katholische Theologie* 113 (1991): 39-51, and Josef Freitag,

"*Sacramentum ordinis*" *auf dem Konzil von Trient*, Innsbrucker theologische Studien 32 (Innsbruck: Tyrolia, 1991).

363 Freitag, *ibid.*, 41-42.

364 *Ibid.*, 44.

365 The question of papal authority was discussed at Trent in this context. "To prevent the cumulation of benefices with the cure of souls, the Spaniards and the French requested the council to declare that the obligation of residence is *jure divino* and both of these national groups supported the thesis that episcopal jurisdiction comes directly from God and not from the pope. The Italians vigourously opposed this opinion. Thus the old controversy regarding *episcopal jurisdiction* and *papal primacy* was revived. Finally . . . it was agreed to dismiss this question without a decision." Bihlmeyer and Tüchle, *Church History* III, 110.

366 Duval, "Council of Trent" 244-245; Freitag, "Schwierigkeiten," 48-50. Freitag goes so far as to say that "Trent did not make any decision about a determinate approach to understanding the sacrament of Order" (50).

367 Thus almost at the end of the Council, which closed December 4, 1563, and after the deaths of Luther and Melanchthon. The decree and canons can be found in *Conciliorum Oecumenicorum Decreta*, ed. G. Alberigo et al. (Bologna: Instituto per le Scienze Religiose, 1973), 742-744, and translations of that text such as *Decrees of the Ecumenical Councils*, ed. Norman P. Tanner (London: Sheed & Ward; Washington, DC: Georgetown University Press, 1990), and in Henrich Denzinger, *Enchiridion symbolorum definitionum et declarationum de rebus fidei et morum*, 37th. ed., ed. Peter Hünermann (Freiburg-im-Breisgau: Herder, 1991) (DHn), 1763-1778.

368 Session 23, chap. 4, canon 7. Ibid., 1768, 1776-1777. *Cf.* L/RC-4, "Reflections of the Roman Catholic Participants," §40: "When the episcopate and presbyterate had become a general pattern in the church, the historical picture still presents uncertainties. . . . For instance, is the difference between a bishop and a priest of divine ordination? St. Jerome maintained that it was not; and the Council of Trent, wishing to respect Jerome's opinion, did not undertake to define that the preeminence of the bishop over presbyters was by divine law. If the difference is not of divine ordination, the reservation to the bishop of the power of ordaining Ministers of the eucharist would be a church decision. In fact, in the history of the church there are instances of priests (*i.e.*, presbyters) ordaining other priests, and there is evidence that the church accepted and recognized the Ministry of priests so ordained." See also §169 above.

369 Harry J. McSorley, "Trent and the Question: Can Protestant Ministers Consecrate the Eucharist," in L/RC-4, 295.

370 Freitag, "*Sacramentum ordinis*," 374, says that canon 6 goes beyond the rejection of any Lutheran claim that there was no fundamental difference of priesthood between priest and lay person: "[n]ow the sacerdotium is seen as a hierarchy of Order and as such is oriented on the bishop, not on the priest," priest being a concept embracing both presbyter and bishop.

371 Karl J. Becker, "Der Unterschied von Bischof und Priester im Weihedekret des Konzils von Trient und in der Kirchenkonstitution des II Vatikanischen Konzils," in

Zum Problem Unfehlbarkeit, ed. Karl Rahner (Freiburg-im-Breisgau: Herder, 1971), 289-327.

372 The privileges granted to abbots to give tonsure and minor orders to members of their religious orders, were not abrogated (canon 10), but even religious order candidates for subdiaconate, diaconate, and presbyterate had to be examined and approved by the bishop (canon 12).

373 Freitag, "*Sacramentum ordinis*," 388.

374 This group of Evangelical and Catholic theologians began working just after World War II; its work formed an important part of the background to the JDDJ. For its history, see Barbara Schwahn, *Der oekumenische Arbeitskreis evangelischer und katholischer Theologen von 1946 bis 1975* (Göttingen: Vandenhoeck & Ruprecht, 1996).

375 Lehmann, Pannenberg, *The Condemnations of the Reformation Era*, 149. The original, LV I, was published in 1985.

376 *Ibid.*, 157.

377 *The Catechism of the Council of Trent for Parish Priests*, trans. with notes by John A. McHugh and Charles J. Callan, 2nd rev. ed. (New York: Joseph F. Wagner, 1934), 330-331.

378 *Ibid.*, 332.

379 "Above all these, the Catholic Church has always placed the Supreme Pontiff of Rome, whom Cyril of Alexandria, in the Council of Ephesus, named the Chief Bishop, Father and Patriarch of the whole world. He sits in that chair of Peter in which beyond every shadow of doubt the Prince of the Apostles sat to the end of his days, and hence it is that in him the Church recognizes the highest degree of dignity, and a universality of jurisdiction derived, not from the decree of men or Councils, but from God himself. Wherefore he is the Father and guide of all the faithful, of all the Bishops, and of all the prelates, no matter how high their power and office; and as successor of St. Peter, as true and legitimate vicar of Christ our Lord, he governs the Universal Church" (*ibid.*, 333). This is one of only two passages in the *Roman Catechism* that discuss the place of the Pope; the other, in the discussion of the unity of the church in Part I on the Creed, refers to him simply as (after the Church's "one ruler and governor, the invisible one, Christ") "the visible one, the Pope, who, as legitimate successor of Peter, the Prince of the Apostles, fills the Apostolic chair. It is the unanimous teaching of the Fathers that this visible head is necessary to establish and preserve unity in the Church" (*ibid.*, 102).

380 *Ibid.*, 334.

381 *Disputationes de Controversiis Christianae Fidei* (Ingolstadt, 1586-1593), cited here from Roberto Bellarmino, *Opera Omnia* (Naples: C. Pedone Lauriel, 1872). In the sections on ministry and the sacrament of Order, he argues with writings by Chemnitz, Calvin, and Melanchthon, as well as Luther himself.

382 *Secunda Controversia* I, 14 (*Opera Omnia* II, 167-169). Chief among the bishops' special powers of order is the power to ordain; among the Fathers, Bellarmine cites Jerome in his Letter to Evangelus ("What does a bishop do beyond what a presbyter does, except ordain?") not only in this section on order but on 170 against Chemnitz,

171 against the Franciscan Miguel de Medina, and in his book *De Sacramento Ordinis* I, 11 (*Opera Omnia* III, 773).

383 II Controv. I, 15 (II, 170-171).

384 Pierre Batiffol, *Études d'histoire et de théologie positive*, 2nd ed. (Paris: Victor Lecoffre, 1902), 265. Batiffol's essay, "La hiérarchie primitive," occupies 223-275 of this second edition; it appeared first in *Revue biblique* in 1895.

385 *Ibid.*, 266.

386 *Ibid.*, 264.

387 Known generally as the "Theologia Wirceburgensis," it represents Jesuit instruction at the University of Würzburg, and Francis Schüssler Fiorenza, "Systematic Theology: Task and Methods," *Systematic Theology: Roman Catholic Perspectives* (Minneapolis: Fortress, 1991) I, 30, calls it the first text to present church teaching in the form of theses, followed by arguments. The first edition in fourteen volumes appeared in that city between 1766-1771; citations are from Holtzclau's "Tractatus de Ordine et Matrimonio," in *Theologia dogmatica, polemica, scholastica et moralis*, 2nd ed., vol. 5, 2 (Paris: Julien, Lanier, 1854), 295-584.

388 Diss. 1, c. 1, art. 3, §30-33, *ibid.*, 325-327.

389 Diss. 1, c. 2, art. 7, §97, *ibid.*, 367; cp. §105, *ibid.*, 374.

390 Diss. 1, c. 2, art.9, §129, *ibid.*, 394.

391 Diss. 1, c. 2, art. 9, §129-142, *ibid.*, 394-401. One is the passage from John Cassian about Paphnutius and Daniel, which was cited also by Arthur Carl Piepkorn, L/RC-4, 221. Holtzclau thought that a priest probably could not even be empowered to ordain a deacon, despite the faculty conceded by Innocent VIII to Cistercian abbots in 1489; one key reason was that the Bull of concession had not been found (§§143-144, *ibid.*, 401-402).

392 *Cf.*, *e.g.*, the manuals of H. Lennerz (see above note); E. Hugon, *De Sacramentis in Communi et in Speciali*, 5th ed. (Paris: P. Lethielleux, 1927), 729-730; Francisco a P. Sola, "De Sacramentis Initiationis Christianae," *Sacrae Theologiae Summa* IV, 3rd ed. (Madrid: B.A.C., 1956), 215.

393 See Francis Schüssler Fiorenza, *Foundational Theology: Jesus and the Church* (New York: Crossroad, 1984), 67-71. Besides the "Theologia Wirceburgensis," many other manuals follow this pattern, such as the often-revised *Manuale Theologiae Dogmaticae* of J. M. Hervé (Paris: Berche et Pagis, 1924-1926 and into the 1950s), where "De ecclesia" is in v. 1, "De ordine" in v. 4.

394 The latter placement may be due to the order in which the sacraments are named in the canons of the Council of Trent, Session 7, canon 1 (D 844 = DS 1601); see page 1 of the volume containing Holtzclau's treatise on order.

395 Some twentieth-century manuals placed the treatise on the church among the means of sanctification, after the Incarnation and before the sacraments, but the disjunction of church and ministry remained and neither parish nor diocese received explicit attention. *E.g.*, Franz Diekamp, *Theologiae dogmaticae manuale*, trans. Adolphus M. Hoffmann from the sixth German edition (Paris: Desclée, 1933-1934),

listed "De Ecclesia" for vol. 3, part 1, between Incarnation and Grace; Ludwig Ott, *Fundamentals of Catholic Dogma*, trans. Patrick Lynch (Cork: Mercier Press, 1963), has "The Church" between "The Doctrine of Grace" and "The Sacraments."

396 *Pastor Aeternus*, chap. 1.

397 *Ibid.*, chap. 2.

398 *Ibid.*, chap. 3.

399 *Ibid.*, chap. 4.

400 Bernard M. Kelly, *The Functions Reserved to Pastors*, Catholic University of America Canon Law Studies 250 (Washington: Catholic University of America Press, 1947), 4.

401 Kelly, *Functions* 8: "This parochial unity of the city (*civitas*) was one of the most characteristic marks of the ancient diocese. The cathedral was the only parish church in the city. Around the ninth century, however, other parishes appeared in the city, administered by collegiate chapters." *DHn* 3857-3861.

402 Pope Pius XII, "Sacramentum Ordinis," AAS 40 (1948): 5-7. The Constitution was dated November 30, 1947.

403 *Sacramentum Ordinis*, 2. This paragraph is not quoted in Denzinger-Schönmetzer or the more recent edition by Peter Hünermann.

404 *Ibid.*, 5. Jean Beyer, "Nature et position du sacerdoce," *Nouvelle revue théologique* 76 (1954): 358, points out that while the 1917 *Code of Canon Law*, canon 949, called the sub-diaconate, diaconate, and the presbyterate "sacred orders," Pope Pius XII in this constitution applies the term to the diaconate, presbyterate, and episcopate.

405 LG, §18.

406 LG, §18.

407 LG, §20.

408 LG, §20.

409 LG, §25, CD, §12.

410 LG, §§19, 22.

411 LG, §22.

412 CD, §5.

413 CD, §38.1

414 CD, §6.

415 LG, §22.

416 LG, §§21, 26 ; CD, §15.

417 See 1 Tim. 2:5; LG, §28.

418 LG, §27.

419 SC, §42.

420 LG, §28.

421 PO, §7.

422 PO, §4.

423 PO, §2.

424 LG, §28, PO, §6.

425 PO, §6.

426 LG, §28.

427 LG, §28.

428 LG, §28.

429 PO, §15. *Cf.* §7.

430 L/RC-4, "Common Observations" §21, 14.

431 Thomas Kaufmann, "Amt," RGG⁴ 1 (1998), 428-429.

432 *Cf.* J. Reumann, "Ordained Minister and Layman in Lutheranism," in Eucharist and Ministry §§38-48, reprinted in J. Reumann, *Ministries Examined: Laity, Clergy, Women, and Bishops in a Time of Change* (Minneapolis: Augsburg, 1987), 36-41.

433 Gottfried Brakemeier, "Amt. 3. Außereuropäisch," RGG⁴ 1, 429-430, where parallels in Roman Catholicism are noted (*e.g.*, base communities in Latin America, with their "Ortsgebundenheit," in light of the Second Vatican Council's "people of God" theology; *cf.* Faustino Teixeira, "Basisgemeinden in Lateinamerika," 1:1156-1157).

434 Hans Martin Mueller, "Bishop," *Encyclopedia of the Lutheran Church* 1:311; Heinrich de Wall, "Bischof, 3. Evangelisch," RGG⁴ 1, 1622-1623, with specific functions that include ordination and in some Landeskirchen even veto power over synodical decisions (Bayern, Württemberg). See for details Schmidt-Clausen, cited above §66, n. 107, who (110-115) treats a VELKD Declaration in 1957 on apostolic succession, of which the bishop not a guarantee, but it is "an essential dimension" of "the Church in its entirety and all its members" (115). In Schmidt-Clausen, n. 112, Gregory Dix is quoted on "that unhappy phrase 'the historic episcopate,'" as one particular theory under which so many "variant manifestations of the episcopate" have been put, when the "apostolate" is the real question (Dix, "The Ministry in the Early Church," in *The Apostolic Ministry: Essays on the History and Doctrine of Episcopacy*, ed. K. E. Kirk [London: Hodder & Stoughton, 1946]), 296-298).

435 Schmidt-Clausen (n. 107 above), 97.

436 Martin Hein and Hans-Gernot Jung, "Bishop, Episcopate," *The Encyclopedia of Christianity* (Grand Rapids, MI: Eerdmans/Leiden: Brill) 1 (1999), 263-264; Gerhard Tröger, "Bischof, IV, Das synodale Bischofsamt," TRE 6 (1980), 694-696.

437 Lowell G. Almen, "Law and Koinonia: An Overview of the Structures and Ministries of the Evangelical Lutheran Church in America" (paper, December 2, 1999), 1. See further *The Lutherans in North America*, ed. E. Clifford Nelson (Philadelphia: Fortress, 1975), where in the section on the years 1650-1790, T. G. Tappert takes up clergy on 43-49, and for 1790-1840, H. George Anderson, 102-105 and 125; see also "Theological Education," 104-108, 129, 204-206, 284-292, 432-434, and 520.

438 *The Journals of Henry Melchior Muhlenberg In Three Volumes*, trans. T. G. Tappert and J. W. Doberstein (Philadelphia: the Evangelical Lutheran Ministerium of

Pennsylvania and Adjacent States and Muhlenberg Press, 1942, 1945, 1958), 1:7. Harvey L. Nelson, "A Critical Study of Henry Melchior Muhlenberg's Means of Maintaining his Lutheranism" (dissertation; Drew University, Madison, NJ, 1980): 373-374, observes how German settlers, "despite the voluntaristic, pluralistic, congregationally oriented religious climate of the Middle Colonies . . . clung to their German views of the pastor and his office."

439   Muhlenberg envisioned especially a gathering of those ordained as pastors and serving as teachers, but even at the first meeting there was an effort to have every congregation represented by members, often elders or deacons. The name "Ministerium," found also in New York and elsewhere, was retained in eastern Pennsylvania until 1962.

440   Between 1840 and 1875, some fifty-nine, listed in *The Lutherans in North America*, 175.

441   *Cf.* Charles P. Lutz, *Church Roots: Stories of Nine Immigrant Groups That Became the American Lutheran Church* (Minneapolis: Augsburg, 1985); J. Reumann, *Ministries Examined*, 71, "presbyterial succession."

442   So Justus Henning Böhmer (1674-1749) and J. W. F. Höfling (1802-1853). *Cf.* Reumann, "Ordained Minister" §44, repr. 39, with encyclopedia references, and Edmund Schlink, *Theology of the Lutheran Confessions*, trans. P. F. Koehneke and H. J. A. Bouman (Philadelphia: Fortress, 1961), 244, n. 13. In Böhmer's work in church law, the influence of Pietism is to be seen; Detlef Döring, RGG⁴ 1 (1998), 1671; Höfling's Erlangen theology distinguished the ordering of salvation (*Heilsgeschichte*) from church orders; the ministerial office rests on the universal priesthood, which is "the only office that exists by divine right"; Hanns Kerner, RGG⁴ 3 (2000), 1830.

443   *The Lutherans in North America*, 155-157, 168-169, 178.

444   "On the Ministry," Thesis VII, in, among other places, D. H. Steffens, "The Doctrine of the Church and the Ministry," in *Ebenezer*, ed. W. H. T. Dau (St. Louis: Concordia, 1922), 152-153; Reumann, "Ordained Minister," §§59-60 = repr. 45-46. *Cf.* So James H. Pragman, *Traditions of Ministry: A History of the Doctrine of the Ministry in Lutheran Theology* (St. Louis: Concordia, 1983), 140-146; *cf. Ministries Examined*, 66-67.

445   *The Ministry: Office, Procedures, and Nomenclature* (St. Louis: Commission on Theology and Church Relations), Thesis 1, 25.

446   "Ordained Minister," §45 = repr. 40; Pragman, 129-131, where Stahl's *Kirchenverfassung* is cited.

447   "Ordained Minister," §45 = repr. 39-40; Pragman, 136-137. K. Scholder, RGG, 3rd ed, 6 (1962), 1401-1403, notes Vilmar's stance against a Kurhessen-Waldeck "Summepiskopat" that introduced the Church of the Prussian Union in some regions and his stand for separation of church and state. Such views led to the "Renitent" or resistence movement in 1873, some of whose members emigrated to America. Vilmar regarded statements in the "Treatise on the Power and Primacy of the Pope" (69-70, 72) about congregations in emergencies electing and ordaining ministers as "superfluous remarks" for an "inconceivable" situation, the absence of all pastors called by pastors (Schlink, *Theology of the Lutheran Confessions*, [n. 442 above] 244, n. 12). At Treatise 72, the Kolb and Wengert edition has not added the phrase to which A. C.

Piepkorn called attention in L/RC-4, 110-111, n. 14, *adhibitis suis pastoribus*, "the church retains the right to choose and ordain ministers *using their own pastors*."

448 "Ordained Minister" §58 = repr. 44-45, stressing Loehe's distrust of democracy and support for episcopacy as found in Scripture, *i.e.*, identical with the presbytery; Pragman, 132-136. See Loehe's *Three Books About the Church* (1845; trans. 1908; Philadelphia: Fortess, 1969); *Aphorismen über die neutestamentichen Ämter: Zur Verfassungsfrage der Kirche* (1849), rev. ed. *Kirche und Amt: Neue Aphorismen* (1851); S. Hebert, *Wilhelm Löhes Lehre von der Kirche, ihrem Amt und Regiment: Ein Beitrag zur Geschichte der Theologie im 19. Jahrhundert* (Neuendettelsau; Friemund-Verlag, 1939); J. L. Schaaf, "Loehe's Relation to the American Church," diss. Heidelberg 1962.

449 Gerhard Schoenauer, RGG⁴ 5 (2002), 502, "eine apostolisch-episkopale Brüderskirche . . . innerhalb deren an der Bedeutung der Ortsgemeinde als primäre Gestalt der Kirche festgehalten wird."

450 *The Lutherans in North America*, 158-159, 180-183, quotation from 181; 228, Missouri alleged "hierarchical tendencies" on church and ministry in the Iowa Synod.

451 *Ministries Examined*, 200-219; Edgar R. Trexler, *Anatomy of a Merger: People, Dynamics, and Decisions That Shaped the ELCA* (Minneapolis: Augsburg, 1991), 63-66, 85-86, 97-100, 112, 116-121, 141-143, 182-183, and passim. Points of debate over ministry lay elsewhere, especially involving parochial school teachers and a wide variety of "deacons" and rostered ministers. There had been a long history of discussion in The Lutheran Church–Missouri Synod on the ministerial status of teachers; *cf.* "Ordained Minister" §§65-66 = repr. 47-48 plus 67-68; Pragman, 171-176. A particular problem here were women day-school teachers; if considered "ordained," the LCMS would immediately have had the largest number of women clergy of any U.S. church.

452 *Together for Ministry*, §§152-163, 23-24. The other two recommendations of the task force related thirdly to the ELCA's officially recognized lay ministries, which include deaconesses, deacons, certified lay professionals, and commissioned teachers, from predecessor bodies; ELCA Associates in Ministry; and the creation of a new category of Diaconal Ministers. Fourth was a recommendation on "Flexibility for Mission" allowing, among other items, for non-stipendiary ("tent-making") ministers and licensed ministers.

453 *Together for Ministry*, §108, 16. Pragman, 154-156, observed that the universal priesthood "was not a significant issue for 20th-century Lutheran theologians." Similarly, J. Reumann, "The Priesthood of Baptized Believers and the Office of Ministry in Eastern Lutheranism, from Muhlenberg's Day to Ours," Lutheran Historical Conference 1999 (forthcoming).

454 *Together for Ministry* §§77, 79, 11.

455 *The Lutheran Understanding of Ministry: Statement on the Basis of an LWF Study Project*, LWF Studies, Reports and Texts from the Department of Studies (Geneva: LWF, 1983), cited in *Together for Ministry*, §123. Recommendations on bishops were purposely limited because of agreement that major discussion should come on proposals from the Lutheran-Episcopal dialogue III (1983-1991) in the *Concordat of Agreement* (1991).

456 *1993 Reports and Records: Vol. 2, Minutes* (Chicago: ELCA, 1995), 691. Lowell G. Almen, "Review of Governing Documents of the Evangelical Lutheran Church in America on the Role and Responsibility of Bishops as an Indication of the Underlying Theology of that Office" (paper, December 1, 2000), 6.

457 Lowell G. Almen, "Review of Governing Documents," 6-7, *Minutes* 692; the term of office of bishops was changed from four to six years, with reelection possible; "constitutional provision †S8.12. was revised 'to reflect more clearly the pastoral and oversight functions of the bishop' in synods,'" Almen, 7, *Minutes*, 692, for the resolution; 424-427, for the amended text of the provision. Almen, 7-9, added a statement adopted by the ELCA Conference of Bishops in 1999 for their collegial guidance, "Relational Agreement Among Synodical Bishops of the Evangelical Lutheran Church in America."

458 *The Ministry of the Church: A Lutheran Understanding*, Studies series, Division of Theological Studies (New York: Lutheran Council in the USA, 1974), where ordination and installation were seen as *kairoi* in "the continuum of ordained ministry"; *The Historic Episcopate* (1984), including definition of *ius divinium* as "divine law" according to God's word, by Christ's institution, with American Lutherans "free to create under the guidance of the Spirit forms of leadership that embody *episcopé* and hold ecumenical promise"; see *Ministries Examined*, 75 and 163.

459 See n. 455 above for the 1983 report on Ministry. *Episcopacy in the Lutheran Church?* (1970) has been cited above in n. 79. *Lutheran Understanding of the Episcopal Office*, Reports and Texts series (Geneva: LWF Department of Studies, 1983). *Women in the Ministries of the Church* appeared under the same auspices, also in 1983. *The Ministry of All Baptized Believers: Resource Materials for the Churches' Study in the Area of Ministry* (Geneva: LWF, Department of Studies, 1980) reprints the 1974 LCUSA study (n. 458 above) and other Lutheran and ecumenical documents.

460 BEM. Michael Seils, *Lutheran Convergence? An Analysis of Lutheran Responses to the Convergence Document "Baptism, Eucharist and Ministry" of the World Council of Churches Faith and Order Commission* (Geneva: LWF, 1988) found less agreement on ministry than on other areas. Cf. also Daniel Martensen, "Ministry," and J. Reumann, "Eucharist and Ministry," in *Lutherans in Ecumenical Dialogues: A Reappraisal*, ed. Joseph A. Burgess (Minneapolis: Augsburg, 1990), 123-135, 136-147.

461 In the extensive literature on the topic, see Krister Stendahl, *The Bible and the Role of Women: A Case Study in Hermeneutics*, trans. Emilie T. Sander, Facet Books Biblical Series 15 (Philadelphia: Fortress, 1966); Brita Stendahl, *The Force of Tradition: A Case Study of Women Priests in Sweden* (Philadelphia: Fortress, 1985).

462 See *Ministries Examined*, 78-100, for the section "What in Scripture Speaks to the Ordination of Women?" originally published in *Concordia Theological Monthly* 44 (1973): 5-30; 120-125, for "The Lutheran Experience," and 131-139, for subsequent discussions, including discussions among Roman Catholics. The LCMS in 1969 acted to allow women to vote in congregational or synodical assemblies and to serve on boards or agencies, provided there is no violation of the orders of creation or women exercising authority over men (1 Tim. 2:11). Cf. Pragman, 158-177.

463 As of September 15, 2002, the ELCA counted 2,738 pastors who were women, out of a total of 17,725 ordained ministers. In 2003 there have been seven bishops in the ELCA who are women.

464 *Ecumenism: The Vision of the Evangelical Lutheran Church in America* (adopted 1991), 14. "Preliminary recognition" can involve eucharistic sharing but "without exchangeability of ministers." Under "full communion" there is not only mutual recognition of ordained ministers but also their "availability . . . to the service of all members of churches in full communion, subject only but always to the disciplinary regulations of the other churches."   ·

465 The Lutheran-Episcopal *Concordat of Agreement*, Lutheran-Reformed *Formula of Agreement*, and *Joint Declaration* (as then framed) were presented together as *Ecumenical Proposals, Documents for Action by the 1997 Churchwide Assembly* of the ELCA.

466 The issues of the presence of Christ in the Lord's Supper and God's will to save (predestination) were treated in terms of "complementarity." Affirmed together were "a ministry of word and sacrament as instituted by God," to which one is ordained once, "usually by presbyters," with recognition of *episcopé* carried out by one ordained person or collegially (presbyteries and synods).

467 *Following Our Shepherd to Full Communion: Report of the Lutheran-Moravian Dialogue with Recommendations for Full Communion in Worship, Fellowship and Mission* (© ELCA, 1997), 38-42, with quotation from 41. The Moravian Church has "a threefold ordained ministry: deacons, presbyters (elders) and bishops," with one ordination (to deacon, "subsequent consecrations to other offices"), and "historic episcopacy." The "historic episcopacy" was retained from the Ancient Moravian Church but with bishops as non-diocesan, so as to avoid competition in Germany with "the established church and their offices" (13), a feature continued in North America; cf. Piepkorn, *Profiles in Belief* 2: 344-348.

468 CCM.

469 *1999 Reports and Records: Assembly Minutes* (Chicago, 2000), 378, revised text as voted 378-87.

470 Porvoo (n. 352 above).

471 *The Meissen Agreement: Texts* (London: Council for Christian Unity [Occasional Paper No. 2], 1992).

472 *Called to Full Communion (The Waterloo Declaration)*, available online at *www.elcic.ca*, ELCIC Documents (May 1, 2004). It was preceded by Canadian Lutheran-Anglican Dialogue 1983-1986 (CLAD I, with Report and Recommendations) and CLAD II, 1989, Interim Sharing of the Eucharist, with agreement in 1995 to take steps toward full communion by 2001.

HISTORICAL ESSAYS

Chapter 1

❄

TWO SACRED ORDERS:
DIACONATE AND PRESBYTERATE

BY MICHAEL SLUSSER

At the time of the Reformation, Martin Luther and others challenged the distinction between priest and bishop with the help of ancient materials preserved in medieval theological tradition. One such instance, the object of the present study, is Distinction 24, chapter 12, from Book IV of the *Sentences* of Peter Lombard:[1]

> *Only two are called sacred.* Although all are spiritual and sacred, yet the canons do very well to hold that only two orders should be called sacred, namely, diaconate and presbyterate, because we read that the primitive church had only these, and we have the Apostle's command concerning these alone.[2]

Lombard's *Sentences* was the standard theological textbook that the Reformers and their contemporaries encountered in their studies. The tradition presented in the quoted passage, on the face of it, does not number episcopal orders among those that should be called "sacred." What can we know about (1) the place of this passage in Lombard's own work, (2) its antecedents, and (3) how it was interpreted in the years between the twelfth century and the Reformation?

I. The Place of the Passage in Lombard's *Sentences*

a. The Passage Itself

What are "the canons" to which the text refers that specify that only two orders should be called "sacred"? Apparently, the reference is to the first canon of the Synod of Beneventum in 1091, convened and presided over by Pope Urban II:

> Let no one henceforth be chosen bishop who is not found living religiously in sacred orders. *Sacred orders* we call the diaconate

and presbyterate. For we read that the primitive church had
only these; we have the Apostle's command on these alone. But
we grant that subdeacons, since they too minister at the altar,
[may be made bishop] if the occasion demands, but very rarely,
if they be seen as men of religion and knowledge. But let this
not happen without explicit permission from the Roman pontiff
or the metropolitan.[3]

Given the context, "sacred orders" is meant as a specification of those
who may be made bishops, rather than as a general statement. Hence
the phrase might not exclude the episcopate from also being a sacred
order. We shall see that matters are more complicated. Meanwhile,
notice that there is a third rank, not a "sacred order," from which bishops may be drawn, however rarely: the subdeacons.

b. The Passage's Context in the Sentences
The whole of Lombard's Book IV, Distinction 24, to which the quoted
passage belongs, is devoted to orders,[4] beginning with the traditional
sevenfold classification from doorkeeper (ostiarius) up to priest (sacerdos). At the points where it first appears,[5] the term sacerdos is not further
specified; neither presbyter nor bishop is mentioned, which raises the
possibility that those two might be regarded as different sorts of priests.
Then, however, Lombard goes up the list in detail, devoting a chapter to
each order,[6] and after deacon, he comes to "presbyter" in chapter 11, not
sacerdos. Most of his treatment of the presbyter deserves to be quoted,
not least because the language he has taken over from earlier writers
becomes classic. He starts with what Isidore of Seville (c. 560-636) has
to say about its etymology as "elder," and then pastes together four more
quotations from Isidore:

> "Therefore presbyters are also called priests (sacerdotes),
> because they 'give holy' (sacrum dant). Although they are
> priests, still they do not have the summit of the pontificate
> (pontificatus apicem) as bishops do, because they neither sign
> the forehead with chrism, nor give the Paraclete; that this is
> owed to bishops only the reading of the Acts of the Apostles

demonstrates." "Whence also among the ancients bishops and priests were the same, because that name is one of dignity, not of age." "The name 'priest' is composed from Greek and Latin: it is 'giving holy'" or holy leader.[7] "For as 'king' (*rex*) comes from ruling (*regendo*), so priest (*sacerdos*) from sanctifying, for he consecrates and sanctifies." "A priest is called *antistites* from the fact that he 'stands before' (*ante stat*): he is first in the order of the church."[8]

Thus even in a section devoted to the presbyter as priest, a distinction is made in passing between the presbyter and the bishop.

The next few chapters are not directly on our subject: chapter 11,3 is from one of the False Decretals and simply describes the ordination ceremony.[9] Chapter 11,4 makes a set of parallels: Aaron as chief priest and his sons as ordinary priests are compared to Christ's designation of the Twelve Apostles, whose role is played in the church by the "greater *pontifices*," and the other seventy-two disciples, whose place the presbyters hold. One of the apostles, Peter, was their leader (*princeps*), and his place is taken by the pope. This passage tends to separate the bishop from the presbyter. Chapter 11,5 takes 1 Timothy, "where [Paul] indicates the presbyter by the word 'bishop,'" to refer to the qualities to be sought in the presbyter.

Then comes Distinction 24, chapter 12,1, the focal passage quoted at the beginning of this paper. It is followed immediately by a brief explanation:

> For the Apostles ordered bishops and presbyters in the different cities. We also read that levites were ordained by the Apostles, of whom the greatest was saint Stephen. With the passage of time, the Church established subdeacons and acolytes for herself.[10]

The term "bishop" appears again in Distinction 24 in chapter 15, where we learn that "it is the name of a dignity and of an office."[11] It is followed by "pontifex" in chapter 16, a term that seems to overlap "bishop": "Pontifex is the chief of the priests, if one regards them as people following a road.[12] He is also called high priest, for he makes priests and levites, he disposes all the ecclesiastical orders."[13] This passage is consistent with Distinction 24, chapter 11,4, as cited above. Finally, Distinction 24, chapter 17 differentiates bishops by rank as patriarchs, archbishops, metropolitans, and bishops, but it gives no amplification of the last-named.

Our focal text, therefore, which speaks of but two sacred orders, diaconate and presbyterate, sits in the midst of texts that envisage more elaborate lists of persons and titles both below and above the deacon and the presbyter. These lists connect with passages in the Torah, the Gospels, and the Pastoral Epistles. Lombard himself does not provide a harmonization of these lists.

II. The Antecedents of Our Passage

The most important source of many of Lombard's texts, the *Decretum* of Gratian, was scarcely a decade old itself.[14] Since the whole complex of material on the clergy in the *Decretum* is so extensive that to try to treat it would overwhelm this paper, I shall restrict myself to its tradition of the canon from the Council of Beneventum.

The canon from the Council of Beneventum (1091) to which *Sentences* IV, Distinction 24, chapter 12,1 seems to be referring appears with only minor, mostly orthographic, differences in Decretum, Distinction 60, chapter 4.[15] Another (and once again slightly different) text of the canon is cited earlier in the *Panormia* of Yves of Chartres (c. 1040-1115), less than a generation after the Council of Beneventum.[16]

When we look for the background of the idea expressed in the canon itself, with Isidore of Seville (c. 560-636) we arrive at a rich source for texts relevant to its theme. As I noted above, Lombard assembled a large part of Distinction 24, chapter 11, "On presbyters," out of passages he drew from Isidore's *Etymologies*. It would be a mistake, however, to see the *Etymologies* as presenting an argument for the equating of presbyter and bishop; in *Etymologies* VII, cap. 12, de clericis, Isidore puts bishops in paragraph nos. 4-12, presbyters much later in nos. 20-21, where he distinguishes them sharply from *episcopi*. Closer to the spirit of the Lombard passage in Distinction 24, chapter 12,1 are texts from another of Isidore's works, *De Ecclesiasticis Officiis*. There we read that "'Bishop,' as one of the prudent says, is the name of a work, not of an honor. . . . Therefore we can say in Latin that the bishop superintends, so that someone who would love to preside but not to assist may understand that he is not a bishop."[17] Isidore also hands on the comparison we saw above, "Old Testament priests are to presbyters as high priests are to bishops." He then proceeds to describe presbyters and bishops as having virtually the same duties with regard to the Eucharist, teaching the people, and preaching, and he adds,

> only on account of authority is ordination and consecration reserved to the high priest, lest if the discipline of the church were arrogated by many it might dissolve concord and generate scandals.[18]

Then Isidore alludes to the same texts from 1 Timothy, Titus, Philippians, and Acts that we saw above in Lombard, Distinction 24, chapters 11,4 and 12,2. The critical editor of Isidore's treatise has traced Isidore's own sources as follows: the line about bishops as superintendents is from Augustine's *City of God*, 19.19; the statement about the common duties of bishops and presbyters, with a purely disciplinary restriction of certain powers to the former, comes from "De VII Ordinibus Ecclesiae" 6;[19] and the comments on scripture are from Pelagius's commentary on 1 Timothy.[20] Thus two of the sources, Augustine and Pelagius, are from the early fifth century, while the "De Septem Ordinibus Ecclesiae" has been dated to the very end of the sixth century.[21]

Two medieval treatises on ecclesiastical offices help fill out the context of this discussion. Johannes Beleth (twelfth century), in his *Summa de Ecclesiasticis Officiis*, treated only briefly of persons (*officia* in the title refers to ceremonies rather than positions in the church). For John, ecclesiastical persons were of two kinds; some were ranked by dignity, others by orders. By dignity they are "pope, patriarch, cardinal, primate, archbishop or metropolitan which is the same, bishop, co-bishop, archdeacon, archpresbyter. . . . The persons of orders are the priest (sacerdos) deacon, subdeacon, acolyte, exorcist, lector, doorkeeper."[22] The two distinct scales of dignities and of orders will persist in later discussion.

A somewhat later writer, Sicard, bishop of Cremona (c. 1155-1215), speaks of orders in his *Mitrale* II, 2. He espouses the theory (later rejected by Aquinas and others) that there are seven orders because there are seven gifts of the Holy Spirit. He classifies ecclesiastical persons as distinguished in three categories: either by religious habit, as monks; or by orders, as clerics; or by dignity, along with habit or orders, as abbots and bishops. Bishops do not otherwise appear in the chapter on order, but they return two chapters later, when the subject is dignities. Sicard repeats the theory that orders were arranged in imitation of Old Testament models, while dignities were fashioned on gentile models; and of the dignities, the episcopal dignity is the greatest. He adds,

> The episcopal office is to ordain presbyters and other ministers of the church, veil virgins, confirm the baptized, consecrate oil and chrism, dedicate churches, excommunicate rebels, reconcile penitents, bless vestments and vessels. And note that more than once bishops were also called presbyters, as is proved by many texts, but later one became the name for age, the other of office. But afterwards, just as the archdeacon is elected by the deacons, and the emperor by the army, so by the priests a greater one was set apart.[23]

The final sentence of that quotation from Sicard is an idea he borrows from Jerome's *Letter to Evangelus*,[24] which became a key text for the Lutheran Reformers.

We can see in these texts that there was an ambiguity about presbyters and bishops. In some respects, the medieval authors considered them together, especially under the category of priesthood (*sacerdotium*), but in others they asserted their distinction and their differing powers.[25] The canon of Beneventum cited by Lombard is symptomatic of this ambiguity, but the canon did not apparently play a role in the discussion.

III. How This Passage Was Treated between the Twelfth Century and the Reformation

What follows is the result of a search for the subsequent interpretation of Lombard, *Sentences* IV, Distinction 24, chapter 12,1 through twenty-eight commentaries on the *Sentences*, supplemented by Thomas Aquinas's Pauline commentaries.

a. Alexander of Hales (c. 1186-1245)

In Alexander's commentary on the *Sentences*, he does not reflect on Distinction 24, chapter 11-12, but in his discussion of the higher orders, he does introduce a source, one which Lombard did not use, that will tend to heighten the distinction between presbyter and bishop. This is pseudo-Dionysius's *De Ecclesiastica Hierarchia*,[26] which insists upon a triple order. He lists them first as bishop-priest-minor orders, saying the the first is perfective, the second illuminative, and the third purgative.[27] A little later, he offers the triad presbyter-bishop-pope, distinguishing both the power and the charity appropriate to each.[28] In general, one may say that Alexander links the presbyter more closely with the lower clergy and clearly distinguishes episcopal ordination from the priestly order.[29]

b. Bonaventure (1217-1274)

Bonaventure, on the other hand, does deal with the text from Distinction 24, chapter 12,1 in his commentary on the *Sentences*. He cites it in a question on whether there are both sacred and non-sacred orders, but he does in a slightly altered form: "In the primitive church there were no orders but sacred ones, namely, presbyterate and diaconate." Bonaventure replies,

> To the objection that in the primitive church there were only sacred orders, we must say that that is false; there were indeed others. But they were given implicitly in the imposition of hands, for the hand is the organ of organs. But the reason why they were not distinguished was because there were few ministers and few faithful, so it was fitting to give all the offices to one person. Now the divine cult has been multiplied, so things are not the same.[30]

The issue here has nothing to do directly with episcopacy or presbyterate; instead, it proposes that orders, both sacred and non-sacred, represent a deployment of a complexity implicit in the simplicity of the primitive church. A little later, he questions whether the episcopate is an order, which became a classic topic in the literature. After citing the list of seven grades of order ending in priesthood (*sacerdotium*), which would leave the episcopate a dignity rather than an order, Bonaventure agrees that there is no order higher than to consecrate the Body of the Lord; but there can still be a distinction of

> dignities and offices, which still do not constitute a new grade or order, such as archpresbyter, bishop, archbishop, patriarch, *Pontifex Summus*, . . . which are not names of orders but of dignities. Also common opinion holds this, that in the episcopate a new character is not impressed, but a sort of eminence is conferred on him which always remains with the character of order itself, even when all jurisdiction is lost.[31]

c. Thomas Aquinas (1224/5-1274)

Our Lombard text appears most clearly in Aquinas's commentary on Distinction 24, quaestio 2, quaestiuncula 2, objectio 2, which claims that in the teaching of Christ and the apostles, there are no other orders except presbyters and deacons. Aquinas replies that

> in the primitive church all the lower ministries were entrusted to deacons, because of the lack of ministers, but all those ministries existed implicitly in each deacon. Later, when divine worship spread, the church distributed explicitly in various orders what she had implicitly in the one. As Lombard says in his text, the church instituted other orders for herself.[32]

The issue for Aquinas was apparently not whether the presbyter and bishop are distinct but whether there were lower orders below that of deacon.

In quaestio 3, article 2, he raises directly the issue of "whether above the priestly (*sacerdotalem*) order there should be some episcopal power"[33] (notice the shift from "order" to "power"). Among the authorities that could be cited in favor is pseudo-Dionysius, *De Ecclesistica Hierarchia* 5, which (as we saw in the section on Alexander of Hales) limits sacerdotal power to purifying and illuminating, but says that the bishop can in addition "perfect" (*perficere*) or complete. Another authority offered is the common-sense observation that every office or duty requires one person in charge, so "priests too ought to be in the charge of someone who is their chief, and this is the bishop."[34] In his own solutions, Aquinas distinguishes between the priest's primary power of consecrating the eucharist and his secondary power of preparing the people to receive it. The latter power, that of absolving people from their sins, presupposes jurisdiction and subordinates the priest to the one who can grant it.[35] Thomas also assigns to the bishop a power over Christ's mystical Body that goes beyond the priestly power.[36]

Finally, in the "Expositio Textus" (that is, where Aquinas clarifies the text of particular passages of the *Sentences*), he has this to say about Distinction 24, chapter 12: "The canons hold that only two orders are called holy: this is because only two orders have power over the sacrament itself; the subdeacon has power only over the sacred vessels." Apparently Aquinas did not see the bishop/presbyter distinction as an issue in our passage.[37]

Before leaving Aquinas, I would like to look at his commentaries on the scriptural passages most frequently brought up in connection with our passage. First, on Philippians 1:1, Aquinas asks why the presbyters were not mentioned. He answers that they are counted together with the bishops, who would not be mentioned in the plural for one city unless the term included the presbyters. And yet the presbyterate

> is another order, because in the gospel itself we read that, after naming the twelve apostles (in whose persons the bishops act), he named seventy-two disciples, whose place the priests hold. Dionysius too distinguishes bishops and priests. But in the beginning, although the orders were distinct, the names of the orders were not, whence this verse [Phil 1:1] includes the presbyters with the bishops.[38]

Aquinas answers a similar question in regard to 1 Timothy 3:1, especially in the light of the fact that Dionysius, allegedly Paul's convert, mentions three orders: "The presbyters are understood along with the bishops—not that the orders are indistinguishable in reality, but only as to the names, because the presbyter is the same as 'elder' and bishop as 'superintendent.'" When Aquinas comes to 1 Timothy 4:14, he repeats the observation that the names "presbyter" and "bishop" are interchangeable. What concerns him more is the fact that his Latin text has "with the imposition of the presbyter's hand," i.e., the hand of one presbyter, when there should have been three to ordain a bishop. He offers two solutions: (1) that even when there *are* three, one is principal and the others only assist; and (2) that in that period, there were so few bishops that one could not always gather a group of three.[39]

Aquinas's comment on Titus 1:5,7 offers us a small surprise in his interpretation of the contrast between "appoint elders" (1:5) and "A bishop . . . must be blameless."

> He [Paul] uses the name "bishops" and "presbyters" indifferently. The heretic who was ambitious to be bishop[40] found a pretext here; when he could not attain it, he separated himself from others and taught many falsehoods, including saying that bishops differ in nothing from priests, which is contrary to Dionysius in *De Eccl. Hierar.*[41]

The authority of Dionysius as the authentic interpreter of Paul's meaning here could not be clearer.

If Aquinas is any indicator, the bishop/presbyter distinction was largely taken for granted, whether it was founded in "order" or in dignity, jurisdiction, or power. The theologian needed to account for its precise nature, and that proved difficult enough. It did not occur to Aquinas to question it, even in connection with our passage from Lombard.

d. Peter of Tarentaise, OP (c. 1224-1276)

At the end of his life, Peter spent nearly six months as Pope Innocent V.[42] When he comments on the *Sentences*, Book IV, Distinction 24, in question 4, article 1, he asks about the episcopal dignity in the church and presents several views. His own determination of the matter matches Aquinas's view that the primary act of the priest is to consecrate the eucharist; the secondary one is to prepare the faithful by "binding and loosing." Peter thinks that a well-ordered regime should come down from one "universal rector"; that is why Jerome said that, after an initial period when presbyter and bishop were the same, a worldwide rule was issued that one should be placed at the top and schisms should be eliminated. "Thus bishops know themselves to be greater than presbyters, more by custom than by the truth of the Lord's dispensation."[43]

Commenting on Distinction 25, Peter asks in question 1, article 1, "Whether only a bishop can ordain?" Peter says yes, though minor orders may sometimes be conferred by someone specially authorized. Our text of focus, Lombard's Distinction 24, chapter 12,1 is not cited in this context. In article 2, Peter of Tarentaise presses further with "Whether a presbyter can ordain a bishop?" After all, presbyters ordained Timothy, Moses consecrated Aaron, and the bishop of Ostia consecrates the pope. Peter cites Hebrews 7:7, Gratian's *Decretum*, and "No one can give what he does not have," and he decides in the negative. To the example of Timothy, on whom the presbyters laid hands, he says, "By the name of presbyters, he understands 'bishops,' says the Gloss."[44] Though Peter of Tarentaise apparently knows of theories that, due to the unity of the priesthood, presbyters can ordain, he does not think that they are sound, and in any case, our focus passage is not cited as part of the argument for such a theory.

e. Richard of Middleton (born c. 1249), a Franciscan
Our text comes up as the third *objectio* in Richard of Middleton's commentary on the *Sentences* IV, article 3, question 3, on Distinction 24: "Whether there are only seven orders." In this context, the statement that there are only two sacred orders argues that there are not even seven orders. Richard answers that in the primitive church there were fewer faithful and no need for so many ministries, but by the inspiration of Christ who had carried out the duties of all the orders in his own person, the church did not "establish" new orders but simply conferred the other five already instituted by Christ.[45] Our focus passage is simply not related to the distinction of the office of bishop as it appears in Richard of Middleton.

Richard does ask the question as to whether there is any power in the church higher than the priestly power, and he answers in the same way Thomas did above: it has mainly to do with jurisdiction and the power to absolve from sins. He does add, however, in his response to an objection, that "the priest represents Christ in this, that through his own person he fulfilled some ministry; the bishop also in this, that he instituted other ministers and founded the church. Whence to ordain others for divine worship belongs to the bishop."[46] For all that, "Episcopacy must not be called an order, which is a sacrament, but rather a kind of dignity of order." It impresses no character, properly speaking, but it is an order (though not a sacrament) in regard to the other sacred actions besides consecrating the Body and Blood of Christ.[47] The closest approach to our issue is in the very next question, on whether one particular bishop is higher in the church. The first objection points out that the bishop of Ostia consecrates the pope, and so must be higher than the pope. Richard points out that this is only in one particular respect, "which can't be said of a priest in comparison with a bishop, because the power of a priest is exceeded by the power of the bishop as if by a power of a completely different kind."[48]

Richard asks in Distinction 26, article 1, question 1, "Whether a presbyter who is not a bishop can ordain?" Richard answers,

> Someone can have the power of conferring orders two ways, either by ordinary power or by general or special commission. In the latter way, conferring minor orders can sometimes be given to to non-bishops, as one of the objections said. In the first way, the power of conferring any order at all belongs to bishops alone. The reason for this is divine institution.

He goes on to say that this is reasonable, and he makes an analogy between general/soldiers and bishop/ministers.[49] Our focus text from the *Sentences*, Distinction 24, chapter 12, is not brought up here, and it was probably not thought to be relevant to the issue.

f. Durandus of Saint-Pourçain, OP (c. 1275-1334)

Durandus, in question 5 on Distinction 24, asks a question that is now familiar: "Whether in the church there is any power greater than the priestly?" His answer makes the usual distinction between power of jurisdiction and power of consecration. The former extends farther and farther the higher we go; in regard to the latter power, however, one may propose a large doubt (*dubium*), based on Jerome, who saw the priestly power as being so lofty

> that every priest, as regards sacerdotal power, can administer all the sacraments, confirmation, all the orders, all blessings, and

do all consecrations. But because of the danger of schism it was ordained that the priests should elect one of their number who would be called the "bishop" as watching over the others, whom the others would obey, and to whom performing ordinations was reserved and other things of the kind only bishops do. Therefore the bishop is greater than the priest as regards jurisdiction, but not as regards the power of order or consecration, but they are equals, even though from church ordinance some things are reserved to bishops and prohibited to priests.[50]

The evidence that Jerome provided came from the group of biblical texts we've seen before (Phil 1:1, Acts 20:28, Tit 1, 1 Tim 4), and was confirmed by reason, since the only power the apostles or bishops had was sacerdotal, according to this thesis.

Durandus disagrees with this view and sides with those others "who say that the power of order or consecration is greater in the bishop than in the simple priest, not only from church ordinance but from the nature of order and consecration by divine institution."[51] He reasons from the special anointing received by the high priest in Leviticus 8 to a corresponding elevation of the bishop. "And this opinion is more common and safer, because more in accord with the doctrine of the church, which is of the greatest authority in what pertains to the articles of faith and the church's sacraments."[52]

Durandus then cites another, even more radical opinion: "Some even say that then [in the primitive church] both kinds of power were conferred on all who presided over the congregations, so that the congregations had at hand an ecclesiastical leader who could administer all the sacraments and institute ministers; but this is not true."[53] It is not true because Dionysius tells us that the distinction between bishop and presbyter existed in apostolic times. Jerome himself should have known better, since the power of jurisdiction was entrusted to Peter alone, and from him to others. And Augustine reports that a certain Aerius said that no difference should be discerned between bishop and priest.[54] Durandus says the reason offered in support of that opinion was invalid for two reasons: first, Christ did many things that were not written down, so that "it doesn't follow that, if Christ is not said to have done this, therefore he didn't do it";[55] second, because Christ had power to such an excellent degree that he could and did give the effect of a sacrament without the full ceremony—e.g., at the Last Supper, where they were ordained without being given the sacred vessels to touch.[56]

g. Peter Aureolus (1280-1322), a Franciscan
Peter, in his commentary on Distinction 25, in a single question, article 1, speaks of the proper recipient and minister of orders, and his words on the minister are relevant:

> Second, I give the rule about the minister: the only suitable minister is a bishop, though by dispensation it might be a priest. Next I say *any* bishop, so as not to exclude one who is wicked, or stripped of rank or excommunicated.

He does not say whether the dispensation here is for giving minor orders (as in Richard of Middleton above) or even for subdiaconate, deaconate, and priesthood.[57]

h. Francis of Meyronnes (c. 1285-1328), a Franciscan
In his commentary on the *Sentences*, Francis makes no mention of our focal passage from Lombard, but he does tell us something about the contexts in which non-bishops were commissioned to confer the minor orders. In his comments on *Sentences* IV, Distinction 25, he says that the pope gave such power to the friars who were headed into "tartariam" (presumably the lands being occupied by the crusaders). He also says emphatically that any bishop can ordain, even one who is a heretic, a schismatic, excommunicated, irregular, both schismatic and heretical (he points out that Greek bishops can ordain truly), or degraded from rank.[58] If it seems puzzling that so much attention was given to the question of whether heretical, schismatic, excommunicated, or degraded bishops could ordain, remember that popes, especially starting with Gregory VII (1073-1085) during the investiture controversy, used those ecclesiastical penalties quite heavily against bishops who accepted their insignia of office from lay princes. If all those bishops' ordinations had been invalid, the church would have been in inextricable confusion.

The examples above should give one a good idea of what the commentaries on the *Sentences* from the late Middle Ages have to offer on the subject of sacred orders as it impinges upon the discussion in this dialogue. Other commentaries consulted either did not treat order at all or said nothing significant beyond the parameters of these examples. Very little in any case turns up in regard to our focal text: it was hardly ever brought up in connection with the presbyter-bishop issue.

There is a fair amount of modern literature that might throw light on our text and its implications.[59] The following may be of particular interest. One article that tackled issues from the side of canon law began its summary of the evidence as follows:

> This study has traced the evolution of the opinion which came to be the common opinion among the medieval canonists. Their investigation of the episcopacy began with the texts cited in Gratian's *Decretum*. Here they found no clearly articulated answer to the question: what is the episcopacy? On the contrary, they found texts which would support either of two conclusions. Certain statements of Isidore of Seville and Jerome emphasized the centrality of the priestly office and power; there was little development of any properly episcopal power in the line of order. Yet other texts, especially concerning the administration of the sacraments, delineated a properly episcopal power in the areas of sacramental administration and various benedictions and consecrations. Finally, there were the difficult passages which contained the commission of this normally episcopal power to simple priests.[60]

It is the last category that comes the closest to showing a possible route to ordination of one priest by another. The canonist Huguccio († 1210) thought that there was one way it could happen: if the pope authorized a priest to do it.[61] This argument presumes a sort of limitless power in the papacy which may not make it very useful in the present ecumenical context.

Concrete instances of such authorization did occur. Ludwig Ott, a conservative Catholic dogmatician, cited several of them even in his brief compendium, under the heading "Extraordinary Minister."[62] Other scholars have dealt with these same fifteenth-century texts in greater detail[63] and associated this pattern of papal documents with the Council of Florence's careful statement that the bishop is the ordinary minister of the sacrament of Order.[64] The instances most frequently quoted involve abbots, but the situation of abbots was peculiar and quite unlike that of ordinary presbyters. They were obliged to attend councils, as bishops were, and many even had the right to vote in ecumenical (i.e. general) councils. Abbots have not been consecrated bishops, but perhaps the abbatial dignity—and remember that for many medieval theologians episcopacy was a dignity rather than an order—was regarded as equivalent, at least as regards the subjects of the abbot; could we say the same of others in presbyteral orders?

A. M. Landgraf has surveyed all of early scholasticism on the subject of whether the episcopate in an *ordo*.[65] He cites Baisi's theory that "the priest possesses all that is needed to ordain from the point of view of *potestas ordinis*, but lacks what is required from the point of view of *potestas jurisdictionis*, and the latter can be given him extraordinarily by the Pope; bishops in contrast possess it in the ordinary way, thanks to their episcopal consecration." Landgraf says that Baisi is right if the ordination of the bishop is instituted by Christ as a sacrament distinct from priestly ordination; even if it is not, he still *may* be right. Was the distinction original, or did it come in later?[66] Citing a large number of texts, but especially Jerome's commentary on Titus 1 and Letter 146 to Evangelus and Ambrosiaster on Titus, chapter 3, Landgraf notes that they give the impression that the distinction between priest and bishop was a later development, arrived at for practical reasons. But then things get less clear, even in terms of medieval exegesis of the Pauline texts usually considered in this connection.[67] For example, Peter the Chanter († 1197) "deals explicitly with the distinction between bishop and priest . . . and sees it in the *unctio*, the conferring of certain sacraments, and in preferment (*prelatura*). But whether for him this distinction also involves orders as such is not clear."[68] After a brief review of canon law, Landgraf pursues the issue through the systematic theologians, citing many more texts than I have above. But his findings are of limited value for our discussion because of his single-minded focus on the way in which Order as such is defined, and whether in those terms episcopacy is a distinct order from the presbyterate. Lécuyer's excellent article[69] is good background for the Second Vatican Council, but it does not really answer the questions of (1) whether episcopacy is essential to the being of the church or (2) whether, in case of need, presbyters can ordain other presbyters.

This paper has not resolved the issue it addresses, nor does a simple resolution seem possible, but perhaps it will enable us to frame discussion in historically appropriate terms.

NOTES

1 Peter Lombard (c. 1100-c. 1160) was an Italian theologian who became archbishop of Paris and whose four books of *Sentences* became the standard compendium of Christian theology until the middle of the sixteenth century.

2 The references implied in "we read" and "we have the Apostle's command" are to 1 Timothy 3:1-13 and Titus 1:5-9. The Latin text of Lombard's passage: "*Duo tantum sacri dicuntur.* Cumque omnes spirituales sint et sacri, excellenter tamen canones duos tantum sacros ordines appellari censent, diaconatus scilicet et presbyteratus, quia hos solos primitiva Ecclesia legitur habuisse, et de his solis praeceptum Apostoli habemus." Magistri Petri Lombardi, *Sententiae in IV Libris Distinctae*, Spicilegium Bonaventurianum 4-5 (Grottaferrata: Collegii S. Bonaventurae Ad Claras Aquas, 1971, 1981), II, 405. The rather clumsy way of referring to the text by "distinctions" is conventional, but not original, say the editors (op. cit. I 143*-144*). In the original division of each book by chapters, ours would be Book IV, chapter 142,1.

3 According to Mansi, *Sanctorum Conciliorum Amplissima Collectio*, t. 20, column 738-739. Mansi says that Phillipe Labbe, SJ, sent him the canons of the Synod of Beneventum; until those showed up, he knew of that synod only from mentions by Berthold of Constance and Caesar Baronius's *Annales*. The Latin text of canon 1 as given in Mansi: "Nullus deinceps in episcopum eligatur, nisi qui in sacris ordinibus religiose vivens inventus est. Sacros autem ordines dicimus diaconatum ac presbyteratum. Hos siquidem solos primitiva legitur ecclesia habuisse: super his solum praeceptum habemus apostoli. Subdiaconos vero, quia et ipsi administrant, opportunitate exigente concedimus, sed rarissime, si tamen spectatae sint religionis et scientiae. (3) Quod et ipsum sine Romani pontificis, vel metropolitani non fiat." (A marginal note in Mansi refers to Gratian's *Decretum*, Dist. 70, chap. 84.) The other three canons have nothing to do with our issue.

4 Distinction 23 is on extreme unction, 25 on the qualities of the recipients of orders and issues like simony.

5 Distinction 24, chap. 1 and 3.

6 And rather surprisingly describes how Jesus Christ himself had exercised each of the seven. For the evolution of this list, see Joseph Crehan, "The Seven Orders of Christ," *Theological Studies* 19 (1958): 81-93. A full study of such lists is in Roger E. Reynolds, *The Ordinals of Christ from Their Origins to the Twelfth Century* (Berlin: Walter de Gruyter, 1978).

7　The editors of the *Sentences* point out that this last etymology comes from the *Glossa ordinaria* on 2 Chronicles 4.9 and is found in Gratian's *Decretum*, Dist. 21, chap. 1. The standard critical edition of the *Decretum* is in *Corpus Iuris Canonici* I, ed. Aemilianus Friedburg (Leipzig: B. Tauchnitz, 1879, reprinted Graz: Akademischen Druck- u. Verlagsanstalt, 1955).

8　*Sentences* 4, Dist. 24, chap. 11,2, quoting Isidore, *Etymologies* 7,12, sections 21, 20, 17, and 16.

9　Though Peter Lombard has forgotten the laying-on of hands and invocation of the Holy Spirit, which are in his sources. On the "False Decretals," ninth-century texts from Normandy, see *Oxford Dictionary of the Christian Church*, 3rd. ed., ed. E. A. Livingstone (Oxford: Oxford University Press, 1997), s.v.

10　Dist. 24, chap. 12,2. It too is taken from Gratian's *Decretum*, Dist. 21, chap. 1.

11　"Dignitatis simul et officii nomen est episcopus." There follows an etymology of the term, taken from Isidore of Seville via Gratian, Dist. 21, chap.1.

12　And therefore presumably needing the occasional bridge (*pons*), though the etymology seems pretty forced.

13　Dist. 24, chap. 16: "Pontifex princeps sacerdotum est, quasi via sequentium. Ipse et summus sacerdos nuncupatur; ipse enim sacerdotes et levitas efficit, ipse omnes ecclesiasticos ordines disponit." This too comes from the same section of Gratian.

14　On the order of Gratian/Lombard, the classic demonstration of Lombard's use of the *Decretum* on this section is by J. de Ghellinck, "Le traité de Pierre Lombard sur les sept ordres ecclésiastiques: ses sources, ses copistes," *Revue d'Histoire Ecclésiastique* 10 (1909): 290-302, 720-728 and 11 (1910): 29-46. The editors of the third edition of the *Sentences* say that the first influence of Gratian appears in *Sentences* III, Dist. 31, chap. 1, then in Dist. 38-39, and then through practically all of Book IV; ed. cit. I 120.*

15　"Nullus in episcopatum eligatur, nisi in sacris ordinibus religiose vivens inventus fuerit. Sacros autem ordines dicimus diaconatum et presbiteratum. Hos siquidem solos primitiva legitur habuisse ecclesia, subdiacones vero, quia et ipsi altaribus ministrant, opportunitate exigente concedimus, si tamen spectatae sint religonis et scientiae. Quod ipsum non sine Romani Pontificis vel metropolitani scientia fieri permittimus." *Decretum*, Dist. 60, chap. 4, ed. Friedburg, 227.

16　Ivo Carnotensis, *Panormia* III 5 (PL 161.1130). The same Yves himself also wrote a *Decretum*, which does not cite the canon from Beneventum. It does, however, offer two other texts along the same line: "Of priests, brethren, the order is two-fold, and no one ought to disturb it from the way the Lord established it" (*Decretum* V, chap. 58 [PL 161.346]: "Sacerdotum, fratres, ordo bipertius est, et sicut Dominus illum constituit, a nullo debet perturbari") and he relays Isidore of Seville's remark that presbyter and bishop are two terms for the same person (*Decretum* VI, chap. 11,2,4 [PL 161.447].

17　"Episcopatus autem, ut quidam prudentium ait, nomen est operis non honoris. . . . Ergo episcopin Latine superintendere possumus dicere; ut intelligat non se esse episcopum qui non prodesse sed praeesse dilexerit." Isidorus Hispaliensis, *De Ecclesiasticis Officiis* II, 5,8, ed. Christopher M. Lawson, Corpus Christianorum Series Latina 113 (Turnholti: Brepols, 1989), 59 (PL 83.782).

18   *De Ecclesiasticis Officiis* II, 7,2 (Lawson, 65): "Praesunt enim ecclesiae Christi, et in
confectione diuini corporis et sanguinis consortes cum episcopis sunt, similiter et in
doctrina populorum et in officio praedicandi; ac sola propter auctoritatem summo
sacerdoti clericorum ordinatio et consecratio reseruata est, ne a disciplina ecclesiae
uindicata concordiam solueret, scandala generaret."

19   The treatise appears among the *spuria* of Jerome in PL 30.148-162; the cited text is
in columns 155-156. J. Lécuyer, "Aux origines de la théologie thomiste de l'Épiscopat," *Gregorianum* 35 (1954), 65, n. 24, says that there is a critical edition by A. Kalff
(Würzburg, 1935). Lest we assume that the unknown author of "De VII Ordinibus
Ecclesiae" thought of bishops as simply presbyters with special duties, we should note
that the quoted words come from section *six* of that little treatise; the seventh section exalts the *ordo episcopalis* remarkably (PL 30.158-159A). In contrast to later lists
of the seven orders, this treatise lists diggers (*fossarii*), porters, readers, subdeacons,
levites or deacons, priests, bishops.

20   These were edited by A. Souter in three volumes (*Texts and Studies* 9, 1-3
[Cambridge: University Press, 1922-1931], reprinted in *Patrologiae Latinae
Supplementum*, 1.1110-1374); the treatment of 1 Timothy 3:8 is at PLS 1.1351.

21   R. E. Reynolds, "The Pseudo-Hieronymian 'De Septem Ordinibus Ecclesiae': Notes
on Its Origins, Abridgments and Use in Early Medieval Canonical Collections,"
Revue Bénédictine 80 (1970): 242-243.

22   Johannes Beleth, *Summa de Ecclesiaticis Officiis*, cap. 13, ed. Herbert Douteil, Corpus
Christianorum Series Latina, Continuatio Medievalia 41A (Turnhout: Brepols,
1976), 32.

23   Sicardus Cremonensis, *Mitrale, Seu De Officiis Ecclesiasticis Summa* II 4 (PL
213.70.AB).

24   Hieronymus, *ep.* 146,1,6, ed. I. Hilberg, Corpus Scriptorum Ecclesiasticorum
Latinorum 66 (Vienna: F. Tempsky, 1918), 310.8-12.

25   According to P.-M. Gy, "Notes on the Early Terminology of Christian Priesthood," in
The Sacrament of Holy Orders (London: Aquin Press, 1962), 115, "In the eleventh
century *sacerdos* normally refers to the priest. Men were still aware that theoretical-
ly it also applied to the bishop." This dated back to Carolingian times, but earlier,
"[b]etween the second half of the fourth century and the sixth *sacerdos* normally
means the bishop, and except where the context indicates the contrary is synonymous with *episcopus.*"

26   Pseudo-Dionysius, or Dionysius the Pseudo-Areopagite (so-called because for a millennium he was thought to be the Dionysius the Areopagite mentioned in Acts
17.34), wrote several works of theology about 500 CE. These survive in Greek, but
medieval translations into Latin, particularly that of John the Saracen (twelfth century), spread the influence of this supposed direct disciple of Saint Paul into
Scholastic theology. See *Oxford Dictionary of the Christian Church*, 3rd ed., s.v.
"Dionysius (6)."

27   Magistri Alexandri de Hales, *Glossa in quatuor libros sententiarum Petri Lombardi* IV,
Bibliotheca Franciscana Scholastica Medii Aevi, t. 15 (Quaracchi: Ex Typographia
Collegii S. Bonaventurae, 1957), 404: "Pontificum Ordo est consummativus et

perfectivus, sacerdotum autem illuminativus et luciducus, ministrantium vero purgativus et discretivus; hierarchico tamen Ordine non perficere tantum, sed illuminare simul et mundare cognoscente; et sacerdotum virtute habente in se ipsa, cum illuminativa, scientiam purgativam. Ipsi vero minores in ea quae meliora sunt transmovere non possunt."

28   Op. cit., 405-406.

29   Op. cit., 414, he quotes the *Decretum* of Gratian, Dist. 40, chap. 8 (I, 147), thinking that it reports the view of Isidore of Seville: "As the worthy union of man and woman makes one marriage, so the clergy and priesthood (*clericatus et sacerdotium*) make one priest, and election and consecration one bishop." On p. 416, "It is otherwise for episcopal consecration than with the priestly order." On the other hand, he knew but did not accept the opinion that a presbyter could be the extraordinary minister of the sacrament of Order; cf. Marie-Joseph Gerlaud, "Le ministre extraordinaire du sacrement de l'Ordre," *Revue Thomiste* 36 (1931): 883.

30   Liber IV, *Sententiarum*, Dist. 24, pars 2, art. 2, q. 1, obj. 1, in *Opera theologica selecta*, editio minor, t. IV (Quaracchi: Ex typographia Collegii S. Bonaventurae, 1949), 618-619.

31   Ibid., q. 3, sed contra and corpus, ed. cit., 621-622.

32   "Ad secundum dicendum, quod in primitiva Ecclesia propter paucitatem ministrorum omnia inferiora ministeria diaconis committebantur. . . . Nihilominus erant omnes praedictae potestates, sed implicite in una diaconi potestate. Sed postea ampliatus est cultus divinus; et Ecclesia quod implicite habebat in uno ordine, explicite tradidit in diversis; et secundum hoc dicit Magister in littera, quod Ecclesia alios ordines sibi instituit." Sancti Thomae Aquinatis, *Commentum in Quatuor Libros Sententiarum*, v. 2, pars altera (Parmae: Typis Petri Fiaccodori, 1858), 896.

33   Ibid., 900. "Utrum supra sacerdotalem ordinem debeat esse aliqua potestas episcopalis."

34   Ibid.: "Ergo et sacerdotibus debet aliquis praeponi qui sit sacerdotum princeps, et hic est Episcopus."

35   Ibid., 901; solutio 1.

36   Ibid., solutio 2.

37   Ibid., 903: "*Canones duos tantum sacros ordines appellari censent:* propter hoc quod hi duo tantum ordines habent actum super ipsum sacramentum; sed subdiaconus super sacra vasa tantum."

38   Thomas Aquinas, *Super Epistolas S. Pauli lectura*, ed. Raphael Cai, 8. ed. revisa (Torino: Marietti, 1953), II, 91, §6.

39   Ibid., 231, §87 and 245, §173-174.

40   The heretic in question must surely be the Aerius described by Augustine in his *De Haeresibus*, 53: "He was a priest, but he is said to have been deeply hurt, because he could not be ordained a bishop. He fell into the Arian heresy and also added some teachings of his own. He said that the sacrifice ought not to be offered for the dead and that the solemnly prescribed fasts should not be observed, but that each one should fast as he wishes so that he does not seem to be under the law. He also said

that a priest should not be distinguished from a bishop in any respect." Translated by Roland J. Teske, *Arianism and Other Heresies*, The Works of Saint Augustine I/18 (Hyde Park, NY: New City Press, 1995), 47.

41 Ibid., 305, §12. "Et utitur indifferenter nomine Episcoporum et presbyterorum. Unde sumpsit occasionem haereticus, qui ambivit Episcopatum, quem quia non poterat adipisci, divisit se ab aliis, et multa falsa docuit. Inter quae dixit, quod Episcopi in nullo differunt a sacerdotibus, quod est contra Dionysium in libro *De Eccl. Hierar.*"

42 His text was printed as Innocenti Quinti . . . qui antea Petrus de Tarantasia dicebatur, *In IV. Libros Sententiarum Commentaria* (Tolosae: Arnaldus Colomerius, 1552), t. 3.

43 Ibid., 269. "et ita Episcopi noverint se magis consuetudine, quam dispensationis Dominicae veritate presbyteris esse maiores."

44 Ibid., 273-74.

45 Ricardi de Mediavilla, *Super quatuor libros sententiarum Petri Lombardi quaestiones subtilissimae* (Brixiae, 1591), IV, 370-371.

46 Ibid., 375.

47 Art. 5, q. 2, ibid., 376.

48 Art. 5, q. 3, ibid., 376-77: "quia potestas sacerdotis exceditur a potestate episcopi quasi a potestate alterius generis."

49 Ibid., 380.

50 Durandi a Sancto Porciano, *In Petri Lombardi Sententias Theologicas Commentariorum libri IIII*, Dist. 24, q. 5.6 (Venetiis: ex typographia Guerrea, 1549), 362: "quod omnis sacerdos quantum est de potestate sacerdotali potest omnia sacramenta ministrare confirmationem, omnes ordines, omnes benedictiones, et omnes consecrationes facere: sed propter periculum schismatis fuit ordinatum, ut sacerdotes unum ex seipsis eligerent qui diceretur episcopus, quasi super alios intendens, cui alii obedirent, et cui reservatum est ordines facere, et huiusmodi quae non faciunt, nisi soli episcopi, episcopus ergo maior est sacerdote quantum ad potestatem iurisdictionis, sed non quoad potestatem ordinis vel consecrationis, sed sunt pares, quamvis ex ordinatione ecclesiae aliqua sint reservata episcopis et prohibita presbyteris."

51 Ibid., q. 5.9, 363: "Alii dicunt quod potestas ordinis, vel consecrationis est maior in episcopo quam in simplici sacerdote non solum ex ordinatione ecclesiae, sed ex natura ordinis et consecrationis secundum divinam institutionem."

52 Ibid.: "Et haec opinio est communior et securior, quia magis est concors doctrinae ecclesiae quae est maximae auctoritatis in his quae pertinent ad articulos fidei et ad ecclesiastica sacramenta."

53 Ibid., q. 5.11: "Dicunt etiam aliqui quod tunc omnibus qui praeferrebatur plebibus conferrebatur utraque potestas, ut plebes in promptu haberent principem ecclesiasticum qui posset omnia sacramenta ministrare, et ministros instituere, sed hoc non est verum."

54 See n. 39 above.

55 Ibid.: "et ideo non est bona consequentia, Christus non legitur hoc fecisse, ergo non fecit."

56   Touching the sacred vessels was at this point treated in the West as the central element in the ordination ceremony. The Reformers replaced this tradition with the earlier practice of laying on of hands with prayer; in 1947, Pope Pius XII made a similar provision for the Latin Rite of the Roman Catholic Church.

57   Petri Aureoli, *Commentariorum in Quartum librum Sententiarum* (Romae: Aloisius Zannetti, 1605), 165. This may be the time to call attention to a problem in using printed editions of medieval texts: elsewhere on the page just quoted, "Peter" makes reference to the Council of Trent! Obviously whoever edited the text for printing has tried to bring it up to date. Short of consulting earlier manuscripts, we have no way to be sure that similar modifications, additions, or emendations have not been made to the other texts presented here.

58   Franciscus de Mayronis, [no title], ed. Mauritius de Hybernia (Venetiis, 1520), 213.

59   See, in addition to the works treated here, N. L. Crumb, "Presbyterial Ordinations and the Church of Rome," *Church Quarterly Review* 164 (1963): 19-33; Franz Gillmann, *Zur Lehre der Scholastik vom Spender der Firmung und des Weihesakraments* (Paderborn: F. Schöningh, 1920); Yves Congar, "Faits, problèmes et réflexions à propos de l'ordre et des rapports entre le presbytérat et l'épiscopat," *La Maison-Dieu* 14 (1948): 107-128; Ludwig Hödl, "Dienst und Vollmacht der Presbyter: im mittelalterlichen Ringen um das Theologische Verständnis der Kirchenverfassung," in *Collectanea Stephen Kuttner* (Bologna: Institutum Gratianum, 1967), I, 529-554; the two new variorum collections of articles by Roger E. Reynolds, *Clerics in the Early Middle Ages and Clerical Orders in the Early Middle Ages* (Burlington: Ashgate, 1999).

60   Robert P. Stenger, "The Episcopacy as an Ordo according to the Medieval Canonists," *Mediaeval Studies* 29 (1967): 67-112 at 110-111.

61   Stenger, 87: "The position which Huguccio takes with respect to ordination is consistent with his explanation of the episcopal *ordo*. He adopts as a general rule that the pope can permit any cleric to confer the *ordo* which he himself possesses. Thus, since a priest has not the episcopal *ordo*, he cannot confer it on another. In line with Huguccio's principle, though, a priest could be permitted by the pope to ordain another to the priestly *ordo*."

62   Ludwig Ott, *Fundamentals of Catholic Dogma*, trans. Patrick Lynch (Cork: Mercier, 1963).

63   John de Reeper, "Relation of Priesthood to Episcopate," *Jurist* 16 (1956): 345-358; Marie-Joseph Gerlaud, "Le Ministre Extraordinaire du Sacrement de l'Ordre," *Revue Thomiste* 36 (1931): 874-885. On the Bull "Sacrae Religionis" (1400) and its withdrawal, one should see E. Hocedez, "Une Découverte Théologique," *Nouvelle Revue Théologique* 51 (1924): 332-340, and Joachin Puig de la Bellacasa in *Estudios Eclesiasticos* (April 1925).

64   Concilium Florentinum, Sessio VIII, November 22, 1439, "Bulla Unionis Armenorum," in *Conciliorum Oecumenicorum Decreta*, ed. G. Alberigo (Basel: Herder, 1962): 525-526; DB, 701, DS, 1326.

65   Artur Michael Landgraf, *Dogmengeschichte der Frühscholastik*, 3. Teil, "Die Lehre von den Sakramenten," Bd. 2 (Regensburg: Friedrich Pustet, 1955), 277-302 = "Die Lehre der Frühscholastik vom Episkopat als *ordo*," *Scholastik* 26 (1951): 496-519.

66   Ibid., 277. He is summarizing the findings of Corrado Baisi, *Il Ministro Straordinario degli Ordini Sacramentali*, Roma: Anonima Libraria Cattolica Italiana, 1935. A later exponent of Baisi's position is Jean Beyer, "Nature et position du sacerdoce," *Nouvelle Revue Theologique* 76 (1954): 356-373, 469-480.

67   Landgraf, 279-286.

68   Ibid., 285.

69   See n. 19 above.

Chapter 2

※

THE OFFICE OF THE BISHOP IN EARLY LUTHERANISM WITH PARTICULAR ATTENTION TO THE IDENTITY AND DISTINCTION OF PRESBYTER AND BISHOP

BY SCOTT S. ICKERT

1. The early Lutheran attempt to preserve an effective *episcope* and the "deep desire" to "maintain the church polity and ranks of the ecclesiastical hierarchy" (Philipp Melanchthon, *Apology* of the *Augsburg Confession* [in BC], Article 14.1) was compromised due to unavoidable circumstances. "The cruelty of the bishops," Melanchthon maintained, "is the reason for the abolition of canonical government in some places, despite our earnest desire to keep it" (Apol. 14.2). Consequently, the reformers made a distinction between *episcope*, which even in some of its jurisdictional aspects is exercised *de iure divino*,[1] and the polity of the church in its historical development, particularly the hierarchy, which they asserted was created by human authority. Moreover, along with this *distinction* came the *identification* of bishop and presbyter, proposed by Martin Luther as early as 1519.[2] This assertion, however, did not mitigate the practical necessity of personal oversight of the presbyterate; nor did the Lutheran stress on the human origin of the episcopal structure contradict the expressed desire to maintain the traditional polity, *including*, if possible, the hierarchy.

2. Lutherans deplored the degeneration of the episcopal office. They regarded the office as corrupt and the sitting bishops as usurpers who sought wealth and temporal power while persecuting the gospel's defenders. "The pope and his fake cardinals and bishops. . . . not only teach against Christ, but they also cruelly persecute and murder those who profess true doctrine."[3] "The bishops either force our priests to forsake and condemn the sort of doctrine we have confessed, or else, in their unheard of cruelty, they kill the unfortunate and innocent men.

This keeps our priests from acknowledging such bishops."[4] The bishops "do not preach the Gospel or concern themselves with saving men's souls. All they try to do with everything they say and do is to establish and maintain their sovereignty over men."[5] "For my ungracious lords, the pope and the bishops, are supposed to be bishops and preach God's Word. This they leave undone, and have become temporal princes who govern with laws which concern only life and property."[6] The Lutherans saw the bishops as "raging against our churches."[7]

Thus a state of emergency existed in which the ministry of oversight somehow would have to be carried out by others, including princes. Yet the crisis was not met with an alternative ecclesiology or doctrine of ministry. Reforms instead focused on basic pastoral responsibilities around which a flexible ministry of oversight could be adapted or improvised to meet emergency requirements.

3. As the reformers were willing to "keep the ecclesiastical and canonical polity,"[8] they did not demand that bishops relinquish their status. "Our churches do not ask that the bishops should restore peace and unity at the expense of their honor and dignity . . . but they ask only that the bishops relax certain unreasonable burdens which did not exist in the church in former times and which were introduced contrary to the custom of the universal Church."[9] "It is not our intention to find ways of reducing the bishops' power, but we desire and pray that they may not coerce our consciences to sin."[10]

Thus Luther, too, could grant bishops honor, power, and wealth, so long as the bishops permitted the preaching of the gospel. "Thus I shall honor the pope and love his position, provided that he leaves my conscience free and does not require me to offend against God. . . . We would be happy to pay our respects to Behemoth and his scales, that is the pope and the bishops, with all the station and position they have, if they let us keep Christ."[11]

> We wish to let you [bishops] remain what you are and teach (as we have done in the past) that you should be allowed to be princes and lords, for the sake of peace, and that your properties should be left alone. . . . Thus you see after all that in us you have not foes, but great friends, yes even protectors. For

what harm does it do us, if you are lords and princes? If you do not want to do what is right for yourself, and your estate and office, well, then it is not we, but you who will give account for that. Only keep the peace and do not persecute us! We do not ask for more, and have never asked for anything else, than that the gospel be free.[12]

In 1530 Luther even proposed that, if the bishops were not interested in exercising spiritual authority, they could retain their temporal power and turn over spiritual responsibilities to those better qualified. "We offer this: we will perform the duties of your office; we will support ourselves without cost to you; we will help you remain as you are; and we will counsel that you have authority and are to see to it that things go right. What more can we do?"[13]

Instances existed in which sitting bishops not swayed to the Reformation appeared to have tolerated the Lutherans and even, possibly, to have provided certain kinds of oversight, as in Silesia and perhaps in part of Hungary (now Slovakia).[14] On the other hand, though there were various moves in this direction (as in Cologne), in the end no bishop of the Empire together with his see was won for the Reformation.

4. To meet the needs of the church in the emergency, the reformers claimed the right of oversight, including the right to ordain. "If the bishops were true bishops, they might be permitted (for the sake of love and unity; but not of necessity) to ordain and confirm us and our preachers. But what if the bishops proved not to be "true"? "Yet, the church must not be deprived of ministers on their account. Accordingly, as we are taught by the examples of the ancient churches and Fathers, we shall and ought ourselves ordain suitable persons to this office. . . . St. Jerome, too, wrote concerning the church in Alexandria that it was originally governed without bishops by priests and preachers in common."[15]

Melanchthon stated the matter in sharper and more precise terms. When the bishops are heretics or refuse ordination, then "the churches are by divine right compelled to ordain pastors and ministers for themselves."[16] By divine right the church *must* do whatever is necessary to see that the gospel is protected and handed on and that a functioning ministry in orderly succession is maintained.

A recourse to presbyteral ordination, then, was clearly a reaction to a crisis, not justification for an alternative ministerial structure; and its implementation was conditional. *"When the regular bishops become enemies of the Gospel and are unwilling to administer ordination,* the churches retain the right to ordain for themselves. For wherever the church exists, the right to administer the Gospel exists. Wherefore it is necessary for the church to retain the right of calling, electing, and ordaining ministers."[17] "So, in an emergency even a layman absolves and becomes the minister and pastor of another."[18]

The reformers, moreover, based presbyteral ordination on the identity of bishop and presbyter (see §7 below). "Jerome teaches clearly that in the apostolic letters all who preside over the churches are both bishops and presbyters."[19] The only distinction between presbyter and bishop is the right to ordain. Yet since the bishops have abused this power, "it is right to restore this jurisdiction to godly pastors and see to it that it is used properly for the reformation of morals and the glory of God."[20]

The intention was not to replace or circumvent the episcopal structure, but to reform it by temporarily co-opting it. The aim was not to do away with bishops, but to recall them to their evangelical foundation; not to exalt the presbyterate structurally, but to ennoble the episcopate spiritually. The right of presbyteral ordination, then, is *de iure divino* because it is a *status confessionis* and demanded by the circumstances, not because it is a permanent institution of the church. The practice of presbyteral ordination was regularized in many Lutheran territories. This was due more to the ongoing nature of the split in the Western church—and the long-term accommodations to it that had to be implemented—than it was due to a theology of ministry that set out deliberately to focus on the presbyterate.

5. The office of bishop is an office of the word. "This is the chief responsibility and duty of the bishop: the ministry of the Word."[21] "He is certainly a bishop who takes the lead in the preaching of the Word."[22] "The chief thing in a bishop is that he set forth the Word correctly, because teaching is his principal work, and is to be devoted above all to the conservation of doctrine."[23] "The bishops are servants of Christ. It is their duty to tend His sheep and give them pasture. Therefore to give pasture

is nothing else than to preach the Gospel, by which souls are fed and made fat and fruitful, and that the sheep are nourished with the Gospel and God's Word. This alone is the office of a bishop."[24]

If a bishop were unwilling or unable to preach the word, then "a bishop should create learned men (if he himself is not gifted) who will preach the gospel clearly and purely in his stead all over his diocese." Here, too, precedent had been established. "Thus we read that St. Valerius, bishop of Hippo, had St. Augustine preach for him before [Valerius] became bishop and protected [Augustine]. Likewise, the custom in many Greek lands was to have priests preach for their bishops in their presence."[25]

6. Luther defined a bishop as a watchman, visitor, inspector, and supervisor as a practical application of his general assertion that the bishop's office is an office of the word. The bishop, above all, must tend to the gospel among his people, Luther maintained. "To be an *episcopus*, or bishop, means to be careful, to be alert, to watch diligently, so that the devil does not take us by surprise."[26] "Bishop means 'watchman,' 'visitor'. . . . He looks around to see what is being taught and how people live. He watches with open eyes that no false doctrine breaks in or that there be no person who does not listen, who holds his teaching in contempt."[27] Thus the image of the watchman also clearly emphasizes pastoral *jurisdiction*.

As the Reformation took hold, canonical bishops were replaced by Lutheran "superintendents." Normally this office was held by one of the leading pastors in a city, and it was thus an embodiment of Luther's linking the offices of presbyter and bishop.[28] As a Latin translation of *episcopus*, the superintendent was meant to retain something of the episcopal tradition and to endorse it, while at the same time distinguishing evangelical from Catholic communities. General oversight by civil authorities, in addition to or in conjunction with the superintendent—a consequence of Luther's endorsement and encouragement of princely *Notbischöfe*—tended to co-opt the ministry of oversight.[29] Yet even as this trend became institutionalized, what was implemented was essentially a personal, rather than synodical or presbyteral, form of oversight (though consistories often were employed, too, as in Wittenberg).

7. An archbishop, a bishop, and a presbyter exercise the same basic ministry of word and sacrament, for there is a single ministry of the word. Bishop and presbyter are thus the same. This assertion complemented Luther's early insistence (in his controversy with the papacy) that all bishops are equal.[30] Luther appealed primarily to the Pastoral Epistles, Jerome's *Titus* commentary, and Jerome's letter 146 to Evangelus.[31] St. Paul, Luther said, clearly considered elders or presbyters to be the same as bishops. In the early church there were several bishops in one city, rather than a single absentee bishop of several cities.[32] "Here [in Titus 1:5-7], I think, no one can deny that bishop and elder are the same. . . . He should provide the church with preaching and sacraments," Luther wrote.[33]

Luther's model was that of an individual congregation and its bishop/presbyter, whose ministry was focused on word and sacrament, the care of souls and discipline. With this stress on the ideal bishop/presbyter as the sole or chief pastor of a city, Luther was appealing to the ancient framework of the bishop in his see/parish.

Luther was not bothered about the structure of ministry or the proper designation of ministers, but rather wanted to reconstitute the ministry's foundation on the basis of the description of the "bishop" as found in the Pastoral Epistles. His accent was always on the spiritual basis of ministry as it is exercised concretely within a specific community, a stress that does not preclude a concern for oversight beyond the local level, though for him such matters were secondary and derivative.

Luther's discussion of bishops, then, normally included a listing of basic functions. Clearly, bishops and priests perform the same basic duties; their common tasks are basically oriented to one ministry of word and sacrament and the pastoral needs of the church. *That* is why there is a single ministerial office.

> Therefore in Paul bishop is the same as elder . . . He is the steward to whom the Lord has entrusted everything. . . . He has been appointed a minister of the Word for this, that he should distribute these things to his family, to his brethren, that is, he should diligently preach the Gospel and administer the sacraments, instruct the ignorant, exhort the instructed, rebuke those who misbehave, moderating and tempering them by the Word and ministering to them with prayer and the sacraments.[34]

"Every minister or spiritual regent should be a bishop, that is, an over-seer or watchman, so that in his town and among his people, the gospel and faith are built up and win out over foe, devil, and heresy."[35]

8. There was also medieval precedent for the identification of presbyter and bishop, the fullness of ministry residing with the presbyterate (as the class of ministers most responsible for the eucharistic sacrifice). Consequently, a principal strain of ecclesiology viewed the episcopate not so much as a separate order, but as a specific dignity and function (for example, Peter Lombard said there were two sacred orders, the diaconate and the presbyterate), and episcopal ordination was not considered a sacrament, but rather a sacramental.

While medieval ecclesiologies were often concerned about questions of powers and orders, Luther concentrated on the New Testament and early church views of ministry, which he saw as rooted in preaching and the sacraments. His ecclesiology was always more descriptive than speculative, more reductive than expansive. From the point of departure in word and sacrament, and with their concentration on the biblical bishop/presbyter as the basis of a more general return to the sources, the Wittenberg reformers proposed a recovery of the ancient and original meaning of episcopacy, which the medieval church also mostly—but not entirely—affirmed.[36]

9. If the congregation is the locus of ministry—because there the proclamation of the gospel, administration of the sacraments, prayer, care of souls, and ecclesiastical discipline take place in concrete terms—then, as Georg Kretchmar maintains, Luther's conception approached what in Orthodox terms is known as "eucharistic ecclesiology."[37] Luther's conception of ministry, as well as all practical and structural implications deriving from it, were grounded in the liturgy. Thus the image of the bishop/presbyter preaching and presiding at the eucharist (as the liturgical president of a local city congregation) could be considered the foundation of Luther's ecclesiology. For his theology of ministry, Luther thus *started* with the biblical and early church model of the "bishop."

Kretchmar claims that the single office of ministry that Luther had in mind is the *episcopal* office in which presbyters also are included.[38]

This is confirmed, Kretschmar maintains, in Luther's *Formula missae* of 1523, where the president is called "bishop," a work Luther dedicated to the pastor of the congregation in Zwickau, Nikolaus Hausmann. In Luther's letters he often addressed city pastors as bishops.

The Wittenberg ordination rite followed the form of episcopal ordination. The ordinands were addressed as future bishops; the ministers of ordination were to be the pastors of neighboring cities, that is, neighboring bishops, as prescribed by canon 4 of the Council of Nicaea, to which the ordination rite explicit refers. Presbyters presiding at ordinations did so as holders of the one, full, episcopal office. Those ordained entered into an episcopal line of succession, which was primarily a succession in teaching and the orderly transmission of the gospel.[39] The ordinands are called to this (episcopal) ministry, "so that many others may be sanctified and reconciled to the Lord through your word and work."[40] Thus did the Lutherans attempt to retain the orderly transmission of the ministerial office through the presbyterate, which originally included bishops (or at least was not originally distinguishable from them). A derivation of the ministry by delegation from the common priesthood of all believers was an idea foreign to the Lutheran tradition.[41]

10. Luther did not completely ignore institutional questions. He stressed that episcopal structure, including succession in office, is set up by God indirectly, through human authority.

> God calls in two ways, either by means or without means. Today He calls all of us into the ministry of the Word by a mediated call, that is, one that comes through means, namely, through man. But the apostles were called immediately by Christ Himself, as the prophets of the Old Testament had been called by God Himself. Afterwards the apostles called their disciples, as Paul called Timothy, Titus, etc. These men called bishops, as in Titus 1:5ff.; and the bishops called their successors down to our own time, and so on until the end of the world. This is a mediated calling, since it is done by man. Nevertheless, it is divine.[42]

While this comment was meant to apply generally to all ministers of the word (not just to bishops) as apostolically based and divinely ordered, a question still might arise about its application to episcopal ministry in terms of the "traditional polity" that the Lutherans said they desired to maintain. For example, is there an ambiguity here that can be helpful in a discussion of the Lutheran insistence that bishops are instituted (merely) by human authority? Admittedly stretching Luther's point, can it be said that episcopacy, too, is a mediated calling "done by man," which is also somehow divine? Even if this question remains open, still it would seem imperative to request some kind of positive response from Lutherans to questions of order, particularly to the office of bishop.

11. Luther did recognize the necessity of episcopal oversight beyond the local parish. In 1523 he even advised the Bohemians how to institute it for themselves. As cities begin to elect their own bishops, Luther said, "then these bishops may wish to come together and elect one or more from their number to be their superiors, who would serve them and hold visitations among them."[43] Such bishops were formed from the bottom up. "According to St. Paul, and also St. Jerome, a bishop and a priest are one and the same thing. But of bishops as they are now the Scripture knows nothing. Bishops have been appointed by ordinance of the Christian church, so that one of them may have authority over several priests."[44] Extra-parish episcopal jurisdiction is a human construction, motivated at least in part by Luther's rejection of the claims of the extreme papalists. Yet it is a necessary task, which by means of the essential process of visitation serves the gospel.

There is no implicit contradiction, therefore, between the identity of pastor and bishop and the need for extra-parochial oversight. Rather, the authority of the bishop rests wholly on the *Predigtamt*. The bishops of the early church are models in this respect; and Luther frequently lifted them up as examples. It was due to their personal integrity and faithfulness to the gospel in the context of their diligent, watchman-like visitation that the church's man-made structure relating to the office of bishop proved to be beneficial. Luther reflected on this in his preface to the *Articles of Visitation* drawn up by Melanchthon in 1528 for Electoral Saxony.

Formerly, in the days of the ancient Fathers, the holy bishops diligently followed these examples [of visitations recorded in Scripture] and even yet much of this is found in the papal laws. For it was in this kind of activity that the bishops and arch-bishops had much of their origin—each one was obligated to a greater or lesser extent to visit and examine. For, actually, bish-op means supervisor or visitor, and archbishop a supervisor or visitor of bishops, to see to it that each parish pastor visits and watches over and supervises his people in regard to teaching and life. And the archbishop was to visit, watch over, and supervise the bishops as to their teaching.[45]

This ordering Luther described as "useful and necessary."[46]

Luther regarded the patriarchs as prototypical bishops. Noah, Abraham, Jacob, and Joseph were all bishops.[47] Abraham was a bishop because "he instructs his church concerning the will of God, admonishes them to lead a holy life, strengthens them in their faith, fortifies their hope of future blessing, and prays with them."[48] Even Abimelech, the king before whom Abraham posed as Sarah's brother, could be considered a bishop in Luther's eyes because he taught the word at his court (Gn 20:8).[49]

12. There were opportunities to test the theory, for evangelical bishops did function for a time. Experiments were carried out in Schleswig-Holstein (1542-1547) and Kammin in Pomerania (1545-1556). Perhaps the most celebrated case was in Naumburg-Zeitz in 1542, when Luther himself ordained Nikolaus von Amsdorf in the cathedral in Naumburg. Luther was assisted by the local abbot and three evangelical superin-tendents. The rite used—basically the Wittenberg ordination rite for pastors with a few variations—included the imposition of hands and an enthronement. The effort eventually failed due to Amsdorf's difficulties in office. The new bishop, who attempted to operate independently of the civil authorities, found himself severely hampered by a lack of coop-eration, interference on the part of the government, and the strength of the Catholic opposition.[50]

Merseburg was another notable example of an evangelical episco-pate where temporal domination went even further. When Bishop

Sigismund died in 1544, Prince George III of Anhalt became the coad-jutor under Duke Maurice's brother August, who was appointed to serve as secular administrator of the diocese. George hoped that Matthias von Jagow, the bishop of Brandenburg who had implemented the Reformation in his diocese in 1539-1540, would install him. Matthias, however, died before the consecration could take place. In 1545 Luther consecrated Prince George, who still could not use the title "bishop." George continued to serve under the duke August, who carried out the princely duties of the bishop and retained the title. Though George dili-gently tried to carry out the duties of bishop, the scope of his work was limited because the purse strings remained in the hands of the duke. Thus did the separation of the temporal and spiritual duties of the bish-op, as CA 28 had proposed, lead ironically to secular domination of the episcopal office. That was, however, the price the church in Germany paid to achieve theological purity on the one hand, and political and ecclesiastical unity on the other. At any rate, imperial victory in the war of Schmalkalden put an end to all such experiments.[51]

Wendebourg draws important conclusions about these develop-ments. As the Wittenberg reformers attempted energetically to retain the episcopal structure in its traditional form and did not shy away from making compromises in order to achieve it, they never held the *existing episcopate* to have been commanded by God (*de iure divino*). Nor did the concept of apostolic succession in the sense of a succession in the office of the diocesan bishop have any binding force for them, "as it hardly played any role in the medieval period."[52] Thus one may conclude from Wendebourg that the Lutherans never thought they had anything to "recover" from those who had retained "the traditional polity." The reformers saw through the eagerness of the princes to deprive the bish-ops of their political power, and they "believed that in the reformed part of Christendom the government of the Church should be exercised as soon as possible by non-political church authorities, and for the Wittenberg reformers that meant first and foremost by bishops."[53]

13. The *Confessions* make a point of distinguishing between divine and human right. In CA 28, a distinction is made between the (prince) bish-ops' temporal authority, as well as some kinds of jurisdictional authority

(e.g., matrimonial cases and tithes), which they possess by human authority; and the office of forgiving sins, judging doctrine, and excluding the ungodly, which is done "not by human power but by God's Word alone."[54]

Melanchthon maintained that the polity of the church as well as the various ranks of ecclesiastical hierarchy were created by human authority.[55] With respect to the question of rank, he made the usual appeal to Jerome. "Jerome teaches clearly that . . . all who preside over the churches are both bishops and presbyters. . . . For apart from ordination, what does a bishop do that a presbyter does not do?"[56] Such an appeal, however, does not mitigate a willingness to recognize and accept the office of bishop in its long-established form, in which the bishop's office is deemed superior to that of the parish pastor.[57]

That which was created by human authority is not rejected because it is distinguished from what belongs to (episcopal) ministry *iure divino*. Rather, historical precedent is established for the Lutheran alteration of existing structures should that become necessary. The result, however, is a positive proposal for re-establishing the spiritual basis of episcopal ministry. Thus, CA 28's sharp criticism of contemporary German prince-bishops is not a claim that the episcopate must be merged with the presbyterate. When bishops and presbyters are identified with the appeal to Paul and Jerome, several things are intended: the current status and power of bishops is identified as an aberration and a departure from the original pastoral intent of the office; an historical/theological justification is made for Lutheran contingency measures; and the authentic ministry of the episcopal office is recovered.

With respect to these intentions, Melanchthon enumerated the "power the Gospel grants to bishops." *Within* this divinely ordained authority, the powers of order and jurisdiction (*potestas ordinis, potestas jurisdictionis*) are to be distinguished. The power of order relates to the ministry of word and sacraments, the power of jurisdiction to excommunication and discipline.[58] Harding Meyer claims that this latter function refers specifically to *episcopal* jurisdiction. The bishop, he says, has a special doctrinal and leadership role within the church that is clearly *iure divino*. However, it is a leadership role, which, if need be, clearly *may* stand apart from humanly conceived structures (including ministerial rank as distinguished from the task of oversight); which *should be*, but does not have to be, distinguished from outward dignity, wealth, and pomp; and which *must be* separated from all coercive power, both temporal and spiritual.[59]

NOTES

1   With CA 28.20-22. See the Latin text in *Bekenntnisschriften der evangelisch-lutherischen Kirche* (Vandenhoeck and Ruprecht [Goettingen], 1930, reprinted 1992), 123-124.

2   *Resolutio Lutherana super propositione* XIII *de potestate papae:* "nec Papa est Episcopis, nec Episcopus est superior presbyteris iure divino," WA 2.240; *To the Christian Nobility of the German Nation:* "According to St. Paul, and also St. Jerome, a bishop and a priest are the same thing," LW 44.175. See also Harding Meyer, "Das Bischofsamt nach CA 28," in *Der Augsburger Reichstag 1530 und die Einheit der Kirche,* ed. E. Iserloh, Reformationsgeschichtliche Studien und Texte, 118 (Münster, 1980): 495.

3   LW 24.122 (WA 45.572, 6-7,14-15); cf. LW 1.184 (WA 42.31-36).

4   Apol. 14.2.

5   LW 26.45 (WA 40/1.102, 17-18).

6   LW 45.109 (WA 11.205, 7-9); cf. LW 36.157 (WA 8.501, 24–502, 22) and CA 28.1; also 28.10.

7   Apol. 14.5.

8   Apol. 14.5.

9   CA 28.71.

10   CA 28.77.

11   LW 26.97 (WA 40/1.177,22-23–178,17-19).

12   LW 34.50 (WA 30/2.341,25-27,29-34).

13   LW 34.51 (WA 30/2.343,17-20).

14   See Wendebourg, "The Reformation," 72, n. 58; Georg Kretchmar, "Die Wiederentdeckung des Konzeptes der 'Apostolischen Sukzession' im Umkreis der Reformation," in *Kirche in der Schule Luthers,* Festschrift for D. J. Heubach, ed. B. Hägglund and G. Müller (Erlangen, 1995), 245.

15   Smalcald Articles, Part 3, Art. 10-13; cf. FC SD 10.19.

16   *Treatise on the Power and Primacy of the Pope* (TPPP), 72.

17   Ibid., 66-67, my emphasis.

18   Ibid., 67, my emphasis.

19   Ibid., 62.

20   Ibid., 76.

21   LW 28.286 (WA 26.52, 30-31).

22 LW 40.41 (WA 12.194, 26-27).

23 LW 29.59 (WA 25.47, 19-21).

24 LW 30.134 (WA 12.388, 24-28). See also P. Brunner, "Vom Amt des Bischofs," in *Pro Ecclesia: Gesammelte Aufsätze zur dogmatischen Theologie* 2 (Berlin and Hamburg: Lutherisches Verlaghaus, 1962), 278.

25 LW 39.295 (WA 10/2.154, 14-16, 18-20).

26 LW 41.85 (WA 50.574, 20-22).

27 LW 28.283 (WA 26.50, 20-22); also LW 39.154-155 (WA 7.630, 34–631,10). Luther and Trent are similarly concerned about regaining and reconstituting the basic *pastoral* role of bishops.

28 See M. Brecht, "Ein Schlusswort Luthers," in *Martin Luther und das Bischofsamt*, ed. M. Brecht, 143: "In der Superattendentenamptes verkörpert sich etwas von Luthers Konzeption der Verbindung von Pfarramt und Bischofsamt."

29 See Axel Freiherr von Campenhausen, "The Episcopal Office of Oversight in the German Churches, its Public Status and its Involvement in Church Decisions in History and in the Present," in *Visible Unity and the Ministry of Oversight*, 173. "With the word *Superintendent*, the Reformers did not only take over a Latin translation of the Greek *episcopus*; they also thereby held fast to their episcopal office. . . . But even under the name *Superintendent* the protestant office of bishop could not develop freely." One should note as well that after 1555 many territorial princes, who had functioned as emergency bishops, took the title *summus episcopus*.

30 LW 39.278 (WA 10/2.140, 14-15): St. Paul said "that every town should have a bish-op and they must all be equals." See also LW 39.74 (WA 6.300, 25-27). This is not, however, to deny that one of the bishops may be superior over the others; but a distinction must be maintained between divine and human ordering. "Therefore, since according to divine order all bishops are equal and occupy the place of the apostles, I can certainly confess that according to human order one is above the other in the external church."

31 Especially Titus 1:5-7 and 1 Timothy 3:1-4; also 1 Peter 5:1-4 and Acts 20:17, 28. In 1538 Luther published Jerome's letter with his own foreword. (WA 50.339-343). See Martin Brecht, "Die exegetische Begründung des Bishofsamtes" and Heinz-Meinolf Stamm, "Luthers Berufung auf die Vorstellungen des Hieronymus vom Bischofsamt," in *Martin Luther und das Bischofsamt*, ed. M. Brecht (Stuttgart: 1990), 10-17.

32 LW 36.155, 158 (WA 8.500, 21-24; 502, 36-39); LW 30.135-136 (WA 12.388, 24-28; 390, 2-3); LW 29.16-17 (WA 25.16, 25-28).

33 LW 39.277 (WA 10/2.139, 4-5, 11).

34 LW 29.22-23 (WA 25.21, 5, 8, 11-14). In this regard, see also M. Brecht, "Ein Schlusswort Luthers," in *Martin Luther und das Bischofsamt*, ed. M. Brecht, 142-143: "Afgrund seiner Exegese beharrt Luther auf der Verbindung von Bischofsamt und Pfarramt mit praktischer Amtsausübung in Predigt, Gottesdienst, Seelsorge und Beaufsichtigung der Gemeinde. Die kircheleitenden Aufgaben sind aus diesem einen Amt abgeleitet. Eine besondere Dignität über das Pfarramt hinaus gibt est nicht. Jedes Amt

ist immer nur Dienst. In der heutigen ökumenischen Diskussion über das Bischofsamt sollte diese Einheit der lutherischen Reformation nicht aufgegeben werden."

35 LW 39.155 (WA 7.631, 1-4).

36 On medieval precedents and on the Lutheran identification of bishop and presbyter, see Wendebourg, 51-52, 67-68; G. Kretchmar, 233-234, 238; A. C. Piepkorn, "The Sacred Ministry and Holy Ordination in the Symbolical Books of the Lutheran Church," Excursus 1, "The Primitive and Medieval Church on the Identity of Bishops and Presbyters," in *The Church: Selected Writings of Arthur Carl Piepkorn*, ed. M. Plekon and W. Weicher, ALPB Books (Delhi, New York: 1993), 65-68; and "A Lutheran View of the Validity of Lutheran Orders," in L\RC-4, 216-226. See also Ludwig Ott, *Das Weihesakrament, Handbuch der Dogmengeschichte* 4, fasc. 5, ed. M. Schmaus, A. Grillmeier, L. Scheffczyk (Freiburg: 1969), 50; also 80-81 (for a Lutheran view, see Kretchmar, 277-278).

37 Kretchmar, 240.

38 Kretchmar, 242. "Er kennt letzlich nur ein einziges Amt, das bischöfliche, in das auch die Pfarrer eingeschlossen sind" [original syntax slightly altered]. Cf. 258.

39 See Wendebourg, 52-53.

40 LW 53.124, n. 4 (WA 38.424-425).

41 See W. Pannenberg, *Systematic Theology* 3 (Grand Rapids, MI: Eerdmans, 1998) 402: "The Lutheran Reformation never even referred to a derivation of church ministry from the priesthood of all believers. The church's ordained ministry is a continuation of the leadership function of the apostles."

42 LW 26.17 (WA 40/1.59, 16-23). See also LW 17.211 (WA 31/2.425, 18-20); cf. LW 24.66 (WA 45.521, 4-9) and LW 27.166 (WA 2.454, 3-8).

43 LW 40.41 (WA 12.194, 14-17).

44 LW 44.175 (WA 6.440, 26-29). In this regard, see also the Wittenberg Reformation of 1545, an opinion (*Ratschlag*) of the Wittenberg theologians, concerning in part the role of a reformed episcopacy. The relevant section reads: "To keep order in the church, one must have bishops, a degree higher than priests and they must have a designated authority; one must have a number of them to ordain, to instruct ordinands, to make visitations, to serve on tribunals, to advise, to write, to represent, and to staff synods and councils, just as Athanasius, Basil, Ambrose, and Augustine had to do all these things in order to preserve correct doctrine in their own and other churches and defend them against heretics. If the existing form of episcopacy were torn apart, barbarism and desolation without end would result, for temporal power and princes are burdened with other matters, and only a few respect the church or reflect on her teaching." Quotation and translation in E. Gritsch, "Episcopacy: The Legacy of the Lutheran Confessions," in *Concordat of Agreement: Supporting Essays*, ed. D. Martensen (Minneapolis and Cincinnati: 1995), 109.

45 LW 40.269-270 (WA 26.196, 1-9).

46 LW 40.270 (WA 26.196, 33).

47 For Noah, see LW 2.165 (WA 378, 5). For Abraham, see LW 2.334 (42.501, 6-9).
Cf. LW 3.314 (WA 43.100, 19) and 346 (WA 43.123, 37) where Abraham is called
the "supreme bishop" (*summus episcopus*). See also LW 4.89 (WA 43.199, 9-12):
"Under [Abimelech] the house of Abraham, in which the church was, had peace
and quiet; and the Word was spread among the heathen by Pope or Bishop Abraham,
who, wherever he went, took with him the Word, the worship, the religion, and
everything." For Joseph, see LW 7.152 (WA 44.411, 32): Joseph was the "bishop of
all Egypt," who is appointed by Pharaoh (LW 7.167-168; WA 44.423, 30-31).

48 LW 2.286 (WA 42.466, 36-39): "*ut exercet Pontificale suum officium.*"

49 LW 3.344 (WA 43.122, 20-22); cf. LW 3.340 (WA 43.119, 20-22).

50 M. Brecht, *Martin Luther: The Preservation of the Church 1532-1546* (Minneapolis:
Augsburg, 1993), 300-308.

51 Wendebourg, 58-60; cf. Kretchmar, 272.

52 Wendebourg, 60, and Kretchmar, 251-252. Such a theory of apostolic succession was
only put on the table in the theological discussions at Worms and Regensburg
through Gropper on the basis of a text from Irenaeus that had appeared in print only
with Erasmus's 1526 edition of Irenaeus's works.

53 Wendebourg, 61; and 62: the reformers sought to achieve "a genuine ecclesiastical
episcopate in the reformed part of Christendom."

54 CA 28.19, 21-23, 29; cf. TPPP, 60, 63.

55 Apol. 14.1.

56 TPPP, 62.

57 H. Meyer, 489-490. Meyer refers to CA 28.69ff.; Smalkald Articles III, 10; FC SD 10,
19; Apol. 14.1. Cf. Erwin Iserloh, "Kirche, Kirchengemeinschaft und Kircheneinheit
nach der Confessio Augustana," in *Evangelium—Sakramente—Amt und die Einheit
der Kirche* (Frieburg im Breisgau and Göttingen, 1982), 21, who claims that
Melanchthon's correspondence reveals that bishops not only are to be distinguished
from pastors, but they also are ranked over pastors *iure divino.*

58 Apol. 28, 12-14.

59 On the last point, this was easier to put into words than into practice. On the bishop's divinely ordained jurisdictional authority, see H. Meyer, 493-494, who enumer-
ates two important limitations: (1) Where the bishops introduce or teach something
that is contrary to the gospel, God expressly commands disobedience (CA 28.23-28).
Thus the command of obedience in Hebrews 13:17 ("Obey your leaders and submit
to them") applies to the gospel itself, not merely the rule of the bishops (Apol.
28.20); (2) Obedience is given by individual congregations freely and cannot be
coerced (CA 28.55-56, 76; cf. Luther, WA 30/2.421). On the other hand, as Iserloh
points out in his chapter (p. 24), it is the responsibility of the bishops *iure divino* to
judge, and condemn if necessary, doctrine taught by pastors (CA 28.21). In this case,
obedience is *required* (CA 28.22).

Chapter 3

❈

THE TRIDENTINE DOCTRINE ON SACERDOTIUM

BY GEORGE H. TAVARD

Seen in their entirety, the decrees of the Council of Trent are shaped like a response to, and an appropriation of, the Reformers' identification of the church as the community in which the gospel is preached in its purity and the sacraments administered according to the gospel (CA, art. VII). They also include corrections of what the bishops considered to be the errors of the Reformers, especially in regard to the traditional sacramental doctrine that had been questioned early in the Reformation, with Martin Luther's *The Babylonian Captivity of the Church* (1520). The decrees of 1546 and 1547 dealt primarily with matters relating to the gospel: endorsement of the Nicene-Constantinopolitan creed (session III); reception of the Scriptures and apostolic traditions (session IV); a decree on *lectio* (of Scripture) and preaching (session V); and a decree on justification (session VI). The decree on original sin (session V) is hardly an exception, for its purpose was to show the necessity of justification as pure grace.

Beginning with session VII (1547), the Council dealt with the sacraments, first in general with canons on baptism and confirmation, then with a focus on the eucharist (session XIII, 1551), on penance and "extreme unction" (two decrees, session XIV, 1551), on communion under both kinds (session XXI, 1562), the sacrifice of the Mass (session XXII, 1562), the sacrament of Orders (session XXIII, 1563), and matrimony (session XXIV, 1563). The last session (XXV, 1563) added a decree on Purgatory and shorter treatments of indulgences, fasts and abstinence, and the index of books.

Along with doctrinal decrees, the Council issued a number of reform decrees, in which it placed particular emphasis on preaching the gospel and on the ties between ordination and preaching. From the beginning, the Council foresaw the post-conciliar publication of a catechism that would assist ordinary priests in preaching the gospel properly.

In the consideration of sacraments, special attention was given to the eucharist (sessions XIII, XV, XXII). What was said in these decrees was presupposed by the decree on the sacrament of Orders (session XXIII).

I. The Sacrament of Orders

Priesthood (*sacerdotium*) was the topic of session XXIII of the Council of Trent. This session took place when the Council under Pope Pius IV (pope from December 1559 to December 1565) transferred to Bologna because of the plague around Trent. The session began on September 18, 1562, the doctrinal debate ended on January 31, 1563. The session produced both a doctrinal decree and a series of eighteen pastoral decrees concerning reform of the clergy, notably in regard to priests who had no care of souls and to the bishops' obligation to reside in their dioceses. The doctrinal decree was not promulgated immediately, but rather published together with the just-finished *decreta super reformatione* on July 15, 1563. Although the doctrinal decree is one of the shortest of the Council, the preparation and discussion were the second longest, coming after the debate over justification at session VI.

At first sight, the length of the debate looks surprising, since the topic had been examined at length twice before: at the sixth session under Pope Paul III (pope from October 1534 to November 1549) in April-May 1547, and at the fifteenth session under Pope Julius III (pope from February 1550 to March 1555) in December 1551 and January 1552. The first two discussions produced no decree. They were nevertheless most influential on the third, and the formulation of the anathemas was largely taken from them. The length of the debate was due to the absence of a common theology of the priesthood (*sacerdotium*) among theologians and bishops. Agreement on what could have been a full treatise on Orders and ordination, especially as it could bear on the nature of the episcopate, was impossible. The papal legates who presided over the Council realized this early, and they steered the discussion away from attempting such a project.

The following is a brief survey of the treatment of the topic in sessions VI and XV followed by a discussion of session XXIII.[1]

II. The Sixth Session

The sixth session was chiefly devoted to the doctrine of justification, the decree *De justificatione Impii* being adopted on January 13, 1547. After this the Council discussed sacraments and on March 3, 1547, adopted a decree in four parts: a short introduction on the sacraments, thirteen canons on sacraments in general, fourteen on baptism, and three on confirmation. However, the plague broke out in Trent on March 6, and the session reconvened in Bologna, in papal territory. The move was protested by fourteen bishops, who were mainly Spanish, and the emperor, who was involved in the Schmalkald war and feared that the relocation of the Council outside the imperial lands would weaken his position.

The discussions in Bologna bore on Orders, matrimony, and extreme unction. The debate was introduced in April 1547 by Cardinal Girolamo Seripando, superior general of the Hermits of St. Augustine, and one of the papal legates, who became the chief guide of the discussions on *sacerdotium*. Seripando handed out a list of nine anathemas, most of which referred to quotations from the writings of Luther (*De Captivitate Babylonica, De Abroganda Missa*) and Philipp Melanchthon (*Apologia Confessionis Augustanae* III, 9, *Disputatio de Sacerdote et Sacrificiis*, nos. 3-5, *Loci Communes* on the number of sacraments). The main points rejected by these canons are as follows: (1) Orders is not a sacrament; (2) Orders is a sacrament in regard to preaching, not to offering; (3) Orders is the ministry of the word, and as such, is only a sacrament; (4) Orders is only a function (*officium*); (5) there is no visible sacerdotium in the New Testament; all Christians are priests, but they need to be vocati to exercise priestly functions; (6) a priesthood that would do something for others in order to appease God would contradict the justice of faith; (7) those who do not preach are not Christian priests; (8) priests do not receive the power (*potestatem*) of sacrificing for the quick and the dead; and (9) bishops are not *de iure divino* and deserve no honor.

Another set of five anathemas had been proposed by a theologian, Ambrosius Pelargius, at some time before March 24. Though this list was not debated, it is indicative of an abiding concern that loomed in the background of the discussions: (1) Orders is only a rite for the election of pastors; (2) Orders is only for preaching, not for offering; (3) The election and institution of pastors by the people is *de iure divino*; (4) All Christians are priests *ex aequo*; and (5) A priest can become a layman again.

The two sets of canons indicate that theologians and bishops were eager to refute the reduction of the priestly ministry to preaching, but they could not do this without insisting that preaching is an integral task of priests and bishops. Their other major concern was to maintain an essential distinction between priest and lay person.

The nine anathemas were revised and presented again by Seripando in the form of four articles. In this list, 1 is identical with (1) above; 2 combines (2) and (7); 3 includes (5) and adds that the function requires both a call by authority and the consent of the people; and 4 includes (9) and adds that bishops have no power to ordain and that an ordination they perform is null (*irritam*). The references for this are to Luther's *De Captivitate Babylonica* and to John Calvin's *Institutio Christianae Religionis*, chapter 19.[2]

These articles were examined by several groups of theologians from April 30 to May 7. Prominent among them were the Jesuits Diego Laynez and Alphonso Salmerón, who had been sent by Julius III as his personal theologians.[3] Although most of the theological opinions were quite hostile to these articles, the milder view of a conventual Franciscan, Joannes de Coregio,[4] is summed up as follows by secretary Massarolli:

> On the first article . . . , there is no sacrament in ordination, inasmuch as the high dignity (*gradus*) given by God in ordination is not a sacrament, but the sacrament is ordination itself . . . Another thought the opposite, asserting that whether it is called order or ordination it is a true sacrament. Again, the first part of the second article is not altogether (*simpliciter*) false, but it is true that the priest has the power to preach; that he has not also the power to offer [the sacrifice] is plainly false.[5]

Following the theologians, the general congregations concentrated on the eucharist. No further decree was adopted at this session, and the decree *de eucharistia* was passed in October 1551, at the thirteenth session.

III. The Fourteenth Session

Decrees on penance and on the unction of the sick, called "extreme unction" by the Council, were adopted at this session (1551), along with fifteen canons on penance and four on the unction. The last of these condemns the notion that the presbyters of the Epistle of James are not "priests ordained by bishops, but seniors in whatever community, and that therefore the minister of the unction is not a priest only."

IV. The Fifteenth Session

Although the fifteenth session (1552) closed without issuing a doctrinal decree, participants spent a great deal of time debating the Mass and the sacrament of Orders. In regard to doctrine, six canons were proposed, again by Seripando. Except for canons 2 and 5, which were new, the canons came in substance from the sixth session, when several of the previous anathemas were combined in canons 3 and 4. Thus the following propositions are condemned: (1) Orders is not a sacrament; (2) Orders is not one sacrament, and the inferior orders are not degrees toward the priesthood; (3) There is no hierarchy; all the baptized are *ex aequo* priests; they may exercise the priesthood only if called by the magistrates and with the consent of the people; priests can become laymen again; (4) There is no visible priesthood in the New Testament; priesthood is not the power to offer the sacrifice or to absolve from sins, but only the function of preaching; those who do not preach are not *sacerdotes*; (5) no unction is necessary in the rite of ordination; and (6) bishops do not exist *ex iure divino*; the ordinations they perform are null if the people do not consent to them.

These canons were discussed by the conciliar theologians from December 3 to December 19, 1551, and by the bishops in general congregations from January 2 to January 13, 1552. From January 14 to 17, a small task force drafted a doctrinal decree followed by canons. On January 21, this draft was presented to all the bishops. It had three chapters and eight anathemas: chapter one was on the necessity and institution of the sacrament of Orders; chapter two was on the visible and external *sacerdotium* of the church; and chapter three was on the hierarchy and the difference between bishop and priest.

The canons condemned the following ideas: (1) Orders is not a true sacrament; (2) it is not one sacrament; (3) there is no hierarchy;

(4) ordination is not valid without the consent of the people; (5) there is no visible, external priesthood in the New Testament; (6) there must be no unction in the rite of ordination; (7) the Holy Spirit is not conferred in ordination; and (8) bishops are not *iure divino*.

No immediate vote was taken on the decree or the canons. Meanwhile, for political and theological reasons, the Council presidents decided to invite the Reformers again to attend the Council and be heard. As had been done already at the thirteenth session, on January 25, 1563, the Council voted to grant a safe-conduct for Protestants to come to Trent, and the session ended.

V. The Council's Documentation

The Council of Trent never condemned persons, but it did condemn opinions. Nevertheless, the council fathers and theologians had in mind several of the Reformers; the proposed anathemas were accompanied by references to writings, chiefly of Luther and Melanchthon, occasionally also of Martin Bucer and Calvin. Historians generally agree that this background information did not come directly from an extended study of the Reformers' works, but rather from extensive lists of assumedly authentic quotations from their writings. In 1525 the German theologian Johannes Cochlaeus had published a list of five hundred errors that he attributed to Luther: *Articuli CCCCC Martini Lutheri*, Cologne, 1525. Another list of more than six hundred errors, printed in 1530, was the work of Johannes Fabri. Also in 1530 Johannes Eck brought a list of 404 heresies to the Diet of Augsburg.[6] The teachings that were condemned in the anathemas were taken from such lists. No attempt was made, however, to verify the exactitude of the quotations or to understand their context.

VI. The Council's Pastoral Concern

Most of the Tridentine sessions carried out two tasks that were both distinct and closely related. The bishops intended to reformulate the traditional doctrines against the denials found in various lists of false teaching. They also were determined to reform the church, most notably the life and ministry of priests and bishops. They were especially eager to promote good preaching. Already in 1546 at the fifth session, after its decree on original sin, the Council had issued a reform decree *super lectione et praedicatione*. With seventeen articles, the decree was very elaborate. Among other points, the decree specified that an adequate stipend must be provided to "lectors in sacred Scripture" who would present the "exposition and interpretation" of the written word (art. 1). Such lectureships should be established in metropolitan and cathedral churches (art. 2). The decree also recommended lectures on grammar that would prepare "poor clerics and other scholars" eventually to pass on to *ipsa sacrae scripturae studia* (art. 3). The decree gave instruction on how to promote these studies in monasteries (art. 4), among regulars (art. 5), in parochial churches, and on how to restrain and discipline erroneous or scandalous preaching (art. 15).

In spite of their eagerness to give an effective response to the accusation of not preaching the gospel, theologians and bishops were not of one mind on some theoretical questions that were relevant to preaching. Many of the pastoral debates turned around whether ordination to the priesthood and the obligation to preach should be tied together. The bishops knew that ordained priests were too numerous to be all entrusted with the care of souls. Many never preached, most of these being, in any case, insufficiently trained for the pulpit. These were "sacrificing" priests in one sense of the expression, their only official task being to celebrate Mass, even with no attendance, for a particular intention and with an appropriate stipend—what Luther called *Winkelmesse*—and presumably the "sacrifices of masses" of Article XXXI in the *Thirty-Nine Articles*. Most bishops agreed that preaching the gospel was an episcopal and sacerdotal task, and admitted that it had often been neglected. Some, however, were persuaded that the old system was not essentially bad, and argued that many non-preaching priests were pious and edifying.

There was no common theology of the priesthood at the end of the Middle Ages and in the sixteenth century.[7] It was not unusual among canon lawyers to consider the tonsure, the minor orders, the subdiaconate, and the episcopate as parts of the sacrament of Orders, along with the diaconate and the priesthood. In 1509, however, Cardinal Thomas de Vio Cajetan, OP, taught that only the priesthood and the episcopate, but not the diaconate, are sacramental. Sylvester Prierias, OP, explained in his own *Summa*, before 1517, that the different orders are theologically distinguished from one another by their specific ties to the eucharist. Only the orders that are the closest to it, namely, the dia-conate and the priesthood, constitute the sacrament.

Thus variations were found even among Thomists. Given the active presence of other theologies there was a degree of what Cajetan called *incertitudo materiae* in regard to the sacrament of Orders. It is hardly surprising that the Reformers wished to clarify the matter, or that the Council could not easily produce a magisterial decree on the ordained ministry.

VII. The Twenty-First and Twenty-Second Sessions

In July 1562, session XXI adopted a decree on communion under both kinds. The decree specified that there is no *iure divino* obligation to receive communion with both bread and wine (ch. 1); that the church has the authority to adjust sacramental practice, as long as the substance of the sacrament is maintained (ch. 2); that the total Christ (*totum et integrum Christum*) is present under each species, and that children before the age of reason have no obligation to receive sacramental com-munion (ch. 4).

On September 17, 1562, session XXII adopted a decree on the sac-rifice of the Mass (nine essentially descriptive chapters). While it did not allow Mass to be said in the vernacular, the decree (ch. 8) encour-aged the celebrant to give frequent explanations during the Mass itself (*inter missarum celebrationem*). The bishops (*Decretum super petitione con-cessionis calicis*) chose to postpone to a later time a debate on two ques-tions relative to authorizing Communion under both species in the case of specific persons or nations.

Session XXIII followed immediately, a list of seven anathemas being distributed by Seripando on September 18, 1562. These anathemas were left over from the previous sessions, except for 6, which was new. The anathemas condemned the following notions:

- Orders is not a sacrament but only a rite.
- It is only a human invention.
- It is not one sacrament and the minor orders are not degrees to the priesthood.
- There is no hierarchy, and all Christians are *ex aequo sacerdotes*.

- There is no visible priesthood in the New Testament.
- The unction given in ordination is a pernicious practice.
- Bishops are not superior to priests.

This was practically identical with the previous list of eight canons, former canon 7 being omitted. Thirty-four theologians working in three shifts studied the list. They ended their discussion on October 2.

The general congregation of October 3 designated eight conciliar fathers to draft a doctrinal decree with canons. The Jesuit Diego Laynez was one of them. This task force presented a draft with seven canons on October 13. Among the new canons, canon 1 was the former canon 5; canon 2 combined the previous canons 1 and 2; canon 3 combined the previous canons 3 and 4; canon 4 was new: "Ordination does not confer *spiritualem et indelebilem potestatem* and a priest can become a layman; or the Holy Spirit is not given by ordination and it is in vain that the bishops say, Receive the Holy Spirit"; canon 5 was the previous canon 6; and canons 6 and 7 resulted from a division of the previous canon 7.

The draft, slightly revised by Seripando, was discussed by the bishops from October 13 to October 20. Some bishops supported the canonical view that all orders are *ex iure divino*. Some wished to use the traditional term—character—instead of *spiritualem et indelebilem potestatem*. The most interesting suggestion came from Laynez, who stated a principle in the light of which one could decide if bishops were superior to priests *iure divino*: *Quae voluit Deus esse immobilia et invariata fecit per se, quae vero variabilia per homines* ("What God wants to be immutable and unchanging, God does by himself; what God wants to be variable, God does through men"). Although this principle is not self-evident, Laynez concluded that bishops are superior to priests *iure divino* because they were instituted by Christ.[8]

The text and canons were revised on November 3, many different forms being proposed for canon 7. The resulting text was debated in general congregations from November 3 to December 6, when a new draft was again presented by Seripando. This had five chapters and eight canons; canon 6 was divided and became 6 and 7; canon 7 became 8.

Again Seripando proceeded to another revision, which he presented on January 11, 1563. It had five chapters and six canons. Canon 6 condemned the belief that there is no hierarchy and that all Christians are *sacerdotes*.

The final version of the decree was brought in by Seripando on January 31. It had five chapters and eight canons, including canon 7 on bishops and canon 8 on the pope. This decree was not voted on at the time, for the debate turned to a reform decree concerning ordained ministers. Both decrees were voted on and adopted by the Council on July 15, 1563.

This session XXIII was attended by four papal legates, three patriarchs, twenty-five archbishops, 185 bishops, four abbots, seven superiors general, twelve delegates of secular princes, 130 theologians, and three canon layers.[9] One of the papal legates, Charles Borromeo (1538-1584), archbishop of Milan and a nephew of the pope, insisted several times that the canons be short and clear, and that nothing be said in the decree about the nature of the episcopate.

VIII. The Doctrinal Decree

In four brief chapters and eight canons, the decree reasserts the scholastic understanding of priesthood. *Sacrificium* and *sacerdotium* go together in the New Testament as in the Old Testament. The Lord himself instituted "the visible sacrifice of the Eucharist," and he gave the apostles and their successors in *sacerdotio* the power, not only to "consecrate, offer, and administer his body and blood" but also to dismiss or retain sins. "The sacred Scriptures show it and the tradition of the Catholic Church has always taught it" (ch. 1). Although the conciliar language on the point has generally not been followed, this chapter makes no mention of bishops, and it regards all those who have received the power to "consecrate, offer and administer the body and blood" of the Lord and to dismiss and to retain sins as the successors to the apostles *in sacerdotio*. It follows that, in regard to the eucharistic celebration, both priests and bishops are successors of the apostles. In this they share one and the same priesthood (*sacerdotium*).

Because of the importance and dignity of this *sacerdotium*, the minor and major orders that led to it were instituted. The diaconate goes back to the Scriptures, and the other orders are mentioned from the beginning of the church (ch. 2). That *sacerdotium* is one of the seven sacraments is based on the testimony of Scripture, the apostolic tradition, and the unanimous consensus of the fathers (ch. 3). As in baptism and confirmation, a character that cannot be destroyed or removed is conferred in the sacrament of Orders. The priesthood of the New Testament is not a temporary power, and the ordained cannot become lay "if they do not exercise the ministry of the word of God." If all Christians were given an equal spiritual power, the hierarchy would be destroyed, which would be against the teaching of St. Paul. Bishops succeed the apostles, not only in *sacerdotio*, but also in *locum apostolorum* ("in the apostles' place"). Thus bishops "principally belong to the hierarchy" and are superior to priests. They confer confirmation and ordination. The consent of the people or of secular authority is not a condition for any ordination, whether of bishops, of *sacerdotes*, or of any other order (ch. 4).

The canons are those of the last revision made by Cardinal Seripando (see above). Canon 1 corresponds to the substance of chapter one; canon 2 to chapter two; canons 3 and 4 to chapter three. Canon 5 stands on its own as a defense of the unction with chrism that is included in the rite of ordination. Canons 6 and 7 affirm the hierarchy of ministers, priests, bishops, and the special authority of bishops. Canon 8 affirms that the Roman pontiff is a true bishop.

IX. The Reform Decrees

The Council was anxious that doctrine and reform go together. The reform decrees of session XXIII give a good idea of the pastoral background of the doctrinal debate. Each decree is in the form of a canon, and two of them—1 and 18—are very long.[10] As in the previous conciliar sessions, the redactors were broadly inspired by the recommendations made in the Consilium *eminentissimorum cardinalium de emendanda ecclesia* of 1537.

Canon 1 affirms the obligation of "all the titulars of patriarchates, primacies, metropolitan and cathedral churches" to reside in their church or diocese, "even if they are cardinals of the Holy Roman Church." Temporary exceptions may be made by the higher ecclesiastical authority, not by secular authority, and for no more than two or three months. Most of the discussion turned around the origin and nature of this obligation. If it is *de iure divino* the rule admits of no exception. If it is *de iure ecclesiastico*, exceptions may be made by the Holy See. The canon does not decide the question directly, though by admitting tem-porary exceptions it implies that the obligation of not *iure divino*.

Canon 2 specifies that bishops who have not been consecrated with-in three months of their election must not receive the benefits of their see.

Canon 3 declares that the task of ordination cannot be delegated to those who are not bishops.

Canons 4 through 6 and canon 11 dealt with tonsure and the minor orders. It was one of the concerns of Trent to respond to the Reformers' denunciation of the minor orders as merely human inventions. The main suggestion was to revitalize each of them to make them relevant again, though their possible suppression was also mentioned in the debates. The tonsure must not be granted to the unconfirmed and the ignorant, or to criminals (canon 4). Minor orders must be given only to those who have a good recommendation from their pastor or teacher; those in minor orders who wish to receive the major orders must be investigated further by the bishop or his delegate, at least one month before ordination (canon 5). No child who has the tonsure or the minor orders can receive the corresponding benefits before the age of fourteen (canon 6). The minor orders must not be conferred on those who do not understand Latin (canon 11). The ordained must fulfill the function received from their bishop unless they are studying and taking grades; they must not be ordained to a major order unless they have the corre-sponding degree of knowledge, and not before staying one full year in minor orders, where they must properly fulfill their tasks and show respect to priests and bishops (canon 11).

Canons 7 through 10 and 12 through 18 deal with the major orders. The candidates must come to the episcopal city no later than the *feria quarta* (Wednesday) before ordination, so that the bishop may, along with wise and prudent priests, diligently investigate their "sex, person, age, status (*institutionem*), mores, doctrine, and faith" (canon 7). Ordinations to major orders must take place in the cathedral at the proper canonical times, the candidates being normally ordained by their own bishop (canon 8). Bishops may not ordain someone they know (*familiarem*) who is not in their jurisdiction, unless this person has stayed with the bishop for at least three months (canon 9). Abbots may not give the tonsure to, or ordain to minor orders, anyone who is not their subject (canon 10). The minimal age for ordinations is twenty-two for the subdiaconate, twenty-three for the diaconate, and twenty-five for the priesthood (canon 12).

Subdeacons and deacons must be instructed to keep continence. Subdeacons should not be promoted to the diaconate if they have not exercised their order for one year. Two sacred orders cannot be received on the same day (canon 13). Deacons should exercise their order for at least one year before being ordained to the priesthood. Their task is to teach the people, administer the sacraments, be pious and chaste, and set an example of good works. Bishops must make sure that priests celebrate Mass on Sundays and feast days, or as often as is needed if they have the care of souls (canon 14). Priests have the power to absolve from sins by ordination, but they cannot do so without the bishop's approval (canon 15). No one may be ordained without being assigned to a church or "a pious place"; vagrant clerics must not be allowed to celebrate or to confer the sacraments (canon 16). All the functions of the major and minor orders must be restored. The tonsured and those in minor orders may be married but not bigamous, that is, remarried after widowhood (canon 8).

Canon 18 is a long instruction concerning the creation of seminaries in each diocese. It is based on the principle that, in order to avoid "the *voluptates* of the world" in their adolescence, boys must be "trained in piety and religion in their young years." The students must be no less than twelve years old and of legitimate birth. Details are given as to the organization and financing of the seminary. The canon specifies that all teachers must be competent, and that scholastic (*scholasteriae*) disciplines must be entrusted only to "doctors, masters, or licensees in *sacra pagina* or canon law."

As the debate shows, the bishops' concern was to refute the contention that minor orders are otiose and useless inventions, that all Christians are equally priests, that only preaching is the essence of ministry, that papal priests do not preach, that offering sacrifice to God is not a Christian function, and that bishops are nothing more than priests. The final vote on the doctrinal decree was delayed from January to July in order to make sure that the two decrees, doctrinal and pastoral, would fit each other.

X. Conclusion on Trent

There were no disagreements at the Council of Trent regarding the obligation of priests and bishops—all of them being *sacerdotes*—to preach the gospel and to offer the sacrifice of the eucharist. The first point was present in the debates on reform from the beginning of the Council. The second point was asserted in the decrees of session XIII on the eucharist and of session XXII on the sacrifice of the Mass and its celebration. There were no disagreements on Orders being one of the seven sacraments, on its conferring an indelible character, or on the authority of bishops over priests.

There were disagreements, however, regarding the necessity and functions of the minor orders, the exact nature of the indelible character, the sacramentality of the episcopate, and the extent of the papal primacy in relation to ecumenical councils. The basic question about the nature of the episcopate was, Is it an *ordo hierarchicus* or an *ordo sacramentalis?* In 1562 at least five opinions were formulated at the Council:

1. Episcopacy is the fullness of the sacrament of Orders; it is not only sacramental, but is also the highest degree of the sacrament.

2. Episcopacy is not a degree of the sacrament of Orders, be it the highest; it is an order by itself, a sacrament in its own right.

3. All orders, minor and major, are sacramental, including the episcopate (Salmerón, SJ).

4. All major orders are directly sacramental, and the minor orders are so indirectly, through their connection with the eucharist (Jean Walter, OP).

5. Episcopacy as such is outside the sacrament of Orders; it is simply a higher degree of jurisdiction than that of a priest, the sacramental priesthood (*sacerdotium*) being oriented exclusively to the eucharist. (This was the classical Thomist position.)

Given this variety of theologies, the writers of the decree had a double intent. On the one hand, they meant to condemn erroneous doctrines attributed to the Reformers. On the other, they wished to preserve the freedom of debate among Catholic schools. These two intentions combined to make the Council's text minimal in what it affirmed and restrained in the explanations it gave. It states the sacramental character of *sacerdotium* and the apostolic successions of priests without deciding anything on the nature of episcopacy other than its institution *iure divino*, the special apostolic succession of bishops, their superiority to priests, and their role in confirmation and ordination. The text describes the twofold task of *sacerdotes*—preaching the gospel and offering the eucharist—without imposing an interpretation of the nature of the eucharistic sacrifice. It affirms the indelible character of ordination without defining its nature. Debates in Catholic theology on all these points, as also on the relative powers of bishops, councils, and popes, continued after the Council as much as before. On the whole, session XXIII was therefore more effective in instituting diocesan seminaries than in determining doctrine. The theologians of the Counter-Reformation were given a largely free hand to develop theories on what makes the Mass a sacrifice.

XI. The Catechism of the Council of Trent

The writing of a catechism had been foreseen from the beginning of the Council. The *Catechismus Concilii Tridentini* was issued by Pope Pius V (pope from 1566 to1572) in 1566.[11] The introduction explains the function of *pastores* or *ecclesiae ministri*, that is, priests and bishops, with their collaborators in the other orders. On the one hand, the word they preach must be received, not as a "word of men," but as "the word of Christ, which it truly is" (*Proemium*, no. IV). On the other hand, they must teach the true doctrine, which is contained in the word of God (no. V), which itself is "distributed in Scripture and the traditions" (no. XII). Given this introductory emphasis on the word, it seems surprising that the treatment of Orders in chapter VII does not mention preaching the gospel among the tasks of priests.

The doctrine of the catechism on *sacerdotium* is much more elaborate than the minimal exposé of the Tridentine texts. It presents a view of *sacerdotium* that would become characteristic of the Counter-Reformation. In thirty-four sections, the chapter explains the importance of correct teaching on the priesthood, as this is the highest dignity in the institution of the church. Ministers are called by God through the bishop. The power of ministry is twofold. The power of Orders relates to "the true body of Christ the Lord in the holy Eucharist." The power of jurisdiction relates to "the mystical body of Christ," that is, to "governing and moderating the Christian people and leading it to eternal heavenly blessedness" (no. VI). The Christian *sacerdotium* is higher than the *sacerdotium* that certainly existed under the law of nature, before the Mosaic law was given, and is higher also than the Mosaic priesthood (no. VIII). The word "order" designates an "organization (disposition) of higher and lower realities which so fit together that each is referred to the other."[12] There is such an Order in the church; it is a true sacrament, and it is one (no. X), though it includes several degrees. The tonsure introduces into the Order. Four minor orders follow, and each are carefully explained. There are the three major orders of sub deacons, deacons, and priests. While all the baptized have an internal priesthood by baptism (nos. XXIII-XXIV), there also exists an external priesthood of the New Testament, the task of which is determined by the rite of ordination: to offer sacrifice to God and to administer the sacraments, including the forgiveness of sins (no. XXV). Ordination confers a grace of "sanctification and also a *potestas* over the sacrament of the Eucharist." This power is "full and perfect in the priest," and it exists in the other orders in proportion to their "nearness to the sacrament of the altar" (no. XXXIV).

This power is also called "a spiritual character, because those who are imbued with it are distinguished from the other faithful by some interior mark imprinted in their soul, and because they are devoted (*mancipantur*) to the divine cult." Priesthood is the "supreme degree of all sacred orders"[13] (no. XXII), the priest being "constituted interpreter and mediator between God and men"[14] (no. XXV). The priesthood has four degrees: of priests, of bishops, of archbishops (though their ordination does not differ from that of bishops), and of patriarchs (nos. XXVI-XXVII). The Catholic Church has always "venerated" the Roman pontiff who sits in the chair of Peter with the highest degree of dignity and has received from God (*divinitus datam*) the widest jurisdiction (no. XXVIII).

The authors of the catechism did not say more about the episcopate than was found in classical scholasticism. In this they followed the injunctions of Charles Borromeo. But they were obviously not satisfied with the doctrinal moderation of session XXIII in regard to *sacerdotium* as such. They spread a notion of the priestly character and of a media-torial role of the priest that had not been taught by the Council of Trent. Largely because of the catechism, such notions became commonplace in the rhetoric and the theology of the Counter-Reformation.

The original version of this text was presented at the meeting "Lutherans and Catholics in Conversation" in December 1999.

NOTES

1   The classic edition of the acts of the council is *Concilium tridentinum. Diariorum, Actorum, Epistularum, Tractatuum nova collectio*, 12 (Freiburg: Goerresgesellschaft, 1901-1930) (CT); I have consulted volumes VI, VII, and IX. Of the many studies of the Council of Trent, I have consulted the following: *Histoire des conciles oecuméniques: Latran V et Trente* (Paris: Editions de l'Orante, 1971); *Trente II* (1981); Ephrem Boularand, "Le Sacerdoce de la loi nouvelle d'après le décret du concile de Trente sur le sacrement de l'Ordre," *Bulletin de littérature ecclésiastique*, LVI (1955), 193-228; André Duval, "L'Ordre au concile de Trente," in *Etudes sur le sacrement de l'ordre* (Paris: Editions du Cerf, 1957), 277-232; *Des Sacrements au concile de Trente* (Paris: Editions du Cerf, 1985), chap. 7: *L'ordre*, 327-404; Jean Bernhard, Charles Lefebvre, Francis Rapp, *Histoire du Droit des Institutions de l'Eglise en Occident*, XIV: *L'Epoque de la Réforme et du Concile de Trente* (Paris: Editions Cujas, 1990); Josef Freitag, *Sacramentum ordinis auf dem Konzil von Trient*, Ausgebledenter Dissenz und erreichter Konsenz (Innsbruck: Tyrolia, 1991).

2   The reference must be to the third edition (Latin in 1543, French in 1545), which had twenty-one chapters; the second edition (1539/1541) had only seventeen chapters.

3   Peter Canisius was also among the conciliar theologians; Laynez would be elected superior general of the Society of Jesus in 1556, and he would then attend the council as a conciliar father.

4   Joannes Bernerius (d. 1553), professor of metaphysics in Bologna from 1543 to 1552, provincial in 1551.

5   CT, VI, 121; longer version, 104-105.

6   I take this from Erwin Iserloh, *Luther und das Konzil von Trient. Die Behandlung der reformatorischen Lehre durch das Konzil* (Karl Lehmann, ed., *Lehrverurteilungen-kirchentrennend?* vol. 2 *Materialien zu den Lehrverurteilungen und zur Theologie der Rechtfertigung* [Freiburg: Herder, 1989], 164).

7   The following examples are given by Duval, 330-331.

8   CT, VI, 95.

9   Jean Bernhard, *L'Epoque*, 203.

10   *Conciliorum Oecumenicorum Decreta* (Basle: Herder, 1972), 720-729.

11   I have used the following edition: *Catechismus ex decreto Concilii Tridentini ad paro-chos* (Ratisbonne, 1883).

12   Est enim ordo . . . dispositio superiorum et inferiorum quae inter se ita aptae sunt ut una ad alteram referatur (240).

13   Tertius omniumque sacrorum ordinum summus gradus est sacerdotium (245).

14   Quibus caeremoniis et verbis interpres ac mediator Dei et hominum constituitur, quae praecipua sacerdotis functio aestimanda est (247).

THEOLOGICAL ESSAYS

Chapter 4

❖

ADIAPHORA, IUS DIVINUM, AND
MINISTRY: A LUTHERAN PERSPECTIVE

BY SCOTT S. ICKERT

While an examination of *adiaphora* and the *ius divinum/ius humanum* distinction may be helpful in any consideration of how Lutherans and Catholics understand ministry, the precise definition of these terms—and thus their application to ministry, as well as bishops—is far from apparent.[1] Each term must be considered in historical context. The Lutheran debate over *adiaphora* ("things that make no difference") was precipitated by a particular political crisis of the sixteenth century, and its application, which varied among Lutherans, was a response to an emergency. The Lutherans' appeal to *adiaphora*, moreover, was somewhat unique and largely without precedent. The distinction between *ius divinum* and *ius humanum*, on the other hand, was traditional. Among Lutherans, this distinction was not the subject of controversy, as was the case with *adiaphora*. Both *adiaphora* and the *ius divinum/ius humanum* distinction, however, originated as responses to various crises that, in one way or another, appeared to threaten the nature and existence of the church.

Adiaphora was developed as a Lutheran response to strictures imposed by imperial forces in the aftermath of the Lutheran defeat in Smalkaldic wars of 1547. The predicament led to fierce inter-Lutheran debates over which reforms could in good conscience be given up or compromised without resistance. Exactly what did and did not constitute *adiaphora* in specific political emergency situations could not be determined in advance; and its precise application became an enduring inter-Lutheran problem, which often was related to a similar debate among Lutherans over what constituted a *status confessionis*.

Ius divinum, on the other hand, a commonly used juridical term, generally was not the subject of major controversy in the sixteenth century. The Lutherans tended to use the expression sparingly and with respect to specific topics. Its meaning mostly was assumed and not precisely defined.

With the concept of *adiaphora*, the question of bishops was almost synonymous with the question of the church's survival under religious oppression. Bishops signified coercion. *Adiaphora* was applied to bishops as a consequence of the imposition of certain ceremonies and practices, which were supposed to be enforced as a result of the reintroduction of the episcopal structure in the *Augsburg Interim* of 1548 (see below). However, it was not episcopal authority per se that was considered an *adiaphoron*. Indeed, under normal circumstances, obedience to the rule of bishops was required by divine law (CA 28.22). In the situation of the *Interim*, however, episcopal ordination could be resisted, because, while it was an important sign of continuity in the apostolic ministry of the gospel, it was also not necessary to ensure that succession. In the crisis, noncompliance became necessary; for the reimposition of episcopal ordination was regarded as a principal means of enforcing the provisions of the Interim and thus of establishing—coercing—an unevangelical counter-reform that would only compromise or obscure the saving gospel.

Ius divinum, on the other hand, played a more fundamental role with respect to a general definition of ministry; and the context of the distinction's use did not arise out of a particular crisis, as in the case of *adiaphora*, but rather out of the general turmoil of sixteenth-century ecclesiastical reform. In this case, one thinks of the definition of the role of the minister of the gospel, to preach the word, administer the sacraments, and maintain discipline (office of the keys), all *de iure divino*, a definition that applies to bishops and pastors equally. The *ius divinum/ius humanum* distinction, however, did touch on bishops with respect to their status relative to that of other ministers. The traditional structuring of ministers, it was said, is established by human right. Here Martin Luther's early and sustained attack on papal primacy, the appeal to Jerome on the humanly devised structuring of the episcopal office, and the justification of presbyteral ordination stand out. Still, what appeared to be a clear distinction between *ius divinum* and *ius humanum* within the context of Reformation polemics pertaining to ecclesiastical structure was not always so obvious once the Lutherans had to set up and maintain their own ecclesiastical structures, when the divinely ordained authority of the prince tended to co-opt the humanly ordered authority of the bishop.

Lutheranism arose out of disruption. Much of its development reflects that turmoil as its theology, and consequently also its ecclesiology, responded to challenge, exception, and discontinuity. If its ecclesiology has any particularly distinctive features, this fact is mainly due to Lutheranism's origins in controversy, crisis, and political maneuvering. *Adiaphora* initially was a response to a particular political emergency and was meant to provide a rationale for dealing with such crises. The *ius divinum/ius humanum* distinction, however, was employed generally as a critical principle. Yet it, too, was forged in the heat of controversy.

One may wonder how what started out as a distinction became a separation, that is, why a line in the sand became such a secure border. To be sure, in a life-and-death struggle for the gospel and the church— for the word of God and the ministry of word and sacrament—it undoubtedly became necessary to draw bold lines between *ius divinum* and *ius humanum*. At the same time, this necessity seems to have prompted an either/or situation whereby a juridical distinction and guideline became a tactical polemical weapon. With the perspective of time and the luxury of hindsight, one can at least pose the question, Do the various ways in which the terms *ius divinum* and *ius humanum* were used in earlier polemical situations preclude the possibility that a greater degree of nuance and flexibility could exist now between these seemingly mutually exclusive categories than the sixteenth-century Lutheran reformers were in a position to acknowledge?[2]

I. *Adiaphora*

A major inter-Lutheran dispute, known as the Adiaphoristic Controversy, arose after Luther's death. The dispute was a reaction to the *Augsburg Interim* (May 1548) proposed by a commission established by Charles V. The dispute also resulted from a subsequent alternative compromise document known as the *Leipzig Interim* (December 1548), which was prepared chiefly by Philipp Melanchthon and implemented by Duke Moritz in Electoral Saxony. These proposals attempted to reestablish certain Catholic beliefs and practices and were imposed on the Lutherans after the defeat of the Schmalkald League one year earlier. The swift response of some prominent Lutheran church leaders was vehemently negative, fracturing Lutheranism into camps that differed over whether and in what circumstances the church could allow such compromises.

Adiaphora is defined in the Formula of Concord (10.1) as "those ceremonies or church usages which are neither commanded nor forbidden in the Word of God but have been introduced into the church in the interest of good order and the general welfare." The chief issue was whether certain ceremonies and church usages, which were challenged, altered or discarded by the reformers, may be allowed to be reintroduced in times of persecution.[3]

This issue created an intense debate among the Lutherans. One party, the "Philippists," appealing to Melanchthon, declared that it was possible for the defeated Lutherans to remain true to their evangelical principles and still conform to the reintroduction of things that were essentially matters of indifference (*adiaphora*). The other party, the "Gnesio-Lutherans," whose chief spokesman was Matthias Flacius Illyricus (1520-1575), maintained that no concessions of any kind could be made. Indeed, resistance was required; capitulation, even in matters that normally were considered indifferent, would lead to the suppression of pure doctrine and to a gradual insinuation of false teaching into the Lutheran churches.[4] The *Formula of Concord* generally endorsed the position of the Gnesio-Lutherans. "In time of persecution, when a clear-cut confession of faith is demanded of us, we dare not yield to the enemies in such indifferent things. . . . In such a case it is no longer a question of indifferent things, but a matter which has to do with the truth of the Gospel."[5] The reassertion of papal primacy (*iure divino*) and the reintroduction of the old episcopal jurisdiction had to be refused, therefore, on the grounds that the hierarchy represented the principal means of the *Interim*'s enforcement. Thus, in the eyes of the Gnesio-Lutherans, since the bishops in this capacity represented the chief exponents and promoters of false doctrine, their authority had to be resisted.

In 1530 the Lutherans had declared that "the bishops to not have power to institute or establish anything contrary to the Gospel."[6] In that context, the matter of *adiaphora* was raised as it touched on the matter of episcopacy, which was assumed to be a necessary precondition of political repression and suppression of the gospel. This does not mean that episcopacy itself—or the continuous and structured exercise of *episcope* over time—was considered to be a matter of indifference. While the traditional structured ordering of the ministry was not deemed necessary for salvation, *episcope* clearly was recognized as necessary for ministerial accountability to the gospel and for the proper functioning and ongoing support of all ministers of the word. That the Lutherans were willing to go to great lengths to preserve and maintain the traditional polity already supports this assertion. That the Lutherans at Augsburg maintained that the pastoral role of the bishop is given by divine right, including certain fundamental aspects of the ministry of jurisdiction, confirms it.[7]

Thus the ministry of word and sacrament (including the maintenance of discipline as a function of the power of the keys) was not among the things considered to be indifferent and unnecessary for salvation. The ministry is not an *adiaphoron*. The office of the word is absolutely essential to the church. Without that ministry, there is no church. For if, as the Lutherans never tired of reiterating, salvation comes through justifying faith (CA 4), then it certainly follows that "to obtain such faith God instituted the office of ministry" (CA 5).

But what about bishops? Since bishops share in this essential ministry, and to that fundamental extent are the same as all other ministers of the gospel, they, too, are not simply an *adiaphoron*, even though the hierarchical structuring of their ministry is by human authority. Nor is their particular ministry of oversight a nonessential element in the economy of salvation, provided that this authority is not abused. Therefore, the particular historical structuring of ministry—especially in times of persecution when a confession of faith is required—may be considered a matter of indifference. In addition, episcopal oversight, like all other aspects of ministry, is limited and conditioned by the word. Should the bishops, therefore, violate their divinely ordained authority, resistance may be required. "It is lawful for bishops and pastors to make regulations so that things in the church may be done in good order, but not that by means of these we make satisfactions for sins, nor that consciences are bound so as to regard these as necessary services."[8] In such cases, especially in times of repression, one must obey God rather than men.

For the most part, then, the question of *adiaphora* for Lutherans arises in crisis situations when the integrity of the gospel appears to be threatened. Indeed, just such a crisis had to be confronted in the sixteenth century. But *adiaphora* also has been applied to various controversial matters of church practice and tradition (e.g., liturgical matters) in nonemergency situations in order to promote good order and to preserve the general welfare.

Adiaphora originally was developed by Lutherans to identify traditions overwhich the church needs to be free to exercise a certain amount of discretion. The exercise of such discretion becomes an urgent matter when resistance or noncompliance is demanded. *Adiaphora* thus functions to distinguish what pertains strictly to the gospel and may not be compromised under any circumstances, and it distinguishes which practices and differences of opinion may be tolerated for the sake of church unity.

In the sixteenth century, episcopal jurisdiction in certain matters, including ordination, qualified as one of those instances in which no compromise could be admitted. However, while the traditional structure of episcopal supervision may not be necessary for salvation and while temporary departures from it can be made in an emergency, what happens after the emergency passes? *Adiaphora* may permit or even require resistance, but does it justify intransigence when cooperation may be demanded at a later time and in different circumstances? Indeed, is it possible that today Lutherans can consider episcopal structures—which they once resisted for justifiable theological reasons—to be functionally necessary, theologically prudent, and ecumenically imperative, and therefore desirable and recoverable? *Adiaphora* is always situation-specific. If once during a crisis it demanded resistance to episcopal structures, does it not now demand, for the unity of the church, a possible accommodation, or at least openness, to those same structures?

II. *Ius Divinum/Ius Humanum*

Luther and Ius Divinum/Ius Humanum

Luther applied *ius divinum* to various topics in order to assert or refute the divinely ordained status of human and ecclesiastical institutions.[9]

With respect to the debate over monastic vows, Luther made an important distinction. He agreed that the offering of vows is *de iure divino*, a general command that was not in dispute.[10] The problem was how one distinguishes among various vows. The freedom of the gospel given in baptism is certainly by divine right,[11] and therefore is a freedom not to be surrendered. Consequently, while the offering of some vows is *de iure divino*, the monastic vow, which Luther viewed as compromising baptismal freedom, is not to be considered *de iure divino*.

Luther also regarded marriage as an institution established by divine right[12] and given for the sake of all human beings as creatures created in the image of God.

Luther's most concentrated and celebrated use of the *ius divinum/ius humanum* distinction as it pertains to ministry, however, arose in connection with his early conflict with the papacy. Prior to the Leipzig debate, a pamphlet war ensued among Luther, Eck, and Karlstadt. It became clear almost immediately that the papacy was going to be a principal issue. Eck had published twelve and then thirteen theses against Karlstadt and Luther. Prior to the debate, Luther published his *Resolution on the Thirteenth Thesis Concerning the Power of the Pope* in which he continued his attack against the idea that the papacy was established *de iure divino.* The papacy, he maintained, was a venerable human institution based on ancient custom. The issue was raised again during the debate, with the result that Luther was identified with Huss, whose position Luther later unequivocally endorsed in his *Defense and Explanation of all the Articles* (1521), written as a response to the bull *Exsurge Domine.*[13]

The debate over the divinely ordained status of the papal office continued after Leipzig. In 1520 Luther responded to attacks by Augustine Alveld in his *On the Papacy in Rome Against the Most Celebrated Romanist in Leipzig.* "This, then, is the matter in question," Luther wrote, "Whether the papacy in Rome, possessing the actual power over all of Christendom, as they say, is derived from divine or from human order."[14] Luther clarified his assertion that the papacy was a human institution. Indeed, it is by divine right that all bishops are equal, and it also is by divine right that they occupy the place of the apostles, he wrote.[15] He clarified the latter assertion, in substance at least, in his 1531 Galatians lectures.[16] According to Luther, by divine right, the bishops as ministers of the gospel, and therefore in conjunction with all such ministers, are charged with the faithful transmission of the apostolic faith. It is precisely their shared commission that denotes their equality. The apostolic office of the bishops is the divinely ordained ministry of word and sacrament, which they have in common with all other ministers, but for which, as overseers of that shared task, they bear a special responsibility.

One may wonder what were Luther's possible assumptions or implied understandings of the office of bishop. Did he also have in mind the ongoing leadership role of the apostles (which all ministers of the gospel share in some way)? And is this role or function established by divine right, too? If one keeps in mind—as George Lindbeck suggests—the Reformation caveat that "the authority and rights of the ecclesiastical office (and of the church as a whole) are not to be viewed in static juridical or ontological terms as attributes that it continues to possess independently of what it does, but rather must be seen as functions of 'service to the word,'"[17] then perhaps Luther's comments may suggest this possibility.

The Lutheran Confessions and Ius Divinum/Ius Humanum

With regard to ministry, the Lutheran Confessions (*The Treatise on the Power and Primacy of the Pope*) confirm, as Luther had insisted, that papal primacy is by human and not by divine right.[18] Even if primacy were by divine right, obedience still would have to be denied to the pope because of the way in which he perverted the gospel, according to the treatise. "Even if the bishop of Rome should possess primacy and authority by divine right, obedience would still not be owing to those pontiffs who defend godless forms of worship, idolatry, and doctrines which conflict with the gospel."[19] Divine right, in other words, does not exist to justify the office, but rather exists to verify the ministry of the gospel for which the office of ministry exists and was established to serve. "The gospel requires of those who preside over the churches that they preach the gospel, remit sins, administer the sacraments, and, in addition, exercise jurisdiction, that is, excommunicate those who are guilty of notorious crimes and absolve those who repent. By the confession of all, even of our adversaries, it is evident that this power belongs by divine right to all who preside over the churches, whether they are called pastors, presbyters, or bishops."[20]

This distinction between office as a static reality and ministry as the dynamic exercise of that office provides a justification for a temporary reconfiguration of that office and perhaps even a departure from traditional structures when necessary, especially in times of crisis, to maintain and preserve the integrity of the gospel. Indeed, when circumstances warrant it, such reconfigurations and departures may be required by divine right. "When the bishops are heretics or refuse to administer ordination, the churches are by divine right compelled to ordain pastors and ministers for themselves."[21] Also, in cases where the bishops are not performing their civil duties (authority they possess by human right), temporal magistrates are compelled, by divine right, to make these decisions if the bishops are negligent.[22] Leadership of the Christian community, whether by bishop or prince, is established by divine right. However, such leaders themselves are always accountable to the divine mandate.

What has been established by divine right, therefore, sometimes can and indeed must change to ensure that, especially in a time of crisis, the church always remains faithful to its message, ministry, and mission. Divine right is not an individual claim in the sense of a personal right, but rather relates directly and primarily to the ordinance and command of God.

The one major positive use of *ius divinum* with respect to the ministry of bishops is found in CA 28.20-22 (Latin text) and relates to all ministers of the word. The context of that passage is the contrast between civil and ecclesiastical jurisdiction. Ecclesiastical jurisdiction is given by divine right, and therefore the obedience that churches owe their bishops is also by divine right. "When one inquires about the jurisdiction of bishops, therefore, civil authority must be distinguished from ecclesiastical jurisdiction. Hence according to the gospel (or, as they say, by divine right) no jurisdiction belongs to the bishops (that is, to those to whom has been committed the ministry of Word and sacraments) except to forgive sins, to reject doctrine which is contrary to the gospel, and to exclude from the fellowship of the church ungodly persons whose wickedness is known, doing all this without human power, simply by the Word. Churches are therefore bound by divine law to be obedient to the bishops according to the text, 'He who hears you hears me.'"[23]

In accordance with this, a later Lutheran document, the Swedish *Church Ordinance* of 1571, presented to the church in 1561 by Lauentius Petri and approved in 1572 and 1593, stressed the importance of episcopacy "as being an irreplaceable order of the church."[24] Petri was trying to preserve the Swedish episcopate in the face of the religious instability of the monarchy and the possibility that the king would abolish or co-opt the episcopacy. Erik XIV (r. 1560-1568) leaned toward Calvinism, and John III (r. 1568-1592) had converted to Roman Catholicism. Thus while "the distinction which now exists between bishops and priests was not known at first in Christendom, but bishop and priest were all one office," nevertheless, the ordinance maintained that the institution of episcopacy "was very useful and without doubt proceeded from God the

Holy Ghost," a ministerial function that has remained in the church "and must remain in the future, so long as the world lasts."[25]

According to this particular sixteenth-century Swedish document, the traditional Lutheran confessional position regarding episcopal ministry is maintained. While the distinction between bishop and priest is *de iure humano*, the function of episcopal oversight as a ministry of the gospel is divinely instituted. But an additional effort seems to be made in this document to push beyond the confessional claim about the ministry of oversight *de iure divino* to a justification of episcopal governance itself (i.e., the traditional office of bishop). If nothing else, this makes the confessional understanding of the precise relationship between the *ius humanum* ordering of ministry and the *ius divinum* institution of *episcope* less clear.

The stress on the permanency of episcopacy in the *Church Ordinance* does not necessarily contradict the Lutheran Confessions, but it does stretch and challenge understandings of the *ius divinum/ius humanum* distinction expressed there. Any consideration of that challenge, however, must take into account the late sixteenth-century Swedish church's own political dilemma, which was very different from what had existed earlier in Germany.

But a similar challenge to the received confessional understanding came through an ecumenical overture to the Church of Sweden on the part of the Anglican communion. This was a statement of the Conference of Bishops of the Church of Sweden in 1923, which in confessional terms is perhaps more conservative than the *Church Ordinance* but subtly reinforces the same kind of ambiguity with respect to the *ius divinum/ius humanum* distinction. The 1923 bishops' statement says that while the structuring of the three orders of ministry is *de iure humano*, the "organizations and forms of ministry which the cravings and experiences of the Christian community have produced" are acknowledged to have been instituted "under the guidance of the Spirit in the course of history."[26]

Ius Divinum/Ius Humanum *as a Theological Problem*

The statements of the church in Sweden clearly raise certain important questions concerning the relationship between *ius divinum* and *ius humanum* as applied to bishops. These questions have been addressed—in general terms and not with any specific reference to or view of the Swedish

proposals—both in international and U.S. Lutheran–Roman Catholic conversations. The Swedish proposals are important because they point
toward the need for a more general re-examination of *ius divinum*, which,
in fact, has occurred to a certain extent within the context of
Lutheran–Roman Catholic dialogue, and which needs to be reviewed again.

A question arises, however, with respect to the reference to the
Holy Spirit in the Swedish proposals (and in other treatments of this
topic), namely, whether it can be considered strictly equivalent to *ius
divinum*. Few would argue today, especially regarding the ordering of the
church, that the Holy Spirit does *not* work also in what is deemed *ius
humanum*. One might wonder, therefore, how an appeal to the Holy
Spirit is helpful in the difficult task of sorting out *ius divinum* from *ius
humanum*. Perhaps this observation only confirms current suspicions
about the usefulness of the distinction in contemporary conversations.
On the other hand, a stress on the Holy Spirit obviously is meant to
indicate and to stress the primacy of the divine agency.

George Lindbeck, in an article prepared for round V of the
Lutheran–Roman Catholic dialogue and reproduced in *Papal Primacy and
the Universal Church* (1974), deals extensively with the Malta Report
(1972) on the topic of *ius divinum*. Lindbeck suggests that "the
Reformation denial and contemporary Roman Catholic affirmation of the
ius divinum [as applied to papal primacy] are not irreconcilable."[27] As an
example of this, he points to what he called a "functional" view of *ius divinum* adopted by some Roman Catholics. This functional, as opposed to
what he calls an "irreversibilist" approach, interprets *ius divinum* "in such
a way that it simply becomes equivalent to historically contingent and
possibly reversible necessity."[28] The Catholic functionalists, who obviously support the *ius divinum* nature of papal primacy, are actually quite similar in viewpoint to Lutherans, who oppose the claim that the papacy is *de
iure divino*. Yet they should "have no difficulty with the functionalist interpretation of the *ius divinum* character of certain post-biblical developments, for this simply affirms that what is historically and functionally
necessary for the welfare of the church is also what God wills that the
church be and do."[29] Lindbeck reiterates that the approaches of Lutherans
and Catholics on this point are not necessarily mutually exclusive.
Lindbeck himself reaches the following conclusion: "Because of this ambiguity [of both Lutheran and Roman Catholic positions], the traditional

controversy over the *de iure divino* character of the papacy is now of only historical interest. The terms of the discussion have changed. When one looks at the ministerial orders of the church functionally and historically (i.e., in terms of their service of the word and of development in time), then the neat sixteenth century dichotomy between either *ius divinum* or *ius humanum* becomes impossible. Concrete post-biblical structures and offices can be inextricably both to a far greater degree than was allowed for by late medieval juridical categories."[30]

The Malta Report already had come to a similar conclusion, which Lindbeck regards as a challenge. Paragraph 31 of that document states the following: "Greater awareness of the historicity of the church in conjunction with a new understanding of its eschatological nature, requires that in our day the concepts of *ius divinum* and *ius humanum* be thought through anew. In both concepts the word *ius* is employed in a merely analogical sense. *Ius divinum* can never be adequately distinguished from *ius humanum*. We have *ius divinum* always only as mediated through particular historical forms." Paragraph 33 reiterates the fact that, while the gospel is always prior, it is conditioned by historical contingency: "The church is permanently bound in its ordering to the gospel which is irrevocably prior to it. It is in respect to this that the Catholic tradition speaks of the *ius divinum*. The gospel, however, can be the criterion for a concrete church order only in living relationship with contemporary social realities."[31] Both Lutherans and Roman Catholics are then presented with this challenge: "Therefore the church must discern the signs of the Holy Spirit in history and in the present, and in faithfulness to the apostolic proclamation must consider the restructuring of its orders."[32]

Edmund Schlink, writing during the same time period as the Malta Report and round V of the Lutheran–Roman Catholic dialogue, made a similar observation from the perspective of *ius humanum*, with a particular stress on the agency of the Holy Spirit. With the concept of human law, he says, we encounter a process indicated in Acts 15:28, "For it seemed good to the Holy Spirit and to us." Thus in the church, which is guided by the Spirit, there is really no such thing as a purely human ordering. Consequently, the *ius humanum* is the historically actualized form (*geschichtlich-aktuellen Gestalt*) of the *ius divinum*, the latter's historical interpretation in the here and now. The essence and center of the *ius humanum*, Schlink maintains, consists in the fact that in *ius humanum* the *ius divinum* becomes concrete and humanity in its present reality is claimed concretely by Christ's commission. He further suggests that the ecumenical problem with respect to the *ius humanum/ius divinum* distinction (I would say task) is not in determining the boundary between the two concepts and thus focusing on the division between them, but rather in approaching the distinction with vigilance, openness, and flexibility regarding how the *ius divinum* presently, i.e., historically, is made effective in the *ius humanum*.[33]

The important theological discussion of nearly thirty years ago, which here is only briefly summarized and highlighted, has implications that are still challenging. Indeed, they would seem to beg important questions under current consideration, namely, the distinction common to both Lutherans and Roman Catholics between *ius divinum* and *ius humanum*, as that distinction pertains to ministry in general and to bishops in particular. This was a theological distinction, basically juridical, initially forged in controversy, which for many historical and cultural reasons within the Lutheran tradition hardened into something of a division, as Lutheranism evolved into a variety of national and ethnic ecclesiastical traditions established following the initial post-confessional period of the sixteenth century. An important exception in the history of Lutheranism to that particular development that deepened the divide between *ius divinum* and *ius humanum* is to be found in Sweden, as described above.

Luther in his Galatians lectures, discussed above, seemed to reflect the difficulty in distinguishing too strictly between *ius divinum* and *ius humanum* as that distinction is applied to ministers. As Luther discussed the orderly transmission of the gospel in history, he declared that whereas the apostles were called and commissioned directly by Christ, their successors in office, designated as bishops in Titus 1:5ff., are called to be their successors in a process that will go on "until the end of the world." At this point, the question arises, Is this second, mediated calling a human effort only, a *ius humanum* that is by definition isolated from and independent of the *ius divinum*? Luther, though he does not deal with the matter in such terms, clearly seems to conclude otherwise: "This is a mediated calling, since it is done by man. Nevertheless, it is divine."

Consequently, perhaps Lutherans should be wary of judging episcopacy in terms of the traditional *ius divinim/ius humanum* interpretation. Perhaps Lutherans should not hastily judge bishops, as some have done, as optional, incidental, or dispensable. Can Lutherans see—precisely in the humanly devised structuring and historical necessity that gave bishops to the church in the first place—an ordering *de iure humano* that was established to serve the gospel? Is it thus a concrete work of the Spirit for the ongoing life and well-being of the church? Luther's own supremely high, even idealistic picture of the early church's episcopal leadership may indicate such an openness. For if the leadership function of the apostles is handed on to the church's ministers pre-eminently through the bishops (i.e., through their primary function as ministers of the word), as Luther maintained, then clearly Lutherans can regard neither that function nor that tradition as only a human creation.

This point, however, should not be regarded as an attempt to obscure the Lutheran argument that while the establishment of the one ministry of the gospel is a *ius divinum* for which the bishops have a special responsibility as leaders in the apostolic tradition *de iure divino*, its particular ordering in history is a human establishment. Here the stark reality of human sin always stands in the background. This gives rise to the Lutheran stress on the *ius humanum* as a salutary reminder of the fallibility of all institutions, especially ecclesiastical ones. The structure of the divinely ordained office of the ministry, therefore, both with respect to the pervasiveness and perdurability of sin and in order to give the *ius divinum* origin of the institution its due, always stands in need of reform, adaptation, and renewal. By the same token—here perhaps Lutherans need a salutary reminder—the humanly established office of bishop, which has served the church for most of its existence, also should be regarded as a gift of the Spirit for the ongoing leadership and preservation of the church in the truth of the gospel. In light of these mutual admonitions, *ius divinum*, which in all circumstances must be distinguished from *ius humanum*, can no longer be viewed as a dichotomy.

From a Lutheran perspective, the *ius divinum/ius humanum* distinction, then, might be regarded as a tension dynamically adaptable to historical contingency rather than as a rigid division. As Lutherans have tended to emphasize caution when it comes to the *ius divinum* character of ministerial structure, they have placed a counter-stress on the *ius humanum*. Still they might be encouraged to pay greater attention to the positive role of the Holy Spirit in preserving ecclesiastical traditions and structures, thus avoiding the temptation either to collapse or polarize the tension.

Finally, Lutherans also might consider *ius divinum* as it pertains to bishops in a way similar to Lindbeck's assessment in his contribution to the earlier round of this dialogue on the related topic of papal primacy. Then the focus would not be on the dichotomy between *ius divinum* and *ius humanum*, but rather on the relationship between *ius divinum* "and a necessity which is historically relative and conditioned, but functionally urgent, i.e., contingently but really necessary 'for the sake of the gospel.'"[34]

NOTES

1 See articles prepared for an earlier round of this dialogue: Arthur Carl Piepkorn, "*Ius Divinum* and *Adiaphoron* in Relation to Structural Problems in the Church: The Position of the Lutheran Symbolical Books"; George Lindbeck, "Papacy and *Ius Divinum*: A Lutheran View," in L/RC-5, 119-127, 193-208. See also Carl Peter, "Dimensions of *Ius Divinum* in Roman Catholic Theology," in *Theological Studies* (TS) 34 (1973). 227-250; and the Report of the Joint Lutheran–Roman Catholic Commission on "The Gospel and the Church" ("Malta Report"), (1972), 31-34, in GA I.

2 Also note Piepkorn, 121: "For the Lutherans divine right and human, including ecclesiastical, right constitute a perfect dichotomy."

3 See FC, *Epitome*, 10.1: "The chief question has been, In times of persecution, when a confession is called for, and when the enemies of the Gospel have not yet come to an agreement with us in doctrine, may we with an inviolate conscience yield to their pressure and demands, reintroduce some ceremonies that have fallen into disuse and that in themselves are indifferent things and are neither commanded nor forbidden by God, and thus come to an understanding with them in such ceremonies and indifferent things?"

4 FC, SD, 10.2-3.

5 FC, *Epitome*, 10.6.

6 CA 28.34.

7 See CA 28.21-22.

8 CA 28.53.

9 Luther offered a general definition of ius divinum in his *Resolutions disputationem de indulgentiarum virtute* (1518). "Christ is without doubt a divine lawgiver and his doctrine is divine law, which no authority can change or dispense with." LW 31.88; WA 1.522, 15-16 (*Christus sine dubio legislator divinus est et doctrina eius ius divinum, id est quod nulla potestas mutare aut dispensare potest*).

10 WA 8.577, 20 (LW 44.252).

11 WA 8.330, 3; 613, 9 (LW 44.309).

12 WA 6.555, 4-5 (LW 36.98); WA 43. 152,17 (LW 4.23); 292, 27 (LW 4.218).

13 See LW 32.82 (WA 7.433, 1-5): "I claim that if St. Peter himself were sitting in

Rome today I would still deny that he is pope and supposed to rule over all other bishops by divine right. The papacy is a human invention of which God knows nothing. All churches are equal, and their unity does not depend on the sovereignty of this one man."

14   LW 39.57 (WA 6.286, 35–287, 2).

15   LW 39.74 (WA 6.300, 25-27): "Therefore, since according to divine order all bishops are equal and occupy the place of the apostles, I can certainly confess that according to human order one is above the other in the external church."

16   LW 26.17 (WA 40/1.59, 16-23). Cf. LW 17.211 (WA 31/2.425, 14-21). Commenting on Isaiah 52:8 ("Your watchmen lift up their voice, together they sing for joy."), Luther says: "[T]he kingdom of Christ is such that He speaks through the voice of pastors, stewards, and apostles. All these lift up their voice and sing praises at the same time. The watchmen and bishops are called ministers of the Word. In their teaching they have nothing but a voice as far as their task is concerned, and with that voice they do not wail and mutter sad words, but they sing praises and lift up their voice, that is, harmoniously, with one mouth, they proclaim joyful news. Therefore, the kingdom of Christ begins with the apostles and then is carried forward by their successors, through the voice of the watchmen. They were not such dumb and bewitched bishops as there are now. True bishops must be 'apt teachers' (1 Tim. 3:2)." See also LW 24.66 (WA 45.521, 7-9), where in this task bishops are on equal footing with other true proclaimers: "Thus the process goes on; the Word is handed down to us through the agency of true bishops, pastors, and preachers, who received it from the apostles." Note also LW 27.166 (WA 2.454, 3-11; 13-14; 16-17): "St Jerome concludes from this passage [1:2] that there are four kinds of apostles. First those who are such, not by men or through man but through Jesus Christ and God the Father, as were formerly the prophets and all the apostles. Secondly, those who are such by God's doing indeed through man, as were the apostles' disciples and those who lawfully succeed the apostles till the end of the world, as do bishops and priests. But this class cannot exist without the first, from which it has its origin. Thirdly, those who are such by a man's doing or that of men and not of God, as when someone is ordained as a result of favoritism and the efforts of men. Thus we now see very many being elected to the office of priest, not by the decision of God but by the favor of the rabble for a price. . . . For to this class must belong all those who offer themselves for bishoprics and priesthoods before they are called. . . . The fourth kind consists of those who are neither called by God nor by men or through man but by themselves."

17   Lindbeck, 198.

18   *The Treatise on the Power and Primacy of the Pope* (TPPP), 1-7, 12.

19   TPPP, 38. Cf. 42, 57.

20   TPPP, 60-61.

21   TPPP, 72.

22   TPPP, 77.

23   For the text of the Latin version, see *Die Bekenntnisschriften der Evangelisch-Lutherischen Kirche* (Gottingen, 1992), 123-124.

24 *The Office of Bishop.* Report of the Official Working Group for Dialogue between the Church of Sweden and the Roman Catholic Diocese of Stockholm (Geneva, 1993) 148. For a translation of a portion of the text of the *Church Ordinance*, see 149-150. In the escursus, "The Swedish *Church Ordinance* 1571 and the Office of Bishop in an Ecumenical Context," Sven-Erik Brodd notes that in Petri's other writings both the monarchy and the episcopacy are divinely ordained institutions.

25 *Church Ordinance,* in *The Office of Bishop,* 149, 150.

26 *The Office of Bishop,* 154-155.

27 Lindbeck, 195.

28 Ibid.

29 Ibid., 203.

30 Ibid., 207-208.

31 See *Growth in Agreement* (GA) I, 175-176. See also C. Peter, 228-229, who agrees with M. Löhrer that *ius divinum* designates an unfinished theological task (see also 236). But this should not simply lead us to a *theologia negativa,* Peter says. In this regard, Peter summarizes, approvingly, the work of E. Schillebeeckx, who maintained that "although there is no direct link between contemporary church offices and an act of foundation on the part of Jesus, still the threefold office of bishop, presbyter, and deacon is the work of the Spirit of the risen Christ." In this sense, the threefold office is certainly based on a *ius divinum,* "but one that does not exclude a reordering of the triadic structure itself." Also in this connection and in keeping with the Malta Report, Peter acknowledges not only the historically conditioned nature of office, but also recognizes an eschatological proviso: "The ultimate validation of truth-claims for Christian faith is in the future" (246-247).

32 GA I, 176.

33 See E. Schlink, "Zur Unterscheidung von *ius divinum* und *ius humanum,*" in *Begegnung: Beiträge zu einer Hermeneutik des theologischen Gesprächs,* ed. M. Seckler, O. Pesch, J. Brosseder, and W. Pannenberg (Graz, 1972), 247.

34 Lindbeck, 202.

Chapter 5

❋

A ROMAN CATHOLIC PERSPECTIVE ON IUS DIVINUM

BY MARGARET O'GARA

Introduction

The use of the category *ius divinum* (divine law) is not the focus of frequent discussion today in Roman Catholic theology. It receives little direct attention in the *Lexikon für Theologie und Kirche*, *Sacramentum Mundi*, the *New Dictionary of Theology*, the *New Catholic Encyclopedia*, or the *Catechism of the Catholic Church*. The *Catholic Guide to Periodical Literature* and the *Religion Index* for periodicals show few articles on the topic for the last twenty-five years.

But earlier and continuing claims about what is part of the church *de iure divino* continue to serve as a source of division among Christians. In this essay, I will offer a brief Roman Catholic perspective on the meaning and viability of the category itself of *ius divinum*. I will not try to make a judgment about whether a particular sacrament or office of the church is or is not *de iure divino*. Instead I will examine what it means to claim anything is *iure divino* and how our Lutheran–Roman Catholic dialogue could approach conflicting claims.

Lutheran–Roman Catholic Dialogue on *Ius Divinum*

The Lutheran–Roman Catholic dialogue has regularly adverted to *ius divinum* claims as a source of past division and has noted a new context for evaluating such claims. The "Malta Report" of the Lutheran–Roman Catholic International Commission for Dialogue (1971), for example, states that "greater awareness of the historicity of the church in conjunction with a new understanding of its eschatological nature requires that in our day the concepts of *ius divinum* and *ius humanum* be thought through anew." In addition, the Malta Report says that the two "can never be adequately distinguished" from each other.[1]

In the discussion of papal primacy by the U.S. Lutheran–Roman Catholic dialogue, the idea of *ius divinum* arose again. In "Differing

Attitudes toward Papal Primacy," the "Common Statement" notes that Roman Catholics have affirmed that "the papacy is a matter of divine law (*ius divinum*)" and "consequently have viewed it as an essential part of the permanent structure of the church," while "Lutherans have held, in opposition to this, that the papacy was established by human law, the will of men, and that its claims to divine right are nothing short of blasphemous."[2] At the end of the "Common Statement," the signers note that they "do not wish to understate" their remaining disagreements. "While we have concluded that traditional sharp distinctions between divine and human institution are no longer useful, Catholics continue to emphasize that papal primacy is an institution in accordance with God's will." But Lutherans find this "a secondary question." The one thing necessary, Lutherans insist, "is that papal primacy serve the gospel and that its exercise of power not subvert Christian freedom."[3]

In their reflections, the Lutheran participants give their opinion that "the traditional distinction between *de iure humano* and *de iure divino* fails to provide usable categories for contemporary discussion of the papacy." Instead, the Lutheran participants suggest a different set of questions: "In what way or ways has our Lord in fact led his church to use particular forms for the exercise of the Petrine function? What structural elements in the church does the gospel require for the ministry which serves the unity of the empirical church?"[4] Roman Catholics, for their part, affirm that the papacy is divinely instituted, "imperative" because "it is willed by God for his church." But since the term *ius divinum* used to mean institution by a formal act of Jesus and a clear apostolic record of such an act, today "the term itself does not adequately communicate what we believe concerning the divine institution of the papacy." Instead, Roman Catholics continue, "we are convinced that the papal and episcopal form of Ministry, as it concretely evolved, is a divinely-willed sequel to the functions exercised respectively by Peter and the other apostles according to various New Testament traditions."[5]

In his discussion of the idea of *ius divinum*, Avery Dulles includes in its meaning the terms "divine right," "divine law," "divine institution," and "divine ordination," which he notes are not synonymous but "may be used almost interchangeably for the purposes of this essay."[6] I will include this broad sense of *ius divinum* here as well.[7] But what is the basic meaning or value intended by *ius divinum* talk? Why is it worth understanding or reconceptualizing? As he notes the difficulties with this older termi-nology and its accompanying worldviews, Dulles suggests that we not eliminate the older terminology until we find substitutes. "After all," he observes, "it is important to find ways of expressing that the Church is not its own Lord."[8] I believe that this is an important function that the idea of *ius divinum* has served: to show that the church is not its own Lord. Dulles explains that "there has to be some terminology that allows us to distinguish what the officers of the Church decide as a matter of free discretion and what they hold because fidelity to God's revelation so requires. The traditional *ius divinum* terminology, for both Protestants and Catholics, provided ways of making this distinction."[9]

The Anglican–Roman Catholic International Commission (ARCIC) provides another suggestion for understanding *ius divinum* talk when, in discussing the primacy of the bishop of Rome, members propose reconceptualizing "divine right" to mean that the primacy of the bishop of Rome is "part of God's design for the universal *koinonia*"[10] or that for Roman Catholics it expresses "God's purpose for his Church."[11] But they continue by noting that Anglicans might be able to affirm the develop-ment of the Roman primacy as a gift of providence, "in other words, as an effect of the guidance of the Holy Spirit in the Church." And ARCIC members suggest, "it is reasonable to ask whether a gap really exists between the assertion of a primacy by divine right (*iure divino*) and the acknowledgement of its emergence by divine providence (*divina providentia*)."[12]

Roman Catholic Conciliar Texts and Roman Catholic Contemporary Theology on *Ius Divinum*

Roman Catholic Conciliar Texts

Roman Catholics inherit the use of *ius divinum* claims in conciliar texts. Dulles draws our attention to its use in three councils. The Council of Trent was "remarkably nuanced" in its discussion of the sacrament of penance, according to Dulles, since Trent "saw the substance of the sacra-ment as having been instituted by Christ, but conceded that the form of its celebration was a matter of human legislation."[13] Carl Peter also emphasizes the nuanced approach the Council used to the sacrament of penance. The Council distinguished between the necessity of confessing serious sin to a priest, which it taught was *iure divino*, and the rules regard-ing frequency of confession, which it taught were required by the church.[14]

In *Pastor Aeternus* (*On the Infallibility of the Roman Pontiff*), the First Vatican Council taught that by the institution of Christ himsef (*de iure divino*), Peter has a perpetual line of successors in his primacy within the church. Dulles finds this approach "a static and objectivistic notion of divine institution," which seems "to refer to the actions of the historical Jesus in his earthly and risen life."[15]

Finally, the Second Vatican Council left open whether the distinction between bishop and presbyter is of divine institution.[16] But it asserted that the variety of ministries in the church is *ex divina institutione*, and that bishops are successors of the apostles by divine institution as well. It also taught that the church has by divine mandate the duty to preach the gospel to every creature. According to Dulles, the Second Vatican Council had a "dynamic" understanding of divine law as "something given only inchoatively at the beginning—that is to say, as something that unfolds in the history of the Church."[17]

Roman Catholic Contemporary Theology

How do Roman Catholics understand *ius divinum* today? Three articles by earlier members of this Lutheran–Roman Catholic dialogue (Dulles, Peter, and George Lindbeck) discuss a wide variety of viewpoints on this question. I will summarize some of their findings.

Dulles finds four schools of thought among twentieth-century Roman Catholic and Lutheran theologians. He calls the first the "neo-Lutheran" view. Exemplified by Edmund Schlink, this view sees four essential elements in Christ's new covenant: (1) the mission of proclamation; (2) baptism; (3) the Lord's Supper; and (4) the power of binding and loosing. All of these elements rest on the word of the Lord and are unexpendable, but the church can regulate from human authority how these actions are to be conducted. According to Dulles, Hans Küng held a position close to Schlink's, which puts a strong emphasis on the apostolic period in its understanding of *ius divinum* but does not read the New Testament in a literal way.[18]

Dulles labels a second view "nonhistorical orthodoxy," which was earlier exemplified by Francisco Suarez, and in the twentieth century is exemplified by J. B. Franzelin and Emmanuel Doronzo. "According to this view, everything essential to the Church in any period of its existence must have been actually contained in the apostolic deposit; for the Lord alone could give the Church what it needed for its supernatural mission, and he would not have failed to supply it with anything truly requisite."[19] Proponents of this approach held that Jesus personally established the Mass as a sacrifice, instituted each of the seven sacraments directly, and conferred primacy upon Peter. While New Testament texts could be used to support such views, their proponents also drew on oral traditions considered to be apostolic.

Dulles identifies a third group, represented by Karl Rahner, as the "developmental theory." This theory holds that *ius divinum* does not necessarily mean that the structure being considered was given directly by Christ himself during his earthly ministry. Instead Rahner thinks the concept of *ius divinum* can be extended to include decisions made by the church in apostolic times that were consonant with the church's nature and now may be irreversible.[20] Rahner argues that such a sacrament or office "may draw its *iure divino* character from its being an indispensable way of insuring the necessary continuation of that which Jesus did found."[21] Rahner finds revelation within this process of free decision making by the apostolic church, and he writes that "the irreversibility of an action and decision is not something particularly strange and surprising, but rather is exactly what one should expect in the light of the nature of freedom."[22]

Carl Peter also comments on Rahner's approach to *ius divinum*, noting that Rahner's writings on this topic before the Second Vatican Council had a major impact on Roman Catholic theology.[23] Dulles places Peter within the third "developmental" school represented by Rahner. But while Rahner left open the question of whether any institutional developments of the postapostolic church were irreversible, Peter holds that some are definitely irreversible. Peter also lays strong emphasis on the process of discernment used by the church to discover whether something is *de iure divino*; such discernment is not "reducible to the laws of inductive or deductive reasoning"[24] nor to the explicit language of the New Testament.[25] Details of application are worked out by the church in history.

Dulles notes that although both Rahner and Peter hold the possibility of irreversible developments in the postapostolic church that are also *de iure divino*, they still "are reluctant to specify exactly what in the later development was in fact irreversible."[26] Dulles continues, "If the episcopate is such a development, does this mean that the monarchical episcopate is forever necessary—or could you, for example, have a college of presbyters collectively filling the office of bishop? If papal primacy is an essential and irreversible feature of the church after a certain date, what exactly does that mean? Must the primacy always be that of the bishop of Rome? Could it be exercised by a group of bishops rather than by a single individual? Could the papacy rotate from see to see according to a cycle of a certain number of years? Could the pope be required always to consult the synod of bishops when he exercises his primacy of jurisdiction or infallible teaching functions? These questions are not easily answered."[27]

In his writing after the Second Vatican Council, Rahner makes clear the flexibility with which he approached even institutions such as the papacy and the episcopate that he regarded as part of the church *de iure divino*. He says that the forms of these institutions could vary greatly in different times. He notes that "the concrete forms in which . . . papal authority" is exercised could "undergo such far-reaching transformations that so far as the average everyday impression of an individual Christian is concerned the directive power of the pope may be encountered in some new form in which it seems to retain only a slight connection with that authority which was once and for all defined in the First Vatican Council as permanently enduring."[28] The episcopal structure of the church as well could perhaps be altered so that it was ascribed to a "small collegiate body" and was complemented by "many structures and institutions . . . built into the Church which give the people of the Church a more active role than that which they have previously had in the life of the Church itself."[29]

In his commentary on the *Dogmatic Constitution on the Church* (*Lumen Gentium*), Rahner leaves as "an open question" the extent to which the later church is bound by the early church's decision to have "two limited degrees" of the office of bishop (priesthood and diaconate)."[30] He comments, "And here we may leave it an open question, whether this decision also binds the Church which came after, that is, is part of the process of revelation of divine law in the apostolic Church, or represents Church law of human institution in the apostolic age."[31] He continues, "The full office in its essence, its collegiate form and its union with the Pope is in any case of divine institution."[32]

Dulles identifies a fourth school of thought, represented by Johannes Neumann and Edward Schillebeeckx, which he calls the "functionalist" approach. Neumann, for example, held that a postapostolic development could be *de iure divino* for a certain period in the life of the church, but then later modified. Schillebeeckx as well "rejects Rahner's suggestion that the development of the monarchical episcopate since New Testament times could be irreversible."[33] Just because postapostolic developments do not come from Jesus in his earthly ministry but rather are influenced by sociological factors, however, does not make them merely human since "the Holy Spirit is continually operative in the Church."[34]

Dulles himself proposes a fifth approach to "what is unchangeable about the Church;" he calls this approach "relational." The church is constituted by its relationship to Jesus Christ, a stable reference point, and its relationship to those to whom it mediates Christ's presence, the changing people of each time and place. While recalling and reliving the mysteries of Christ's life, death, and Resurrection, the church must relate and adapt to various ages and cultures. Dulles explains, "The abiding structures of the Church, therefore, must undergo ceaseless modification, not in order to weaken or dissolve its bonds in Christ, but precisely in order to keep them intact."[35] With this in mind, Dulles presents four spheres or concentric circles that are each related differently to the concept of *ius divinum*: (1) the inner core of the church's mission demanding a ministry of proclamation, baptism, eucharist, and binding and loosing; (2) institutional features that appeared after the apostolic age but are irreversible—such as the anointing of the sick or the episcopate—and "may be called *iure divino* in a somewhat more extended sense than structures that pertain to our first category;"[36] (3) temporary, reversible developments "truly willed by Christ and inspired by the Holy Spirit"[37] could also be envisioned, such as collegiality of the bishops or greater cultural pluralism; and finally, (4) discretionary matters that are provisional and subject to the church's decision. Eric Doyle makes a somewhat similar suggestion, saying that "it is evident on historical grounds that there must be a hierarchy of elements of divine institution in the church of Christ on an analogy with the hierarchy of truths."[38]

Dulles notes the difficulty of distinguishing between the second and third spheres—between the irreversible and the reversible postapostolic developments. He sees the papacy as an example of an irreversible sphere, while he sees (writing in 1977)[39] the exclusion of women from ordination as perhaps a reversible development. Commenting on the latter, Dulles writes, "As with the papacy, so here, it would not be enough to argue simply from apostolic precedent or from unbroken continuity with the past. If the exclusion of women from ordination is to be sustained, a justification must be given in terms of the biblical and liturgical symbolism and the need of the Church as a sign of Christ in the world today."[40]

Finally, Dulles suggests an alternative terminology, in which the most essential sphere be seen as *ad esse ecclesiae* (for the very being of the church), the second, irreversible sphere as *ad plene esse* (for the fullness of the being of the church), and the third, reversible sphere as *ad bene esse ecclesiae* (for the well-being of the church); the fourth sphere would not be seen as part of the church's being. Whether these or other terms are found, Dulles points out, "it will be necessary to differentiate . . . between the biblical and the nonbiblical, the apostolic and the nonapostolic, the reversible and the irreversible." Dulles ends his discussion by calling for "a more modest and nuanced view of *ius divinum*," noting that continuity and mutability are both required in his suggestion. "The Church's abiding essence actually requires adaptive change; and such change, if it is healthy, serves to actuate and express more vividly the true and permanent nature of the Church itself."[41]

In his article on *ius divinum*, Lindbeck notes that discussions of *ius divinum* when applied to papal primacy show many agreements between Lutherans and Roman Catholics. He notes five points about contemporary Lutherans: (1) they recognize the importance of the Petrine function; (2) they are open to the possibility that it should be more effectively institutionalized in Lutheranism; (3) they do not exclude the possibility that the papacy could rightly exercise this function; (4) to do this, however, the papacy must be reformed theologically and practically to make clear its subordination to the primacy of the gospel; and (5) even if this were to happen, however, "Lutherans do not agree that the papacy is the necessary institutionalization of the Petrine function."[42] But in fact many Roman Catholics share the same views as Lutherans on the first four points, Lindbeck emphasizes. For instance, Roman Catholics also insist on the Reformation thesis "that the authority and rights of the ecclesiastical office (and of the church as a whole) are not to be viewed in static juridical or ontological terms as attributes which it continues to possess independently of what it does, but must rather be seen as functions of 'service to the word.'"[43] Thus, Lindbeck concludes, "the one remaining point of dispute on the level of theological principle is whether it [the papacy] is a necessary instrument (Thesis 5)" for carrying out the Petrine function.[44]

But even this fifth thesis is uninformative, Lindbeck continues, since the word "necessary" could have two meanings: (1) the papacy could be the "contingently (and perhaps only temporarily) necessary means for carrying out the Petrine function simply because it happens at present (and we don't know about the future) to be the only historically available instrumentality which could effectively do this job for the church as a whole;" or (2) "unconditional necessity" of the papacy.[45] But Lindbeck notes that there is nothing un-Lutheran in attributing the first, contingent kind of necessity to papal primacy. And Lindbeck wonders, Are Roman Catholics actually obligated to affirm an unconditional necessity for papal primacy, the kind that Lutherans must deny?[46]

Surveying contemporary views on *ius divinum*, Lindbeck sees only two really distinct schools of thought: (1) functionalists, who might call something *de iure divino* if it is a historically and functionally conditioned necessity, as he suggested (see above) might be thought about papal primacy; or (2) irreversibilists, who hold that a *de iure divino* structure must be irreversible or permanent. "Lutherans see no biblical grounds for asserting this irreversibility, at least not as a matter of faith, and consequently deny that the papacy is *de iure divino* in this second sense. In contrast, they have no difficulty with the functionalist interpretation of the *ius divinum* character of certain postbiblical developments, for this simply affirms that what is historically and functionally necessary for the welfare of the church is also what God wills that the church be and do."[47] In fact, *ius divinum* in contemporary discussion differs so much from earlier understanding that its meaning has become fluid. "Perhaps some things which were prohibited by divine law in biblical and post-biblical times are now in our day commanded (e.g., the ordination of women)," writes Lindbeck.[48] Because the difference between Lutherans and Roman Catholics on *ius divinum* has narrowed so much and the terms of the discussion have changed, Lindbeck concludes that "the traditional controversy over the *de iure divino* character of the papacy is now of only historical interest."[49] Lindbeck argues that "the only meaningful contemporary manner of posing the question of papal primacy is to ask whether it is a possible—or perhaps even the best or only—way of effectively institutionalizing the

Petrine function now or in the foreseeable future. On this point," he continues, "Lutherans are open to persuasion."[50]

A final perspective was provided by an interesting discussion of *ius
divinum* within canon law. Although canon law is outside the scope of
this essay, one article should be mentioned. In the article "*Ius Divinum*
as a Canonical Problem: On the Interaction of Divine and Ecclesiastical
Laws," Joseph J. Koury compares the canons of the 1917 Code with the
revised 1983 Code regarding claims and comments about what is "divine
law" or "by divine institution."[51]

He finds examples where something attributed in the 1917 Code to
divine law lacks such a claim in the 1983 Code, e.g. some liturgical matters.[52] In addition, sometimes the 1917 Code speaks of divine law in one
way, but the 1983 Code attributes it in another way to the matter discussed. For example, the more recent Code shifts its claim of divine
institution from the distinction between clergy and laity in the church
to the existence of both clergy and laity in the church.[53] As another
example, a rule regarding sanations of marriage is actually reversed,
although the same reference to impediments from divine law is maintained.[54] In a discussion on *communicatio in sacris*, the boundaries of
what divine or ecclesiastical law forbid "have been dramatically
redrawn."[55] The 1983 Code also adds some new uses of "divine law;" for
example, it states that all of the Christian faithful are bound to do
penance "in virtue of divine law."[56] Another section of the Code on marriage impediments and dispensations shows a movement in the "boundaries" of "divine law." Koury gives several examples of this boundary
movement, including the deletion of "forbidden by divine law." The
1917 Code refers to the divine prohibition of a mixed marriage where
there is a danger of perversion of the Catholic spouse and the children.
The phrase "forbidden by divine law" has been deleted in the 1983
Code's treatment of this point. Finally, sometimes a claim to divine law
is maintained but its object is changed. For example, the 1917 Code
affirms a divinely ruled right and duty to acquire knowledge of doctrine
and embrace the true church of God. The 1983 Code says that all persons "are bound to seek the truth in matters concerning God and God's
Church" (canon 748.1) and that they also have a divinely ruled duty
and right to embrace and observe the truth that they have recognized.[57]

At the end of his article, Koury notes that "rigid and exaggerated claims for *ius divinum* have in the past created and contributed to divisions among the churches."[58] Knowing and communicating the boundaries between divine and ecclesiastical laws and "the different ways in which they are recognized, enacted, or changed" remains "an unfilled yet important task of church officials and ministers," he continues. He also offers the opinion that claims of *ius divinum* "should not be easily made," lest in later changes of them, "the claim and language lose some of its weightiness, the rule being urged lose some of its effectiveness, and the Church lose some of its credibility."[59]

My Reflections

By now it must be clear that, as ARCIC states, in Roman Catholic conviction "there is no universally accepted interpretation" of *ius divinum* language.[60] In discussing the primacy of the bishop of Rome, ARCIC notes that "it means at least that this primacy expresses God's purpose for his Church."[61] Beyond that basic meaning, a number of different interpretations of *ius divinum* coexist today in Roman Catholic theology. At the same time, claims about *ius divinum* from past conciliar documents and present understandings continue to cause division between Roman Catholics and Lutherans. In this situation, I offer reflections on three points: (1) a consensus in Roman Catholic theology; (2) a range of meanings within this Roman Catholic consensus; and (3) a way forward.

A Consensus in Roman Catholic Theology

Roman Catholic theology has officially made the shift in understanding from what Bernard Lonergan calls a "classicist" worldview to "historical-mindedness." In its commitment to historical-mindednesss, Roman Catholic theology enjoys a genuine consensus.

Lonergan describes the contrast between knowing "man . . . abstractly through a definition that applies *omni et soli* and through properties verifiable" in everyone. He writes, "In this fashion one knows man as such; and man as such precisely because he is an abstraction, also is unchanging."[62] By contrast, Lonergan continues, one can know humankind as "a concrete aggregate developing over time, where the locus of development and, so to speak, the synthetic bond is the emergence, expansion, differentiation, dialectic of meaning and of meaningful performance. On this

view intentionality, meaning, is a constitutive component of human living; moreover, this component is not fixed, static, immutable, but shifting,
developing, going astray, capable of redemption; on this view there is in
the historicity, which results from human nature, an exigency for changing forms, structures, methods; and it is on this level and through this
medium of changing meaning that divine revelation has entered the world
and that the Church's witness is given to it."[63] By historical-mindedness,
Lonergan does not mean relativism, as he emphatically points out; he
means rather the recognition of the historicity of human understanding
that characterizes contemporary thought and that profoundly affects the
way we think about our knowledge of the truth.

Ladislas Örsy puts it more simply when he describes our time as "the
age when the Church was coming to grips with the law of evolution,
especially in doctrinal matters."[64] Or again, we could describe it with
Rahner as the recognition that there dwell in the church together
"changeable and unchangeable factors," some part of the permanent
witness to the faith and some not.[65] Once the shift to historical-mindedness is made, Frederick Crowe notes, we can see that the church is
not only a teacher but also a learner. He argues that for the church, even
for the writers of Scripture and for the magisterium, learning comes
before teaching,[66] and that "we have laid so much stress on the teaching
Church—and this not as a function related to and integrated with a
learning function, but as an office belonging to certain people—that we
have not attended to the learning function, though it is primary."[67]

In its official teaching, the Roman Catholic Church is in the process
of making the shift from a classicist worldview to historical-mindedness.
We can see this shift symbolized in the emphases of the two Vatican
councils. The First Vatican Council taught that "the meaning of the
sacred dogmas is perpetually to be retained which our Holy Mother
Church has once declared"[68] and spoke of definitions that are
"irreformable."[69] The Second Vatican Council affirmed—without denying the earlier points—that "there is a growth in the understanding" in
the church "of the realities and the words which have been handed
down." It continues, "For as the centuries succeed one another, the
Church constantly moves forward toward the fullness of divine truth
until the words of God reach their complete fulfillment in her."[70] At the
Second Vatican Council, the historicity of understanding is affirmed,

and some practical implications of this insight are embraced in the endorsement of historical critical tools for the study of Scripture. This shift to historical-mindedness is confirmed more thoroughly in the 1973 teaching *Mysterium Ecclesiae* of the Congregation for the Doctrine of the Faith when it notes that "the meaning of the pronouncements of faith depend partly upon the expressive power of the language used at a certain point in time and in particular circumstances," that "some dogmatic truth is first expressed incompletely (but not falsely), and at a later date . . . it receives a fuller and more perfect expression," and finally, that truths taught through dogmatic formulas sometimes "bear traces" of "the changeable conceptions of a given epoch."[71]

In its theological reflection and in its official documents, then, the Roman Catholic Church has made the shift from classicism to historical-mindedness. This is a real consensus.

A Range of Meanings within This Roman Catholic Consensus

But sometimes Roman Catholics differ about how to apply this shift to questions of *ius divinum*. While they affirm historical-mindedness in general, they may treat particular questions out of a classicist worldview. Or again, they may affirm historical-mindedness, but then be left with the range of historicity-affirming views Dulles listed above, which can include both those with a developmental irreversible viewpoint and those with a developmental and reversible viewpoint on church structures.

Two examples may help us see such variety in action. The first comes from comparing arguments about the papacy and the ordination of women. In the Lutheran–Roman Catholic dialogue on papal primacy, the Roman Catholic participants explain that traditional views of *ius divinum* emphasized institution of a structure by a formal act of Jesus and the clear witness of this act in the New Testament or in some apostolic tradition.[72] But such an understanding is inadequate, according to the Roman Catholics. In the New Testament, they have not found a clear and direct affirmation about the papacy itself, but this does not "surprise or disconcert" them, they say. "We believe that the New Testament is given to us not as a finished body of doctrine but as an expression of the developing faith and institutionalization of the church in the first century. . . . As Roman Catholics we are convinced that the papal and episcopal form of Ministry, as it concretely evolved, is a divinely-willed sequel to the functions exercised respectively by Peter and the other apostles according to various New Testament traditions."[73] Here we see a clear argument for the papacy, well grounded in historical-mindedness, probably drawing on the developmental school of thought represented by Rahner's position. ARCIC members state this more explicitly: "Yet it is possible to think that a primacy of the bishop of Rome is not contrary to the New Testament and is part of God's purpose regarding the Church's unity and catholicity, while admitting that the New Testament texts offer no sufficient basis for this."[74]

But if we compare this position's rationale to the discussion on why women cannot be ordained, we see an interesting contrast in the argument's foundation. In *On Reserving Priestly Ordination to Men Alone* (*Ordinatio Sacerdotalis*), Pope John Paul II bases his own argument against women's ordination on the conscious will and practice of Christ in choosing "the 12 men whom he made the foundation of his Church."[75] The gospels and the Acts of the Apostles show that "this call was made in accordance with God's eternal plan: Christ chose those whom he willed . . . after having spent the night in prayer," explains John Paul II. He continues, "The Church has always acknowledged as a perennial norm her Lord's way of acting."[76] While avoiding the argument from Christ's maleness and using instead this biblical argument from Christ's conscious will and practice, John Paul II also declares "that the Church has no authority whatsoever to confer priestly ordination on women and that this judgment is to be definitively held by all the Church's faithful."[77]

I am not here discussing the content position of these three documents, but I note that they present a striking contrast in argument foundations. The first two, on papal primacy, use a kind of developmental notion of *ius divinum* that grounds the primacy not in acts of the historical Jesus but rather in a divinely willed sequel to New Testament gestalt, seeing the Spirit active in the postapostolic church. The second, on the exclusion of women from ordination, uses a kind of biblical interpretation of the historical Jesus himself and emphasizes the limits of the church's authority for any postapostolic deviation from the conscious will and practice of Jesus on this matter. The two arguments present an interesting contrast.

Another example showing the range of Roman Catholic application of historical-mindedness comes from within the Doctrinal Commentary on the Concluding Formula of the Profession of Faith (June 29, 1998) by Cardinal Joseph Ratzinger and Archbishop Tarcisio Bertone, which was issued coincident with the promulgation *Ad Tuendam Fidem*. In the commentary, the authors set out to explain the meaning of the category "taught definitively" that has been officially inserted into the *Code of Canon Law* by *Ad Tuendam Fidem*. A definitive teaching, Ratzinger and Bertone explain, is not a part of revelation, yet it is connected with revelation and proposing it is an exercise of infallibility. Why should believers accept such definitive teaching? The authors emphasize that assent to a definitive teaching is based "on faith in the Holy Spirit's assistance to the magisterium and on the Catholic doctrine of the infallibility of the Magisterium."[78] While such a teaching is not a part of revelation, it is necessary for the support of revelation.

Furthermore, Ratzinger and Bertone explain, definitive teaching is, as it were, inside a kind of "Waiting Room" (my term) for revelation; while the church may not yet have recognized that a given definitive teaching can be known infallibly to be part of divinely revealed truth, in time it may come to do so. Ratzinger and Bertone give an example from the past—the teaching on papal infallibility—which was once definitive teaching, they say, because it seemed at least connected to revelation. But then, at the First Vatican Council, the teaching on papal infallibility moved out of the "Waiting Room" to be recognized and infallibly taught as divinely revealed truth. Another example, they suggest, may be the exclusion of women from ordination. This teaching is now taught only definitively, in *Ad Tuendam Fidem*, but perhaps some day it might be taught infallibly as divinely revealed truth.

Within this unusual presentation can be found a clear statement of historical-mindedness (though applied wrongly here to the question of women's ordination, I believe): "Moreover, it cannot be excluded that at a certain point in dogmatic development the understanding of the realities and the words of the deposit of faith can progress in the life of the church, and the magisterium may proclaim some of these doctrines as also dogmas of divine and catholic faith."[79] Some truths have been defined, the authors explain; "other truths, however, have to be understood still more deeply before full possession can be attained of what God, in his mystery of love, wished to reveal to men for their salvation."[80] These statements use different arguments and manifest a different worldview than that of *Ordinatio Sacerdotalis*, even though they aim to defend the conclusion and reasoning of that document.

These two illustrations serve to show a range of meanings within Roman Catholic theology in the interpretation of *ius divinum* within the framework of historical-mindedness. While the term *ius divinum* is not always used, the two illustrations reveal different views and applications of its meaning.

A Suggestion for a Way Forward

When reading Lindbeck's article, I was struck by some similarities with the successful method of the "Joint Declaration on the Doctrine of Justification."[81] Like the "Joint Declaration," Lindbeck emphasizes that many points affirmed by Roman Catholics are not denied by Lutherans. Lutherans, he says, "have no difficulty with the functionalist interpretation of the *ius divinum* character of certain postbiblical developments, for this simply affirms that what is historically and functionally necessary for the welfare of the church is also what God wills that the church be and do."[82] Many Roman Catholic theologians as well as Lutherans "now emphasize the primacy of the gospel and employ chiefly functional categories when dealing" with questions about papacy or ministerial orders in general.[83] For instance, both see papal primacy as necessary "only as a means, only as an instrument, for the proclamation of the gospel."[84] According to Lindbeck, even Lutherans who criticize the views of their irreversibilist Roman Catholic colleagues may not really be denying their viewpoints, since the irreversibilists "insist on the difficulty of specifying exactly what is *de iure divino* and therefore irreversible in any given development."[85]

Lindbeck's position suggests a way forward for our Lutheran–Roman Catholic dialogue. Rather than trying to adjudicate among the many historically-minded approaches to *ius divinum* now being used in both of our communions—some of them internally inconsistent—perhaps we could take the more modest route of clarifying that the denials of one church do not contradict the affirmations of the other church on the issue of *ius divinum*. So, for example, we might argue: (1) when Roman Catholics affirm that the primacy of the bishop of Rome is *de iure divino*, they do not deny that this primacy and all office in the church must be under the word of God and must serve it; (2) when Lutherans deny that the primacy of the bishop of Rome is *de iure divino*, they do not deny that papal primacy could be conditionally necessary today for the effective proclamation of the gospel in the contemporary world; and (3) when Roman Catholics affirm that the episcopate is *de iure divino* part of the ordained ministry, they do not deny that the exercise of the episcopate must be reformed.

The Anglican–Roman Catholic Commission's discussion of *ius divinum* gives additional suggestions for such an approach. "*Jus divinum* in this context need not be taken to imply that the universal primacy as a permanent institution was directly founded by Jesus during his life on earth," ARCIC comments. "Neither does the term mean that the universal primate is a 'source of the Church' as if Christ's salvation had to be channeled through him. Rather, he is to be the sign of the visible *koinonia* God wills for the Church and an instrument through which unity in diversity is realized. It is to a universal primate thus envisaged within the collegiality of the bishops and the *koinonia* of the whole Church that the qualification *jure divino* can be applied."[86] Commission members go on to note that "the doctrine that a universal primacy expresses the will of God does not entail the consequence that a Christian community out of communion with the see of Rome does not belong to the Church of God."[87] In addition, they note, Anglican theologians have sometimes affirmed "that, in changed circumstances, it might be possible to recognize the development of the Roman primacy as a gift of divine providence—in other words, as an effect of the guidance of the Holy Spirit in the Church."[88] And they ask "whether a gap really exists between the assertion of a primacy by divine right (*jure divino*) and the acknowledgement of its emergence by divine providence (*divina providentia*)."[89]

These points suggest two other possible theses besides the three enumerated above: (4) when Roman Catholic affirm that the papacy is *de iure divino* part of the church, they do not deny that a Christian communion out of communion with the see of Rome may belong to the one church of Christ; and (5) when Lutherans affirm that God will always provide instruments for the proclamation of the gospel in every age, they do not deny that the episcopate could be an instrument chosen by God for this age.

This approach would allow us to draw on *ius divinum* traditions in a positive way, while also responding to the fears and misunderstandings that such traditions carry. In addition, it would absolve us from choosing among the different, sometimes conflicting, approaches to *ius divinum* used today in the Roman Catholic communion and, I suspect, in the Lutheran communion as well. And it would help clarify which issues related to *ius divinum*, if any, still divide us.

Conclusion

Dulles is correct when he underlines the importance of what is intended by the idea of *ius divinum*. This idea is a way to emphasize the permanence of the gospel and the Church's dependence on the Lord. At the same time, Roman Catholic theology now attributes a variety of meanings to *ius divinum*. I suggest that a way forward involves clarifying what is affirmed and what is denied by each of our communions in this regard, suspecting that on this matter we are not finally at odds.

NOTES

1   Lutheran–Roman Catholic [International] Study Commission, "The Gospel and the Church" (The Malta Report), GA I, 175, no. 31.

2   L/RC-5, no. 7.

3   Ibid., no. 30.

4   L/RC-5, "Differing Attitudes toward Papal Primacy: Reflections of the Lutheran Participants," no. 35.

5   L/RC-5, "Differing Attitudes toward Papal Primacy: Reflections of the Roman Catholic Participants," nos. 34-35.

6   Avery Dulles, "*Ius Divinum* as an Ecumenical Problem," *Theological Studies* (TS) 38 (1977): 681-708, at 681.

7   Discussions of moral theology and its relationship to the divine command tradition focus on a different set of issues from those of this paper; e.g., Oliver O'Donovan, "How Can Theology Be Moral?" *Journal of Religious Ethics* 17 (1989): 81-94; Jean Porter, "Christianity, Divine Law and Consequentialism," *Scottish Journal of Theology* 48 (1995): 415-442.

8   Dulles, 698.

9   Ibid., 698.

10   ARCIC I, "Authority in the Church I," *The Final Report* (London: SPCK & Catholic Truth Society, 1982), no. 24b, GA I, 97.

11   ARCIC I, "Authority in the Church II," *The Final Report*, no. 11, GA I, 108-109.

12   Ibid., no. 13.

13   Dulles, 687.

14   Carl J. Peter, "Dimensions of Jus Divinum in Roman Catholic Theology," TS 34 (1973): 238-239; cf. André Duval, "Le 'droit divin' de l'intégrité de la confession selon le canon 7 'De Poenitentia' du Concile de Trente [P. A. Amato]," *Revue des Sciences philosophiques et théologiques* 63 (1979): 549-560; Pierre M. Gy, "Le précepte de la confession annuelle et la nécessité de la confession," *Revue des Sciences philosophiques et théologiques* (1979): 529-547.

15   Dulles, 689.

16   Ibid., 689.

17   Ibid., 690.

18   Ibid., 690-691.

19   Ibid., 692.

20   Ibid., 693.

21   Ibid., 694.

22   Karl Rahner, "Reflections on the Concept of *Ius Divinum* in Catholic Thought," *Theological Investigations*, vol. 5, trans. Karl-H. Kruger (Baltimore: Helicon Press & London: Darton, Longman & Todd, 1966), 237.

23   Peter, 227.

24   Ibid., 246.

25   Ibid., 248.

26   Dulles, 695.

27   Ibid., 695.

28   Karl Rahner, "Basic Observations on the Subject of the Changeable and Unchangeable Factors in the Church," *Theological Investigations* 14, trans. David Bourke (New York: Seabury Press, 1976), 17.

29   Ibid., 19.

30   Karl Rahner, Commentary on Article 20 of the Dogmatic Constitution on the Church [*Lumen Gentium*], in Herbert Vorgrimler, ed., *Commentary on the Documents of Vatican II*, vol. 1, trans. Kevin Smyth (New York: Herder and Herder, 1967), 192.

31   Ibid.

32   Ibid.

33   Dulles, 696.

34   Ibid.

35   Ibid., 700.

36   Ibid., 701.

37   Ibid., 703.

38   Eric Doyle, "The Essential Unity of the Church: Some Consequences for Ecumenism," *Journal for Ecumenical Studies* 20 (1983): 253.

39   In 1978, the Congregation for the Doctrine of the Faith issued "Declaration on the Question of the Admission of Women to the Ministerial Priesthood" (*Inter insigniores*) (*Origins* 6 [1977-1978]: 520); in 1994, John Paul II issued "*Ordinatio Sacerdotalis*" (*Origins* 24 [1994-1995]: 49, 51-52).

40   Dulles, 705.

41   Ibid., 708.

42   George Lindbeck, "Papacy and *Ius Divinum*: A Lutheran View," in L/RC-5, 196.

43   Ibid., 198.

44   Ibid., 198-199.

45   Ibid., 199.

46   Ibid.

47   Ibid., 203.

48   Ibid., 204.

49   Ibid., 207.

50   Ibid., 208.

51   Joseph J. Koury, "*Ius Divinum* as a Canonical Problem: On the Interaction of Divine and Ecclesiastical Laws," *The Jurist* 53 (1993): 104-131; cf. Ad. Van Der Helm, "Le droit divin dans une perspective oecuménique," *Praxis Juridique et Religion* 3 (1986): 225-231; Marie Zimmermann, "Le chrétien catholique romain face au droit de son église," *Praxis Juridique et Religion* 5 (1988): 72-81.

52   Ibid., 106.

53   Ibid., 108.

54   Ibid., 114.

55   Ibid., 116.

56   Ibid., 120.

57   Ibid., 115.

58   Ibid., 130.

59   Ibid., 131.

60   ARCIC I, "Authority in the Church II," no. 11.

61   Ibid.

62   Bernard Lonergan, "The Transition from a Classicist Worldview to Historical-Mindedness," *Second Collection* (London: Darton, Longman and Todd, 1974), 5.

63   Ibid., 4-5.

64   Ladislas Örsy, "Magisterium: Assent and Dissent," TS 48 (1987): 473.

65   Rahner, "Basic Observations on the Subject of Changeable and Unchangeable Factors in the Church," 3.

66   Frederick E. Crowe, "The Church as Learner: Two Crises, One Kairos," *Appropriating the Lonergan Idea*, ed. Michael Vertin (Washington, DC: The Catholic University of America Press, 1989), 371.

67   Ibid., 373.

68   DS 3020; translation is from Josef Neuner and Heinrich Roos, trans. Latin into German, *The Teaching of the Catholic Church*, ed. Karl Rahner, trans. into English by Geoffrey Stevens (Staten Island, NY: Alba House, 1967), 38.

69   DS 3074; translation is from Neuner and Roos, 229.

70   *Dei Verbum*, in *The Documents of Vatican II*, ed. Walter M. Abbott (New York: America Press, 1966), no. 8.

71   Congregation for the Doctrine of the Faith, *Mysterium Ecclesiae*, *The Tablet* 227 (July 14, 1973), 668.

72   L/RC-5, "Differing Attitudes Toward Papal Primacy: Reflections of the Roman Catholic Participants," no. 34.

73   Ibid., nos. 34-35.

74   ARCIC, "Authority in the Church II," no. 7.

75   John Paul II, *Ordinatio Sacerdotalis*, no. 2.

76   Ibid.

77   Ibid., no. 4.

78   Joseph Ratzinger and Tarcisio Bertone, "Commentary on Profession of Faith's Concluding Paragraphs," *Origins* 28 (1998): 116-119, see no. 8.

79   Ibid., no. 7.

80   Ibid., no. 3.

81   JDDJ.

82   Lindbeck, 203.

83   Ibid., 194.

84   Ibid., 199.

85   Ibid., 205.

86   ARCIC, "Authority in the Church II," no. 11.

87   Ibid., no. 12.

88   Ibid., no. 13.

89   Ibid.

Chapter 6

※

RECENT LUTHERAN REFLECTIONS ON UNIVERSAL MINISTRY

BY SCOTT S. ICKERT

As consensus forms among Roman Catholics and Lutherans on fundamental matters of faith and doctrine, the question of ministry increasingly dominates the conversation. Universal ministry often stands out (even when avoided) as an inescapable and intractable problem. There are obvious historical reasons for this: The papacy, an office meant to serve the church's unity, often found itself at certain critical moments in the vortex of controversy—often of a political nature—that led, ironically, to the church's fragmentation.

For the churches of the East and West, the role and nature of universal ministry is unavoidable because, to one degree or another, the church's visible unity is at stake. The issue is also intractable because both Orthodox and Protestant opposition to the papacy, no less than Catholic championing of the papacy, has become, justifiably or not, an important aspect of their respective self-identities.

Papal Primacy in Lutheran–Roman Catholic Dialogue

Inevitably, then, the Lutheran–Roman Catholic dialogue has dealt with the topic of universal ministry. On the international level, the Joint Lutheran–Roman Catholic Study Commission noted the unavoidable nature of papal primacy in the "Malta Report" of 1972 (nos. 66-67). The issue was taken up in 1981 by a new Roman Catholic–Lutheran Joint Commission in the document *The Ministry in the Church*, section 3.5, *The Episcopal Ministry and Service for the Universal Unity of the Church* (nos. 67-73). The final paragraph (no. 73) of that 1981 document sounds a positive note, though it concludes with a caveat from the Malta Report (no. 66), an emphasis that continued to stand out as a Lutheran theme in the ensuing dialogue: "But in the various dialogues, the possibility begins to emerge that the Petrine office of the Bishop of Rome also need not be excluded by Lutherans as a visible sign of the unity of the church as a whole 'insofar as [this office] is subordinated to the primacy of the gospel by theological reinterpretation and practical restructuring.'"

Lutherans and Catholics in round V's *Papal Primacy and the Universal Church* (1974) took up the theme of universal ministry, excluding the question of papal infallibility. Papal infallibility is addressed in round VI's *Teaching Authority and Infallibility in the Church* (1978).[1]

The Common Statement of the *Papal Primacy* document (round V) speaks of a "Petrine function" to describe "a particular form of Ministry exercised by a person, officeholder, or local church with reference to the church as a whole," a function that "serves to promote or preserve the oneness of the church by symbolizing unity, and by facilitating communication, mutual assistance or correction, and collaboration in the church's mission" (no. 4). This emphasis on a Petrine *function* became the conceptual basis for Lutheran–Roman Catholic convergence on universal ministry. Moreover, by distinguishing a Petrine function from the jurisdictional authority of the bishop of Rome, *Papal Primacy* provides a useful means for furthering the discussion. This was an important step toward a theological reformulation of the papacy called for in the Malta Report. It became clear that, while the historical institution of the papacy could not be circumvented in any plan for reunification, neither could the topic of its reform. The discussion of Petrine function, therefore, acknowledged as given the papacy's Roman incarnation, without glossing over the problematic nature of its historical development. It did so without isolating papal ministry from that of the rest of the church.

Lutherans, who originally wanted to maintain the historic structures, now in round V's *Papal Primacy* "increasingly recognize the need for a Ministry serving the unity of the church universal." Here Rome's historical preeminence is recognized: "For the exercise of this Ministry, institutions which are rooted in history should be seriously considered [because] the church should use the signs of unity it has received, for new ones cannot be invented at will." The document also recognizes the contemporary situation of global communication and international cooperation, where the question of universal ministry is regarded as an opportunity to serve the church's unity and further its cooperation, communication, and mission. Finally, *Papal Primacy* reiterates a caveat of the international Joint Commission: "The one thing necessary, from the Lutheran point of view, is that papal primacy be so structured and interpreted that it clearly serve the gospel and the unity of the church of Christ, and that its exercise of power not subvert Christian freedom."[2]

Thus, while the link between Petrine function and the bishop of Rome can be endorsed by Lutherans, the jurisdictional power of that office can never be allowed to betray the basic function of service to the church's unity, mutual assistance or correction, communication, and mission. The function of service is becoming increasingly important in an era of instantaneous global communication and international political and economic interdependence.

In round V of the dialogue, Lutherans and Catholics thus found themselves in agreement on the following points: the unity of church must be a visible unity; special responsibility for such unity may be entrusted to an individual minister, under the gospel; and the bishop of Rome can be that minister.[3] Finally, in *Papal Primacy* the Lutheran dialogue members ask the Lutheran churches if they are prepared to affirm that papal primacy, "renewed in light of the gospel, need not be a barrier to reconciliation." The Lutheran dialogue members also ask whether Lutherans are able to acknowledge "the possibility and the desirability of the papal Ministry, renewed under the gospel and committed to Christian freedom, in a larger communion which would include the Lutheran churches" (L/RC-5: no. 32, 23).

Yet in the same document Lutherans identify two problems: the use of the term "antichrist" and papal jurisdictional claims. With regard to the term "antichrist," the Reformers did not reject the Petrine function, "but rather the concrete historical papacy as it confronted them in their day." The epithet was already part of a tradition of protest common to pre-Reformation reformers to condemn papal abuses of power. The term was often linked with a denial that the papacy exists by divine right.[4] With regard to jurisdictional power, historic concern centered on the pope's claims to secular power, considered to be an abuse of authority. That the Reformers found themselves outside papal jurisdiction was not problematic, for they regarded themselves "as being on par with those parts of the church, especially in the East, which did not recognize the jurisdictional primacy of the bishop of Rome" (L/RC-5, II, no. 30, 26). In consideration of this history, Lutherans justified the human institution of the jurisdictional authority of the bishop of Rome. This was not an outright denial of papal jurisdiction. But by reminding Rome of it historical limitations, the Reformers sought to justify their rejection of unwarranted expressions of papal power.

Taken together, Lutherans' charge of antichrist and the identification with the Eastern churches functionally defined Lutheranism as anti-papal despite significant confessional arguments to the contrary. Nevertheless, the dialogue participants expressed confidence that, by giving proper attention to these historical problems, a way forward could be forged toward a greater degree of visible unity. It would include a commonly recognized universal ministry to serve the church's mission.

> We ask our churches earnestly to consider if the time has not come to affirm à new attitude toward the papacy 'for the sake of peace and concord in the church' [Melanchthon] *and even more for the sake of a united witness to Christ in the world*. Our Lutheran teaching about the church and the Ministry constrains us to believe that a recognition of papal primacy is possible to the degree that a renewed papacy would in fact foster faithfulness to the gospel and truly exercises a Petrine function within the church.[5]

Contemporary Lutheran Theological Reflection

The challenge to deepen Lutheran appreciation of universal ministry for the sake of the church's mission, as proposed by the dialogue, has been addressed by several theologians, including Robert Jenson, Harding Meyer, Wolfhart Pannenberg, and David Yeago. Their contribution to this topic is, in part, an extended commentary and further reflection on the work of the dialogues.[6]

Antichrist

Martin Luther's use of the term "antichrist" is an obvious stumbling block to a Lutheran recognition of papal primacy. Of the four theologians mentioned above, Meyer has dealt with the issue in relative depth, pointing out that Luther criticized the popes of his time on three basic counts, all of which essentially castigated the papacy for its promotion of a righteousness of works.[7] The pope was the antichrist according to Luther because (1) the pope retained the exclusive right to interpret

Scripture; (2) he established new articles of faith, requiring ultimate trust on the part of the faithful; and (3) he claimed that Christians could not be saved apart from their obedience to the pope and his power. But Meyer claims that as these problems could be addressed positively, a limited openness also is suggested. Whenever the pope takes up the concerns of the Reformation, when he places himself under the authority of Scripture, when he allows and approves the evangelical preaching of the gospel, then, Luther said, Christians shall willingly place themselves under his authority (Meyer, DPL, 318).

Luther's denial of papal power and his accompanying critique of the institution was aimed at the ongoing exercise of the office. Yet his critique, and even his persistent use of the term "antichrist," did not prevent Luther from a conditional willingness to recognize papal primacy. Meyer notes that "even in his last and sharpest writing against the papacy . . . (*Against the Papacy in Rome, instituted by the Devil*, 1545), Luther nevertheless affirms that the pope might enjoy a primacy of 'honor and superiority' and 'of oversight over teaching and heresy in the Church'" (Meyer, LAP, 16-18).

Therefore, despite their criticism, "the issue of papal primacy remains for the Lutheran Reformers, in a somewhat surprising and peculiar manner, an 'open question'" (Meyer, LAP, 20). Such a "conditional openness," which Meyer thinks is also appropriate today, does not thereby repudiate the Reformers' primary concerns, including the depiction of the papacy as the antichrist.[8] Such openness is consonant with what Lutherans maintain in the dialogues: namely, the acceptability of a reformed papacy that serves the gospel and does not arbitrarily restrict Christian freedom.

Ius Divinum

Meyer, Jenson, and Pannenberg are among those theologians who take up the question of *ius divinum* as it applies directly to the papacy. For Meyer, the matter of *ius divinum* is part of a larger question, which he calls the real center of Lutheran criticism as well as its expectation: *the problem of theological understanding and "reinterpretation" of papal primacy*. Meyer maintains that for Lutherans, "this problem requires an answer even if and after the ecclesiological, structural and juridical problematic of papal primacy has found a satisfactory response." But just what is meant by "theological understanding" and "theological reinterpretation?" Lutherans have raised two principal concerns: (1) the claim of papal primacy *de iure divino*; and (2) the theological claim of papal primacy that its doctrinal decisions or definitions *ex cathedra* are "infallible" and "irreformable" (Meyer, LAP, 28; emphasis in original).

Meyer asks two fundamental questions under *ius divinum*. The first and most obvious question is whether papal primacy is necessary. The Reformers placed this concern in the context of salvation. Today, however, the issue is that of *ecclesial* necessity, whether papal primacy is indispensable, whether it is of the church's essence. This question, Meyer says, "raises for Lutherans great difficulties, for it cannot be answered in a way which questions the former and present ecclesial status of the Lutheran churches" (Meyer, LAP, 29). Meyer suggests a way forward:

> Could, perhaps, a distinction between "necessary for being a church" and "necessary for *the unity of the church*" move us closer to an answer? . . . Is it not true that . . . the present ecumenical openness for primacy is grounded in an understanding of primacy as a "ministry *of unity*" and in the hope that it might serve the "*communion* of churches?" What is affirmed about primacy and what is expected from it, what can even be considered as "needed" is exactly this "Petrine function" or "Petrine ministry" for the unity of the church universal. In short, the entire non-Roman Catholic expectation with regard to papal primacy, it seems to me, ultimately drives us towards such a distinction between "church" and "unity of the church" and focuses on the latter. (Meyer, LAP, 29-30. Emphasis in original.)

The second question deals with infallibility. The two concepts of necessity and infallibility are inseparable precisely because infallibility is rooted, according to the Reformers, in the papacy's *ius divinum* claim. Meyer concentrates on Philipp Melanchthon's *Treatise on the Power and Primacy of the Pope* (1537), in which this issue was crucial. "Even if the bishop of Rome did possess primacy by divine right, he should not be obeyed inasmuch as he defends impious forms of worship and doctrines which are in conflict with the Gospel. On the contrary, it is necessary to resist him as Antichrist."[9] Melanchthon was repudiating an exaggerated understanding of the pope's *de iure divino* status. Meyer concludes that "in this perspective the Reformation insistence on the *ius humanum* character of papal primacy basically, and in its main intention, is not the categorical denial of the *ius divinum* but the correction of its maximalistic interpretation," a helpful distinction that can lead to fruitful dialogue on a "theological interpretation" of the papacy (Meyer, LAP, 29-30).

Jenson discusses *ius divinum* obliquely with respect to the papacy, taking up the term as it applies generally to episcopacy.[10] Jenson highlights an article George Lindbeck prepared for round V of the Lutheran–Roman Catholic dialogue.[11] Quoting Lindbeck, Jenson argues for a redefinition of *ius divinum*, which he applies to episcopacy. He writes that "historically relative and conditioned" institutions may be considered divinely instituted as long as two conditions are fulfilled. First, they must be "contingently but really necessary 'for the sake of the gospel.'" Second, their appearance must be irreversible (Lindbeck, L/RC-5, 202-203). Episcopacy fulfills these conditions, Jenson believes, substantiating his claim with a further quotation from Lindbeck: "It is to the episcopally united church . . . that all . . . Christian traditions owe their creeds, their liturgies, and above all their scriptural canon. If these later are inexpugnable, why not the episcopate?" (Jenson, 239). Jenson adds that the episcopacy is a *ius divinum* because the church is led by the Spirit.[12]

The question for Jenson is whether Lindbeck's conditions for a divinely instituted office are met by the bishop of Rome (especially the condition of irreversibility). Jenson affirms unhesitatingly[13] that there must be (*de iure divino?*) a universal pastor. But the pastor must be the bishop of *Rome*, Jenson demurs.

> It is clear that the unity of the church cannot in fact now be restored except with a universal pastor located at Rome. And this is already sufficient reason to say that churches now not in communion with the church of Rome are very severely "wounded." Just so it is sufficient reason to say also that the restoration of those churches' communion with Rome is the peremptory will of God. Yet such considerations do not provide quite the legitimation we look for in systematic theology and that we found for the episcopate and for universal pastorate simply as such. (247)

Why is the necessary legitimacy lacking? Jenson admits it is because "identification of the universal pastor with the Roman episcopacy is not strictly irreversible" (248).[14]

In his discussion of *ius divinum*, Pannenberg focuses on Peter and what he does or does not represent for the church as a whole. In Pannenberg's estimation the question is one of divine right. Does the assertion of the primacy of the bishop of Rome over the whole church rest on a direct institution of the apostle Peter as "visible head" of the church by Christ himself (Mt 16:16-18; Jn 21:15-17; see also DS 3055, 3058)? Divine right must be based solely and directly on Scripture. Roman primacy cannot be *de iure divino*, because

> Today theological exegesis of the NT [New Testament], including Roman Catholic exegesis, has reached widespread consent that these NT sayings about Peter, no matter how else we might assess them, refer only to Peter, not to any successors in his office. . . . from a Reformation standpoint the authority of such an office, and those who hold it, can be one only of human law because we cannot trace it back to any express institution by Jesus himself. (Pannenberg, 429-430)

Pannenberg admits that from the earliest time Peter was seen as a model bishop. Moreover, given the special importance of Rome as the capital of the empire and the martyrdoms of Peter and Paul in that city, it can be understood why the bishops saw themselves in a special sense as Peter's successor. Although a substantiation of Roman primacy must be sought in the early history of the church *de iure humano* and not in the New Testament itself (*de iure divino*) nevertheless, according to Pannenberg, "as a representation of the unity of the whole church, [the papacy] is not just an expression of human arbitrariness but a special instance of all church ministry as a ministry to the church's unity at every level of its life" (430).

Expanding this theme, Pannenberg concludes with a conditional endorsement.

> The authority of a ministry to the universal unity of the church of Christ cannot consist in claims to a power of office that is in

competition with that of other bishops or local churches, but only of the weight that attaches to what has historically become Rome's function as a representative of all Christianity and of the commission that its Lord has given it. (431)[15]

Infallibility

In round VI of the Lutheran–Roman Catholic dialogue, *Teaching Authority and Infallibility in the Church*, the Lutherans affirm a universal teaching office. "We share the conviction that decisions about the truth of the gospel have to be made for the sake of the gospel's life in the world. Consequently, we affirm a Ministry which has the responsibility of reformulating doctrine in fidelity to the Scripture when circumstances require" (L/RC-6, III, 19).[16]

On the other hand, they were wary of speaking of the church's teaching office as infallible, for "infallibility suggests something above and beyond that indefectibility of the Church which we also accept." The Lutherans instead stressed a preaching and teaching authority, "which exists to serve the proclamation of the Word and for the sake of order and discipline in the Church. . . . Such order and discipline are, in part, the responsibility of the Ministry, which exists to ensure that the gospel is transmitted and preserved," but the only guarantee of that transmission is the Holy Spirit (L/RC-6, III, 20).

Subsequent Lutheran reflection has been less hesitant about infallibility without departing in substance from earlier words of caution.

In his discussion of the universal pastorate, Jenson deals with infallibility, which he endorses in principle. Taking his cues from the First Vatican Council, which spoke of the church as one flock under one supreme pastor, Jenson accepts such a ministry while stressing the essentially *pastoral role* of the church's universal bishop. With respect to infallibility, the authority of the pope is exactly that of any bishop or parish pastor, except that it is exercised universally. Jenson operates with the same kinds of restrictions applicable to all pastors—and councils. Jenson emphasizes what Lutherans have said traditionally about bishops, that "the pope's role in the universal church is of the same *sort* as that of a pastor in a local church" (Jenson, 243).[17]

A similar point is made by Yeago:

> For the main tradition of Lutheran ecclesiology, the relationship of shepherd and flock, pastor and people, is structurally essential to the form of the church's life in history. . . . If this *Gegenüber* of pastor and people is an essential, concrete form of the church's ontologically crucial dependence on the gospel, we can then say that in whatever way the church's communion takes concrete form in history, it always does so in some analogical reiteration of the relationship of shepherd and flock. The church exists, for Lutheran ecclesiology, in the basic form of worshiping assemblies presided over by pastors. If the church is also to exist concretely as a communion of such assemblies, then that communion will also take form as a flock with a shepherd. It will be historically actual as a real ecclesial community insofar as it is gathered by a pastor who speaks the word of God to it. . . . But what applies to the worshiping assembly and to the communion of churches in a region must also apply to the church universal. (Yeago, 104-105)

In his attempt to sort out the controverter question of how, when, and under what circumstances the pope's *ex cathedra* decisions are irreformable, Jenson again adverts to the essentially pastoral role of the universal ministry. With an appeal to Cardinal Joseph Ratzinger, Jenson offers a positive assessment. While the First Vatican Council claimed that the pope's definitive decisions could be made by himself, *ex sese*, clarification of that statement had to wait until the Second Vatican Council. "It is now said," Ratzinger claimed, "that the work of the teaching office always takes place on the background of the faith and prayer of the whole church. Yet at the same time it cannot be restricted only to the expression of an already established common opinion but . . . must under certain circumstances take the initiative . . . over against the confusion of a church without consensus" (Jenson, 245; Jenson's translation).

Jenson regards this statement as fundamental description of all pastoral ministry per se, again with the same restrictions. "Exactly the same," Jenson maintains, "must be said, *mutatis mutandis*, of any pastorate; were it not so, it should not be said of pope or council." And, as with all pastors, while it might be necessary to act over against the community for the sake of the gospel, the authority so exercised cannot be said to be simply their own.

> For a presbyteral pastor or a bishop in the local diocese of course cannot say, "This is what *the* church teaches" in such a fashion as to settle the matter, unless the church has in fact taught it. All pastors sometimes must speak with "that infallibility which the divine Redeemer willed his church to enjoy," but they do so as they speak in concord with the whole church, a concord ascertainable only as the one church speaks through her organs of unity. This does not empty the charism of individual bishops and presbyters; in actually addressing the church's teaching to a local church's unique concerns and questions, a bishop or presbyter cannot simply recite dogma but must explain and apply and therein must rely on the same promise of the Spirit as does pope and council. And a local pastor's teaching about a matter not dogmatically settled may determine the church's eventual, and perhaps then irreversible, consensus. (Jenson, 245-246)

Here it would appear that Jenson is merely carrying through to a logical conclusion with respect to the papacy. This is the standard Lutheran teaching that pastors and bishops are the same, that they derive their authority from the same source, that they are equally responsible to it, and thus that their ministries of teaching and preaching and the administration of the sacraments (including the office of the keys), are basically identical. Jenson, in fact, *grounds* papal authority, including its jurisdictional and infallible teaching authority, in that authority common to all ministers of the gospel.

Infallibility is also a principal concern of Pannenberg's. Pannenberg, like Jenson, maintains not just the acceptability but also the necessity of a universal pastor. "In addition to leadership at the local and regional levels, is there needed also at the universal level of the church as a whole a ministry to the unity of Christians, not merely in the synodical form of ecumenical councils at which the regions of Christianity are represented by their bishops, but also by the ministry of an individual who can be active as a spokesperson for Christianity as a whole?" (Pannenberg, 420).

He points out, too, that the Lutheran Reformation "never rules out in principle a ministry to protect Christian unity on the universal level of Christianity as a whole" (421).

Pannenberg regards the claim of infallibility as dubious, and expresses a greater degree of caution than does Jenson. Pannenberg emphasizes the crucial importance of tradition and reception on the part of the church as a whole. He makes a pointed criticism of the Catholic Church for its persistent and overly optimistic view of papal magisterial authority.

> From the days of the first apostolic preaching Christian church-
> es have accepted the teaching of their bishops and councils in
> the light of the link to Jesus Christ and the gospel that is a
> given factor in the faith awareness of all Christians. Involved is
> an explicit testing of the agreement of the proposed doctrine
> with this basic norm of Christian faith awareness, and this is
> what finally decides the reception or not of a doctrine in
> Christ's church (cf. John 10:27). . . . The teaching office is not
> above the Word of God but serves it by teaching only what has
> been handed down (*Dei Verbum*, no. 10). The implication here
> is that the gospel functions as a standard evaluation by which
> to judge proposed doctrine in the process of its reception. But
> thus far the statements of the Roman Catholic teaching office
> about this theme have not stressed this function of the Word of
> God as a criterion of doctrine. They have not denied it, but
> they have focused only on the positive case of agreement with
> the Word of God on the one side and with the faith awareness
> of the church on the other. (Pannenberg, 425-246)

Like Jenson, Pannenberg maintains that infallibility is something promised, not to an individual pastor, but to the church as a whole. The related claims of the teaching office are "tied to the premise that his office is in fact stating the agreed faith of the church that is bound to the gospel of Jesus Christ" (423-424; 427-428). Pannenberg finds the papal claim to jurisdictional primacy in the whole of the Christian world as objectionable as the concept of an infallible teaching office. Echoing the international and American dialogues, Pannenberg says that "there is especial need of a readiness for papal self-criticism in the course of a practical restructuring of the universal teaching office of the church in subordination to the gospel." A starting point would be the separation of the functions of the pope as primate of the whole church and as patriarch of the West (428).[18] Pannenberg regards papal claims of universal jurisdictional primacy and infallibility as having become too closely identified with each other.

Meyer agrees with Pannenberg. Meyer sees infallibility, from the perspective of the Reformers, as indicative of a questionable and objectionable transference of responsibility from the church to the hierarchy.[19] While the Reformers never required papal primacy to give up its claim for authoritative teaching, they did expect the papacy to acknowledge and respect in its teaching what the recent document, *Church and Justification*, calls the "dialectical tension between the claim of its binding nature and the reservation relating to that binding nature" (Meyer, LAP, 33. See also n. 53).

Meyer suggests two possible avenues for exploring a "theological reinterpretation" of papal primacy. The first—and here he reiterates one of Pannenberg's major themes—is to explore further the theology of reception. The second task is to consider "the attempt of some Roman Catholic theologians to understand what Vatican I said about the *binding of the papal magisterium to the 'depositum fidei' contained in Scripture and tradition* not only as indicative, i.e., as something always given but as something *normative*, i.e., as necessary precondition for the legitimacy of papal teaching (Meyer, LAP, 33; emphasis in original).

For these German Lutheran theologians, infallibility is the neuralgic issue. Primacy—not just the ecclesial possibility of a universal ministry, but concretely the primacy of the bishop of Rome—is not a deeply contested theological or confessional problem. Despite the serious criticisms and tensions surrounding it since the time of the Reformation, Roman primacy itself never really was denied. It is still possible, even desirable, today for Lutherans to recognize such primacy.[20] What seems to be of greater importance and more difficult to sort out is the matter of infallibility—how primacy came to be justified and exercised?—and the related question of the extent to which irreformable magisterial authority and universal jurisdictional claims have tended to overlap. Thus on the one hand, the U.S. dialogue was wise to treat infallibility separately, as "conceptually distinct" from primacy.[21] On the other hand, especially in the opinion of the Germans, it does not appear possible to solve the matter of primacy or actually enter into "full communion" with the bishop of Rome, until finally coming to terms with infallibility.

But is this necessarily the case? Yeago, at first glance, would seem to disagree. He sees infallibility as something of a "red herring" in ecumenical discussion, which instead should have been focusing on teaching authority per se. He says infallibility is a "red herring" also because "the Catholic Church does not turn out, upon examination, to be claiming any of the preposterous things that the term tends to suggest" (Yeago, 113). Catholic teaching, which is reflected in what Catholics consistently maintain in ecumenical dialogue, should allay fears about what is *meant* by infallibility, i.e., the limits and the context in which infallible teaching takes place. Yeago resonates the fears of Pannenberg, Meyer, and Jenson when he says that the essential problem is not to be found so much in what is *said* about teaching authority as in how that authority continues to be *exercised*. "The critical ecumenical issue," he says, "is not the philosophical hermeneutics of infallibility but the essentially *ecclesial-political* problem of authority (Yeago, 114; emphasis added).

Here Lutherans also contribute to the problem. They, too, act in a manner inconsistent with what is taught. Lutherans do not fully appreciate their own confessions: "So long as Lutherans boggle at the teaching of the Augsburg Confession that it belongs to the office of a bishop *by divine right* 'to judge doctrine and to condemn doctrine that is contrary to the gospel,' no really fruitful discussion will be possible of the claim of the Roman Bishop to judge doctrine definitively as universal pastor" (Yeago, 114).

There may be some validity, however, to such "boggling." It may be related to a legitimate Lutheran concern, shared by contemporary Catholics, that there not be a "one-sided dependence of the faith on the teaching office, a clerical monopoly on the true knowledge of Christ." The gospel belongs to the whole church, and all the faithful take part in its reliable transmission. No *a priori* validity, therefore, attaches to the judgments of the teaching office; but those judgments "must appeal for recognition by the faithful on the basis of shared standards of legitimacy, in particular Holy Scripture" (Yeago, 114). Lutherans, rightly, have been suspicious of arbitrary authority and "dictatorial power" (115).

For these Lutheran commentators, the temptation to exercise a universal jurisdictional authority, and the claims of an infallible teaching authority have become interdependent. The Germans display a greater wariness than the Americans, who acknowledge a Catholic appreciation, and appropriation, of these concerns.[22] *Both* the relative hesitation of the Germans and the relative openness of the Americans can be said to fall *within* the confessional tension between acknowledgment of primacy and wariness of infallibility.

Confronted, then, with this impasse, we come up against the problem of reception.

What Is to Be Done?

Yeago concentrates on the theme of reception as the critical problem currently facing Lutherans and Catholics on the issue of the papacy. He suggests moving beyond the impasse pragmatically. "We must temper our hopefulness [of possibilities outlined in ecumenical literature] with the recollection that we are seeking the reconciliation of churches, actual communities in the untidiness of history" (115-116). We must proceed with the understanding that "the ecumenical task is . . . never simply a conceptual task; it is an irreducibly political task" (99). Thus the dialogue on papal primacy correctly identified the "horizon of concern" as the church's *mission* (Yeago, 101, cf. 107-108).

Common mission can be carried out only on the basis of agreement on, and commitment to, the truth of the gospel. If the urgency of magisterial authority becomes clear in light of the mission of the church, then Lutherans have a problem; in the northern hemisphere, Lutherans are neither willing nor able to make doctrinal and moral decisions for the sake of the church's mission. On the contrary, such decisions are objected to as a *distraction* from mission (117). "In other words," Yeago says, "mainline Lutheran churches in Europe and North America typically conceive of themselves not as heralds of the gospel but as providers of the consolations of religion" (118). They focus more on questions of *identity* than on the *truth* of the gospel. Infallibility, therefore, is a "red herring" as far as Lutheranism is concerned. Lutheranism is simply too muddled, not only in its understanding of teaching authority as such, but also more important, in its preoccupation with the question of Lutheran identity at the expense of what used to be Lutheranism's overriding concern for the *evangelica veritas*. However one might evaluate this charge, it leads to Yeago's major theme, which he applies particularly to the Lutherans:

The reconciliation of the churches will require not only advances in theological insight but also profound changes in their lived and practiced sense of mission. With particular reference to the Lutheran churches . . . as long as we proceed on our current deep assumptions about our mission, about the ends of our existence, there will be no real prospect of our reconciliation with a Petrine ministry which takes the task of magisterium seriously. (118-119)

Given these circumstances, Yeago is not sanguine about prospects for reconciliation. "The ecumenical problem of the papacy cannot be resolved . . . apart from far-reaching changes in the ethos and practice of all our churches, changes which none of us has the wisdom to define precisely or the power to bring about" (120). He does, however, suggest some concrete steps. First, "we could and should give greater symbolic weight and formality to our communion in prayer." For Lutherans this would mean an "explicit recognition of the pope's leading role in the world Christian community, and an acknowledgment that we too have a stake in the health of the papacy." The Evangelical Lutheran Church in America also could communicate the names of its newly elected bishops to Rome with a request for prayer. This action that "would constitute an acknowledgment that Lutheran bishops are (or should be) engaged in ecclesially significant tasks, however defined, and that Rome too has a stake in their integrity and effectiveness" (Yeago, 120-121).

Yeago's second suggestion expands upon a proposal from *Teaching Authority and Infallibility in the Church*. It concerns "magisterial mutuality" as an intermediate step to develop structures of mutual consultation and colloquy in matters of teaching and discernment (L/RC-6, III, 21). Yeago sees the problem essentially as a practical matter of ecclesiopolitical intransigence (as the other Lutherans have observed, though with somewhat less emphasis than Yeago on the *Lutheran* contribution to the problem). He also suggests practical methods that can contribute to an eventual solution. If Yeago is correct that the impasse concerning the papacy is essentially—though not exclusively—a political matter (the other theologians do not appear to disagree fundamentally), then clearly one of the principal problems to be faced is the reception of the agreements and understandings thus far achieved.

Conclusions

Despite Luther's depiction of the papacy as the antichrist, neither he nor the Lutheran confessions were opposed to papal primacy in principle. Lutheran participants in the international and U.S. dialogues also have maintained a limited openness to such primacy, provided the papal office eschews centralized power, embraces collegiality, demonstrates an openness to criticism (including self-criticism), is willing to consider "theological reinterpretation and practical restructuring" (Malta Report), demonstrably serves the church's unity, and is, in essence, style, and practice, subordinated to the gospel. Contemporary Lutherans, not unlike their sixteenth-century predecessors, have declared themselves willing to accept the primacy of a reformed papacy. But it must be one whose role and authority is essentially *pastoral*, emphasizing the often-reiterated Lutheran claim that bishops and pastors are the same—that they exercise essentially the same ministry of word and sacrament—and that their respective authority (including jurisdiction) derives solely from this source.

According to Pannenberg, such an approach might lead to the "theological reinterpretation and practical restructuring" (422) that Lutherans have demanded. Inasmuch as "church leadership on every level of the church's work [i.e., parish pastors, bishops, popes] is a teaching office (*ministerium verbi*)" (423), so the reform of the papacy has the same starting point "with the question of the form of a teaching office for the church in its totality" (422). Precisely in this regard, Jenson is willing to accept infallibility. He maintains that all pastors must claim it when they teach the faith of the church.

But this does not solve the political problem of the tension between the church as communion and how authority is exercised on the universal level (Yeago). With regard to both teaching and jurisdiction, the church's universal mission requires an authoritative universal *voice*. But whose?

A solution stressed here is the requirement of reception as a true test of papal primacy and universal teaching authority. What, then, about the question of infallibility? Is this the "red herring" Yeago suggests, diverting attention from the underlying issue of teaching authority per se?

Perhaps, but by pushing this issue to the limit, is it not precisely the question of teaching authority that infallibility begs? Unfortunately, despite all the explanations, caveats, and safeguards, infallibility connotes not just spiritual authority, but political authoritarianism. This gives credence to Yeago's argument. A red herring thus becomes a red flag when the issue is reduced to jurisdictional power. At least this is the way most of the respondents, the Germans especially, have reacted.

There is a tendency among them to draw a connection between infallibility and questions of jurisdiction, and the ways in which these questions have tended to complement each other to the detriment of the church's visible unity. As such, the reception of infallibility bears directly on the reception, or non-reception, of primacy.[23] The question many of these Lutherans seem to be asking is, To what degree does infallibility feed a kind of power politics (e.g., direct universal jurisdiction) that has tended to frustrate efforts to achieve a unity in which Lutherans otherwise might be willing to accord the papacy its (rightful?) claim to primacy?

Reception is therefore a principal theme and an urgent problem. Lutherans are being asked to reaffirm an openness to papal primacy— expressed tentatively at the time of the Reformation and subsequently suppressed by a history of polemic and violence—provided certain reforms are instituted for the sake of the church's mission (a "non-starter" according to Yeago unless Lutherans, too, are willing to reform) (see Yeago, 107, 114-120, especially 119). Catholics are urged, more subtly, to receive a notion of reception itself that touches upon the teaching office directly,[24] and which—considering both the First and Second Vatican Councils—goes to the heart of the papal exercise of leadership.

NOTES

1   On papal infallibility, see third section under "Contemporary Lutheran Theological Reflection" in this essay.

2   Paul C. Empie and T. Austin Murphy, eds., *Papal Primacy and the Universal Church* (hereafter cited as L/RC-5) (Minneapolis: Augsburg Publishing House, 1974), I, no. 28, 21. The concluding statement on abuse of power and Christian freedom is repeated in paragraph 30. With regard to historic Lutheran insistence about maintaining, if at all possible, the church's polity, see paragraph 31.

3   Ibid., II, no. 29, 24. With respect to the congruence of these three items, see especially II, no. 32, 28.

4   Ibid., II, no. 30, 25. On the question of divine right, see below paragraph 35: "Rather than using the traditional terminology of divine and human right, therefore, both Lutherans and Roman Catholics have been compelled by their historical studies to raise a different set of questions: In what way or ways has our Lord in fact led his

church to use particular forms of the exercise of the Petrine function? What structural elements in the church does the gospel require for the ministry which serves the unity of the empirical church?"

5   Ibid., II, no. 41, 33. Emphasis added. J. Zizioulas, typically espousing a *communio* ecclesiology, offers what might be termed an "orthodox" postscript. See his article "Primacy in the Church: An Orthodox Approach," in *Petrine Ministry and the Unity of the Church: Toward a Patient and Fraternal Dialogue*, ed. James F. Puglisi (Collegeville, MN: Liturgical Press, 1999), 123-125.

6   See Robert Jenson, *Systematic Theology 2* (New York: Oxford University Press, 1999), 242-249; Harding Meyer, "'*Suprema auctoritas ideo ab omne arrore immunis*': The Lutheran Approach to Primacy" (hereafter LAP), in *Petrine Ministry and the Unity of the Church: Toward a Patient and Fraternal Dialogue*, ed. James F. Puglisi (Collegeville, MN: Liturgical Press, 1999), 15-34; H. Meyer, "Das Papsttum bei Luther und in den lutherischen Bekenntnisschriften" (hereafter DPL), in *Der Dialog der Kirchen 6*, ed. Wolfhart Pannenberg (Freiburg: Herder, 1990): 306-328; Wolfhart Pannenberg, *Systematic Theology 3*, trans. Geoffrey W. Bromiley (Grand Rapids, MI: Eerdmans, 1998): 420-431; David Yeago, "The Papal Office and the Burdens of History: A Lutheran View," in *Church Unity and the Papal Office: An Ecumenical Dialogue on John Paul II's Encyclical Ut Unum Sint (That All May Be One)*, ed. Carl Braaten and Robert Jenson (Grand Rapids, MI: Eerdmans, 2001), 98-123.

7   Pannenberg's brief treatment of the antichrist issue in *Systematic Theology 3*, 421-422, relies in substance chiefly on Meyer's "Das Papsttum."

8   "Not only the polemical equation of pope and 'Antichrist,' also the idea of a rightly exercised primacy are part of the Lutheran theological legacy" (Meyer, LAP, 22).

9   Philipp Melanchthon, "Treatise on the Power and Primacy of the Pope," in *The Book of Concord: The Confessions of the Evangelical Lutheran Church*, trans. and ed. Theodore G. Tappert (Philadelphia: Mühlenberg Press, 1959) no. 330, 57.

10   Jenson, *Systematic Theology 2* (New York: Oxford University Press, 1999), 237-240.

11   George Lindbeck, "Papacy and *Ius Divinum*: A Lutheran View," in L/RC-5, 193-208.

12   "If the Spirit has been leading the church, then if the episcopate has been in fact established in the history of the church, and if this establishment can dramatically have been the leading of the Spirit, then we must judge that the establishment was the leading of the Spirit. And, as we have just argued, given the scope of the decision made as the episcopate became established, if this particular decision was in its time proper it is also irreversible" (Jenson, 240).

13   "If communion ecclesiology is anywhere close to the truth, then plainly the 'one church' of its slogans must have her own pastor" (Jenson, 242).

14   On the question of Roman primacy, apart from the matter of it *ius divinum* status, see also Pannenberg, *Systematic Theology 3*, 420-421. See also Carl E. Braaten, *Mother Church: Ecclesiology and Ecumenism* (Minneapolis: Fortress Press, 1998), 34.

15   On the historical and ecumenical importance of a Roman primacy, see Yeago, "The Papal Office," 106: "Christian unity without Roman primacy would in a real sense be

unity without reconciliation, unity that evaded the burdens of history instead of confronting them."

16   Reference here is made to the Common Statement in L/RC-5, no. 41.

17   See also Yeago, "The Papal Office," 102: "The pope is therefore not in the first instance a sovereign invested with supreme power, but a pastor called to a critically important concretion of a necessary task of Christian ministry. . . . Papal *power* can therefore be considered in subordination to this Papal *ministry*." Emphasis in original.

18   Pannenberg cites an observation of Ratzinger's. See note 1008 in Pannenberg: "As he [Ratzinger] sees it, failure to distinguish between the Petrine office and the patriarchal power of the pope in the West might be responsible for the centralized image that Rome presented up to Vatican II and, we might add, that it has begun increasingly to present [this image?] again in the more recent past. Ratzinger's deliberations also point the way in their brief allusion to the possibility of future autocephalous status for the Reformation churches within renewed ecumenical unity." Cf. Jenson, 248.

19   Meyer, LAP, 31-32. See especially 31: "The real difference between Roman Catholic thought and that of the Reformation is seen only where, according to the Reformers, the responsibility for perseverance in the truth is transferred to and concentrated in the hierarchical office—the bishops and the pope. Ultimately it is taken away from the Church as a whole although it is precisely the whole Church which has been given the divine assurance of and the responsibility for remaining in the truth."

20   Gunther Wenz, "Papsttum und kirchlicher Einheitsdienst nach Massgabe evangelisch-lutherischer Bekenntnistrtadition" *Catholica* 50 (Munster, Westfalen: Aschendorff, 1996): 148, who cites Pannenberg favorably, "Einen grundsäzlichen Widerspruch gegen das Papsttum als universalkirchliches Leitungsamt hat die Reformation nicht erhoben." Cf. *The Condemnations of the Reformation Era. Do They Still Divide?*, ed. Karl Lehmann and Wolfhart Pannenberg, trans. Margaret Kohl (Minneapolis: Fortress Press, 1990): 158.

21   Common Statement in L/RC-5, no. 1.

22   See especially L/RC-6, II, "Catholic and Lutheran Emphases," no. 33.

23   Meyer says that "it has rightly been said that for Vatican I papal infallibility is 'the necessary qualification of the primacy of jurisdiction'" (LAP, 31). See also Pannenberg, 428.

24   In the sense of Jenson's comment (244): "For a presbyteral pastor or a bishop in the local diocese of course cannot say, 'This is what *the* church teaches' in such a fashion as to settle the matter, unless *the* church has in fact taught it." Cf. Pannenberg, 425.

Chapter 7

❖

THE UNIVERSALITY AND PARTICULARITY OF THE CATHOLIC CHURCH

BY PATRICK GRANFIELD

The ecclesiology of communion is especially valuable in helping us to understand the relationship between the universal church and the local or particular churches. The 1992 letter from the Congregation for the Doctrine of the Faith *Communionis Notio* observed that the concept of communion can be applied to the union that exists among particular churches. It said that particular churches "have a special relationship of 'mutual interiority' with the whole, that is, with the universal Church."[1] The particular church, which is truly church and not a subdivision of the universal church, is primarily a diocese, but it may refer to several dioceses in the same region, or rite.[2] The universal church is not an abstraction, nor the sum or federation of local churches, nor the church of Rome. The universal church is the communion of local churches united in faith and charity (see *Lumen Gentium*, nos. 13 and 23).

The purpose of this article is to examine how the church of Rome, the *prima sedes*, is connected to the many Catholic churches throughout the world. Related topics will include centralization and relative autonomy, universalism and regionalism, and unity and pluriformity. How are universality and particularity manifested in the Catholic Church?

Universality

Two factors influence our interpretation of the universality of the contemporary Roman Catholic Church, which comprises all those Christians in union with Rome. The first is that the Roman Catholic Church is a supranational and not a national church. The three hundred member churches of the World Council of Churches, for example, are national churches. A second factor is the size of the Roman Catholic Church, which now has one billion adherents or about 17 percent of the world's population. How, then, has the Roman Catholic Church come to understand and structure its universal character? We shall first present a brief survey of the development of universality and then assess the strengths and weaknesses of such a large, institutionalized, ecclesial body.[3]

The Development of Universality

Diverse ecclesiologies, church orders, and theologies existed among the different New Testament communities, but the unity of the church was ultimately preserved.[4] Raymond E. Brown, in his study of the churches in the sub-apostolic period (the last one-third of the first century) made this insightful observation:

> No one can show that any of the churches I have studied had broken *koinonia* or communion with another. Nor is it likely that the [New Testament] NT churches of this Sub-Apostolic Period had no sense of *koinonia* among Christians and were self-contained conventicles going their own way. . . . We modern Christians have broken *koinonia* with each other; for, explicitly or implicitly, we have excommunicated each other and/or stated that other churches are disloyal to the will of Christ in major issues. Such a divided situation does not have NT approbation.[5]

In the post-apostolic age, the church was not a large, centrally structured institution. Rather it was a loosely organized network of local churches under bishops who recognized each other's ministry. The reception of the eucharist was a sign of communion with God, with the bishops, and with other Christians. Christian travelers of good reputation were given letters of communion from their bishops, which they presented to other bishops who allowed them to share in eucharistic fellowship. Bishops could excommunicate other bishops for cause, and thus separate them from the communion of the bishops.

From its earliest days, Rome occupied a special role in the church, with good reason. It was the burial place of Peter and Paul, the only apostolic see in the West, the symbol of orthodoxy, and the capital of the Roman empire. By the end of the fourth century, the bishops of Rome, such as Damasus I (+384) and Leo I (+461), began to assert universal primatial claims. The widening jurisdiction of Rome tended to weaken the concept of communion. The emphasis became less on the church as a communion of local churches and more on a universal church with the bishops united to the church of Rome. Ludwig Hertling notes that "a Church in communion with Rome is in communion with the whole Catholic Church."[6] By the end of the first millennium, the churches in the West generally accepted the jurisdictional primacy of Rome. Individual bishops more and more looked to the see of Rome for advice and approval.

During the Middle Ages, many popes advocated a centralized universal church under papal authority.[7] Popes Gregory VII (+1085), Innocent III (+1216), and Boniface VIII (+1303), for example, affirmed the Roman pontiff's authority over all Christians, and promoted a grandiose version of papal sovereignty.[8] The pope emerged as the undisputed head of the church and as a unifying force in medieval Europe.

From the sixteenth century to the twentieth, a series of historical events of major significance—the Reformation, the unprecedented missionary activity in the age of discovery, the French Revolution and its disruptive aftermath, the loss of the papal states, and the threat of modernism—prompted bishops, clergy, and laity to look to Rome for support and direction. The restructuring of the Roman curia by Sixtus V (+1590), the Council of Trent (1545-1563), and the 1917 *Code of Canon Law* all strengthened the centralized structure of the Roman church. Theologians portrayed the universal church as a kind of monarchy under papal control and the local church as simply an administrative section of the universal church. The description of the pope by an earlier theologian, St. Peter Damian (+1072), was not far from the mark: "The Pope alone is the universal Bishop of all the Churches."[9] This move toward centralization peaked at the First Vatican Council (1869-1870).

The origins, mission, and scope of primatial authority in the Catholic Church differ from international institutions in other Christian communions, such as the Lutheran World Federation, the Baptist World Alliance, the World Methodist Council, or even the role of the patriarch of Constantinople or the archbishop of Canterbury. The unique claims of the papacy are readily apparent in the teaching of the First Vatican Council.

Convoked by Pope Pius IX, the First Vatican Council issued two dogmatic constitutions: *Dei Filius* on revelation and faith and *Pastor Aeternus* on papal primacy and infallibility.[10] The latter taught that the papacy is of divine right and that the pope's primacy of jurisdiction is supreme, full, universal, ordinary, immediate, and truly episcopal.[11] Each of these characteristics of papal authority are explained below.

First, the pope has full and supreme power of jurisdiction (*tota plenitudo potestatis*). The pope is subject to no superior human power in the church. His authority extends not only to matters of faith and morals but also to the discipline and governance of the church throughout the world. His decisions are subject to review by no one, not even an ecumenical council. The pope also has the supreme power of teaching, and under some circumstances, of teaching infallibly.

Second, the pope has universal power of jurisdiction. It extends to all the faithful. Bishops, clergy, and laity in all the particular churches in communion with the see of Rome are subject to him.

Third, the pope has ordinary power of jurisdiction. This power belongs to him properly in virtue of his office. "Ordinary" here does not mean quotidian, as if the pope were continually and habitually involved in the life of the local church, but rather it means proper or not delegated.

Fourth, the pope has immediate power of jurisdiction. In theory, he can exercise his authority without having to go through any intermediary—civil or ecclesiastical. In practice, he actually governs the church with the help of the curia.

Fifth, the pope has truly episcopal power. He is a consecrated bishop who is a member and the head of the college of bishops, and his authority of teaching, ruling, and sanctifying extends over the universal church. The pope's role is primarily pastoral and not administrative.

The Second Vatican Council, with its teaching on communion and collegiality, presented a far different and more enlightened ecclesiogical vision. Nevertheless, the Second Vatican Council "following in the footsteps of Vatican I" (*Lumen Gentium* [LG], no. 18), was clearly in agreement with the First Vatican Council concerning the primacy of Peter among the apostles and the authority of the pope as the successor of Peter. "And all this teaching about the institution, the perpetuity, the force and reason for the sacred primacy of the Roman Pontiff and of his infallible teaching authority, this sacred Synod again proposes to be firmly believed by all the faithful" (LG, no. 18). The Second Vatican Council taught that the pope was the permanent and visible foundation of the unity of the bishops and the faithful (LG, no. 23).

The 1983 *Code of Canon Law*, not surprisingly, reflects both the First Vatican Council and the Second Vatican Council in its affirmation of papal sovereignty. The *Code* lists a wide range of rights pertaining exclusively to the pope in his role as ruler, teacher, and sanctifier in the universal church:

- The pope, according to the needs of the church, determines how he will exercise his primatial authority, either personally or collegially (canon 333, 2).
- The pope freely selects men to be cardinals (canon 351, 1).
- The pope freely appoints bishops or confirms their election (canon 377, 1).
- The pope conducts the business of the universal church through the Roman curia, which fulfills its duty in his name (canon 360).
- The pope alone can convoke an ecumenical council, preside over it, transfer, suspend, or dissolve it, and approve its decrees (canon 338, 1).
- The First See is judged by no one (canon 1404).
- No appeal or recourse is allowed against a decision or decree of the pope (canon 333, 3).

Despite this imposing array of papal prerogatives, the pope is not without limits. He does not have absolute power but is limited by the very constitution of the church and by divine and natural law. At the Second Vatican Council, Pope Paul VI suggested that the phrase "accountable to the Lord alone" (*uni Domino devi[n]ctus*) be added to the text that described the exercise of papal primary. The Theological Commission rejected this intervention because, "It is an oversimplified formula. The Roman Pontiff is also bound to revelation itself, to the fundamental structure of the Church, to the sacraments, to the definitions of earlier councils, and other obligations too numerous to mention."[12]

The Assessment of Universality

Over the centuries, the Roman Catholic Church, for a variety of reasons, has become a centralized institution. The power of the pope and the curia increased, and the power of the local church under the pastoral care of the bishop tended to decrease. What are the strengths and weaknesses of such a situation?

The *strengths* of a centralized church under papal leadership are numerous. An institutional approach emphasizes corporate and societal stability. A united church with clear lines of command and uniformity of doctrine may be better able to control internal and external pressures. In a church with vast numbers of adherents throughout the world, strong papal leadership can bring together the many local churches and give the faithful a sense of belonging to the "Great Church." A pope with substantial authority may well be able to prevent factions, unify believers in a common mission, and inspire loyalty and pride. Effective papal authority can help prevent exaggerated episcopalism that would isolate local churches from the wider *koinonia*. It has been said that if Christianity did not have a pope, it would have had to invent one. John Henry Newman observed that without a pope "there would be a legion of ecclesiastics, each bishop with his own views, each with extraordinary powers, each with the risk of misusing them. . . . It would be an ecclesiastical communism."[13]

The value of a pastor for the universal church is affirmed in the common statement in round V of the Lutheran–Roman Catholic dialogue. Both the Lutheran and Roman Catholic participants spoke of the benefit of a "Petrine function," which they described as "a particular form of Ministry exercised by a person, officeholder, or local church with reference to the church as a whole."[14] The role of the Petrine function would be "to promote or preserve the oneness of the church by symbolizing unity, and by facilitating communication, mutual assistance or correction, and collaboration in the church's mission" (L/RC-5, 12).

A centralized church order with dynamic papal leadership can, at times, benefit the local church. A good example of this is the ultramontane movement of the nineteenth century.[15] Ultramontanism ("beyond the mountains"), which appeared in postrevolutionary Europe, vigorously stressed the doctrinal and disciplinary authority of the pope. Many local churches sought help from Rome to protect them from the interference of the state. A recent book on this subject, *Varieties of Ultramontanism*, shows how the hierarchies of France, Germany, Italy, England, Ireland, and the United States appealed to ultramontane ideas to resolve problems in their own dioceses.[16] Extreme ultramontanism often encouraged a cult of the pope, and the philosophy was used by some as an instrument of political expediency. Yet ultramontanism also had legitimate ecclesiological concerns. Many bishops viewed moderate ultramontanism positively because they felt that it stood for freedom of the church from state interference, uniformity of belief and practice, and unity and certitude.

The *weaknesses* connected with highly centralized church governance are not directed to the universal papal authority itself, but rather to those attitudes that a centralized church may engender. A good example of these is found in the stirring speech given by Bishop Emile De Smedt of Bruges, Belgium, at the Second Vatican Council, in which he criticized a preliminary draft of *Lumen Gentium* for its clericalism, juridicism, and triumphalism. By clericalism, he meant the dominating role of the clergy and the passive role of the laity. Juridicism referred to a preoccupation with the legal aspects of the church, which leads to the neglect of its inner spiritual reality. Triumphalism pointed to that separatist and elitist attitude that made dialogue with other Christians all but impossible. De Smedt preferred the way John XXIII spoke of the church as "the loving mother of all."[17]

A highly institutionalized church may resemble a modern multinational corporation with its chain-of-command structure more than a spiritual communion of believers. A very large organization can easily be overbearing and discourage constructive dialogue, creative ideas, and legitimate diversity. The church, with its elaborate structures of church authority at the local, national, and international levels, may appear to be impersonal and, at times, even threatening.

A final objection to a concentration of authority in Rome is that centralization tends to diminish the authority of the local church. The bishops of local churches appear more as emissaries of the pope than as genuine pastors of their flocks. Many of these objections were addressed at the Second Vatican Council.

Particularity

Karl Rahner and others have argued that the Second Vatican Council ushered in the era of the world church.[18] Attended by a significant number of non-European bishops, the Second Vatican Council affirmed the theological character of local churches, the need for the church to adapt to various cultures, and the positive salvific value of other Christian and non-Christian communities.

Christianity has begun to move from a Western, European model to an actual world religion. It is no longer simply a Western export; it is adaptable to peoples throughout the world. In the world church, the substance of the faith will remain, but it will be shaped anew in diverse cultural situations. Fresh formulations of the Christian message will appear along with a variety of theological, legal, and liturgical forms.

This vision of the church is not simply a postconciliar phenomenon. In 1944, long before the Second Vatican Council, the French ecumenical pioneer Abbé Paul Couturier described the future Church in terms quite similiar to the present concept of the world church:

> The day will come when the peoples of India, China, and even Africa, will face the reality and implications of the message of Christ: then within the Church there will be throngs of Asians and Africans, rivaling the peoples of the Old World and the New in numbers, influence, and sanctity; many things will be changed but nothing essential. The same creed will be stated in different ways, wide horizons of scriptural study, at present hidden, will be revealed; new forms of spirituality will make their appearance far different from our own in their psychological approach; organization and discipline will be modified.[19]

The emerging world church is not a mega-church with monolithic authority. On the contrary, particularity will be one of its major characteristics. Regional churches that exist in a particular cultural milieu will preserve their unique local character and, at the same time, be in harmony with the wider church. These local churches will be in communion with other local churches throughout the world, contribute to the vitality of the universal church and participate in its governance.

One of the pressing problems facing the contemporary Catholic Church is the centralization of authority in Rome. Cardinal Franz König, for example, argued that bishops should be brought more fully into the governance of the church and that the curia be reformed, "We have to return to the decentralized form of the Church's command structure as practiced in earlier centuries. That, for the world Church, is the dictate of today."[20]

Three principles, rooted in the teachings of the Second Vatican

Council, may help address this question, since they concern the relationship between universality and particularity. The three principles are legitimate diversity, subsidiarity, and collegiality.[21]

The Principle of Legitimate Diversity

The unity of the church exists in and with diversity. In the Catholic Church, there are diverse customs, laws (two Codes of Canon Law), theologies, and liturgical practices. A good example of this diversity is the presence of the twenty-two Eastern Catholic communities, all of which are in union with Rome.[22] These Eastern Catholic churches are not simply tolerated by Rome; their distinctiveness is affirmed and appreciated. Thus the Second Vatican Council noted, "The Catholic Church holds in high esteem the institutions, liturgical rites, ecclesiastical traditions and the established standards of the Christian life of the Eastern Churches."[23]

Considerable diversity among the churches existed in the first millennium of Christianity, but the tendency toward greater centralization and control by Rome accelerated in the second millennium.[24] Pope John Paul II, in speaking of ecumenical relations with the east, has appealed to "the unity which, in spite of everything, was experienced in the first millennium and in a certain sense now serves as a kind of model."[25]

Lumen Gentium discusses diversity within unity in the church. It acknowledges that great differences exist among members of the church. But it insists that the church is one, and that all the faithful are in communion with each other in the Holy Spirit (no. 13). The church, then, "takes to herself, insofar as they are good, the ability, resources, and customs of each people." The richness of gifts in individual churches should be shared with the whole church. John Paul II has explained the value of such interaction: "Communion is made fruitful by the exchange of gifts between the churches insofar as they complement each other."[26]

In a church of one billion believers, extensive diversity is obvious at several levels: ethnic, cultural, sexual, economic, educational, ideological, political, and theological. The church seeks to promote authentic unity and discern what acceptable diversity is. Unity, not uniformity, is the goal. John Paul II stated that "legitimate diversity is in no way opposed to the church's unity, but rather enhances her splendor and contributes greatly to her mission."[27] Diversity is legitimate only when it is not opposed to the gospel message nor weakens the unity of faith and charity.

The pope is the guardian of legitimate diversity and communion within the church. *Lumen Gentium* teaches that individual churches can retain their own traditions without diminishing the primacy of the Chair of Peter. "This Chair presides over the whole assembly of charity and protects legitimate differences, while at the same time it sees that such differences do not hinder unity but rather contribute toward it" (no. 13).[28]

The Catholic Church is aware of diverse approaches to Christianity and the regrettable divisions among Christians. It is, however, committed to the cause of ecumenism—that dialogic process working for the eventual reunion of Christians. As the opening words of the *Decree on Ecumenism* affirm, "The restoration of unity among all Christians is one of the principal concerns of the Second Vatican Council."[29] The Council taught that despite serious obstacles to unity, "all those justified by faith in baptism are incorporated into Christ; they therefore have a right to be called Christians."[30] The support that the Catholic Church gives to the bilateral consultations and other ecumenical activities indicate the high value it places on Christian unity.

The Principle of Subsidiarity

The principle of subsidiarity is a call to individual and small group responsibilities. In 1931, Pope Pius XI described it more precisely: "That which individuals can accomplish by their own initiative and by their own industry should not be taken from them and assigned to the community; in the same way, that which minor or lesser communities can do should not be assigned to a greater or higher community."[31] Pope Pius XII argued in 1946 that the subsidiary function "is valid for social life in all its organizations and also for the life of the Church."[32]

Subsidiarity means that decisions should be taken at the most appropriate level. The legal profession refers to this as "exhaustion of remedies." It is unnecessary to immediately bring a complaint to the highest judicial body in the church for resolution. There may be a tendency among some in the church today to bypass the episcopate and to go directly to the pope, as if he were the sole bishop in the world. Subsidiarity means to first go through the proper channels. There is no need to appeal to Rome until recourse is first made to the pastor, bishop, or the United States Conference of Catholic Bishops (USCCB).

The principle of subsidiarity can also be applied to the Roman curia with its congregations, councils, offices, and tribunals. The pope governs the church through the curia. But the curia should serve the bishops and not control them. Some bishops complain that the exercise of power by the curia is a prime example of exaggerated centralization in the church. The curia, in its tendency to micromanage, often interferes with the life of the local church. There have been calls for a reform of the curia according to the spirit of the Second Vatican Council, which would help make the curia more pastorally sensitive and service-oriented.[33]

The issue of subsidiarity was raised by several episcopal conferences in preparation for the Extraordinary Synod of Bishops in 1985.[34] Despite this concern, the final report of the Synod made only a minor reference to subsidiarity. It recommended that a study be made of the principle of subsidiarity to determine whether it is applicable to the church.[35] So far there has been no published report of that study.

The Principle of Collegiality

The Second Vatican Council supplied what was lacking at the First, a theology of the episcopacy. This theology taught that the episcopacy is of divine right (LG, no. 20), that a bishop has proper, ordinary, and immediate power in his particular church (LG, no. 27), that the bishop is the foundation and visible principle of unity in his particular church (LG, no. 23), and that bishops are not to be regarded as vicars of the pope, for they exercise an authority that is proper to them (LG, no. 27). Each bishop, as a member of the college of bishops, should be solicitous not only for his own church but also, in a non-juridical manner, for the whole church (LG, nos. 22, 23).[36]

The Council's teaching of the doctrine of collegiality has had far-reaching effect in the postconciliar church. Collegiality in the strict sense, or effective collegiality (*verus actus collegialis*) (LG, no. 22), is the worldwide solidarity of bishops who—through their sacramental consecration and hierarchical communion with one another in the college of bishops and with their head the pope—possess full and supreme authority in relation to the universal church (LG, nos. 18, 22). An ecumenical council is the clearest example of effective collegiality. Collegiality in the broad sense, or affective collegiality, is the exercise of the collegial spirit (*affectus collegialis*) (LG, no. 23) that encourages collaboration among the bishops with the pope on the national, regional, and international levels. Two examples of this kind of collegiality are episcopal conferences and synods of bishops.[37]

Collegiality is primarily a theological concept. According to the 1985 Synod of Bishops, "The ecclesiology of communion provides the sacramental foundation of collegiality. Therefore, the theology of collegiality is much more important than its mere juridical aspect."[38] Furthermore, collegiality depends on the papacy; the college of bishops cannot act without the pope, since he is both fellow member and head. The critical text is *Lumen Gentium*, which states, "Together with its head the Roman Pontiff, and never without this head, the episcopal order is the subject of supreme and full power over the universal Church. But this power can be exercised only with the consent of the Roman Pontiff" (no. 22). Finally, collegiality is dialogic. A united episcopate in genuine dialogue with the pope constitutes authentic church governance.

The Second Vatican Council did not give a detailed plan for the implementation of collegiality. It did not explain precisely how the papal and episcopal offices should be coordinated. Collegiality, then, is a work in progress that will develop through trial and error. As Cardinal Leo Suenens once remarked, "Collegiality is an art that must be learned in common or not at all."[39]

The two major organs of collegiality in the church today are episcopal conferences and synods of bishops. They express concretely the unity and diversity of the church.

The Episcopal Conference

From the early days of the church, in both the East and the West, bishops have gathered in councils and synods to discuss common concerns. In the last two centuries, many countries have formally established episcopal conferences to deal with specific issues in their geographical regions. Unlike councils or synods which meet irregularly, episcopal conferences have a stable and permanent character. The Second Vatican Council urged the establishment of conferences in the universal Church. It taught that it is "supremely fitting that everywhere bishops belonging to the same nation or region form an association which would meet at fixed times."[40] In 1966, Paul VI mandated that each nation or territory establish a permanent conference of bishops, if one did not already exist. He gave norms governing their activity.[41]

The 1983 *Code of Canon Law* devoted a separate section to episcopal conferences in canons 447 to 459.[42] Episcopal conferences must meet at least once each year. The United States Conference of Catholic Bishops (USCCB) meets twice yearly, and the members elect a president and vice president to serve a three-year term only from among the diocesan bishops.

Episcopal conferences have been an especially important feature in the postconciliar church. They are effective signs of the particularity and universality of the church. It is beneficial for bishops in the same country or region to come together to address specific pastoral challenges and to share resources, expertise, and experience. Since the Second Vatican Council, the bishops in the United States have issued hundreds of documents on a variety of subjects. The two that are perhaps the best known are *The Challenge of Peace* (1983) and *Economic Justice for All* (1986).[43]

The most authoritative recent teaching on episcopal conferences is the apostolic letter *Apostolos Suos* of John Paul II in 1998.[44] It makes several important points regarding the nature and functioning of episcopal conferences.

First, *Apostolos Suos* notes that episcopal conferences have become "the preferred means" for bishops of a particular area to consult with one another. Conferences are "a most helpful means of strengthening ecclesial communion" (no. 6).

Second, the episcopal conference is an example of the collegial spirit (*affectus collegialis*), not an example of collegiality in the strict sense. The authority of the bishops who gather in an episcopal conference is not the same as the teaching authority of the entire college of bishops. An episcopal conference, therefore, does not exercise supreme teaching authority.

Third, an episcopal conference is not meant to be a substitute for the teaching of the individual bishop or to infringe on the autonomy of the local church and the "inalienable responsibility" (no. 24) that each bishop has in relation to the universal church and to his particular church.

Fourth, the members of an episcopal conference are all diocesan bishops in the territory, those in law equivalent to them (e.g., diocesan administrators or vicars apostolic), coadjutor bishops, and those titular bishops "who exercise a special task entrusted to them by the Holy See" (no. 17). A deliberative vote is given to diocesan bishops and those equivalent to them in law and to coadjutor bishops. The conference itself decides whether auxiliary and other titular bishops have a deliberative or a consultative vote. In the USCCB, auxiliary bishops have a deliberative vote except in financial issues. Bishops emeriti (retired bishops) may be invited to the conference. They are given a consultative vote.

Fifth, the pronouncements issued by an episcopal conference are binding on the faithful only when they are approved unanimously or when, after being approved by a two-thirds majority, receive the *recognitio* (approval) of the Holy See. Some view this provision as unusual, since it is not required in any other deliberations in the church, not even in an ecumenical council. It could tend to limit the doctrinal role of the conference. Binding statements can come only from the plenary assembly of the conference and not from any smaller groups within it.

The Synod of Bishops

"Collegiality is without doubt an expression of decentralization," wrote Cardinal Godfried Daneels, "especially as it is practiced through synods."[45] Paul VI formally established the synod of bishops in 1965 in order to bring the bishops closer together, to provide information regarding issues facing the church, and to seek consensus on doctrinal matters.[46] The synod is a consultative body; it is not a mini-ecumenical council, since it does not represent the entire episcopate. Three types of synods exist: the ordinary synod deals with any important matter that requires the attention of the episcopate; the extraordinary synod addresses subjects that concern the entire church; and the special synod discusses matters affecting one particular region in the church.

Twenty-one synods have been held in Rome from 1967 through 2001: ten ordinary synods (1969, 1971, 1974, 1977, 1980, 1983, 1987, 1990, 1994, 2001); two extraordinary synods (1967, 1985); and nine special synods (1980 [two], 1991, 1994, 1995, 1997, 1998 [two], 1999). The synods usually meet from two to four weeks with some two hundred participants in attendance. The usual process of communicating the results of the synod to the wider church is by an apostolic exhortation written by the pope. The document appears a year or so after the close of the synod and is based on the secret list of recommendations—or "propositions"—

prepared by the synod fathers and submitted to the pope.

Many bishops and theologians have urged that the synod be reformed, since they consider the synods to have been a disappointment. Cardinal Daneels, for example, writes that "the way the synod takes place is unsatisfactory. The synod's function of collaboration and participation in the exercise of the primacy must be emphasized more."[47] Archbishop John R. Quinn notes that "the tendency since the Council would appear to be to restrict the synod as much as possible."[48]

The debate over the reform of the synod focuses on several issues. First, all the synods have been held in Rome. Should not, occasionally at least, the synods be held in other places to convey better the notion of the church's universality? Second, a deliberative and not simply a consultative vote may be desirable on occasion. It is permitted by canon 343, but no pope has yet allowed it. Third, granting its advisory nature, the synod seems to be very much under papal control. The pope calls the synod, sets the agenda, appoints 15 percent of its members in addition to curial officials, and issues its final report. Fourth, the present procedure mandates too many short speeches by the synod fathers with little or no time for any serious discussion or reflection.

Conclusion

The relationship between the universality and particularity of the church is a delicate one. What we seek is the correct balance between unity and diversity, between the authority of the center and the authority of the local church. On the one hand, the central administration should not dominate the local church or fail to respect its unique ecclesial character. The principles of legitimate diversity, subsidiarity, and collegiality are not meant to weaken the bonds with Rome, but to strengthen them. Rome, of course, can always intervene in the life of the local community to protect the unity of faith and communion. Such interventions, however, should not be made regularly but occur only in times of necessity. They should be made in the spirit of assistance and not domination.

On the other hand, the local church is not, in the words of Paul VI, "free, detached, and self-sufficient."[49] The local church is in communion with other local churches and recognizes the unique mission of the church of Rome in the universal church. Some universal authority is needed, along with a measure of reasonable autonomy on the local level.

The central administration of the church should not engage in absolutism, nor should the local church tend toward church-dividing isolationism. Ideally both should live in a "symphony of concord" mentioned so often by the Fathers of the Catholic Church. When that occurs, mutual interiority is present at a high degree, and the entire church functions truly as a *communio ecclesiarum*.

NOTES

1   Congregation for the Doctrine of the Faith, "Letter to the Bishops of the Catholic Church on Some Aspects of the Church Understood as Communion" (*Communionis Notio*) (hereafter CN) in *Origins* 22 (June 25, 1992): 109.

2   See Second Vatican Council, *Dogmatic Constitution on the Church* (*Lumen Gentium*), in *Vatican Council II: The Conciliar and Postconciliar Documents*, Austin Flannery, ed. (Northport, NY: Costello, 1996), no. 26; *Decree on the Pastoral Office of Bishops in the Church* (*Christus Dominus*), in Flannery, no. 11; *Decree on the Church's Missionary Activity* (*Ad Gentes Divinitus*), in Flannery, no. 22; and *Decree on the Catholic Churches of the Eastern Rite* (*Orientalium Ecclesiarum*), in *The Documents of Vatican II*, Walter M. Abbot, ed. (New York: Guild Press, 1966), no. 2.

3   For other discussions of this topic, see Avery Dulles, "The Church as Communion," *New Perspectives on Historical Theology: Essays in Memory of John Meyendorff*, ed. Bradley Nassif (Grand Rapids, MI: Wm. B. Eerdmans, 1996), 125-139; Patrick Granfield, *The Limits of the Papacy: Authority and Autonomy in the Church* (New York: Crossroads, 1989); "The Church Local and Universal: Realization of Communion," *The Jurist* 49 (1989): 449-471; and Joint Working Group, "The Church: Local and Universal," *One in Christ* 27 (1991): 267-284.

4   See Pontifical Biblical Commission, *Unity and Diversity in the Church* (Vatican City: Libreria Editrice Vaticana, 1991).

5   Raymond E. Brown, *The Churches the Apostles Left Behind* (New York: Paulist, 1984), 147-148.

6   Ludwig Hertling, *Communio: Church and Papacy in Early Christianity*, trans. Jared Wicks (Chicago: Loyola University Press, 1972), 55.

7   On this point, see the classic article by Yves Congar, "De la communion des églises à une ecclésiologie de l'Église universelle," *L'épiscopat et l'Église universelle* (Paris: Cerf, 1962), 227-260.

8   Not everyone approved of an imperial papacy. St. Bernard of Clairvaux wrote to Pope Eugene III (+1153), "When the Pope, clad in silk, covered with gold and jewels, rides out on his white horse, escorted by soldiers and servants, he looks more like a successor of Constantine than of St. Peter." St. Bernard, *De Consideratione* in Jacques-Paul Migne, *Patrologia Latina Database* (CD-ROM ed.) (Alexandria, VA: Chadwyck-Healey, 1995), IV: 3, 6; PL 182:776. (Hereafter cited as PL.)

9   St. Peter Damian, *Opusculum* 23, cap. 1. PL 145: 474.

10   The Latin and English texts of these constitutions can be found in ed. Norman P.

Tanner, ed., *Decrees of Ecumenical Councils* (London: Sheed & Ward; Washington, DC: Georgetown University Press, 1990), vol. II: 802-816.

11   Tanner, II: 813-815.

12   *Acta Synodalia Sacrosancti Concilii Oecumenici Vaticani II* (Vatican City: Typis Polyglottis Vaticanis, 1973), vol. III, part 1, 247.

13   John Henry Newman, *Letter to the Duke of Norfolk*, in Alvan S. Ryan, W. E. Gladstone, and John Henry Newman, *Newman and Gladstone: The Vatican Decrees* (Notre Dame, IN: University of Notre Dame, 1962), 101.

14   Paul C. Empie and T. Austin Murphy, eds., *Papal Primacy and the Universal Church: Lutheran-Roman Catholic Dialogue V* (hereafter cited as L/RC-5)(Minneapolis: Augsburg Publishing House, 1974), no. 11.

15   For a detailed treatment of this movement, see Roger Aubert, *Le pontificat de Pie IX (1846-1878)*, rev. ed. (Paris: Bloud & Gay, 1963).

16   Jeffrey von Arx, ed., *Varieties of Ultramontanism* (Washington, DC: The Catholic University of America Press, 1998).

17   *Acta Synodalia*, 142-144.

18   See Karl Rahner, "Basic Theological Interpretation of the Second Vatican Council," in *Concern for the Church* (New York: Crossroad, 1981), 77-89 and Walbert Bühlmann, *The Church of the Future: A Model for the Year 2001* (Maryknoll, NY: Orbis, 1986). For other reflections on the world church, see *Proceedings of the Catholic Theological Society of America 39* (Washington: 1985). The theme of the 1985 convention was the world church.

19   Abbé Paul Couturier, "Prayer and Christian Unity: The Ecumenical Testament of Abbé Paul Couturier," *One in Christ* 2 (1966): 229. This article was originally published anonymously and *ad usum privatum*. It was later republished shortly before Couturier's death under his name.

20   Cardinal Franz König, "My Vision for the Church of the Future," *The Tablet* (March 27, 1999): 426.

21   These principles were referred to as "Norms for Renewal" in round V of the Lutheran–Roman Catholic dialogue. See L/RC-5, 19-20.

22   See Ronald Roberson, *The Eastern Christian Churches: A Brief Survey*, 6th ed. (Rome: Orientalia Christiana, 1999).

23   Second Vatican Council, *Decree on the Catholic Churches of the Eastern Rite (Orientalium Ecclesiarium)* (Vatican City: Libreria Editrice Vaticana, 1964), no. 1.

24   For a theological analysis of this development see Yves Congar, "Autonomie et pouvoir central dans l'Église vus par la théologie catholique," *Irénikon* 43 (1980): 291-313.

25   *Ut Unum Sint*, in *Origins* 25 (June 8, 1995): 62, no. 55.

26   Ibid., 62, no. 57.

27   *Origins* 25:61, no. 50.

28   The Roman Catholic/Lutheran Joint Commission in 1981 summarized the position

of the Catholic Church on this issue: "The ministry of the Bishop of Rome is to serve the unity of the universal Church and legitimate diversity in the Church." L/RC-6, GA I, 269.

29   Second Vatican Council, *Decree on Ecumenism (Unitatis Redintegratio)*, in Flannery (1964), no. 1.

30   Ibid., no. 3.

31   Pius XI, *Acta Apostolicae Sedis* (hereafter AAS) 23 (Vatican City: 1931), 203.

32   Pius XII, AAS 38 (Vatican City: 1946), 145.

33   See Archbishop John R. Quinn, *The Reform of the Papacy: The Costly Call to Christian Unity* (New York: Crossroad, 1999), 154-177.

34   For the texts of fifteen of these preparatory reports see *Synode extraordinaire: Célébration de Vatican II* (Paris: Cerf, 1986).

35   Extraordinary Synod of Bishops, "A Message to the People of God and The Final Report," *Origins* 15 (December 19, 1985): 449. For further information on the principle of subsidiarity, see Ad Leys, "Structuring Communion: The Importance of the Principle of Subsidiarity," *The Jurist* 58 (1998): 84-123.

36   See also *Christus Dominus*, nos. 3 and 5.

37   Although the term "collegiality" is most properly used in reference to episcopal solidarity, the same collegial spirit can also be found in other ecclesial structures: diocesan pastoral councils, presbyteral councils, and parish councils. John Paul II mentioned this wider spirit of cooperation in his first encyclical *Redeemer of Man (Redemptor Hominis)* (Vatican City: Libreria Editrice Vaticana, 1979), no. 5.

38   John Paul II, *Redemptor Hominis*, no. 4.

39   José de Broucker, *The Suenens Dossier: The Case for Collegiality* (Notre Dame, IN: Fides, 1970), 36.

40   Second Vatican Council, *Decree Concerning the Pastoral Office of Bishops in the Church (Christus Dominus)* (Vatican City: Libreria Editrice Vaticana, 1965), no. 37.

41   Paul VI, *Motu proprio Ecclesiae Sanctae*, AAS 58:11 (October 24, 1966), 773-774.

42   Canon 447 gives a precise description of the episcopal conference: "The conference of bishops, a permanent institution, is a grouping of bishops of a given country or territory whereby, according to the norm of law, they jointly exercise certain pastoral functions on behalf of the Christian faithful of their territory in view of promoting that greater good which the Church offers humankind, especially through forms and programs of the apostolate which are fittingly adapted to the circumstances of the time and place." *Code of Canon Law: New English Translation. Trans. of Codex Iuris Canonici* (Washington, DC: Canon Law Society of America, 1998).

43   United States Conference of Catholic Bishops, *The Challenge of Peace* (Washington, DC: USCCB, 1983) and *Economic Justice for All*, 10th anniv. ed. (Washington, DC: USCCB, 1988).

44   John Paul II, *The Theological and Juridical Nature of Episcopal Conferences (Apostolos Suos)* in *Origins* 28 (July 30, 1998): 152-158.

45   Cardinal Godfried Daneels, "On Papal Primacy and Decentralization," in *Origins* 27 (October 30, 1997): 339.

46   Paul VI, *Apostolica Sollicitudo* 57 (Vatican City: Libreria Editrice Vaticana, 1965): 775-780. See John Johnson, "The Synod of Bishops: An Explanation of its Nature and Function," in *Studia Canonica* 20 (Ottawa: St. Paul University Press, 1986): 275-318.

47   Daneels, "On Papal Primacy and Decentralization," 340.

48   Quinn, *The Reform of the Papacy*, 111.

49   Paul VI, AAS 64 (1972): 498-499.